Regenerating the Ecology of Place

Regenerating the Ecology of Place

First Edition

Wayne S. Teel
James Madison University

cognella
SAN DIEGO

Bassim Hamadeh, CEO and Publisher

Clare Kennedy, Associate Acquisitions Editor

Tony Paese, Project Editor

Abbey Hastings, Production Editor

Emely Villavicencio, Senior Graphic Designer

Trey Soto, Licensing Specialist

Natalie Piccotti, Director of Marketing

Kassie Graves, Senior Vice President of Editorial

Jamie Giganti, Director of Academic Publishing

cognella | ACADEMIC PUBLISHING

3970 Sorrento Valley Blvd., Ste. 500, San Diego, CA 92121

Contents

Acknowledgments

N O BOOK IS WRITTEN ALONE. I enjoyed the writing process largely because of my wife, Alta Brubaker's constant encouragement and occasional grammatical advice. Many people have educated me on the contents in this volume beyond the referenced works in this text. Key people include Harold Miller, Gideon Mutiso and Joshua Mukusiya in Kenya; Jim Lassoie and Louise Buck at Cornell; and many of my colleagues at James Madison University including Jennifer Coffman, Tom Benzing, Robert Brent and Gene Tucker. My thanks to all of you and to many I have not named here.

Two people have read the entire book and made considerable editorial contributions: Anna Maria Johnson and Daude Teel. Others have read one or two chapters and done the same including Jennifer Coffman, Alta Brubaker and a number of students in my Sustainability: An Ecosystem Perspective course. This book was written for that class. Steven Johnson contributed many of the photos found in the book. Austen Linder developed a set of illustrations found in some of the chapters. The late Terry Hirst, also of Kenya, provided four illustrations in the Trillion Tree chapter with the permission of his wife, Nereas Hirst. Again, many thanks.

While these and many others contributed to the contents of this volume, I remain responsible for any and all errors found within. I have enjoyed writing this book and I hope all of you who read it find something in it you can remember and use.

Wayne S. Teel
November 26, 2020

Introduction

Regenerating the Ecology of Place

I T IS AN ODD EXPERIENCE TO sit and write nearly every day for three months. I had never tried this before. Writing allows the internalized thoughts to seek a public hearing that endures. Lecturing quickly fades in the minds of students and anyone else who happens to listen, but writing sticks; people can see it again, so it behooves one to get it right. Whether I have or not is for others to judge, though the errors are mine to own.

The topic chosen arose from two sources: the lectures and content of my course at James Madison University (JMU), Sustainability: An Ecological Perspective, and my time in Africa (Sudan, Kenya, and Mozambique), both as a volunteer from 1980 to 1985 and from 1990 to 1993, and later as a JMU professor during trips in 2009, 2011, and 2013. Travelling troubles me these days. Flying uses more fossil fuels than any other mode of transport, spraying carbon dioxide and other gases in the upper troposphere and contributing to global warming. It is this that causes the trouble. Climate change outweighs all the other problems we have on the planet, and many of these are severe too. Like everything on Earth, all the problems are interconnected. Our planet, as we presently know it, is dying. It is hard to watch. Knowing that I contribute to this dying by using air conditioning, driving a car, heating my house, cooking and lighting with coal-powered

FIGURE 0.1   A view over the Atlantic

electricity, and flying around in airplanes is deeply disturbing. The very means I use to identify and to help solve environmental problems are part of the problem itself. How do you stop a billion-ton train when you are riding it?

Sustainability means doing things now in ways that allow future generations to do it too without harming the planet. This cannot happen if we maintain things as they are; we have to heal the damage already done and make the environment healthy again at every scale. That is why the word *regenerating* replaced the original word *sustainability* in the title of this book. Practicing what I preach is nearly impossible within the context of where I teach. It is not hopeless, but it is very hard. The task requires me to change the habits of a lifetime and requires me to help others change their own lifetime habits. This is not a task for some future generation, or for my children; it is a task for me. This book at its core is about the means and ends we must choose in order to halt and even reverse climate change to keep the planet habitable for ourselves and most other life as we know it. Yet this goal interconnects with every other aspect of our lives at the same time.

The process of reversing climate change has two distinct parts. The first is stopping our addiction to fossil fuels, which means, for Americans, at least an 80% reduction in the amount of energy used per capita in the United States. This reduction will require much more than just changing lightbulbs or buying a more energy-efficient refrigerator, though these simple acts are both good, necessary things. But even more, it means deliberately choosing to live without a car, to live closer to one's workplace, to eat food grown closer to home or even in the backyard, to keep indoor temperatures warmer in summer and cooler in winter, to work more with our hands and less with machines, and to be content with what we have for far longer than we have done in the past. David Holmgren calls this the five Rs: refuse, reduce, reuse, repair, and recycle (Holmgren 2002). Manufacturers will have to make things that last, are repaired easily, and are able to be recycled using less energy. All of these tasks are doable but require a rapid change of mindset since we do not have much time. Our best minds now say we have less than two decades to implement dramatic changes to our energy use (McKibben 2011; Brown 2009; Shiva 2008). At present, the train has not begun to slow down.

The second part, after reducing fossil fuel use, is even harder, though perhaps simpler. We have to let nature grow again. Wherever we have gone upon this planet, nature has suffered impacts. "The soil is bare now, nor can foot feel, being shod." That line from Gerard Manley Hopkins's poem "God's Grandeur" reveals the depth of our disconnection from the natural world.[1] This disconnection allows us to directly or indirectly promote deforestation, sow monocultures, employ chemical agriculture, exploit farmworkers, destroy cultures, and disrupt entire ecosystems. We have severed our own roots with the land. It is time to take our shoes off and feel the soil. Where it is found hard, we need to work to soften it; where it is found scarred, we need to work to heal it; where it is found empty, we need to work to fill it. The salvation of the planet is found in deeply rooted plants and in people deeply rooted in their places. Rootless people cannot heal the planet.

---

1   http://www.poemhunter.com/poem/god-s-grandeur/

FIGURE 0.2   Converting a lawn to a garden.

Our ongoing task, to borrow Wes Jackson's words, is "becoming native to this place." We need to take our cue from Wendell Berry and resettle America. To heal the planet, we cannot remain uprooted. The World Bank once promoted the phrase "Think Globally, Act Locally." It is a good sentiment—but sadly, incorrect. Every ecosystem is a local ecosystem. I can't think globally and fix my backyard. To fix my backyard, I have to think and act locally. The actions of others thinking about their backyards in other places will provide me with clues, but I have to take those lessons and apply them to the unique nature of my place. Every ecology of place is different. The seemingly endless plains of Iowa, of Kansas, and of Saskatchewan may appear the same everywhere, but there are subtleties of soil, moisture, plant communities, and fauna that make for significant variation. We are fooled by our promotion of sameness with endless fields of corn, soybeans, wheat, Douglas fir, and yellow pine. The desire to have everything look the same and produce the same thing has left us blind to the productivity of diversity and the healing of community. Recapturing our vision for diversity will inform our ability to change the rootedness of the land. It is only in the healing of local landscapes and seascapes that we can solve our global crisis.

The book is comprised of 13 chapters, starting with some background on the language of ecology and ending with an extended essay on the potential of trees. These chapters, sometimes subdivided by theme, follow the path that I used in my courses and tell many stories about how others have walked these paths in local settings. The underlying theme throughout the text is the necessity of understanding the local ecology of the place where you live and acting on that knowledge to develop new ways of interacting with living systems on the planet.

FIGURE 0.3   Beavers, architects of their own environment.

The Chapters

1. Ecology: The Language of the Planet

We live in a world of complex systems, and no one has articulated this better than Donella Meadows. She developed an understanding of the state of our planetary system based on the language of ecology and systems thinking: the study of how life works. Explaining this language and the stories of ecosystem dynamics forms the core of this chapter. It provides the foundation for the other chapters in the book by giving details on biotic and abiotic factors, symbiotic relationships, keystone species, biogeochemical cycles, biomes, and more.

2. Learning What Not to Do

Living in Africa for nine years taught me one very important lesson: You have to learn what you should not do before you are open to learning what you should do. Nature has some fixed rules, and if you violate them, consequences are inevitable. Duncan Brown realized this when he looked at the negative impact that the city of Sydney, Australia, was having on its harbor. Karl-Henrik Robèrt, a pediatric oncologist from Sweden, realized this while trying to untangle the why of so many childhood cancer problems. In the process, they developed ways of understanding environmental problems that are lessons for us all.

3. The Rise and Pending Fall of Conventional Agriculture

Food is central to all of us. We all need to eat. The production of food was once the province of nearly half the population in most counties, and well over half of the population lived in what we now consider rural areas. But with the discovery of coal, the cheap processing of steel, advances in understanding the chemistry of life, and the unravelling of the genetic code, profound changes entered the agricultural domain. At least in so-called developed nations, agriculture shrank as the primary vocation of a large portion of the population, freeing labor for other areas of productivity. Yet these profound changes are also impacted by the same ecological laws described previously. What is agriculture's role in the degradation of our environment? This chapter provides a brief glimpse of agriculture's changes and their impact.

4. From Lawns to Sustainable Perennial Agriculture: Making Permaculture Part of Your Landscape

We are connected to the ecosystems in which we live, and our actions in these ecosystems determine its health. Nothing represents our unintended negative relationship with ecosystems better than the nearly ubiquitous lawn. At the same time, there is no more-appropriate starting place for change than that lawn. In it lies the key to moving from a high-maintenance unproductive monoculture to a productive and ecologically thriving permaculture. This chapter provides a glimpse of how this process can happen.

FIGURE 0.4   Converting a lawn to a garden, amending soil.

5. Reducing Your Personal and Global Carbon Footprint

All of us impact the planet in some way simply as participants. The type of impact is important. My own footprint proved uncomfortably large mostly through the use of fossil fuel energy, especially air travel. Reducing this energy footprint is not simple, but substantial strides toward this goal are possible. Moving from ancient stored fossil energy sources to direct dependence on today's solar power is the key. It will involve conservation, resource reduction, solar capture via plants, and generating needed power from the sun, wind, and other natural sources.

6. Water: A Global Issue with Local Solutions

Water is essential to life, and it lies at the heart of many social conflicts. How we obtain, use, and misuse water is something we commonly ignore, yet climate change and increasing population demand that we pay attention to patterns of water supply, demand, and use. Too often in the two centuries of industrial development, we have relied on big-project solutions to our water problems. Long-term answers will require us to come up with thousands of local answers, unique to each ecology of place. Two local approaches to water supply are given in this chapter, one in the Shenandoah Valley and the other in Kenya.

7. Managing Manure: Following Nature's Nutrient Cycles

Human waste commonly goes with water in industrial societies. This is a mistake, since it takes the biogeochemical cycles involving nitrogen, phosphorus, and other nutrients and turns it into straight-line pipes dumping in the ocean. Manure is not a waste; it is a natural resource and food for thousands of organisms that we ignore. Regenerating these nutrient cycles is crucial for healing local ecosystems. We have to rethink the management of our animals and our own waste to make this happen.

FIGURE 0.5 Pigs managing a manure and woody bedding compost pile at Polyface Farm in Swoope, Virginia.

8. Rice, Records, and the Potential for Alternative Agriculture

Food production is a crucial activity in an age of rising population and lack of new agricultural land. No one has done more to improve production than Dr. Norman Borlaug, a Nobel Peace Prize–winning plant breeder. Although Borlaug's contributions are laudable, there is a problem with the green revolution he founded in that it depends heavily on chemical inputs and fossil fuels. New methods based on understanding the original ecological place of plants like rice are rewriting this revolution; and out of this new understanding, an agroecology of place is beginning. This chapter looks in some detail at the System of Rice Intensification and the ideas of Masanobou Fukuoka.

9. Why Say No to Genetically Modified Organisms?

Some people claim that the only way to solve the world's problem with food supply is to intensify chemical agriculture and to engineer new crop varieties with genes extracted from other organisms. Though there are a few success stories, the dangers of genetically modified crops are already realized. Our first step is to recognize that nature has already developed systems to overcome productivity threats. The key to agricultural fecundity does not lie with corporate controlled seed; it lies in the biological diversity of ecosystems and the genetic diversity already found within our crop plants. Unfortunately, the corporate model is eroding this diversity.

10. Putting Carbon Where It Belongs: An Introduction to Soil

At present, the atmosphere is passing the 400 parts per million (ppm) level of carbon dioxide. Scientists like Dr. James Hanson are calling for a reduction to 350 ppm. Where is this carbon supposed to go? The answer is back into the soil. Soil has long held a lot of carbon, but agricultural practices, deforestation, and development have caused soil carbon levels to drop. This chapter proposes that soil carbon retention is not only possible but also essential for regeneration of the biomes of the planet.

11. A New Type of Black Gold: An Introduction to the Making and Use of Biochar

The deep red soils of the Amazon are notoriously infertile, but the native peoples of that region solved the problem using charcoal and waste. We now call this charcoal used as a soil amendment biochar, and it is proving a soil additive worthy of some consideration, especially on marginal soils. This chapter explains how charcoal is made, how it is used as a soil amendment, and what impact it can have on agriculture and local ecosystems.

12. The Problem of Brittle Landscapes: A Deeply Rooted Solution

Tropical savannas, temperate prairies, and other semiarid landscapes are easily degraded. Development and overgrazing are cited as culprits in this process. Environmentalists and cattle ranchers battle over this question, but nature has a different take on the problem. According to Allan Savory, grasslands and grazers coevolved in these ecosystems, but we do not follow nature's pattern in our management strategies.

FIGURE 0.6   A piece of biochar made from waste pine wood.

FIGURE 0.7   A covered spring in Kakamega County, Kenya.

New thinking about rangeland management using ecological tools like intense grazing, restorative rest periods, fire, and the added technology of good electric fencing make rethinking grazing both restorative and productive.

13. The Trillion Tree Project: Tree Crops and the Benefits of Agroforestry

About 40% of the land surface area of the planet was once forest, and much of it still is, though humans have done a lot to shrink this base. J. Russell Smith was one of the first to address this problem, but not by denouncing deforestation—though he did that, too. Rather, Smith's focus was on tree crops like fruits, nuts, and fodder trees. His look at trees helped inspire the field of agroforestry, the reintegration of trees into an agroecosystem. The planet has potential for a lot more trees: not only in forests, but also in backyards, on farms, and in a variety of different management systems. This chapter looks at these systems and their potential locally and across the planet. Getting a trillion trees in the ground is a function of millions of local projects.

FIGURE 0.8   A Fall acorn drop in the forest of western Virginia

A Guiding Principle

No book or paper influenced me more than Aldo Leopold's *A Sand County Almanac*. In his book, Leopold lays out the changes he saw in the land over the course of his life and what he thought needed to be done. His is a call to treat the land and water with respect, a respect absent from the dominant economic thinking of his and our generations. At the heart of his thinking is his development of a Land Ethic, by which to assess every action you take upon the land:

> Examine each question in terms of what is ethically and esthetically right, as well as what is economically expedient. A thing is right when it tends to preserve the integrity, stability, and beauty of the biotic community. It is wrong when it tends otherwise.

It is time for us to go and do likewise.

FIGURE 0.9

References

Berry, Wendell. 1977. *The Unsettling of America*. San Francisco: Sierra Club Books.

Brown, A. Duncan. 2003. *Feed or Feedback: Agriculture, Population Dynamics and the State of the Planet*. Utrecht, the Netherlands: International Books.

Brown, Lester. 2009. *Plan B 4.0: Mobilizing to Save Civilization*. New York: W.W. Norton. (Available as a free download at: http://www.earth-policy.org/images/uploads/book_files/pb4book.pdf.)

Holmgren, David. 2002. *Permaculture: Principles and Pathways Beyond Sustainability*. Hepburn, Victoria, Australia: Holmgren Design Services.

Jackson, Wes. 1990. *Becoming Native to this Place*. Berkeley, CA: Counterpoint.

Leopold, Aldo. 1986. *A Sand County Almanac*. New York: Ballantine Books.

McKibben, Bill. 2011. *Eaarth: Making a Life on a Tough New Planet*. New York: Henry Holt.

Robèrt, Karl-Henrik. 2002. *The Natural Step Story: Seeding a Quiet Revolution*. Gabriola Island, British Columbia: Canada: New Society Publishers.

Shiva, Vandana. 2008. *Soil Not Oil: Environmental Justice in an Age of Climate Crisis*. Cambridge, MA: South End Press.

Credits

Chapter 1

Ecology
The Language of the Planet

Introduction

In this chapter we will examine the key concepts and words of ecology, the study of *oikos*, the Greek word for "house." This language is the cornerstone for the rest of the book. Each key word in the ecological lexicon will be defined and explained using a relevant example and story. Without a common language, we cannot fully understand our impact on ecosystems and the various cycles of energy, water, and nutrients that are the basic building blocks of living systems. Once a common language is established, we can move on to the specifics of human actions on these systems and dive into details of how the systems are impacted.

We often impact systems because we wish to extract some resource for our use. Examples include energy for mobility; water for irrigation or municipalities; minerals for our computers, phones, cars, or buildings; and land to grow food. Yet we do this extraction without properly considering the effect on the ecosystems. If we wish for an ecosystem to heal, we have to know how it works—using a language that accurately describes these processes. Thus this chapter gives us the tools to understand how our house is designed and how it operates.

Living on a Finite Planet

As I started writing this opening chapter, an e-mail arrived from the Roots Action Team, a group of highly respected environmental, political, and social activists, concerning Fukushima Plant #4; one of the five nuclear reactors damaged during the earthquake and tsunami that hit Japan in 2011. As of June 2020, 1,300 spent fuel rods still rested in a pool of water 100 feet above the Pacific Ocean, requiring continuous cooling to prevent meltdown and the release of "15,000 times as much radiation than was released at Hiroshima." Testing is now underway to see if it is safe to remove them.[1] It is a scary thought. Even a little radiation can do a lot of damage. The nuclear bombing of Hiroshima killed 100,000 people. The potential Fukushima disaster would not be in the form of a nuclear explosion, but would compromise vast stretches of our planetary ecosystem already weakened by the combined actions of humanity. And we don't know what to do in the long term. Perhaps we will have done something by the time you read this. Why did we ever put ourselves in this predicament in the first place?

Originally this book was about sustainability, a concept much discussed and defined over the past half century. Perhaps the introduction to the subject came from The Club of Rome in 1972. The Club of Rome was founded as an informal group of scientists, businesspeople, politicians, and other leaders to develop a coherent idea about the direction of the planet.[2] Donella Meadows[3] headed some of their first efforts to produce models that could answer the basic question, "What will happen to the planet if we do not change?" The answers they found were not pretty. Their response was recorded in the book *Limits to Growth*, the first comprehensive critique of the concept of unlimited economic growth on a finite planet. The book raised a firestorm of protests from economists, political thinkers, and the business community, who operated on the assumption that the vast resources of the planet were too great for humanity to deplete. In spite of this protest, there exists no effective and conclusive counterargument to the points laid out in *Limits to Growth*. The fact that we do live on a finite and small planet was dramatically portrayed for all of us by the photograph of Earth Rising, taken by the Apollo 8 astronauts as they came around the back side of the moon. It illustrates our need to shift to more sustainable models of living than those we have turned to in the past (Figure 1.1).

So what is sustainability? What are sustainable systems, and why are they important? Asking these questions is probably the greatest gift that the authors of *Limits to Growth* gave us. To address them, they used the language of ecology, literally "the study of our house," from the Greek word *oikos*, meaning "house." What makes a house last? How does the living system of the planet work? This is the study of ecology. Life has evolved a complex set of systems that are self-correcting, adjusting to the interplay of abiotic factors like climate, soil, minerals, and solar energy input, with biotic factors in the form of producers that capture

---

1   "Tepco finds no obstacle to removing fuel rods from Fukushima reactor." Kyodo News, June 10, 2020. https://english.kyodonews.net/news/2020/06/17d23c757314-tepco-finds-no-obstacles-to-removing-fuel-rods-from-fukushima-reactor.html

2   The Club of Rome was founded in 1968 and continues today.

3   For a more complete picture of Donella Meadows, one of the most important environmental and political thinkers of the twentieth century, go to the Academy for Systems Change website, at https://www.academyforchange.org/, and click "Donella Meadows Project."

FIGURE 1.1   Earthrise. This is the name given to a photograph of the Earth that was taken by astronaut William Anders in 1968 during the Apollo 8 mission. Nature photographer Galen Rowell declared it "the most influential environmental photograph ever taken."

energy from the sun and consumers that feed on that energy for their own actions. As the systems remain in balance over the long term, they are considered sustainable. If the systems go out of balance, they can destroy themselves or be destroyed by whatever outside energy enters the system and disturbs that balance. According to *Limits to Growth* (1972), and its sequels *Beyond the Limits* (1992) and *Limits to Growth: The 30-Year Update* (2002), Earth's systems are badly out of balance and are in danger of collapse. The 1,300 fuel rods of Fukushima are just one symptom of that dangerous input of uncontrolled energy that makes our planetary trajectory unsustainable.

So how is *sustainability* defined? Frequent attempts at definitions came out after *Limits to Growth* stimulated the conversation. The United Nations put together a commission, under the leadership of former Norwegian prime minister Gro Brundtland, called the World Commission on Environment and Development. The Commission came up with this definition:

> *A sustainable society is one that meets the needs of the present without compromising the ability of future generations to meet their own needs.*

While every definition of a complex system will be imperfect, this one has a simplicity that helps it hold true. The depth it needs comes from the language of ecology. How do systems that last a long time really work? And how do they recover a state of working balance after a severe shock?

The Language of Ecology

Ecology is the study of Earth's systems as stated above. Thankfully, these systems are scalable. Since the earth is a spherical planet, the incoming energy from the sun varies according to the sun's distance from the equator, which can be defined as the line of maximal input of energy from the sun. Because of earth's 23.5-degree rotational tilt away from perpendicular to the direction of solar energy input, we have a climate system that varies on an annual cycle. The nature of that variation, combined with differences in topography and shape of land masses on the planet, produces the vast diversity of climate types, varying with latitude (distance from the equator), altitude, wind direction, and continental shape in relation to ocean currents. These abiotic factors help mold the membership of the biotic community across a particular landscape or water body. The result is subsets of the planetary system, which we call ecosystems.

The particular language used to describe these ecosystems is important to know in order to join the conversation. The following section is a list of key words and concepts used in this book on a regular basis. This is not an exhaustive list—for that you need an ecology text. Rather, it is an attempt to define things in relation to what makes a system sustainable. Keep in mind that sustainable systems are dynamic ecosystems. Change over time is not a bad thing in and of itself; systems tend to swing like a pendulum from times of relative stability, to bursts of change, and back to stability. It is the ability to recover from change—resilience—that is the crucial dimension. In the following subsections, each keyword is accompanied by a definition and sometimes an example. Any one of these can be pursued in greater depth.

Abiotic Factors

The term *abiotic factor* describes any component of the nonliving aspects of an ecosystem that is critically important in defining and shaping the living systems in a particular place. Abiotic factors include climate and all its variables, such as temperature, precipitation, and wind. Equally important are the physical characteristics on which climate acts: from rocks, soils, topography, water bodies, and minerals down to the ratio of elements found in that place. Powering everything is energy input coming from the sun. Solar input drives every system on the planet, and it varies according to latitude and aspect (Figure 1.2). In the Northern Hemisphere, a south-facing slope receives more energy than a north-facing

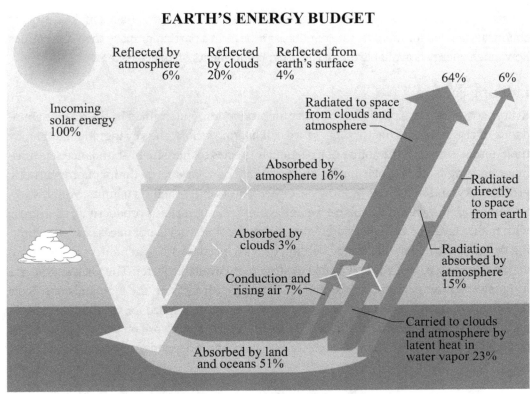

EARTH'S ENERGY BUDGET

Reflected by atmosphere 6%

Reflected by clouds 20%

Reflected from earth's surface 4%

64%

6%

Incoming solar energy 100%

Radiated to space from clouds and atmosphere

Absorbed by atmosphere 16%

Radiated directly to space from earth

Absorbed by clouds 3%

Radiation absorbed by atmosphere 15%

Conduction and rising air 7%

Carried to clouds and atmosphere by latent heat in water vapor 23%

Absorbed by land and oceans 51%

FIGURE 1.2 Incoming solar energy. The fate of incoming sunlight among reflection and absorption in the atmosphere, land surface, and bodies of water.

slope. This difference affects temperature, moisture availability, species type, and rate of growth. Abiotic factors define the parameters of an ecosystem community native to a particular place. Becoming familiar with these factors is critical to understanding what makes an ecosystem work.

Biotic Factors

Biotic factors include anything living in a system, and the range is enormous. On land in healthy soil, you can find bacteria numbering over five billion in a single teaspoon. At the other end of the scale, you can also find footprints, made by an elephant in soft mud, that hold over 4 liters of water. That elephant will provide a habitat for trillions of bacteria living in its gut, on its skin, and in its waxy ear canals. Life is abundant at every scale. Yet all of this life depends on the unique ability of some life forms to capture energy from the sun, to absorb carbon dioxide from the atmosphere or from a water body, and to combine this with water to make simple sugars in the process called photosynthesis, the most important chemical equation on the planet. From these sugars, plants and all other organisms make the other chemicals needed for life. The rate of photosynthesis in a particular place then determines how much energy is available for all the other components of an ecosystem.

Limiting Factors

Every ecosystem has a particular capacity for production, constrained by the relative abundance of critical abiotic factors. These we call *limiting factors*, the key ingredients that, by their absence, restrict the ability of a particular species to increase in abundance. The ultimate limiting factor is solar input. The fixed rate of solar energy limits photosynthetic productivity, and this varies by location. Other factors exert their own limits. Water is key. Systems with low levels of available water have less photosynthesis productivity than areas with higher levels of available water. Notice that precipitation is not necessarily the limiting factor. You can have abundant, verdant growth in a desert if water enters a place from an outside source, or if the soil is able to store more available water. The Okavango Delta in Botswana is an outstanding example (Figure 1.3). Rivers from the highlands of Angola feed the region with water during its dry season, creating a space for wildlife to thrive in an otherwise harsh, semiarid climate. Other limiting factors work on smaller scales. The availability of nitrogen can restrict growth of species that depend on environmental input

FIGURE 1.3   Okavango Delta, Botswana.

of that nutrient. The same is true for phosphorus, potassium, calcium, and the whole range of macro- and micronutrients essential for life. Other limiting factors of note include temperature, soil type, and soil depth.

Habitat

A *habitat* is the combination of abiotic and biotic factors that comprise conditions that can lead to the success of a *species*, defined as the population of an organism that can successfully reproduce in a place through time. This does not mean that a particular species is trapped in a particular place; it just means that all the conditions are right in that place if the species were to be there. For example, we know that Northern California has the right habitat for the gray wolf, but until a gray wolf travelled to that area from Oregon recently, gray wolves did not reside there.

Niche

A biological *niche* is the place and role of a specific species in a particular ecosystem. The niche of a species can be very broad, as is the case with many omnivores, or very specific. An example of this comes from Charles Darwin, who received a package of Madagascar orchids from a collector friend. Darwin examined the flower, *Angraecum sesquipedale*, and predicted that there must be a moth having a tongue 25–30 cm long, that could pollinate the flower while reaching the nectar. It took 40 years to discover the pollinator, but a moth was found that had exactly those characteristics: the African hawk moth, *Xanthopan morgani*, which specializes in extracting food from orchids with hard-to-reach nectar while pollinating them (Kritsky 1991).

Producers

It is easy to think of plants as the key *producers*, and indeed they are on land. No one can doubt the amazing ability of a giant sequoia in the Sierra Nevada foothills of California or the stout, fat, odd-looking baobab in Africa to capture

FIGURE 1.4   Giant sequoia. The "Grizzly Giant" tree in Mariposa Grove, Yosemite National Park.

sunlight, carbon dioxide (CO_2), and water and turn them into massive physical structures. In water, however, especially in oceanic ecosystems, the lowly algae become the foundation of the system, even though algae are seldom the most abundant organism by weight in aquatic ecosystems. They reproduce rapidly but are also consumed rapidly, yet their rate of reproduction necessarily underlies the growth and abundance of most oceanic species—from zooplankton to blue whales.

On land, producers thrive most abundantly and diversely in areas with high available water and year-round warm temperatures. Tropical rainforests, estuaries of river systems, and inland swamps produce more consumable organic material than other areas. Typically, as you move north or south from the equator, ecosystem productivity tends to drop until finally limited by temperature in the Arctic and Antarctic. In water, on the other hand, the reverse holds true. Colder water, especially temperatures near the maximum density of liquid water at 39°C, are generally richer in nutrients (the major limiting factor of oceanic ecosystems), especially the nutrients nitrogen and iron.

Gross Primary Productivity and Net Primary Productivity

In any ecosystem, there are a number of factors that determine the productivity of a given place: water, temperature, light exposure, soil texture, soil nutrients and availability, pH, and more. Plants growing in this place are able to catch energy from the sun and, via photosynthesis, combine water and carbon dioxide to make simple sugars. This is termed the *gross primary productivity* (GPP) of an ecosystem, a measurement of how much sugar the ecosystem can make in a given time period, usually in one year. Not all of this productivity results in a new tissue for the plants, however; energy is needed for the plant to make this sugar and combine it with nutrients sucked from the soil in order to make new tissue. As an approximate value, 50% of the produced energy, or GPP, is needed to make new tissue in the plant, called *net primary productivity* (NPP). Since plants are the primary producers in most ecosystems, this NPP value is what determines the ultimate population of organisms in ecosystems.

Consumers

Any organism that is dependent on another organism for providing the energy for life is a *consumer*. Even some plants are consumers. An example of a consuming plant is the pitcher plant. Its central stem is modified into a cup that holds a sweet solution that is attractive to flies and beetles. When these critters land in the solution, they are trapped and the digestive enzymes also found in the liquid break them down, giving nitrogen to the plants, which thrive in acidic, swampy, nutrient-poor locales. Pitcher plants still photosynthesize for their energy, but they depend upon the insects to bring in the necessary nutrients.

Most consumers do not have the capacity to provide any energy input. Unlike *autotrophic* (self-feeding) plants, they are *heterotrophs* that must consume autotrophs for sustenance. Consumers are divided into categories according to their preferred diet. Primary consumers eat plants directly. These can be very selective feeders, such as an aphid species, the diet of which is restricted to the juices of a particular host plant; or they may be generalist feeders such as elephants, which will eat grass by the trunkful or consume the branches and bark of an acacia tree when little else is available. Primary or first-order consumers become food for secondary consumers, the predators that eat consumers. Again, size is not necessarily an indication of the specie's position as a consumer. Lions are secondary consumers, but so are copepods, one of the most abundant organisms in the ocean, most of which cannot be seen with the naked eye. Copepods subsist on zooplankton, first-order consumers of phytoplankton or algae. In fact, an oceanic ecosystem can be quite complex in consumption levels. Small copepods can be eaten by larger copepods like krill, which are then eaten by small fish like menhaden, anchovies, grunions, or sardines. These forage fish serve as food for larger fish, which can, in turn, be eaten by tuna, marlin, swordfish, or, ultimately, killer whales. The last could be seventh-, eighth-, or ninth-order consumers. On land, however, it is rare to get beyond the third-order consumer level.

The final category of consumer is the *detrivore*. This group is dominated by

FIGURE 1.5 Pitcher plants in Linn Run State Park, Pennsylvania.

FIGURE 1.6 A common shiner in North Fork Shenandoah Watershed.

FIGURE 1.7 Saprophytic fungi fruiting material on a branch removal site of a damaged tree. Fungi are the most important detrivores in forest ecosystems.

bacteria and fungi, but larger organisms may get into the act as well. Our bodies are, after all, food for worms. Detrivores get their energy from dead organic material, whether it is a producer or any level of consumer. Detrivores take this food, turn it into energy for themselves, and release CO_2 back into the atmosphere. Just to make things complicated, detrivores are consumed too; just think of robins eating an earthworm, or of a person eating a mushroom. The dance of life is complex. One further caveat: The largest known organism on the planet is a variety of honey mushroom in the western United States, spreading across 500 acres of forest land. This mushroom is parasitic, meaning that it lives and weakens the evergreen forest species dominant in that region.[4]

Food Web

While it is fairly easy to think of producers to consumers at various levels, including detrivores, as a linear progression, nature does not lend itself to easy categorization. It is better to think of an ecosystem as a food web woven around the producers (Figure 1.8). While some species, such as ladybugs, might specialize in eating only aphids that live on one category of plants, other species are less discriminating. Bears will happily eat huckleberries and salmon in the same day. Squirrels, those cute consumers of acorns and hickory nuts, are not shy about eating an egg or even a newly hatched baby bird. Omnivores are abundant, and humans are perhaps the best representative of that group. Drawing lines of relationships in an ecosystem is a complex task.

Food Pyramid

One aspect of a food web that is linear is the flow of energy through an ecosystem. Energy comes from the sun, of course, and is captured by plants or other autotrophs. A substantial portion of the energy captured is consumed by the plant in order to make the components of its own tissues. Plants manufacture amino acids, fats, oils, cellulose, DNA, and a host of other biological molecules using sugar as the energy to drive the system. Over half the energy captured by a plant is used by the plant. The rest becomes the plant itself, which is potentially consumed.

Consumers, as they eat, grow, and reproduce, use a great deal of the energy for maintenance. Not all energy ends up as part of the organism. Usable energy for the organism is obtained through respiration, the process of breaking down tissue from the organism consumed and releasing energy. The rate at which you exhale CO_2 is your respiration rate,

---

4   Priya Chaudary. "Honey fungus: World's largest living organism on Earth". Science Reporter. September 2018 http://nopr.niscair.res.in/bitstream/123456789/44964/1/SR%2055%289%29%2062-63.pdf

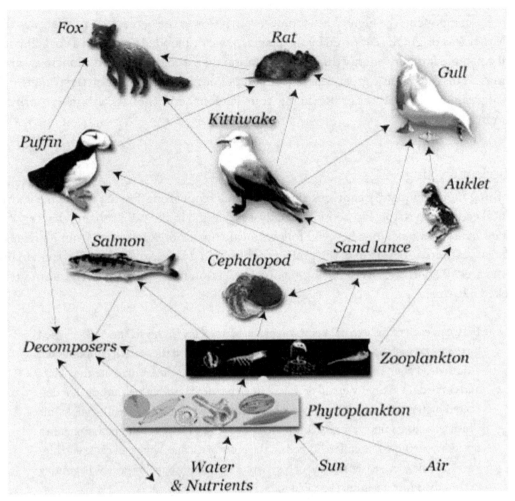

FIGURE 1.8 Food web. A food chain is simply "who eats what." A food web weaves together many food chains to form a complicated network of feeding relationships among different plants and animals. Many animals eat more than one thing, and each link in each chain is important and integral to the entire system. Pictured here is an example of a marine food web in Alaska. Notice that this food web illustrates the relationships between producers (plants that make their own food using chlorophyll and the sun's energy) and consumers (animals that eat producers and other animals). It also shows the relationship between predators (animals that hunt and eat other animals) and prey (the animals that are hunted).

a measure of your energy consumption. All organisms respire. As a general rule, only about 10% of the energy consumed by an organism is available for the next trophic level. The actual value varies according to the organism and its environmental conditions. The term *trophic level* is a synonym used by ecologists for consumer levels. It has an energy content component: the higher the trophic level, the lower the percentage of energy available that was originally captured by the plants. A warm-blooded animal in a cold climate will consume far more energy through respiration than a cold-blooded animal in a warm climate. This factor has a great deal to tell us about our human impact on the planet, and it will reappear in Chapter 5, "Reducing Your Personal and Global Carbon Footprint," later in this volume.

Nutrient Cycling

Nothing more eloquently captures the adventures of an atom flowing through a continental ecosystem than Aldo Leopold's "Odyssey," found in the "Wisconsin" chapter of *A Sand County Almanac*. In it Leopold follows a calcium atom, X, starting from its release from a weathered rock deep in the prairie soil through its cycle over the ecosystem in his home area of southwest Wisconsin. Picking a selection from "Odyssey," the atom's trip looked like this:

> Between each of his excursions through the biota, X lay in the soil and was carried by the rains, inch by inch downhill. Living plants retarded the wash by impounding atoms; dead plants by locking them to their decayed tissues. Animals ate the plants and carried them briefly uphill or downhill, depending on whether they died or defecated higher or lower than they fed. No animal was aware that the altitude of his death was more important than his manner of dying. Thus a fox caught a gopher in a meadow, carrying X uphill to his bed on the brow of a ledge, where an eagle laid him low. The dying fox sensed the end of his chapter in foxdom, but not the new beginning in the odyssey of an atom. (Leopold 1966, 113)

In Leopold's story, X ends its odyssey in its ancient prison, the sea, after washing down the Mississippi River. Even Leopold might be surprised to find that the sea does not imprison an atom away from land. A scientist in British Columbia, Canada, studied salmon that migrate from the sea, examining their growth years back to the altitude of their hatching high in the coastal mountains and found that these spawning adults, which die and are consumed by bears, eagles, raccoons, and other species, are responsible for bringing enough available nitrogen upstream to influence the growth of coastal forests (Reimchen 2001). Along with the nitrogen come phosphorus, calcium, and a host of other macro- and micronutrients. These then join the long march back to the sea through land-based ecosystems. The sea is not a prison; it serves only as a long-term residence until a mobile member of its ecosystem brings nutrients back to their starting point.

Symbiosis

Though the term *symbiosis* is generally considered to mean an association between two species that has mutual benefit, the term in ecology carries a broader meaning. It is more appropriate to consider *symbiosis* an obligatory relationship between two species, even those relationships that on the surface appear to benefit only one species. The broader definition includes the four terms that follow.

Predation

Predation is straightforward; one species eats another species, resulting in the death of the individual of the other species. Hundreds of examples are immediately apparent. My yard near Keezletown in Virginia is prime habitat for praying mantises (Figure 1.9). These green insectivorous giants congregate on the south wall of the house in the fall, basking in the warmth and often chowing down on whatever insect happens their way. Mantises are not highly discriminating predators. These days the exotic and disgusting invasive stink bug is their most readily available prey, much to my delight.

Predation is not a one-way benefit, though, which is something we need to understand about the working of ecosystems. The story that best illustrates this comes from Yellowstone National Park. During the twentieth century, our human desire to eliminate predator species succeeded in eradicating wolves from the entirety of their Rocky Mountain homeland. We exterminated wolves in the name

FIGURE 1.9 Praying mantis attacking a mating pair of grasshoppers. Photo by Steven Johnson.

of protecting our cattle and sheep from the ravages of this predator, but the results came at a cost. In the park, elk are the largest of the wolves' regular prey. Without wolves, the elk population became lazy, congregating near rivers, chewing on their favorite aspen, poplar, and willow foods, and generally becoming a weak parody of themselves. As a result, riparian

FIGURE 1.10   Bull elk, Oregon.

habitat was stripped of young trees and declined, the beavers disappeared, birds left, and, as a later result, streams became more erosive in spring floods and summer downpours.[5]

Then, in the 1990s, the wolf was reintroduced to the park from Canada. The lazy, slow, or sick elk that did not respond to this new reality became food for wolves, while the remainder learned to eat, drink, and move. As time passed, riparian ecosystems recovered, beavers returned, bird habitat reappeared, erosion stopped, and fish numbers grew in the cooler, shaded streams. Elk numbers did not decline as expected, but they did become harder to see and their range expanded over more of the park. Sick, old, or injured elk were thinned from the population, but the overall population was more robust. Predation has a mutual ecosystem benefit for a population, if not for the individual.

Parasitism

Parasites are organisms that live off another species to their own benefit and to the detriment of their host. Parasites take many different forms, and most of the time we do not like them.

---

5   There are many sources for this information, including the rangers of Yellowstone Park: Brodie Farquhar, "Wolf reintroduction changes ecosystem in Yellowstone. June 30, 2018 https://www.yellowstonepark.com/things-to-do/wolf-reintroduction-changes-ecosystem.

   There are also detractors, who say that the recovery is not nearly as far along as suggested and that there is still damage in the ecosystem not associated with wolves and elk. See Arthur Middleton, "Is the Wolf a Real American Hero?" *New York Times*, March 9, 2014. http://www.nytimes.com/2014/03/10/opinion/is-the-wolf-a-real-american-hero.html?_r=0.

   The truth is that all of this is hard to pin down. Good science exists on both sides of the debate. What we do know is that climate change is having an impact on aspen ecology and that the recovery of these places will not look equivalent to what it was when the wolf was exterminated.

How many times have you heard the idea that all species are created for a purpose? The inevitable response is "What about the mosquito? I don't know what good they are." It may be a hard struggle to find a beneficial aspect of a mosquito with its potential to spread parasitic diseases like malaria, dengue fever, yellow fever and more, yet some parasites are extremely important and, ultimately, beneficial.

In the 1980s and early 1990s, a tiny fuzzy arthropod called the cassava mealybug (*Phenacoccus manihoti*) spread across the continent of Africa (Figure 1.11a). This mealybug thrives on the growing tip of cassava branches, sucking juice from the plant like aphids. The withdrawal of nutrient reduces the plant's transfer of energy to the cassava roots where they produce large starchy tubers. In Mozambique at that time, these tubers supplied up to 50% of the human diet in rural areas. Cassava is not native to Africa; it originated in South America, most likely in the rainforests of southern Brazil and eastern Paraguay, and it was thought that the plant parasite came from there and was introduced accidentally to Africa over 300 years after the crop arrived.

Scientists from the International Institute of Tropical Agriculture in Ibadan, Nigeria, found a parasitoid wasp, *Epidinocarsis lopezi*, in Paraguay that specifically preyed on the mealybug (Figure 1.11b). The wasp is very small and reproduces by laying an egg in the back of the mealybug. The wasp larva feeds on the mealybug, making it unable to reproduce. Upon maturity, the wasp exits, mates, and begins laying more eggs. Within a decade after introduction in Africa, the *E. lopezi* wasp had reduced the impact of the mealybug to an inconsequential level (Gutierrez et al 1988). The bug was not eliminated—nature does not work that way—but the population was reduced to a level at which the plant parasite was effectively controlled by the parasitic wasp and the threat to the cassava was eliminated.

This type of biological control is very effective, but it is also very specific. Other attempts to introduce biological control have not worked as successfully, such as the cane toad in Queensland, Australia. Scientists are now very careful to test biological control organisms

FIGURE 1.11   Two photos showing (a) the cassava mealybug and (b) its associated parasitic wasp.

before introducing the agents to a new area. Often the problems caused by the introduction are greater than the problems they were meant to solve.

Commensalism

There are numerous examples in nature of *commensal* relationships, probably many happening on your body right now. These are relationships in which one species benefits while the other is essentially unaffected. One example is the tiny mites that live in various places on our skin, most famously on our faces. One species, *Demodex folliculorum*, especially likes the hair follicles of our eyebrows, eyelashes, and beards. Mites are tiny members of the Arachnida class, Acari subclass, so are distant relatives of spiders. They eat the oils produced by sebaceous glands during the growing of hair, and occasionally may eat dead skin cells. They cause no problems in the way that lice do; they just live off what are essentially waste products that we wash off with soap. Human babies have no mites, while we adults may have over 1,000 individuals on our faces alone.[6]

Commensal relationships are not just invisible. Among plants, some species, such as the marigold, put out chemicals that cause insects to avoid them. In the process, other plants benefit simply by their proximity, with no corresponding benefit to the marigold. Remoras live near, and are often seen attached to, large predators like sharks. They travel with sharks, and when the larger animal makes a kill, the remoras detach and feed on the leftovers. The sharks don't even notice. The same is true of cattle egrets. They like to hang out with cattle and other large herbivores that scare up and expose insects and other critters, on which the egrets feed. Again, there is no direct benefit to the herbivore, but the egrets thrive in their presence. It is possible that the egrets reduce the parasite load of the cattle, but the literature on this is scanty.

Mutualism

Mutualism deserves a longer explanation, because it is arguably the most important product of evolution. It is essentially the relationship established between two organisms—distinct species, often from different kingdoms, that are mutually beneficial. Perhaps the most famous of these is the relationship between nitrogen-fixing bacteria, in the families called *Rhizobia* or *Frankia*. *Rhizobia* are usually found in association with legumes in the family *Fabaceae*, in plants such as alfalfa, clover, beans, peas, soybeans, and peanuts, or in trees such as acacia, *Leucaena leucocephala*, or black locust. *Frankia* are bacteria of a different type, referred to

---

6   Hadley, Debbie. "Do You Really Have Bugs Living in Your Eyelashes?" ThoughtCo. https://www.thoughtco.com/bugs-in-our-eyebrows-1968600.

as actinomycetes that form nodules on the roots of trees like alders and casuarinas. Many farmers take advantage of these relationships in order to increase the nitrogen available to the crop plants in their fields.

Another set of mutualistic relationships exists between plants and fungi. This relationship was not recognized as important until after World War II and has gained economic importance only in the past 25 years. The details of the following story come through Chris Maser, formerly a faculty member in Oregon State University's College of Forestry and a participant on a team uncovering the secrets of old-growth forests in that state. In the early 1980s, forest managers were concerned that forests that were managed to provide timber for companies like Weyerhaeuser, Boise Cascade®, and Georgia-Pacific on private land or the National Forest, which were harvested twice and then replanted for a third crop of trees on a 50-year rotation, were not thriving. The team felt that old-growth forests might hold the answer to the problem (Maser 1994). This was a major economic concern, as it could reduce supplies and drive up costs at many levels.

The Oregon State team found an answer in the form of two fungi growing in association with the roots of old trees that produce the Oregon white truffle and Oregon black truffle. A *truffle* is the fruiting body of ectomycorrhizal fungi. These fungi form a close relationship with the root hairs of the trees: The trees exude sugars produced through photosynthesis in their needles, and the fungi exude nutrients captured in their miles of tiny white threads, called mycelia, that weave throughout the soil. Fungi as a kingdom are external digesters, meaning they excrete digestive juices to their sources of food or nutrients, which break those sources down to an available form, then reabsorb the nutrients for movement to the rest of the organism.[7]

It turns out that the third-generation forest was not establishing these root/ectomycorrhizal relationships consistently throughout a new stand of trees, and the plants that did not establish these relationships early in their growth failed to thrive. To understand why, the scientists had to uncover the life cycle of the fungi, which is not an easy thing to do. The white Oregon truffle, *Tuber oregonese*, and its black cousin, *Tuber gibbosum*, do not fruit above ground. Instead they fruit only near the base of Douglas fir trees, the dominant commercial timber species in the Pacific Northwest. These truffles are produced only near trees more than 60 years old, but the rotation for forest growth was 50 years. Even though researchers found Douglas fir with mycorrhizal associations in younger trees of the second generation,

---

7   It is a mistake to think that nutrient transfer is solely the movement of simple sugars and fats from tree to fungi, and inorganic salts from the fungi to tree. It is more complex and interesting than that. See the following section on Endocytosis.

these fungi had not yet reproduced, so there was no source of fungal spores for third-generation forests, except for the isolated stand where some spores had reached.

How do these spores spread from underground fruiting bodies? While pigs love snuffling with their nose plows for truffles, a favorite food, pigs are not native to Douglas fir forest. The local species responsible for their spread turned out to be the red-backed vole, a small mouse like rodent that lives in the surface layer of dead organic material, called duff, which can be very thick in old-growth forest. The voles make tunnels through the duff, searching for food, and truffles are a favorite. The spores of the truffle are not digested well when passing through a vole's digestive tract, and they are defecated into the environment wherever the vole passes. This explains the spread of fungal spores near old-growth trees, but the range of a vole in the environment is not great, so scientists felt it was unlikely that voles were responsible for the isolated cases of fungal attachment to trees in the third-generation forest.

In fact, it turns out that another species is responsible for this, the northern spotted owl, a bird long on the endangered species list because of habitat loss and fragmentation. Northern spotted owls gained fame during the Reagan administration because the Endangered Species Act protected their habitat from logging companies wanting to continue logging the old-growth forests. The conflict became so heated that loggers came out with a bumper sticker saying, "Save a logger, eat an owl." Needless to say, the environmentalists and scientists were not amused. Although it was in the loggers' interest to continue logging, these jobs could not last forever because the old-growth forest is now vanishingly small. The scientists realized the owls held the key to longer-term forest survival. Why? The owls have an odd habit. They nest in the hollows near the top of old-growth forest trees and fly through the forest for their prey at night, listening for the scraping of the voles in the duff. They are effective hunters and consume their prey in the trees. They do not, however, defecate in the trees. Instead they prefer defecating away from their nests, while in flight, commonly over clearings. The voles they eat have spores from the fungi in their guts, and these pass through the birds without loss as well. When the owls defecate over a newly planted forest, some of the spores find the roots of new transplanted trees and a successful relationship begins, but the success rate is low. Foresters have used this information to come up with better reforestation strategies and a better defense of the remnant old-growth forest, advocating for mixed-age stands of trees that can provide these reproductive services for free. Mutualistic relationships like these are found throughout the plant and fungal kingdoms.[8] We ignore them to our own detriment.

---

8   For more information on the role of fungi in ecosystems, the work of Paul Stamets (2005) provides an excellent starting point. This YouTube video of a presentation by Stamets in Australia is another great source: http://www.youtube.com/watch?v=cwLviP7KaAc.

Endosymbiosis

Every species interacts with members of its own kind, yet also interacts with other species in a variety of ways, as defined above. But how all the species evolved is a fascinating question. Evolution by natural selection is the prevailing theory that best explains how organisms as we know them now arose. But some steps in evolution are less well known; noteworthy among these is the discovery that all complex organisms evolved from an earlier mutualism, which became a partnership, which eventually merged into a new set of kingdoms. All early life began as relatively simple cells called prokaryotic cells. These archaea and bacteria kingdoms have no cell walls, just membranes, and no differentiated organelles. They do have DNA and RNA, but it is scattered through the cell, not centered in a nucleus. All of these early organisms had the ability to gain energy by capturing energy-rich molecules in the organic soup of early oceans, and a few of these evolved ways to capture solar energy and make their own food via photosynthesis. These blue-green algae then became the base of the early food web: producers. At some point, competition for resources gave rise to cooperation among some types of bacteria. Lynn Margulis first articulated and popularized the notion that this cooperation eventually gave rise to the eukaryotes—organisms sometimes with cell walls, always with internal organelles and a distinct nucleus housing its DNA. Evidence for this endosymbiotic theory is found in the chloroplasts and mitochondria of each cell. These organelles carry their own DNA in much the same way as bacterial cells. The theory states that eukaryotic cells are the result of a complex mingling of two or more distinct types of archaea or bacteria to form new, more complex cells—a mutualism so complete that the resulting combination cannot survive independently. Margulis used this understanding to support her claim that living systems, ecosystems, have evolved via natural selection more to develop better cooperative relationships or mutualisms than they have from competition (Margulis 1991). To fail to understand this aspect of ecosystems when managing them is to contribute to their decline.

Endocytosis

Cells eat, but the way they eat varies. An individual cell has no permanent oral or anal opening, but some cells are able to channel food to certain intake points and channel waste to vacuoles at exit points in the cell wall or membrane. Other cells can surround their food, essentially making a bubble in the cell wall that captures the food in the bubble, then break it off internally, most prominently demonstrated by amoeba. This method of food intake, called *endocystosis*, is more common than most people realize. The fresh root hairs of plants and the mycelium of fungi also use endocytosis (Pommeresche 2019). In this way they can consume food that is larger than the molecular constituent parts, such as simple sugars (glucose and fructose), amino acids, essential fatty acids, and nucleic acids. It also means

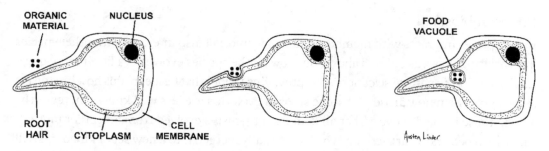

FIGURE 1.12 Endocytosis showing the sequence of intact organic material touched by the root hair of a plant cell. Drawing by Austen Linder.

that plant nutrition is not just a function of absorbing inorganic salts like nitrates, phosphates, and potassium salts. In addition, they can absorb long-chain molecular structures like starches, proteins, fats, and DNA and RNA strands, or perhaps even entire bacteria, as shown in Figure 1.12. They do this by drawing these larges molecules or bacteria into depressions in the cell membrane, surrounding them with membrane material, then breaking off this bubble internally. It can then be broken down internally without ever having to deal with inorganic material. Any material that is unusable then gets tucked back into a membrane-surrounded vacuole and moved out through the cell membrane, where the waste becomes food (raw material) for bacteria and fungi. This latter process is called *exocytosis*. These two processes are an essential part of the entire nutrient cycle. Unfortunately, they have not received the attention they deserve, and some of our environmental management actions have damaged this portion of nutrient cycles, as will be further explained in later chapters.

Exponential Growth

Any population of a given organism, upon entering a habitat with a niche conducive to its own growth and reproduction, will experience a period of exponential growth. *Exponential growth*, is the type of growth that follows the mathematical formula $N_t = N_o \times e^{rt}$, where N_t is the population at a given time, N_o is the population at the start of the growth cycle or first measurement, e is the base value of the natural log, r is the rate of population growth, and t is the time period of that growth. This formula produces what is known as the exponential growth curve, illustrated in Figure 1.13. Exponential growth has received a lot more attention recently with the novel coronavirus, COVID-19. Infection rates and deaths have risen during the first portion of the outbreak following an exponential curve much like the one illustrated.

As you can see from the growth curve, population rises nonlinearly. In most cases, this growth period lasts only until the species reaches a saturation point, and then it either levels off or crashes. The unknown at the beginning of the cycle is the limit of the food supply.

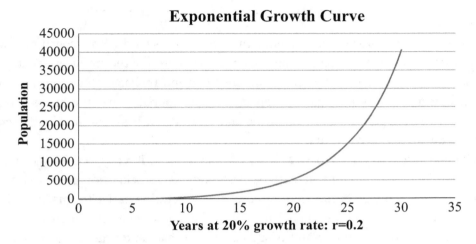

FIGURE 1.13 Exponential growth. An example of an exponential growth curve starting at year zero, with a population of 100 individuals and a growth rate of 20% per year.

Carrying Capacity

When ecosystems have a boundary some type, within that boundary is a limited capacity for production. The availability of food from producers in this area then limits the capacity of other species to grow. The producers' ability to grow is determined by the abiotic factors in the system combined with the nutrient cycling ability of the detrivores. Each species operates with a limit on its ability to reproduce. The maximum population of a species within an ecosystem that can successfully thrive through time without negatively impacting its food supply is referred to as its *carrying capacity*.

Donella Meadows applied this ecological concept to human population and human resource use. She and the *Limits to Growth* team recognized the exponential pattern of human growth and the corresponding patterns found in many aspects of economic growth, and they included with this the idea of carrying capacity inherent in a closed system. They recognized that humans were startlingly close to reaching what ecologists deemed the carrying capacity of the planet. Many economists, politicians, and other academics of the time did not recognize the implications of exponential growth; they were still using as their mantra the objections to Malthus's dire warnings in the early nineteenth century about population exceeding food supply.[9] Yet 40 years later, the warnings of Meadows and company have proven accurate and the planet is in much worse shape than it was in 1972.

---

9   Perhaps the best purveyor of this viewpoint has been the University of Maryland economist and writer Julian Simon, whose book *The Ultimate Resource* (1983) provides an argument against the notion of limits to economic growth.

Overshoot

Overshoot occurs when a population temporarily exceeds its food supply, consuming what economists would call the capital rather than just the interest of the producers it eats. This can cause a loss of productive capacity in an ecosystem and a collapse of the consumer population, as well as any other organism dependent on the population of producers. A prime example of this happened on St. Paul Island and St. Matthew Island in the Aleutian chain of Alaska during the past century.

Reindeer were introduced to St. Matthew Island in 1944. Twenty-four female and five male animals, originally from Siberian domestic reindeer stock, were introduced to the island to take advantage of the arctic tundra-type vegetation native to this low-rainfall island. This type of vegetation can be quite dense, but it seldom reaches more than 30 cm high. About half the 128-square-mile island has suitable habitat for the reindeer, and since the vegetation was dense, the population thrived. According to Klein (1967), by 1957, 13 years after their introduction, the population of reindeer was 1,350 animals, most of which were in excellent physical shape.

By 1963, however, the situation had changed. The population of animals had increased to nearly 6,000 animals, but the average body weight had declined by 38%. Forage availability also notably declined and the largest plant, a type of willow with a recumbent form, showed intense damage after the winter foraging season. Then the winter of 1963–1964 hit, with heavy snows and harsh conditions. The already weakened condition of the animals and the poor forage situation during the winter combined to induce a population collapse. By the time a count could be made again in the summer of 1966, only 42 animals were left. These females were in relatively good condition, but they were not reproducing because no males had survived. This is a classic case of overshoot and collapse initiated by introduction of a species into an area with the right habitat but no consistent predation.

Overshoot is another of the terms used by Meadows in *Limits to Growth*. The authors claim their models show that human population and human use of natural resources follows an exponential growth curve, and furthermore, they predicted that we would exceed the carrying capacity of the planet sometime in the 1980s. This overshoot of carrying capacity will lead to collapse at some point, though their models were unable to identify precisely when.[10]

---

10   The idea of potential collapse is highly controversial, and the discussion about why it has not happened is beyond the scope of this tome. My own hypothesis is that the massive use of fossil fuels and other energy sources like nuclear, hydropower, and now even wind and solar energies has staved off collapse. I do not think it is inevitable, though; we can cut back on energy and consumption especially in developed nations. The real key is developing ecologically appropriate ways of meeting our needs. Subsequent chapters discuss these ideas more fully: see Chapter 5, "Reducing Your Personal and Global Carbon Footprint"; Chapter 8,

Logistic Growth

Thankfully, not all growth follows an exponential curve. Nature has a number of ways to control the growth of a particular species. Competition with other species for the same niche reduces reproductive success. Predation and parasitism reduce populations, as their numbers usually climb with the rise in population of prey species. These effects result in a different kind of curve called the logistic curve, shown in Figure 1.14. The curve starts off like the exponential growth curve, but at a point, usually at one-half the carrying capacity, there is an inflection that prevents the growth from exceeding the carrying capacity of the habitat.[11]

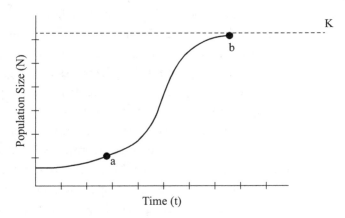

FIGURE 1.14 Logistic growth. The logistic growth curve showing population through time, with the red dotted line showing the carrying capacity.

The implication of the logistic growth curve is that, in any ecosystem where a population exceeds the long-term carrying capacity, there will be a collapse to below that carrying capacity until the system has time to recover. This happened on St. Matthew Island. The reindeer may have reached carrying capacity in 1957 when their population was robust, growing, and healthy and lacked any predation or other limiting factors, but they had certainly exceeded it by 1963 when their larger population was underweight and vulnerable. While it is possible to blame the harsh winter for the rapidity of the collapse, the underlying cause was decline in the food supply. How many other ecosystems on the planet are in a similar state?

Succession

Ecosystems are not static. They can appear so on a human timescale, but this is deceptive since we witness only a limited fraction of the time that an ecosystem exists. An old-growth forest in the Pacific Northwest, for example, can be home to Douglas fir, Sitka spruce, western hemlock, and western red cedar that live to be, on average, over 500 years old. In the Amazon rainforest, trees commonly reach 300 years before falling. Change in either ecosystem

---

"Rice, Records, and the Potential for Alternative Agriculture"; and Chapter 13, "The Trillion Tree Project: Tree Crops and the Benefits of Agroforestry."

11   For a mathematical explanation of the Logistic Equation, see http://mathworld.wolfram.com/LogisticEquation.html.

happens on a timescale not readily apparent to short-term observers. Perturbations do occur, though, and at different scales. Sometimes these changes, like a forest fire or a major storm, wipe out everything in a wide swath. Other times the changes can be as small as a canopy tree falling in the forest, opening a small space so that light reaches the forest floor. In both cases the change induces a sequence of events that ecologists call *succession*: the pattern of vegetative recovery and change in an ecosystem.

Succession starts with an event that causes either superficial loss or total loss of the surface vegetation. The superficial loss could be from a low-intensity fire or a storm that knocks the trees down, but the root systems or lower-level vegetation still survives. In this case, some soil will be open to pioneer species that specialize in covering bare soil. These are commonly annual plants that have lightweight seeds or seeds that are animal-dispersed, allowing them to colonize open territory very quickly. However, in the scenario called secondary succession, some of the perennial plants are still able to grow and these soon reoccupy the landscape, eventually shading out the shorter annuals and bringing the landscape back to a point at which the trees can reoccupy the land, provided there is an available seed source in the ecosystem.

Primary succession occurs when the vegetation dies back completely. The hot fires around Yellowstone National Park in 1989 or the explosion of Mount St. Helens in 1980 left landscapes denuded of vegetation. In the case of Yellowstone, the seed sources for some species, like lodgepole pine, survived and were able to germinate quickly, while annuals quickly colonized the million-acre fire site, so park visitors were able to see growth rather quickly. In the case of Mount St. Helens, most seed sources were lost. The previous evergreen forest was buried or blasted away. The soils were now sterile rock fragments, particles, and dust from the decapitated volcano. Colonization took time, but eventually the annuals came, organic matter started soil formation processes, and this in turn attracted primary consumers bearing seeds of other species on their bodies or deposited in fecal material. These species will slowly take over from the initial succession species. Eventually the Douglas fir–dominated forest will come back, but it will be a long process.[12]

Keystone Species

The wolf in Yellowstone National Park is a perfect example of a keystone species. Without this predator, the elk's behavior changed, damaging the ecosystem and leading to a steady

---

12   For an excellent video on Mount St. Helens, see https://www.youtube.com/watch?v=Ifohb8_2WhE. One of the key findings is that animals such as gophers, when in their holes during the explosion, survived the blast and burial in many locations and were able to bring seeds in their burrows back to the surface, reseeding the local site. The US Forest Service and the Weyerhaeuser Company also did large-scale reforestation outside the main blast zone, which is now a national monument.

decline. Reintroducing the wolf reversed the problem. *Keystone species* are defined as those species that, by their removal or significant reduction in population, induce a change in status in that ecosystem to the detriment of most of the inhabitants. No description in environmental and ecological literature better describes the impact of a keystone species than Aldo Leopold's piece "Thinking Like a Mountain," in the chapter about Arizona and New Mexico in *A Sand County Almanac*. I urge you to read the entire section, if not the entire book. In this passage Leopold describes the killing of a wolf, where he saw the "fierce green fire dying in her eyes." He said that mountains were the only things old enough to understand the meaning of the wolf's cry and that the mountain itself reveled in this since the major threat to the mountain was not the wolf, but rather the overpopulation of deer.

Another keystone species that inspires a lot of attention is the sea otter. The otter is less threatening than the much-maligned wolf and inspires admiration for its undeniably delightful dining habits. The sea otter prefers eating shellfish of various types that require some effort to extract. On its dives to fetch the clams, mussels, and sea urchins that dominate its diet, it also brings a stone to the surface. The otter then places the clam on its belly and proceeds to bash it with the stone until it can extract the flesh for its meal. How many tourists from California to Alaska have enjoyed watching the otter simultaneously at work and play is impossible to count, but the otter's impact on the environment is far more important than its attraction of tourists.

Sea otters prefer the habitat identified by Pacific continental shelf kelp beds. Kelp is a type of algae that attaches to the bottom of the sea, usually tying itself to rocks. Its buoyant stem extends toward the surface, along the way producing leaflike fronds that photosynthesize. The kelp provides a habitat that protects sea otters and numerous fish species from predation by larger fish or even killer whales, which cannot swim well through the fronds. Sea otters have another problem, though: They are covered with the thickest, softest, most luxuriant fur in the animal kingdom. This fur attracted Russian and later American and Canadian fur trappers, reducing the otter population throughout their range. This depopulation allowed one of the sea otters' favorite foods, the sea urchin, free range to eat its favorite food, kelp. When the kelp forest diminished, habitat for the other species hiding in its fronds also dropped and the ecosystem nearly collapsed. Thankfully, the market for sea otter pelts also collapsed. Later Congress passed the Endangered Species Act, which protected the sea otters. The sea otter population has rebounded through much of its range, so much so that native Alaskans are allowed to hunt the animals now, with monitored restrictions.

Sadly, in 1989, another disaster adversely affected the animals in Prince William Sound, an important part of the otters' range and an important fishery in Alaska. The Exxon Valdez crude oil spill was devastating to the entire ecosystem in that region of Alaska, not least of all the sea otter. [13] While the full recovery of Prince William Sound may take a long time, the sea otter population has recovered. It took two full decades for the population in the region to reach a normal life expectancy, and by 2014 scientists determined that the populations showed characteristics of healthy populations in areas not impacted by the oil spill. [14]

Ecological Footprint

Bringing up the Exxon Valdez oil spill leads to another term of importance that emerged after *Limits to Growth* was published: the idea of the *ecological footprint*. The authors of *Limits to Growth* were asking these additional critical questions: How much of the planet is affected by the action of humans? Do the actions of some humans have greater impact than others based upon their degree of consumption? Measuring this impact is the core principle of an ecological footprint. It asks what the impact of society is on the planet and how each of us contributes to that impact. How much land and water, how many trees and oceanic resources, does it take to supply us, corporately and individually, with our lifetime of resource use? The answer can be quite surprising and uncomfortable.

I used an ecological footprint calculator online to find my own ecological footprint and was not pleased with the answer. [15] This one was from the Global Footprint Network. It examines your eating habits (how much meat, poultry, and dairy), your household type and size, your water use, your energy use (mobility, airline flights, car type, motorcycle), and your consumption of goods and use of services in order to calculate how many acres you require to support your lifestyle. I have a passive solar home; drive a Prius [16], ride an electric bike; eat meat (but only grass-fed beef from my own farm), poultry, and dairy; rarely buy major appliances or furniture; recycle everything possible; and compost all vegetative waste. Yet my impact was very high. It would take 7.1 planets to supply all of humanity's needs if everyone lived like me. I require 31 acres of land to support my lifestyle. Scary, because I had thought I was doing rather well. For a typical American the score is lower; it would take 4.3 planets, or about 19 acres. The main impact I have is derived from two

---

13 See *Sound Truths and Corporate Myth$* by Dr. Riki Ott for more depth on this topic. Dr. Ott's website, http://www.rikiott.com, is another resource in the ongoing saga of the spill.

14 25 years after Exxon Valdez spill, sea otters recovered in Alaska's Prince William Sound. John R. Platt, March 5, 2014. Scientific American. https://blogs.scientificamerican.com/extinction-countdown/25-years-after-exxon-valdez-spill-sea-otters-recovered-in-alaskae28099s-prince-william-sound/

15 http://www.footprintnetwork.org/en/index.php/gfn/page/calculators/

16 A Prius does get better gas mileage than other cars its size, but it also has a larger energy cost of production due to the batteries. By the end of its expected lifetime, its ecological impact is probably about equal to that of a car getting 35 miles per gallon, so you could call it less bad than most.

FIGURE 1.15

sources: my mobility because of the car and flying to Africa, and my house, which at 2,300 square feet is rather large (though not by American standards). I drop below the American average with no airline flights.

I could quibble with these results. I don't have air conditioning; my house is super-insulated with straw bales and it passively heats itself, using less than one-quarter the energy of normal houses of equivalent size; and I now have a 4.4-kilowatt solar system on the roof. Yet I have no reasonable argument. Flying remains the single most energy-intensive thing I do, and the most costly to the planet. I recognize that I need to change lifestyle even more than I already have, but I also know that to do so will require broad changes not just by my family and me, but also by the community in which I live and by the United States in general. Reducing our ecological footprint is essential if we are to avoid overshoot and collapse, but it will take communitywide and nationwide work to accomplish. More on this topic is found in Chapter 5, "Reducing Your Personal and Global Carbon Footprint."

Biodiversity

In 1992, E. O. Wilson, renowned student of ant behavior and proponent of the ideas of sociobiology, published a book called *The Diversity of Life*. In this book Wilson eloquently describes the width and breadth of knowledge about organisms on the planet and makes quite clear how little we know with certainty. He tells a story that took place in the Yasuni rainforest near Iquitos, Peru, not far from the Amazon River to illustrate his points most dramatically. The forests in that area are documented to contain over 300 different species of trees per hectare, with the record being over 600 tree species. Another scientist, a colleague of Wilson's, working in Panama, selected one large canopy species, *Luehea seemannii*, and fogged it with a broad-spectrum insecticide. The dying insects and other arthropods fell into funnels that channeled the insects into jars for later identification. The researchers found 163 species of beetles living exclusively in this one tree species. There were thousands of bugs, from centipedes and millipedes to beetles, flies, and lepidopterons (butterflies and moths). This does not even touch the bacterial species that may be native to the gut of each. Biodiversity is the name for this abundance.

The Yasuni rainforest is obviously exceptional, having all the conditions to maximize life in a small area, good water, equatorial solar input, and deep, though not nutrient-rich, soils. Yet diversity is found everywhere that humans have not touched. Natural systems tend toward diversity if given sufficient time to develop. North American forests are less diverse. Part of this stems from the periods of glaciation that episodically extinguished all life from the Ohio and the Missouri Rivers and north. Part of this is from the cooler temperatures and other extreme conditions that organisms must adapt to throughout the continent. Yet diversity is still here, obscured only by the human tendency to promote economically or culturally valued species and grow them exclusively—think corn, soybeans, yellow pine, and lawns. We have, as Vandana Shiva (1993) puts it, a "monoculture of the mind" that detests the messiness of diversity in favor of an order of our own choosing.

Ecologists have recognized that ecosystems tend toward diversity out of necessity. Daniel Janzen, an ecologist at Pennsylvania State University who studies the Guanacaste area of northwestern Costa Rica, observed that trees in wet tropical forests tend to reproduce better when they are farther away from the parent tree in the midst of different species. He hypothesized that insect species specializing in eating the seeds of the tree are denser near the tree itself and diminish in density the farther away you get from the parent tree. Thus, seeds transported farther away have a better chance for survival. This particular hypothesis has proven true in the Yasuni situation where species are evenly and relatively distantly spaced, but it did not hold in the dry forest of Guanacaste. Scientists found that distribution of trees was either clumped or random, but was seldom determined by distance from others of the same species (Hubbell 1979). The range of biodiversity is conditional to the place where one is looking.

The point of these examples is two-pronged. First, we don't really know that much about *biodiversity*. The term itself showed up in the literature only in 1988, and it has not been a major subject for direct study in science for very long, given our penchant for studying individual species or even narrower aspects of biology. Second, biodiversity on the planet is shrinking rapidly. Those who do study it are now calling our age the "sixth great extinction." The previous five were caused by physical disasters internal or external to the planet, but this is the first extinction caused by a particular species on the planet. We ignore the loss of species to our peril.[17] What would be Africa's plight if the wild population of cassava in Paraguay had been lost due to deforestation, causing the loss of the *E. lopezi* wasp, the only known effective agent to control the cassava mealybug? What we do to biodiversity, we may be doing to ourselves.

Genetic Diversity

As biodiversity is the measure of the number of species living in an ecosystem, genetic diversity is the abundance of traits within a given species across the ecosystems in which it thrives. The importance and ultimate necessity of genetic diversity is illustrated by our experiences with agricultural crops like wheat, the second most-consumed species on the planet by humans, trailing only rice. In 1999, a new variety of the wheat stem rust pathogen (*Puccinia graminis* f. sp. *Tritici*), a fungal parasite causing significant to near-total crop loss, entered the agricultural system in Uganda (Figure 1.16). Not long afterward, the disease spread to Kenya, Ethiopia, Eritrea, and across the Red Sea to Yemen, steadily marching north. It was feared that it would reach the breadbaskets of Iraq, Iran, and Pakistan before any resistance could be found. None of the narrow range of varieties in Africa proved resistant to the fungus.[18]

Stem rust has been a problem with wheat for a long time. The late Norman Borlaug, perhaps the world's best-known plant breeder and a 1970 Nobel laureate, first worked on this disease with a team in Mexico starting in 1944. By the early 1950s, they

FIGURE 1.16   Wheat stem rust.

---

17   Richard Dawkins made a valid but hypothetical point during a televised interview relevant to this topic. What if we are not seeing signs of other intelligent life in the universe because before they reached the level of intelligence and technological sophistication that could communicate across the cosmos, they killed themselves off first—through nuclear war, environmental pollution, or planetary warming? Are we following a universal pattern of intelligent life that gets to knowledge before it gets to wisdom?

18   Eduard Akhunov, "Resistance gene found against Ug99 wheat stem rust pathogen", *K-State News*, June 27, 2013. http://www.k-state.edu/media/newsreleases/jun13/sr3562713.html.

had developed wheat varieties containing two genes that conferred resistance to the stem rust pathogen. Most global varieties of wheat in commercial production contain these two genes. The new stem rust, named Ug99, proved capable of avoiding the plant's mechanism to resist stem rust and raised a stir throughout the plant-breeding world. Teams of scientists from Africa, the Middle East, Australia, Europe, and North America responded and began a search for a new genetic trait that could block the disease.

Scientists found the necessary genetic trait in an einkorn wheat variety (*Triticum monococcum*) grown in Turkey. Einkorn wheat is a direct descendent of wild wheat varieties in what we call the Fertile Crescent, the area of land along the Iraq–Iran border that runs in an arc through southeast Turkey and down the Mediterranean Coast toward Egypt. The wheat grasses in this region were primary succession species, rapid colonizers of open soil with large seeds that attracted early hunter-gatherers, and they are arguably one of the first domesticated crops. A gene in einkorn wheat, SR35, was identified as a key component in helping the plant to identify the Ug99 fungus as a threat and to turn on the plant's immune system. Only the breadth of available genetic diversity kept us from an impending agricultural disaster (Saintenac et al. 2013).

The range of genetic diversity is another area of ecological concern. As humanity expands our ecological footprint, turning native vegetation into single-species plantations of agricultural crops, trees, or grass, we reduce the space available for biodiversity and, within that limited scope, further reduce the genetic diversity of each member species. The process makes us more vulnerable to pests and diseases and therefore increases the apparent need to use inputs like fertilizer, insecticides, herbicides, and fungicides that have many known and unknown side effects. There is little doubt that we have one of the most productive agricultural systems in history in certain spots around the planet, but we also have the most vulnerable because we sustain this agriculture, and to a lesser extent our forestry, by fighting with nature rather than by cooperating with it. It is not an accident that most of the relationships between species on this planet are ones of cooperation rather than competition. An adjustment of our dominant strategy is needed; more on this to come.

Study Questions

1. The brief ecological list of terms and examples given here is by no means exhaustive. Can you think of anything you would add to the list?
2. Each of the terms in this list has numerous examples. Pick one, and find and write about an alternative example. What makes a good example of an ecological term?

3. Of all the ecological examples given here, which one strikes you the most? Is there something in particular that you would like to concentrate on and study? Why that particular one?

4. Humans are the most abundant large mammal on the planet, and our domestic animals are not far behind in abundant and total biomass. Are we and our domesticated associates in overshoot on earth? If yes, how is this being exhibited?

References

Gutierrez, A.P, P. Neuenschwander, F. Schulthess, H. R. Herren, J. U. Baumgaertner, B. Wermelinger, B. Lohr, and C.K. Ellis. 1988. "Analysis of Biological Control of Cassava Pests in Africa: II. Cassava Mealybug Phenacoccus manihoti." *Journal of Applied Ecology* 25 (3): 921–940. https://doi.org/10.2307/2403755.

Hubbell, S. 1979. "Tree Dispersion, Abundance, and Diversity in a Tropical Dry Forest." *Science*, New Series 203 (4387): 1299–1309. https://doi.org/10.1126/science.203.4387.1299.

Klein, David R. "The Introduction, Increase, and Crash of Reindeer on St. Matthew Island." *Journal of Wildlife Management* 32, no. 2 (1968): 350–67. https://doi.org/10.2307/3798981.

Kritsky, Gene (1991). "Darwin's Madagascan Hawk Moth Prediction". *American Entomologist* 37 (4): 206–210. https://doi.org/10.1093/ae/37.4.206.

Leopold, Aldo (1986). *A Sand County Almanac.* New York: Ballantine Books.

Margulis, Lynn, ed. (1991). *Symbiosis as a Source of Evolutionary Innovation: Speciation and Morphogenesis.* Cambridge, MA: MIT Press.

Maser, Chris. 1994. "Ancient Forests, Priceless Treasures." In *Restoration Forestry: An International Guide to Sustainable Forestry Practices*, edited by Michael Pilarski, pp. 76–86. Skyland, NC: Kivaki Press.

Meadows, D. H., D. L. Meadows, J. Randers, and W. W. Behrens III. 1972. *Limits to Growth: A Report for the Club of Rome's Project on the Predicament of Mankind.* New York: Universe Publishing.

Meadows, D. H., J. Randers, and D. L. Meadows. 1993. *Beyond the Limits.* White River Junction, VT: Chelsea Green Publishing.

————. 2002. *Limits to Growth: The 30-Year Update.* White River Junction, VT: Chelsea Green Publishing. (See also http://donellameadows.org/archives/a-synopsis-limits-to-growth-the-30-year-update/.)

Norgaard, Richard. 1988. "The Biological Control of Cassava Mealybug in Africa." *American Journal of Agricultural Economics* 70 (2): 366–371.

Ott, Riki. 2005. *Sound Truth and Corporate Myth$: The Legacy of the Exxon Valdez Oil Spill.* Cordova, AK: Dragonfly Sisters Press.

Pilarski, Michael (ed). 1994. *Restoration Forestry: An International Guide to Sustainable Forestry Practices.* Skyland, NC: Kivaki Press.

Pommeresche, Herwig. 2019. "Humusphere: Humus, a Substance or a Living System?" Translated by Paul Lehmann. Greeley, CO: Acres USA.

Reimchen, Tom. 2001. "Salmon Nutrients, Nitrogen Isotopes and Coastal Forests." *Ecoforestry* (Fall 2001), 13–16. http://www.web.uvic.ca/~reimlab/reimchen_ecoforestry.pdf.

Saintenac, C., W. Zhang, A. Salcedo, M. Rouse, H. Trick, E. Akhunov, and J. Dubocovsky. 2013. "Identification of Wheat Gene Sr35 That Confers Resistance to Ug99 Stem Rust Race Group." *Science* 341 (6147): 783–786. https://doi.org/10.1126/science.1239022

Shiva, V. 1993. *Monocultures of the Mind: Perspectives on Biodiversity and Biotechnology.* London: Zed Books.

Simon, Julian. 1983. *The Ultimate Resource.* Princeton, NJ: Princeton University Press.

Stamets, Paul. 2005. *Mycelium Running: How Mushrooms Can Help Save the World.* Berkeley, CA: Ten Speed Press.

Wilson, E. O. 1992. *The Diversity of Life.* Cambridge, MA: Harvard University Press.

Yasuni Rainforest Campaign. (n.d.). Save America's Forests®. http://saveamericasforests.org/Yasuni/Maps/Tree.html.

Credits

Chapter 2

Learning What Not to Do

Introduction

Ecology obeys the same laws that govern the universe. The first law of thermodynamics is that energy cannot be created or destroyed. There are no known exceptions. The same is true for the second law, which is that the total entropy of an isolated system can never decrease over time. This is sometimes popularly phrased as "everything tends toward maximum disorder." Earth by itself is not an isolated system; we are included within the larger system dominated by the sun. Because the sun is constantly bathing us in energy, at the expense of increasing disorder in the sun, order can increase through time on the earth, and this increasing order is produced by life on our planet. Yet within these ecosystems the laws still hold, and if we are not careful we can destroy that order built up by the ecosystems on the earth. It is these systems that dominate the focus of this book, and it is these actions—which are either destructive or constructive—that we want to highlight. The best rule to follow is perhaps the one attributed to Hippocrates, the Greek physician: "First do no harm."

On Ecological Bloodymindedness

In 2003, A. Duncan Brown of Australia wrote a book called *Feed or Feedback: Agriculture, Population Dynamics and the State of the Planet*. It is not a widely read book, but it deserves more attention. The title comes from feedback loops, which are described with eloquence by Donella Meadows in the books mentioned previously and are an important part of the modeling systems developed in *Limits to Growth*. Brown focuses on the element phosphorus as used in agricultural systems and on its relationship to human consumption of agricultural products in cities. Our cities dispose of human waste through water-based sewage treatment systems that do not go back to the farm, but rather exit the 1970s-era wastewater treatment facilities, usually into nearby water bodies and, ultimately, the ocean. It is there that the problems accumulate. For Brown, this problem was illustrated by the impact of the population of Sydney, Australia, and by the disposal of treated human waste in Sydney's famous harbor. In this case, as in the examples below, the story involves the impact of increased phosphorus and nitrogen on ecosystems.

It is worthwhile to follow Brown's feedback system further, using an example from North America. I live and work in Rockingham County, Virginia, the leading agricultural county in the state, located in the Shenandoah Valley, not far from West Virginia. Rockingham County boasts of being the turkey capital of the United States, and at one time the county was the leading US producer of domestic turkeys. The vertical integration of turkey production started here, following the lead of vertically integrated chicken production that started in Maryland following World War II. In a vertically integrated production system, turkeys are never seen outside the poultry houses—40 feet wide and 500–900 feet long—dotting the landscape. The Shenandoah Valley does not have enough land to produce the grain to feed so many birds, so most of the feed comes into the valley by train from Ohio, Indiana, and Illinois, primarily in railcars owned by Cargill®, ADM®, Norfolk Southern RR, and ConAgra®. Over one million metric tons of feed come into the county each year. This feed is then processed and sent to the poultry houses, where the birds eat, drink, and defecate for five months before being sent to slaughter. The manure stays on the farm.

This is a problem in the valley. Poultry manure is high in nitrogen and phosphorus. Nitrogen is highly mobile in soil, and it will move through the soil and in groundwater to streams if spread on fields too often or at the wrong time of year. According to the EPA, Rockingham County ranks second to Lancaster County, Pennsylvania, in sending nitrogen compounds downstream to the Chesapeake Bay. Phosphorus travels to the bay, too, but much more slowly. In most soils, phosphorus, in the form of phosphate ions, is essentially immobile. A farmer spreads the fertilizer, whether in chemical form or as manure, on a field, where it gets tied up with soil and stays there until a plant, often in association with mycorrhizal fungi, sucks the element up to use for its own growth. In Rockingham County, however, we import so much feed and so many birds defecate the waste that the soil profile is full of phosphorus to a depth that the crops cannot reach. Soil scientists have noted that this phosphorus eventually reaches groundwater and starts moving through the hydrological system. In water, as Brown notes, phosphorus combined with nitrogen causes algal blooms that degrade aquatic ecosystems and form dead zones that oxygen-dependent organisms must flee or die.[1] The bay is heavily troubled by these dead zones.

---

[1] Ecologists call this "anthropogenic eutrophication," or human-induced nutrient enrichment. Other places experiencing this problem include, but are not limited to, the mouth of the Mississippi River, the Baltic Sea, the North Adriatic Sea, and the mouth of the Yangtze River. Interestingly, the Black Sea, which had

This is not the only source of the problem. Turkey meat contains additional phosphorus in the form of DNA, RNA, ATP, and other biochemicals. The birds become food in cities and suburbs all around the Chesapeake Bay, where they are eaten, digested, and defecated into the aquatic waste treatment system that Brown describes. That water goes to the Chesapeake Bay as well. The feedback we get from these combined traumatic impacts on the ecosystem is the loss of biodiversity and productivity across the entire ecosystem. For years, people in the EPA, the Chesapeake Bay Foundation, and many other groups have tried to solve the problem, but they have made little headway because we ignore the fundamental problem: We have created a positive feedback loop between people and the agricultural system that encourages the very behavior that creates the problem. Centralized production of turkeys (and chickens) feeding centralized populations of people living far away from the areas of food production destroys the ecosystems where the centralization occurs. Meanwhile, the land where the corn and soybeans are grown gradually becomes more dependent on imported phosphorus fertilizers.

Brown, in his book about Australia, introduces two laws into his discussion that help us to comprehend what is going on in our own place. He terms these, with dry humor, the "Laws of Ecological Bloodymindedness." They parallel the laws of physics and thermodynamics and, in their own ways, are equally immutable. Law number 1 is this:

> *For every action on a complex, interactive, dynamic system, there are*
> *unintended and unexpected consequences. In general, the unintended*
> *consequences are recognized later than the intended ones.*

In our local example, the action on the complex, interactive, and dynamic system is the centralized production of turkey. The positive consequence of that action is the supply of food to all the cities, suburbs, and towns in the Chesapeake Bay watershed. This was immediate and known. The unintended consequence of that action, however, is the deterioration of the Chesapeake Bay ecosystem, not solely from the production of turkeys, but also from the increased population of humans in the watershed fed by the newly developed, centralized production of food. In other words, we have an unintended mess that requires fixing.

Law number 2 is a direct outgrowth of law number 1:

> *Any system in a state of positive feedback will destroy itself unless*
> *a limit is placed on the flow of energy through that system.*

---

one of the largest dead zones on the planet, has improved since the fall of the Soviet Union, which resulted in reduced nitrogen pollution in rivers flowing from Russia through Ukraine to the sea.

For our example, the state of positive feedback is the flow of nutrients from phosphorus mines in Morocco to farms in the Ohio Valley to poultry houses in Rockingham County to the treatment plants for bird and human waste, and finally, into water bodies. This cheap food enables people to live in concentrated settlements in the Chesapeake Bay watershed, which attracts more people, who then need more food, increasing the need for production in Rockingham County, which then must import more grain from the Midwest. The cycle does not end unless you find some way to reduce the energy input to the system. So how do we do that?

Lessons from The Natural Step

We are not the first to ask the question: How do we reduce the excess inputs into a system? In the late 1970s and early 1980s, Dr. Karl-Henrik Robert of Sweden was asking this question too. He did not come at the issue from the angle of an environmental scientist or an ecologist; rather, he questioned the direction the planet was heading from the perspective of a pediatric oncologist. At the time, he was perhaps the leading pediatric oncologist in his country, working at one of its leading hospitals in the capital Stockholm. "Why are children getting cancer at such an early age?" was the initial question tormenting him. His tentative conclusion was that the environment in which the children were living was contaminated with chemicals that stimulated cancer cell growth in children who were genetically susceptible to the disease. These children had a predisposition to cancer, but the disease was triggered by environmental sources, not simply problems internal to the child. Dr. Robert's question became this: How do we address and correct the problems that trigger the cancer?

Part of his answer came from his own patients. When a child has cancer, a whole network of caregivers forms almost spontaneously; the family is at the core, but relatives, friends, colleagues at work, fellow church members, and more gather to support the family and the sick child. What happens if the environment gets the same treatment? Can processes for designing a sustainable system arise in the same way as the caring community around a cancer patient if it is stimulated the right way?

Dr. Robert decided on a very broad strategy to encourage people throughout Sweden to address the question of creating a sustainable society together. At that time, *Limits to Growth* and reports from the World Commission on Environment and Development were available, and this literature fed into his effort to get Sweden thinking. He developed a set of questions that he then sent to over 50 leaders in the country from a wide spectrum of society that included politicians, business executives, writers, academics, journalists, social scientists, and physical scientists. His timing was good. Many in these communities were ready to respond, and they did so. Dr. Robert took the answers, condensed them into common themes, and developed a response, which he then sent back to the respondents for critique and reappraisal. This process went through 21 iterations and involved over 700 people, until it was reduced to four basic system conditions sent to every household and school in Sweden. Through time, it was given the name "The Natural Step" (Robert 2002).

The four system conditions and corresponding sustainability principles are given in the text box entitled "The Natural Step." The four principles are what I dub "the negatives of sustainability"—that is, what you should not do. If we are going to survive on the planet, we have to stop doing these negative things as soon as possible. It is not always clear what the negatives are from the narrow perspective of our homes, neighborhoods, or towns. In the text box, each of the four principles is repeated with slightly different wording and a key example is described. It is quite easy to think of multiple examples for each.

Box 2.1 The Natural Step*

The Four System Conditions

In a sustainable society, nature is not subject to *systematically increasing*:

1. concentrations of substances extracted from the earth's crust
2. concentrations of substances produced by society
3. degradation by physical means
4. and, in that society, people are not subject to conditions that *systemically* undermine their capacity to meet their needs

... reworded as The Four Sustainability Principles

To become a sustainable society we must eliminate our contributions to ...

1. the *systematic increase* of concentrations of substances extracted from the Earth's crust (for example, heavy metals and fossil fuels)
2. the *systematic increase* of concentrations of substances produced by society (for example, plastics, dioxins, PCBs and DDT)
3. the *systematic* physical degradation of nature and natural processes (for example, overharvesting forests, destroying habitat and overfishing); and ...
4. conditions that *systematically* undermine people's capacity to meet their basic human needs (for example, unsafe working conditions and not enough pay to live on).

* From https://www.naturalstep.ca/four-system-conditions.

1. Don't Take Excess from the Ground and Spread It on the Earth's Surface.

In essence, this refers to mining. Hundreds of examples could function here, including mountaintop-removal coal mines, hydraulic fracturing or "fracking" for natural gas and oil, copper mining in Zambia, iron mining in northeast Brazil, aluminum ore strip mines in Guinea or Jamaica, diamond mines in Sierra Leone, or coltan, a columbite tantalum ore, extraction in Eastern Congo. No matter where you go on the planet, you can find something extracted from the crust. In this case, an example that has not yet begun will suffice. On the Alaskan Peninsula, southwest of Anchorage, is a region of rugged volcanic mountains, pristine lakes, grizzly bears, and salmon runs. It is a region barely spoiled by the actions of humans, though we are present there. In the 1980s, a company called Northern Dynasty Minerals discovered a deposit of copper and gold on the western slopes of the Alaska Peninsula's mountains. This area drains west to Bristol Bay, one of the largest and most productive fishing areas still functioning on the planet. The rivers there host a great migration of sockeye salmon, so thick at times that the lakes appear red, the color of the spawning fish.[2]

Northern Dynasty calculated the value of this reserve they call Pebble Mine at approximately $300 billion. This number is based on notoriously unstable commodity prices that rise and fall with market demand and available supply. Both the Anglo American mining company and the Rio Tinto mining company partnered with Northern Dynasty on the project, and both sought permission from the US government and the state of Alaska to exploit the reserve. As expected, opposition groups arose almost immediately. Environmental groups were quick to point out the impact of mines on water quality, because these waters are among the cleanest on the planet. If the mines are not monitored closely, and the companies involved do not place priority on low-impact mining, the salmon of the rivers and lakes and the fish of Bristol Bay could suffer. Unfortunately, such arguments do not commonly work. They have not worked for stopping the mining of coal, oil, natural gas, uranium, gold, or other extractive products, and the companies do not have good reputations for environmental impact. So the environmental groups fought back, and the state of Alaska, burned badly by the Exxon Valdez spill, proceeded with caution.

Today the status of the mine is on hold, though the present administration (in office through 2020) is more in favor of the mining companies on this issue. The environmental objections are part of the reason; the other is funding. Until the 2018 election of the present

---

2   Read more about the salmon and gold conflict in Alaska here: Edwin Dobb, "Alaska's Clash over Salmon and Gold Goes National." *National Geographic*, November 18, 2012. http://news.nationalgeographic.com/news/2012/11/121116-bristol-bay-alaska-salmon-gold-pebble-mine-science-nation/

Alaskan governor, Mike Dunleavy (whose term ends in 2022), and the advent of the Trump administration, politicians had backed mining only tepidly, so banks did not flock to loan financial resources to the effort. The major mining companies involved had lost a considerable amount of money because of the global economic slowdown that began in 2008, but now the demand for the minerals is no longer soft, primarily because of the global switch to renewable energy and electric cars. Northern Dynasty, the company pursuing mining rights, lacks the means to implement the project by itself. The support of Governor Dunleavy and the superficial regulatory efforts of the EPA under Andrew Wheeler are opening up avenues for funding that were not available a decade ago when the mine was first proposed. At this time, thoughts of sustainability are not the issue. The concern is monetary. As yet, corporations and governments seemingly have not recognized the danger of taking things from the ground and spreading them on the surface. However, they are hearing about these dangers from environmental groups concerned that a mine will destroy the largest remaining healthy salmon fishery in North America.[3]

2. Don't Make New Things (Unknown to Nature) and Spread Them on the Earth's Surface.

Carbon is a marvelous element. It has an ability to attach to other carbons and other elements in a myriad of ways through covalent bonding. Nature builds just about all of its molecules on a backbone of carbon. It is this ability to form very complex structures or simple repeated structures, called polymers that chemists have used to create thousands of new molecules with a wide variety of uses. Some have become herbicides, insecticides, and fungicides used in agriculture. Some have become inks, dyes, or detergents. Above all in abundance are the plastic polymers, long chains of simple molecules that become chairs, ropes, polyester cloth, or plastic packaging, including plastic bags. No one can doubt their usefulness. One scientist even stated that we are fools for using petroleum as fuel when it can be used to make plastics and a whole range of useful chemicals. Unfortunately, the first law of ecological bloodymindedness has played its hand.

In July of 2013, I travelled through a small town along a road between Nairobi and Mombasa in Kenya. As we drove, it became clear that a town was nearby, evidenced by all the plastic bags in various stages of disintegration choking the ditch and lodged on thorn trees. It was a messy, nauseating site. Plastic is not known to nature. While it will disintegrate in sunlight from ultraviolet radiation, no bacteria or fungi has yet learned how to eat

---

3   Ariel Wittenberg and Dylan Brown (2019). "How Investors Got a Heads-Up on EPA's Pebble Mine Reversal." *Greenwire*, July 26, 2019. https://www.eenews.net/stories/1060792305.

FIGURE 2.1   Scene from an Atlantic beach.

it.[4] It does not return to carbon dioxide and water the way natural polymers will; the pieces get smaller and spread out, but they do not disappear. Though the durability of plastics is exactly the reason why people like them, the unintended consequence of that durability is felt and seen nearly everywhere.

In the Kenyan village, the impact is just messiness. In the Pacific Ocean, however, the impact is deadly. In the middle of the North Pacific, north of the Hawaiian Islands, is the North Pacific Gyre, an endlessly cycling flow of water into which objects enter but seldom escape. Captain Charles Moore was crossing this region of ocean in 1997 when he found a large soupy mix of plastic bits and pieces, some identifiable but most not.[5] While some of

4   Though success remains elusive, progress on developing plastic eating bacteria that will work outside a laboratory setting is occurring. The prospects are far better for these enzyme carrying bacteria on land than they are in the ocean. "Scientists are making progress with better plastic-eating bacteria." Sarah Scoles, Popular Science, July 1, 2019. https://www.popsci.com/plastic-eating-bacteria/

5   *Discover* Magazine has more information about this. See Thomas Kostigen, "The World's Largest Dump: The Great Pacific Garbage Patch," *Discover* Magazine, July 9, 2008. Another, more recent article also explains the situation well, "Great Pacific Garbage Patch. National Geographic, Resource Library, Encyclopedic Entry. https://www.nationalgeographic.org/encyclopedia/great-pacific-garbage-patch/

the plastic attracts birds like albatross and kills their young, most of the debris is broken down almost to microscopic levels and just floats. It is nearly impossible to remove the plastic in this state, but it impacts the bottom of the food chain. Whether it will ever go away is a matter for speculation, but it won't ever end if humans do not stop adding to it. The shopping bags, plastic bottles and lids, packaging, and discarded plastic lawn chairs all have potential to end up in an oceanic garbage pool. We put it there, and we can stop it by following the edict of this principle.

3. Don't Harvest Renewable Resources at a Faster Rate Than They can Recover.

Any living organism is a possible renewable resource. We have thousands of such resources—and countless examples of the abuse of them. Passenger pigeons in North America once flew in the billions from Canada to Florida. Now they are gone. By 1915, they had been over-hunted and wiped out, perhaps in part because they lost their eastern deciduous forest home range as well. Dodo birds on the Island of Mauritius in the Indian Ocean were wiped out quickly after the island's discovery by the Portuguese. They could have become a food fowl as valuable as the turkey, but we will never know. The great redwood is now flourishing on only 5% of its former range, and we barely saved that in just the last 40 years. Everywhere we turn, examples are found of resources we exploit when economics dictates—sometimes to extinction.

In the 1960s, a chemical called paclitaxel, harvested from the Pacific yew, one of a number of species of an understory bush growing in coniferous forests around the Northern Hemisphere, was found to have properties useful in treating ovarian cancer. It was discovered by the National Institutes for Health in a screening for plants with potential to treat cancer, and the drug was not patented. Subsequent attempts both to test the drug and to use it clinically had a major impact on wild yews in the forests of the Pacific Northwest because the drug is best extracted from bark. At the time, few thought about the reproductive cycle of the tree, which is both slow-growing and slow to reproduce from seed. We were outstripping the ability of the tree to produce the resource at a renewable rate. Thankfully, Bristol Meyers Squib™ discovered a way to semisynthetically produce the drug, known by its brand name Taxol; as a result, the tree, with help from the Native Yew Conservation Council, was able to begin a slow recovery.[6]

---

6   The Native Yew Conservation Council. Additional information can also be found at https://www.fs.usda.gov/treesearch/pubs/31615, and at https://www.nytimes.com/1991/05/13/us/tree-yields-a-cancer-treatment-but-ecological-cost-may-be-high.html

4. Don't Allow a Skewing of Resources to Select Parts of the Human Population.

In 2012 Jamie Dimond, CEO of JPMorgan Chase, took a hit on his salary because his company took a $6 billion loss speculating on a risky financial investment. He made only $6 million—as compared to the $20 million he had been paid the previous year, not including stock options and other perks. Congress would get on his case, but the Republicans shut down the government so there was no one watching the foxes chase the chickens. By comparison, the employees at McDonalds in New York City where JPMorgan Chase & Co. has its headquarters, make minimum wage, presently $7.25 an hour (in 2014). They are seldom employed for more than 29 hours per week, absolving the company of any responsibility to supply health insurance and other benefits. If this is the employee's only job, she will make $10,500 per year with two weeks of unpaid vacation, before taxes and social security are subtracted. This means this employee makes 1/570th of what Jamie Dimond makes in a bad year. Dimond takes home more pay in one day than the person serving him hamburgers makes in one year. That is what is meant by skewing wealth to one part of the population, the top 1% in this nation.

The wording of The Natural Step on this point is unsatisfactory to me. While what the steps say is correct, in that we should not create conditions that prevent people from working to meet their own needs, this still allows people to make extreme profits as long as they pay enough to their workers. This does not recognize the limits of a finite planet or the limits in our capacity to actually benefit from the wealth we may or may not earn. Wealth gained in financial speculation, as is done by most of the big banks globally, is not really earned. Bankers need to eat like all of us, but are they fairly paying for their food so that the pickers, processers, and packers—the ones who actually touch the food to get it to us—make a living wage to do it? These days, in the United States, the answer is most likely that they are not. We have one of the most skewed income distributions on the planet. Thankfully, Thomas Piketty, a French economist, has documented and exposed the reasons behind this increasing disparity of wealth in his recent book *Capital in the Twenty-First Century*.

Former secretary of labor Robert Reich is not afraid to speak his mind. He has just come out with a movie on this subject called *Inequality for All*. In it, he documents the extent of inequality in the United States and names the consequences. What can a corporation do if its employees are too poor to buy its own products? For Reich, the goal is not perfect equality, but rather that the gap be narrowed so that participation itself helps the economy stay sustainable. When income gaps are too large, some people are forced to opt out, becoming drags on the system. And if there are enough drags, the system collapses. Injustice is not sustainable.[7]

---

7   For a link to the movie, Inequality for All go to YouTube: https://www.youtube.com/watch?v=fjYlr5G22IY

This reality exists on college campuses. Students now feel lucky if they get a summer job that pays slightly above minimum wage, and many take the minimum wage. At the same time, federal and state governments have cut back on aid for higher education, either through grants or direct school funding. Thus, students now leave college with an average of $30,000 in education debt, even after their parents have assisted with their tuition and housing. The debt is crippling, while the job market for most fields is poor. As a result, the middle class shrinks; and the rich, no longer saddled with taxes or restraints, gamble with money they did not earn. Then when they win, they keep the money. If they lose, they lay off more employees. It is an unsustainable system that dimly resembles a true democracy. This is why the message of Reich, Piketty, and many others is so powerful: They expose the problem so that a broader spectrum of society can act to do something, though it is a long process.

Moving Toward Sustainability

The Natural Step provides these four principles not to make us gloomy or upset. Rather, the goal is to move toward an approach that is sustainable. In this, the organization shares the goals of the authors of *Limits to Growth*, Robert Reich, and most ecologists. The question is, how to do it? Donella Meadows helps to point the way with models. A model is a way of compressing reality into a formula. The formula is derived from the way things have progressed to date. It draws from real data, such as income distribution, commodity extraction numbers, extent of forests through time, agriculture production, agricultural input use, value-added production, and industrial production. If you take these numbers and develop a model that can follow the trends in historic time accurately from, say, World War I to the present, then inserting numbers for future possibilities can lead to clues as to how to move society toward more sustainable systems.

It is the assertion of this volume that ecosystems provide our best clues to how to move forward. Meadows would not disagree. Nature made the planet what it was until the point when humans started farming, and within that context lies the key to how we should remodel our planet. In the coming chapters of this book, I will describe some of the ways these natural systems work and how we can work with them to

FIGURE 2.2   The death of a tree, a symbol for our time?

remake things. It all starts with the sun: the ultimate energy source for life on the planet, and the one inexhaustible and steady resource that we have. Everything else depends on how we capture, maintain, and control the flow of that energy. We have not done that very well over the last 250 years, and we are now paying the price for that problem. At the same time, we have all the tools we need to do things right. So let's get started.

Study Questions

1. In the area where you live, is there an example of a nutrient problem similar to the one described in this chapter? What are the sources of the problem? Is anything being done about it at present, by environmental groups, government, or business?
2. What inspired you to take an interest in environmental questions? Think about the kinds of things that made you interested in how people impact your local environment. Which of the four things we should not do snaps you to attention?
3. Examine your area at different scales. What examples can you see of people, the government, or companies acting in ways that violate one of the four principles? Are they doing this in ignorance, or do you think they are doing this to avoid costs and save money?
4. Can you think of anything else we should not do? Does that thing fit one of these broad themes of The Natural Step, or would you advocate for making a new category?

References

Brown, A. Duncan. 2003. *Feed or Feedback: Agriculture, Population Dynamics and the State of the Planet.* Utrecht, the Netherlands: International Books.

Meadows, Donella, Dennis Meadows, Jorgen Randers, and William Behrens III. 1972. *Limits to Growth.* Washington, DC: Potomac Associates Group.

Meadows, Donella, Jorgen Randers, and Dennis Meadows. 2004. *Limits to Growth: The 30-Year Update.* White River Junction, VT: Chelsea Green Publishing.

Robèrt, Karl-Henrik. 2002. *The Natural Step Story: Seeding a Quiet Revolution.* Gabriola Island, British Columbia: Canada: New Society Publishers.

Credits

Chapter 3

The Rise and Pending Fall
of Conventional Agriculture

Introduction

Food is without doubt central to our lives. We all have to eat regularly. Yet for many of us an understanding of where our food comes from, how is it grown, and who moves it from the farm to the stores is an unknown. Most people do not even think about it. At the same time, that food production system is one of the most energy-intensive and polluting activities on the planet, as is described eloquently by David Montgomery in *Dirt: The Erosion of Civilization* (2007) and Jared Diamond in *Collapse* (2005). So how did it get this way, and why? That is the subject of this chapter. It is not exhaustive; that would take volumes. It focuses on three major aspects of how we grow food in our era using mechanical, chemical, and genetic knowledge that completely separated production from the native ecology of place, and why that separation leads to problems that are haunting us at a distance in our present food system.

The Problem of Conventional Agriculture

Almost wherever you turn these days you'll find a statement, article, book, or proposal involving some aspect of the problems with modern agriculture. A recent example from *The Nation* is entitled "How Carbon Farming Can Help Stop Climate Change in Its Tracks."[1] Another example is a book by Timothy Wise of the Small Planet Institute and Tufts University entitled *Eating Tomorrow: Agribusiness, Family Farmers, and the Battle for the Future of Food*.[2] The double meaning

---

1   Wood, Wilbur. 2019. "How Carbon Farming Can Help Stop Climate Change in Its Tracks." *The Nation*, May 2027, 2019. https://www.thenation.com/article/agriculture-carbon-farming-ranching-soil/
2   Timothy Wise. 2019. *Eating Tomorrow: Agribusiness, Family Farmers, and the Battle for the Future of Food*. New York: The New Press.

of the book's title is purely intentional. First, there is legitimate concern that food production cannot keep up with population growth and the high demand for meat as exemplified by the typical American diet. How are we going to feed all these people the food that they will demand? This is a different form of the same question that has crept into discussion since Thomas Malthus in early nineteenth-century England. The argument is simple: Population grows exponentially while agricultural production grows arithmetically, and one day those lines will cross. Malthus got the time frame wrong—partly because he underestimated the availability of farmland beyond England, and partly because he underestimated the ability of scientists to bolster food production through chemistry—but his basic argument is sound.

The second meaning of Wise's title is subtle but has deeper implications. Modern agriculture, as developed since the eighteenth century, has become a monster devouring the source of its own sustenance: the soil. We are destroying the basic resource that produces all of our food. This also is not a new idea. Critics of modern or conventional agriculture dot the historic landscape. F. H. King saw problems in the United States and sought answers to agricultural problems in the Far East and documented them in his book *Farmers of Forty Centuries: Or, Permanent Agriculture in China, Korea and Japan*.[3] Sir Albert Howard and his wife Gabrielle, regarded as the founders of organic agriculture, recognized that the kind of farming he grew up with in England did not work in colonial India, so he and his Indian farmer colleagues developed an alternative detailed in *An Agricultural Testament*[4] (Howard 1940). Closer to our era is Wendell Berry, an articulate and wise farmer from Kentucky, wrote what became a seminal book of agriculture critique in 1975 entitled *The Unsettling of America: Culture and Agriculture*. In this work he lamented the disconnect happening in agriculture between the farmer and the land and between farmers and their neighbors. We have become a nation, and perhaps in part a globe, where farming is an industry that produces food that is disconnected from the land it grows on and the people who eat it, thus becoming just a commodity for sale. Agriculture is unhitched from the ecosystem where it operates.

So how did we get to this point? How did agriculture evolve from the hunter-gatherer peoples of our distant past to the global monolith that produces food for the 7.5 billion and growing population of our planet today? And why are so many people claiming, with legitimate reasoning, that it is failing? To answer that question, we have to look both at the distant past and understand the cycles of success and failure among cultures and empires when it comes to food production, and at the more recent developments in agriculture that came

---

3   King, F. H., 1904. *Farmers of Forty Centuries*. Mineola, NY: Dover Publications.
4   My addition of Gabrielle Howard here is a recognition that women are commonly left out of the picture even though they may be recognized in the documentation or the public acclaim of their time (Mann 2018).

about with the mechanization of the industrial revolution, the understanding of chemistry, and the newer science of genetics. These three areas have their own story to tell, and all contribute to the present predicament of what is now called conventional agriculture.

The Mechanization of Agriculture

In terms of time sequence, the oldest of these three areas is the mechanical development of agriculture. The tale goes back perhaps even more deeply into unrecorded history. While we do know that agriculture began somewhere between 12,000 and 8,000 years before the present, we do not know exactly how it started or who started it. Archeologists know from work with human settlement patterns and the evidence found in middens that agriculture has origins in a number of places, perhaps independently, but all following the retreat of the glaciers of the last ice age and the loss of the great mammals of that era. It may be that agriculture was made possible by the demise of these great mammals, or perhaps made necessary by their loss. It is also hypothesized, based on good but not yet conclusive evidence, that drying conditions made it harder to find game and may have reduced the availability of commonly gathered plant-based foods.[5] In any case, hunter-gatherer people ceased moving, because they had found another reliable way to feed themselves. It is also quite likely that women were the ones who developed the earliest forms of agriculture. They did the gathering, the collection of fruits, nuts, roots, and leaves of plants that provided 90% of the calories in a typical hunter-gatherer diet, which probably relied more heavily on perennials than on annuals.

That last sentence requires additional clarification. Gathering is a skill set acquired with experience and handed down from generation to generation. The gatherer learns what to look for, what plants are edible in what season. Many things, like pokeweed in the eastern United States, are edible only when emergent after a winter dormant period, becoming inedible in summer. Other plants provide seed or tubers only at specific times. In the Fertile Crescent of what is now Israel, Jordan, Syria, Turkey, and Iraq, the ancestors of many modern grains were abundant. These ancient annual varieties of wheat, barley, and millet—which are now undergoing something of a revival as emmer, einkorn, spelt, and more—became available as edible seed in the summer and fall. Because they are annuals, they expend a lot of energy producing larger seed to guarantee successful reproduction year after year. The larger seed makes them easier to collect than most herbaceous plant seeds, and as such they offered

---

5   Elic M. Weitzel, 2019, "Declining Foraging Efficiency in the Middle Tennessee River Valley Prior to Initial Domestication," *American Antiquity* 84, no. 2: 191–214. https://doi.org/10.1017/aaq.2018.86.

some advantages to other gathered foods: They were relatively easy to collect and store for long periods without rotting if kept dry. Thus, they enabled human groups to stay in one place with an adequate food supply.

As women observed the plants, they noted characteristics that make collection easier. Plants that ripen simultaneously in dense patches offer abundant product with less labor. Plants that do not fall over easily, non-lodging, are easy to collect at hand height. Seed heads of plants that stay intact when touched, non-shattering, make it easy to collect numerous seeds at once. Plants that do not require a lot of pretreatment to get rid of toxins before cooking and eating are preferred. The ancestors of modern grains offered all these advantages. It is easy to speculate that people noted the places these plants grew best and came back to the same places regularly. Perhaps they dropped seed in places by accident, but then observed a dense patch of grain in those spots the next year. It is not a great leap to think that these people, when granted a surplus of seed, may have even intentionally dropped the seed in places they identified as having good soil conditions. They may have even noted what type of planting worked best to avoid losses to birds and insects. Over time, they developed the first agricultural tool, which archeologists have identified as the dibble stick, a pointed stick with a fire-hardened tip used to make planting holes for grains and other seeds. This was the birth of agriculture.

Annuals are early successional species. They dominate lands that are often subject to erasure of woody competition for a time. They evolved to quickly colonize openings created by disturbances, like a fire, deposition of new soil in a flood, or an opening in a forest following a windstorm or a tree fall. As early agriculturalists observed the physical characteristics of what they collected, they also observed the conditions where the plants grew. At first, they simply chose sites to live where these conditions were relatively constant and predictable. Fire and floods are conditions common in river valleys of relatively flat landscapes, commonly grassland environments. Fire keeps the trees at bay, while floods deposit new soils and create the open conditions ideal for growth of early successional species, the annual grasses and legumes dominant in early agriculture. It is no accident that the first agricultural communities that developed into early civilizations were in river valleys; the Tigris and Euphrates of Mesopotamia, the Nile of Egypt, the Indus of Pakistan, the Ganges of India, and the Yangtze of China are prime examples. In all of these areas, people developed techniques to mimic and expand the ecological conditions ideal for growing annual plants.

Dibble sticks and wooden or wood-and-stone hoes were likely the first agricultural tools used to open soil for planting annuals. While agriculture likely began as a local village-level activity, where people stored food for periods when the nearby land was unproductive, it gradually expanded to a larger endeavor with increased population densities. Two developments at the agricultural level gave rise to the first civilizations, where there is historic evidence of legal obligations in relation to agriculture. The first of these is the increasing reliance on animal power to open up soil, using a tool called an ard. The ard originally was a long wooden pole with a hook on the end that was fire-hardened to scratch open the soil. People trained oxen to pull the ard as they guided it from behind. These techniques are still used in places like Ethiopia. This technique enabled farm size expansion, so that one farmer could feed two to five people for a year.

The second and equally important development is the expansion of irrigation. By being able to control water, farmers could further expand cultivation, enabling the creation of cities with those people now liberated from the demands of production agriculture. The surplus production now required storage and protection. The expansion of irrigation required labor, organized management, development of engineering skills, and defense in case outside

FIGURE 3.1   A young Ethiopian boy using an ard pulled by two oxen on black cotton soils in the highlands of Ethiopia, not far from Dese.

forces attempted to capture the surplus production. From this came the rise of cities, and eventually civilizations with codified laws. Perhaps the best-known of these legal systems is the Code of Hammurabi in Mesopotamia, about half of which deals with agriculture and protecting irrigation systems throughout his kingdom.[6]

Not all early agriculture followed this pattern, but it is harder to find direct evidence of more decentralized forms of agriculture that did not lend themselves to the formation of centralized governance with strict legal codes. Just north of Mesopotamia, in what is now Turkey, agriculture developed in more decentralized forms, not dependent on irrigation and with reliance on a greater diversity of crops. Ancient wheat relatives were developed there, along with barley, lentils, and peas. In addition, there were tree crops, perhaps the most important being the hazelnut, which may have comprised a quarter of the diet. On

6   Scott Michael Rank (ed.), "King Hammurabi and His Code of Law," *History on the net*, https://www.historyonthenet.com/king-hammurabi-and-his-code-of-law.

the other side of the world, in what is now California, native peoples in and around the Sacramento–San Joaquin River valley relied on acorns in the same way. These balanocultures used the acorns like people in the Middle East used grain, but it required no irrigation system (Anderson 2013).[7] There is strong evidence that the intentional selection of improved varieties of both hazelnuts and acorns took place. In neither case did a kind of centralized and militant system arise from cultures dependent on perennial agriculture.

Over a period of at least five millennia, the ard became the dominant agricultural implement. It was key to opening the crusted soils of floodplain agriculture dominant in many regions. Yet it also moved out of floodplains into the rain-fed agriculture of hill country. This brought with it a set of problems that has been well documented in two books: *Collapse: How Societies Chose to Fail or Succeed* by Jared Diamond in 2005, and *Dirt: The Erosion of Civilization* by David Montgomery in 2007. Both books look at the rise and fall of cultures in various parts of the planet and explain from existing evidence on the landscape, and historic documentation if available, just why these cultures failed. Diamond focuses on deforestation and the loss of resources necessary for a society to function. Essentially, societies consume their own resource base, especially forests. Many of his arguments are disputed, especially his chapter on the demise of the culture of Easter Island, which he blames on the overexploitation of a large palm tree used to move the large stone heads around the island. In Diamond's view, the pollen record collected from the mud deposits at the bottom of the island lakes indicates that the palm became extinct around 200 years after the natives started building and transporting the heads, leading to erosion and loss of access to fishing since the palm was also their primary supply of canoe building material. Simultaneously, the loss of this and other trees led to a collapse of agriculture due to soil erosion. Other researchers think the main cause of palm extinction was the accidental importation of rats that fed on the palm seed. In either case, the result was the same: Food supplies collapsed, as did the population of the island and its culture.

Montgomery's book is more focused on soil erosion. He goes all the way back to Hammurabi and successive Mesopotamian civilizations that went through cycles of increase and collapse, usually by attack from outside after the infrastructure of irrigation deteriorated. The Tigris–Euphrates River valley is surrounded by hills to the west and north, and by the Zagros Mountains to the northeast and east. In the hills and foothills, people took the technology of the ard from the valley to the slopes. Unlike the continually refreshed soils of the floodplains, these hills did not tolerate the continuous plowing by ard, and when rains struck bare soil

---

7   Ian M., "Blanophagy for Beginners," *Frequently Found Growing on Disturbed Ground* (blog), 2011, https://ondisturbedground.wordpress.com/2011/11/04/balanophagy-for-beginners/.

they loosened soil particles, precipitating erosion. This erosion led to increased sedimentation in the floodplain, which is a good thing for crop fields, but it necessitated continuous dredging of irrigation systems to keep them functioning. If this dredging was not enforced by government, then overall productivity dropped and emboldened outside forces to attack. This pattern of rise and collapse was not followed by Egypt, which has a narrower geography that is entirely dependent on the Nile and its more distant water sources in Ethiopia and the East African Highlands.

Montgomery goes on to explain that other civilizations followed a rise, erode, and collapse pattern. Among these are both Greece and Rome. The Greek landscape is notoriously hilly and subject to the Mediterranean climate pattern of winter rainfall and dry summers. Farmers in this region relied heavily on tree crops like olive, oak, hazelnut, carob, and pomegranate, along with winter rainfall–oriented crops like wheat, barley, lentils, and peas, with lots of different greens and herbs. By carefully using terrace structures, they operated well for centuries. However, as centralized governance gave rise to more militant forms that removed young men from the labor pool, terraces that require continuous maintenance began to crumble. With farmers still using the ard, their plowing further weakened soil structure on the hills and rainfall led to erosion. The cycle became worse as Greek leaders further militarized in order to guarantee a food supply to the major city-states of the region, Athens and Sparta among them. The continuous disputations allowed Philip of Macedon and his son Alexander to expand their influence beyond their capacity to control, leading to both a widespread Greek cultural influence and a collapse of the central state.

Rome followed Greece as the dominant governing state of the Mediterranean. The Roman rulers knew well the power of a highly productive agriculture, destroying Carthage and its competitive power by destroying its agricultural base to ensure that it could not rise again. Rome itself was blessed with a valley of highly productive agricultural soils. The Tiber River winds its way from the mountainous central spine of the peninsula through a relatively wide valley that runs parallel to the mountains and the coast for a while, before turning west through the city of Rome to enter the Mediterranean. Even today that valley is filled with farms on both sides of the Tiber, relying on the river for irrigation and the replenishment of the valley's soils. According to Montgomery, the Romans loved to plow. He quotes various sources from the time of the Roman Empire that indicate the average farmer plowed three to four times a year. The rich soils in return gave a bountiful supply of food, easily transported downstream to Rome. Eventually, though, the labor required to maintain the agricultural system was extracted by the emperors to maintain a standing army and governance across the empire. Fields exposed by constant plowing eroded, and agriculture declined, necessitating reliance on a large military to extract food from far-flung provinces of the empire. Stretched too thin, the empire became vulnerable to outside forces, eventually leading to its collapse. Erosion should not be underestimated as an underlying cause for the demise of both the Greek and the Roman systems, even though the philosophy of governance and the legal mechanisms they created live on in our social systems. If we fail to keep erosion in mind, our own reliance on that heritage may be doomed as well. As Rome collapsed, agriculture still went on, but for local consumption, not to supply some faraway metropole. Since our heritage in terms of agriculture is primarily, though far from completely, European, we will focus next on what developed in the thousand years between ancient Rome and the connection to the Americas.

Once you pass north of the Alps, climate changes. The climate becomes maritime, and rain can fall at any time of the year—perhaps more in winter than in summer, but the spread is relatively equal. It also falls differently. Instead of heat-induced formation of thunderclouds and subsequent heavier rain, maritime rains are often gentle and longer, allowing time for the soil to absorb the water without significant runoff. Farming is primarily a three-season phenomena, with the growing season getting shorter as you move north. In most cases, in those early years farming also involved animals, not just to pull the plows, but also to become part of the food storage system, consuming things people could not eat so as to provide food in seasons when the land was dormant. It was not an agriculture that led to large surpluses; one farmer basically fed two to three more people, and farms were extended family operations, often tied to a landlord or local ruler of some type (whether called a count, a baron, a prince, or a duke). These feudal landlords protected the farmers and farmland they occupied, in return for a share of production and occasional extraction of labor for the manor or castle dominating the town. These landholding leaders were sometimes bound together in loose affiliation with other fiefdoms, ultimately with loyalty to the church. The only country that was readily identifiable throughout the period was France, and even that association was rather loose (Tuchmann 1987).

Farmers had plots of land identified as their own managed area. Often, the land was owned by the local lord but was granted to the family. On this land the family would grow crops, small grains being dominant, along with legumes (peas and lentils), vegetables of various types, some fruits (apples, pears, cherries), and tubers like beets, turnips, parsnips, and carrots. All these crops evolved in the region and functioned well in that climate. Animals were there too. Cattle, mainly castrated males as oxen, supplied power for pulling the evolving plow. Sheep were common, providing a lot of the fiber on which the population depended. Goats and cows supplied milk, an important winter food supply. Pigs provided something that we now get primarily from other sources: cooking fat, raw material for soap, oil for light, and some protein for the table. These animals were not raised on land that was used for crops; they grazed, browsed, or nosed their way on land held in common to all by the landlord. These were areas of forest, meadow, and stream where the animals foraged for their own foods: grass and herbaceous meadow plants for the cattle and sheep, bush and tree leaves for the goats, and acorns, grubs, roots, and entire plants going to the pigs. The commons land was controlled by all users, under the organizing control of the landlord. The system worked well, but it seldom produced large surpluses; nor did it frequently fail, though poor years were common.

Soil, always important, was something that would deplete over time if not cared for properly. Slowly, by fits and starts, a method developed to keep soil healthy and even increasingly productive. It involved, especially, the cattle, but all the animals and plants participated in producing the raw material: manure.[8] Having a long dormant season, anywhere from five to nine months depending on location, meant that collecting food for the animals was essential. The barn was invented for this. Sometimes the barn was simply the basement of the family home, other times it was separate. Food for the animals was stored above their living space, and daily it was flung down to them in their mangers. By providing bedding for the animals, the manure that mixed with other organic material became the main agricultural input in farming. When the temperature warmed and the animals could go back to pasture and woods, farmers took the now-composted and stirred (by the pigs) manure to the fields and spread it. The ard as used in the Middle East and the Mediterranean did not work well for this purpose, so farmers began to adapt the technology, making it more of a soil-stirring device or plow, often wood with metal attached for strength, which mixed the manure into the soil to the depth of the plow. Soil scientists call this a *plenum* horizon, an anthropogenic soil horizon that has both a good texture and nutrients to enhance agricultural production. This plenum horizon is found throughout the soils of northern Europe from England and France all the way to Russia (Brady 1984).

Improvements in Agricultural Technology and Mechanization

The Renaissance started a major shift in Europe that, while not changing farming directly or quickly, brought science into the forefront of thinking. This eventually produced tectonic shifts in agriculture, thereby creating what we term conventional or modern agriculture. These shifts took three forms: the use of steel tools and increasing mechanization, the understanding of the chemistry of soils and their impact on plant growth, and finally, the advent of genetics along with the ability to rapidly select and breed new characteristics in plants. Mechanization happened first, chronologically, but all three interacted to produce today's low-labor, high-energy-input agriculture. It is good to remember that even at agriculture's

---

8   I expand on this in Chapter 7, "Managing Manure: Following Nature's Nutrient Cycles."

peak of productivity, before the invention of the steam engine, an individual farmer could rarely feed more than five people, meaning that somewhere between 25% and 50% of the population was involved in agricultural production. At least in the Western world, this began to change rather rapidly after 1750.

Meanwhile, the Northern European agricultural system crossed the ocean, landing with Smith and company in Jamestown and in New England with the pilgrims and the Puritans. But the plenum horizon did not exist in these colonial areas. What the settlers found instead were the rocky soils of postglacial floodplains in the north and old soils under deciduous forests in the south. It may have been a new world, but unless scoured and redeposited by glaciers, the soils were old. In fact, soil scientists give the dominant soils of the southeastern United States the name *ultisols*, based on *ult* from the German for "old." Climate differed as well. Instead of the gentle summer rains of maritime regions, thunderstorms and accompanying downpours washed unprotected soils away, or leached away nutrients, making agriculture a hardscrabble operation that often led to periods of deprivation. In addition, while the economics encouraged rapid expansion of agriculture on land formerly worked by native peoples—many of whom died off from smallpox and measles epidemics to which they had little resistance—the new farmers also chose for export such crops as tobacco and cotton, which rapidly lead to soil nutrient depletion.

Tobacco was native but, as we know now, highly addictive, and it also required a lot of labor to grow. Cotton was introduced because the growing season in the southeastern region was long enough. It, too, was labor-intensive. So in 1619 colonial Americans introduced slaves to their agriculture system. At first, these came from active slave markets in the West Indies, brought from Africa to help England and France grow sugarcane, increasingly a major source of calories in the European diet. It was not a stretch to have these same Africans work to grow tobacco and cotton. But the plantation owners soon found that their soils, in the absence of the European style of manure inputs, could not support the continuous growth of these crops. By the late eighteenth century, the US Founding Fathers wrote and said as much about soil nutrition using manure and compost as they did writing the documents used to govern the new nation (Wulf 2011). However, few farmers and plantation owners instituted the ideas that Washington, Jefferson, and Madison promoted. Instead, they pushed west to new, unopened land that promised better fertility, using slave labor and driving out American Indians in the process. The Louisiana Purchase was done as much for this as for any reason given at the time. The limiting factor was ultimately not land, or even soil nutrients; it was labor.

Jefferson was one of a number of people who recognized this and sought ways to improve the productivity of his soil at Monticello. His use and promotion of manure and compost is well-documented, but less well-known is his work to improve the plow. The mathematics of the curve used to make plows was developed during the eighteenth century. Up to that point, plows were mainly used to stir and prepare soils for planting, but they did not work well to flip soil or open up uncultivated land. The tough herbaceous perennials of the eastern prairies, often burned deliberately by Indians to keep the forest at bay, were impossible to break with existing plows. Jefferson helped perfect the curve of the plow. The newly emerging Industrial Revolution, using coal as a power source, enabled production of enough iron—relatively inexpensively—to make them. They were not without flaws. Being made of cast iron, the Jefferson-style plow was brittle, prone to breakage when it hit a rock. It also plugged easily, requiring operators to pull them up and clean the surface of sticky clays before the oxen or horses could pull again. So, in the early nineteenth century people kept tinkering with the design.

The most famous and successful of these tinkerers was John Deere, a name known to anyone in agriculture, or even to owners of lawn equipment. Deere was the first to recognize that cast iron was the problem. Instead he developed a plow made of softer, less-brittle steel, which actually sloughed off a little iron as it passed through the soil. This enabled the plow to move faster through soils; it also meant the farmer did not have to stop frequently to clean the plow's surface. Farmers could open more land with less labor. A second innovation came along to address the breakage problem. Instead of making a plow with one piece, the Deere Company developed a three-piece plow with a bottom cutting edge and point that could be replaced. If you hit a rock hard enough to break the steel, you could simply remove the broken piece and attach another to the still-intact plow curve and support. This saved both money and time. The rhizomatous and fibrous rooted plants of the newly occupied prairie states stood no chance of resisting John Deere's plow.

Around the same time that John Deere was improving Jefferson's plow, Cyrus McCormick was at work on another labor-intensive operation: reaping. The sickle and the scythe are two of the oldest agricultural tools. Simple sickles of stone date back to the beginnings of settled agriculture. The ability to harvest grains with the stalk gave farmers a number of advantages. Bundling seed heads and stalks together and bringing them back to the farmhouse for threshing and winnowing meant farmers had both seed and straw for use. But cutting grain was laborious work, and also a race against the weather, birds, rats, mice, and insects. Ripe grain is prime food for many critters. It is also primed and ready to germinate as soon as conditions are right. Wet weather at the wrong time can result in large losses. Leaving ripe grain standing in a field for too long gives a variety of animals an opportunity too easy to pass up. Farmers watched their crop carefully, and as soon as a field was ready, with sickles or scythes in hand, harvested as fast as available labor would let them. Labor was the limiting factor. In the newly opened lands of the United States, labor was in short supply. Not everyone could afford slaves in the South, and in the North the Industrial Revolution was drawing labor away from the farms. While mechanical innovations were coming quickly, now that steel was cheaper and engineers had a power source in coal and the steam engine, they were not mobile yet in the 1820s when McCormick starting tinkering with reaper designs.

The key to the horse-drawn reaper is a bar that can move back and forth, powered by a ground wheel geared to make the movement quicker. On the bar are a series of triangle-shaped knives that move between fixed teeth that catch the stalks of grain a few inches above the ground, while the swiftly moving knives cut them. Another moving part is a rotating rake that pushes the stalks into the teeth and blades, dropping them onto a platform where all the seed heads face the same direction. This made it easy to bundle the straw and stand the sheaves upright for collection by wagons later. McCormick's first design was working in 1831, when he was 22 years old, but it took a decade before he was able to sell many, because his first trials required even ground. By 1845, he was able to sell 50 reapers a year from his shop in Steeles Tavern, Virginia, but it was only when he took the manufacturing to Chicago that it expanded rapidly in the flat grainlands of Ohio, Indiana, Illinois, and further west.[9] Eventually McCormick's descendants, with financing from J. P. Morgan & Co., established the International Harvester Company, one of the largest farm equipment manufacturers of the twentieth century.

FIGURE 3.2 McCormick's reaper, showing the ground wheel that drives both the unseen sickle bar and the visible rake, creating the easily bundled sheaves of grain. At this time, straw was nearly as important as grain for farmers, providing feed and bedding for animals, and sometimes roofing material for houses and barns.

Plows and reapers set the tone for continued development of agricultural equipment. Agriculture remained an animal-powered endeavor throughout the nineteenth century. Steam engines were large and bulky, requiring management of a bulky fuel, coal, so were better suited to fixed power supply or rail transport. Though impressive steam-powered tractors were invented and used, it was not until the invention of pneumatic tires and the internal combustion engine that power on farms fully transitioned from animals to fossil fuels, which is when farm innovation really took off. Through most of the nineteenth century, harvest involved

9   "McCormick Reaper," http://www.american-historama.org/1829-1841-jacksonian-era/mccormick-reaper. htm,

a series of separate operations. Reaping and bundling was the first step, but the labor continued. The plow and the reaper enabled farm size expansion in terms of land, but it once again was limited by the labor supply due to other factors. The grain then must be separated from the seed heads, usually with a flail or whip device, or, as is still done in Africa, by having animals tread around on the seed heads, breaking the seeds lose. Threshing machines reduced this labor, allowing seeds to drop away from the lighter straw and chaff of the seed heads. Winnowing was still required to get the last of the inedible material away from the seed, usually using a blower of some kind to remove the lightweight chaff. The combination of all three of these processes into one machine, called a *combine*, was the ultimate step in labor reduction of the harvesting process. Figure 3.3 shows an early type of combine in Eastern Washington.

FIGURE 3.3   This picture was taken in 1919 in Lincoln County, Washington, near the town of Harrington on a wheat field where yields averaged between 15 and 25 bushels to the acre. The combine was pulled by 18 horses, but had a gasoline engine powering the mechanics of the combine. Earlier versions used a ground drive wheel, but these required more horses and more frequent repairs. The author's grandfather stands over the belt that carries the grain stalks into the body of the combine. It took about one-third of the crop area farmed to grow the feed for the horses and mules.

The first major constraint that was overcome by the use of mechanical inventions was not plowing or reaping. Sowing seed by broadcasting had many disadvantages, since it was vulnerable to birds and ground-feeding animals. In 1701, Jethro Tull invented a device that greatly reduced that problem: A horse-drawn and ground wheel–powered rotating device dropped seed from a trough-shaped storage bin through a funnel into a slice in the ground made with a sharply pointed hoe; then the device closed the slice with a harrow, a type of fixed flat hoe. This dramatically increased productivity of grain in relation to the amount of seed sown. Tull's earliest models planted three rows of seed at a time.[10] The interesting thing about the invention is that it did not take off in Europe, with its smaller fields and gentler conditions, in part because Tull did not accept the value of manuring fields. Instead, his device was first widely adopted in North America, where fields were larger and manure not widely used.

Seeders, reapers, and plows greatly increased the area that one farmer could manage. Other devices, like cultivators for mechanically reducing weeds in the fields, also aided agriculture expansion. But the major expansion of agriculture to what we know today came about through the expanded use of internal combustion engines, diesel- and gasoline-powered tractors, trucks, combines, and crop-specific equipment. It was fossil fuels that accelerated the movement of labor from farm to city to meet the labor needs of the twentieth century. But mechanical invention alone did not address the limiting factors in agriculture. Two other lines of thinking were required to bring us to agriculture as we know it today.

The Rise of Chemistry in Agriculture

The term *limiting factor* was used a couple of times in the previous section, specifically in regard to labor. The concept of limiting factors was coined by a German agricultural chemist of the mid-nineteenth century. At that time, chemists were rapidly filling in gaps about our knowledge of atoms and were building the first periodic table. Oxygen was identified in the late eighteenth century by J. B Priestly and Carl Wilhelm Scheele independently. Other elements, like nitrogen, were discovered around the same time, but were not named or even fully understood. Nitrogen gas was tricky because it is not reactive, so early chemists did not associate it with living matter. Chemicals containing nitrogen were already widely known, but nitrogen's connection with air was not formally identified until the nineteenth century. Justus von Liebig's contribution was to recognize the critical importance of

---

10   Tom Ricci, "Jethro Tull," *ASME*, 2012, https://www.asme.org/engineering-topics/articles/history-of-mechanical-engineering/jethro-tull.

nitrogen-containing chemicals in agriculture; these involved nitrogen in combination with oxygen as nitrates, or with hydrogen as ammonium ions or amines attached to carbon. Liebig was a pioneer in understanding that inorganic nitrogen compounds and the nitrogen found in organic materials were related. Plants could get inorganic nitrogen compounds from soil and transform them into organic material.

As a result of his studies of the sources of elements in agriculture, Liebig refined, popularized, and quantified the German botanist Carl Sprengel's observation that agricultural productivity is limited by its least available mineral.[11] Liebig developed the model of a barrel made with staves of different lengths. The shortest stave, representing an important nutrient, determined the volume of water the barrel could contain. In soil, Liebig's Law of the Minimum indicated, "The productivity of an agricultural field is determined by the least available nutrient." Figure 3.4 shows water as the limiting factor on a farm. The other staves are the various nutrients Liebig and later scientists identified as both macro- and micronutrients in agriculture.

Liebig was not making a case for fertilizer as the best source of nutrients for crops. He was convinced that manure and other organic sources were valuable. Manure and soil humus were not the source of carbon in living plants. He helped confirm that carbon primarily came from carbon dioxide in the atmosphere, but that both manure and humus supply nitrogen, phosphorus, and most other nutrients. Liebig was perhaps the first scientist to show that inorganic fertilizers had value in agriculture and the first to advocate for their use. At the same time, Liebig vacillated on this position; he became, at various times, both an advocate and an opponent of chemical nitrogen in the form of ammonia. In part, this was because he was not able to make ammonia from raw material in his laboratory. He did, however, promote the use of guano, from deposits of bird droppings, which became an important

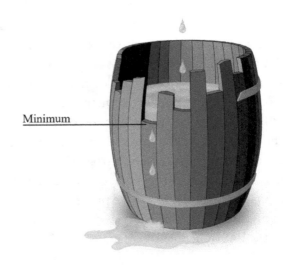

Minimum

FIGURE 3.4   Justus von Liebig's limiting nutrient model.

---

11   Mann (2018) writes that Liebig was something of a showboat and a plagiarist, so it is highly probably that Sprengel should get full credit for the idea of limiting factors. Sprengel was likely the better chemist as well.

agricultural amendment in the late nineteenth century, most of this coming from the Pacific coast of South America (Mann 2012).

While many countries pursued the use of guano as a fertilizer, Germany was likely the most enthusiastic user, but there were a couple of problems to overcome. Germany was newly united as a country from a collection of city-states, larger kingdoms, and provinces, all formerly part of the Austro-Hungarian Empire. Germany was just beginning to build up a military and did not have much of a navy or a merchant marine as the United Kingdom and France did. Germany felt vulnerable on a variety of fronts, even as the new nation asserted itself on the global stage, staking claims in Africa, among other places. Germany felt its supply of guano was vulnerable and wanted a different source of nitrogen; the Bismarck government put up the funding to pursue this, but in 1890 no one, including Liebig, had succeeded.

Meanwhile, a well-known Swedish engineer by the name of Alfred Nobel had won a contract to build a rail line in France. During its construction, which involved breaking through some rock to build a bridge, four construction workers were killed in an explosion of nitroglycerine, the dominant and highly unstable explosive used at that time. Nobel went into his laboratory and came up with a solution. He developed a compound of nitroglycerin into a paste that could be rolled into a stick that would ignite only with a fuse. Dynamite proved a safe and effective alternative to the problem of premature explosions, giving Nobel notoriety beyond his engineering skills. It also attracted the interest of militaries. The easiest source of nitrogen for the explosive was also guano. The military angle prompted an even more intensive pursuit of synthetic nitrogen.[12]

By that time, in the late nineteenth century, it was known that lightning released enough energy in the atmosphere to break the powerful N_2 bond and combine nitrogen either with oxygen to make nitrogen oxides, or with hydrogen from water to make ammonia. Some efforts were made to use electricity from Norwegian hydroelectric projects to make ammonia, but these proved economically inefficient and hard to control (Smil 2001). Eventually the challenge was picked up by a chemist named Fritz Haber, pushed by the BASF chemical company (*BASF* is an acronym for *Badische Anilin und Soda Fabrik*, which is German for "Baden Aniline and Soda Factory"). He was convinced that putting the right amount of temperature and pressure on two reactants—N_2 gas and H_2 gas—in the presence of a catalyst would do the trick. He also recognized that the reaction was reversible, so you had to find a way to draw off the ammonia as it was produced in order

12   Most of the material in these paragraphs is based on the work of Vaclav Smil, *Enriching the Earth: Fritz Haber, Carl Bosch and the Transformation of World Food Production* (Cambridge, MA: MIT Press, 2001).

to keep the very slightly exothermic reaction from reversing in the reaction chamber. It took a number of years for him to develop the correct combination of high pressure, elevated temperature, and an osmium/uranium catalyst to get a consistent and economically viable product (Smil 2001).

While Fritz Haber was the primary scientist behind finding the method to fix nitrogen in the laboratory, it was Carl Bosch who really developed the industry, first by finding a cheaper and less-dangerous catalyst, then by improving the reaction vessel so it was not rapidly degraded by hydrogen, and finally by extracting the produced ammonia without stopping the continuous reaction. He then scaled it up and made it economically viable. Ramping up production happened relatively quickly, but not for agriculture. The primary demand was military, and the main driving force was World War I. Bosch industrialized the war, while Haber continued work in the lab, this time looking for chemical weapons useful on the two-front war the Germans were fighting. Only at the end of the war did industrially derived ammonia and nitrates become widely used in agriculture, though not everywhere and not very quickly because it was still expensive. The energy costs of making ammonia were very high. At first, most of the cost went into extracting the tightly chemically bonded hydrogen from coal; later, although more abundantly and more cheaply, the cost went into extracting the hydrogen from methane in natural gas (Smil 2001). Smil shows that the energy cost of producing one metric ton of ammonia dropped from 96 gigajoules/ton (GJ/ton) in 1920 to just under 50 GJ/ton in 2000, with the best plants dropping the cost to under 30 GJ/ton. A lot of the development of lower-cost ammonium took place during World War II, and the real expansion of fertilizer derived from the munitions-grade ammonium happened after the war because the output was no longer needed for the war effort.

Fritz Haber was not idle after the World War I. He became politically active, revealing an extreme anti-Semitism and becoming an ardent supporter of Adolf Hitler and the Nazis. In his zeal, he started developing more sophisticated chemical weapons, one of which was Zyklon B, notorious for its use in the Nazi concentration camps to exterminate the Jews. The class of chemicals he helped originate, organophosphates, later were developed into a wide variety of insecticides to control agricultural pests and disease-carriers like mosquitoes and bedbugs. Smil makes the highly supported claim that the use of fertilizer and other agricultural chemicals that developed following the model established by Haber and Bosch is behind the human population explosion after World War II. Without the food supply enabled by these chemicals, we would not be able to feed the present global population. While there is considerable merit to this conclusion, the mechanization of agriculture made its own contribution, and the third leg of this increased agricultural production stool is also extremely important: the understanding of plant breeding and genetics.

Understanding Plant Breeding and the
Corporate Control of Seed

The nineteenth century produced a number of people who reshaped the landscape of our age, and none more so than Charles Darwin. Darwin's biography is best described by others, and there is much written about him and his theory of natural selection, commonly called evolution. While there are some who claim that this theory is false, there is much evidence available that it is true, so it is not worth even touching the controversy. Stephen Jay Gould and Richard Dawkins have written books on this with a skill and eloquence that are unmatched. The basic concept Darwin first articulated is very simple: To the best of our knowledge, mating in species is random, but of course only happens when two members of a species of opposite genders survive to maturity. Darwin called the survival a sign of fitness. Each gender contributes 50% of its traits to its offspring. The offspring then is a mix of traits inherited from its parents. If at least two offspring survive to maturity, then this new set of traits contained in that organism is deemed fit. Failure to reach reproductive stage for any reason is a sign of unfitness, or just bad luck. Traits that lead to fitness tend to survive in an overall population, and traits that fail to thrive and reproduce disappear. Darwin termed this process natural selection, while others who followed him sometimes called it "Survival of the Fittest." Darwin did not like that term, nor the storm of controversy his ideas generated, especially after his book *The Descent of Man* hit the shelves in 1870. You will note that there is no mention here of the mechanism for transmitting traits, just random mating and evolutionary pressure on the selection process that determined success in a particular ecosystem.

The mechanism of natural selection was actually discovered around the same time, in the 1860s, by Gregor Mendel, working quietly in a monastery in Hungary. Plant breeding as an area of study did not really exist until Mendel's work on genetics became public knowledge early in the twentieth century. Mendel showed that the phenotype of a plant, which is the expressed or observable characteristics of the plant, is based on an underlying genotype that is subsequently shaped by environmental conditions. Breeders attempt to shift the genotype, the underlying genetics of the species, by selecting phenotypic characteristics that they want, like resistance to a specific disease, and crossing that plant with another that has similar characteristics. Because many characteristics are not controlled by a single gene, the way that petal color in pea plants is controlled, breeding takes many attempts in crossing plants to develop the full expression of the desired phenotype from the underlying genotype. This gets even more complex when there are multiple phenotypic traits desired.

The earliest success of plant breeding for crops using Mendel's techniques happened with corn. Corn has a long, interesting history, starting most likely as the grass teosinte, which does not resemble modern corn. Then, through thousands of plant generations of selection by farmers in the Oaxaca region of Mexico, it evolved via the environmental pressure of selection by farmers. The resulting crop that we call corn, and that most of the rest of the world calls maize, is unique in many ways, facilitating its rapid spread to other parts of the world, especially Africa. Maize, like most grasses, is wind-pollinated, but unlike most other grasses it has separate female and male parts. The female flower is buried at the base of a leaf on the stem and only appears as a bundle of silks, which are stamens that receive the pollen. From there it produces an ear, or seed head, which is covered by a sheath protecting it from birds or other potential consumers. A single plant commonly has one ear, but can have up to three. The male flower stands at the top of the plant and is called the tassel. This separation makes it very easy to control pollination, limiting or eliminating the potential for self-pollination. If the female flower is also shielded, a plant breeder can easily control the parental genetics of the next generation of the plant. This allowed plant breeders to develop hybrid seeds, plants that are crossed between two distinct varieties with traits chosen by the breeder to develop the new characteristics, or phenotype, desired. Often this meant improved yield. Up until then, the average yield of maize had topped out at less than two tons per hectare. The first successful hybrids were developed around 1918, but they did not reach commercial sales until 1926.

In 1924, a farmer in Iowa named Henry A. Wallace developed a hybrid corn variety that he dubbed the "Copper Cross," and in 1926, he established the Hybrid Corn Seed Company to market the hybrid.[13] This brings up a specific aspect of hybrids that really produced seed companies: Hybrid seed does not reproduce true to type. The cross has to be genetically specific or you do not get the phenotypic characteristic desired. Farmers have to purchase the seed again from the same company. Since yields for hybrids are commonly significantly higher, yield covers the costs of procuring the seed, so farmers do not mind the expense. Wallace's company soon changed its name to the Pioneer Hybrid Seed Company and became widely known in the seed business, as did Wallace, who became the Secretary of Agriculture during President Franklin Roosevelt's second term in office.[14] Plant breeding proved more of a challenge for other grains.

Plant breeding is not a field that normally produces famous people. It is long-term, tedious work requiring careful attention to detail and skilled observation of plant characteristics in the field. Yet there is one plant breeder who is regarded by some as the most important scientist of the twentieth century—which, when you realize that includes Albert Einstein, is saying something. Norman Borlaug's story is an intriguing one. He was not a man bent on

---

13   "Pioneer Hi Bred International." https://en.wikipedia.org/wiki/Pioneer_Hybrid_International.
14   Thomas Hoegemeyer, "History of the US Hybrid Corn Seed Industry," University of Nebraska-Lincoln 2014. http://imbgl.cropsci.illinois.edu/school/2014/11_THOMAS_HOEGEMEYER.pdf.

receiving attention or becoming famous. He was born in Iowa in 1914, grew up in a farming community, and pursued his education at the University of Minnesota, earning a PhD from that institution in late 1942. He first studied forestry, getting a bachelor of science degree, but he was attracted by the work of Elvin Stakman, a well-known plant pathologist working on breeding wheat strains that were resistant to a disease called wheat stem rust, a parasitic fungus devastating to the crop.[15] During this time, Henry Wallace, who was now a progressive politician and a supporter of Franklin Roosevelt, became secretary of agriculture and then, from 1941 to 1945, vice president of the United States. Roosevelt and Wallace were concerned that unrest in Mexico was a major issue, and they feared that the rising tide of fascism in Germany would infect the country if something were not done to improve the agricultural situation there. In Mexico during the 1930s, president Lázaro Cárdenas had broken up the large estates dominating the dryland agriculture regions of the north, and distributed the land to small farmers. After he left office, the stem rust began reducing farm yield and Mexico suffered food deficits that contributed to the country's political instability. Wallace, as secretary of agriculture, knew Stakman and tapped him to lead the effort to fight the rust. Stakman then recruited Borlaug as the man to partner with him in the effort (Mann 2018).

Borlaug went to Mexico in 1944, working out of a lab not far from Mexico City, but planting wheat along the northwest coast in a drier region of the country just east of the Baja California Peninsula. He quickly recognized that this region gave a great advantage to plant breeders: two growing seasons. The Yaqui Valley of Sonora has a Mediterranean climate warmed by the Pacific, rendering it perfect for a winter crop of wheat. The central highlands, at nearly 5,000 feet, with cool summers, were just right for a summer wheat growing season. Borlaug worked on the wheat stem rust problem by crossing numerous varieties of Mexican and North American wheat and growing them alternatively in the two locations. Along the way, he and Stakman trained Mexican colleagues in breeding techniques and scientific methods of research. Progress was slow, but Borlaug was not the type to give up easily. He had great patience and was determined to find the right combination of characteristics to tackle a complex problem like disease resistance in wheat. All the researchers' cross-breeding work yielded a number of different varieties that tolerated a variety of different climatic and soil conditions while increasing resistance to the rust.[16]

---

15   "The Father of the Green Revolution: Norman Borlaug Biography" American Academy of Achievement. http://www.achievement.org/autodoc/page/borobio-1.

16   The story is described in much greater detail by Charles Mann in *The Wizard and the Prophet* (New York: Alfred A. Knopf, 2018). Norman Borlaug is the wizard in the title, and he also represents what is the broader conventional wisdom in agricultural science.

At the same time, with the conclusion of World War II, nitrate fertilizer became widely available. While corn responded well to fertilizer, increasing its yield, wheat responded differently, growing thin, elongated stems and more leaf growth, but with stems too weak for the seed heads it produced, resulting in a problem called lodging, the collapse of the stem causing grain to rot on the ground before ripening. As Borlaug's team succeeded in improving resistance to stem rust, they then switched their focus to this second problem.

Wheat, like many small grains, is an annual crop. It starts its growth by producing a number of leaves that feed its root system. Once the root system is sufficiently developed, the plant produces tillers, stems that are eventually capped by a seed head. Borlaug realized that if a plant responded to increased nitrogen fertilizer by increasing the number and strength of tillers instead of the number of leaves, yield would dramatically increase. It took some time and experimentation, but eventually the team found a short-stemmed Japanese wheat that, when crossed with a Mexican variety that had been improved by the team already, responded well to the increased nitrogen in the presence of sufficient water. Lodging was reduced, yields jumped, and the new variety spread rapidly in Mexico and beyond, transforming the country into a net wheat exporter. This is what some have dubbed *the Green Revolution*. By 1963, over 90% of Mexico's wheat was from Borlaug's developed stem rust and lodging-resistant varieties. Borlaug's reputation as a plant breeder extraordinaire spread like the wheat.

Borlaug also had good funding. It came from the Rockefeller Foundation—specifically at the request of Roosevelt, since the government was heavily into deficit spending for the war effort. The funding system became something of a hybrid, relying on the Rockefeller Foundation for core funding, but governments and corporations also contributed. The model developed in Mexico was named CIMMYT, the Spanish acronym for the *International Maize and Wheat Improvement Center*.[17] Scientists came and went from the center, some as doctoral students, some doing postdoctoral work, and some on leave from universities where they served as professors in plant breeding. The model was something of a revolving door: work in two institutions—an applied field lab and a university research center. At the same time, there was a second revolving door. Seed companies recognized that CIMMYT was doing work with novel combinations of genetic material; and novel innovations are patentable—therefore able to be controlled by whoever holds the patent. By funding scientists to work at CIMMYT, or even at a university in exchange for rights to the patent on successful seed development, companies were enabled to bulk up production of the new variety and make a profit on the sales. In return, the companies helped fund the research and infrastructure of both the research station and the university. During the 1960s, the number of research

---

17   https://www.cimmyt.org/

stations like CIMMYT expanded, with increased funding from the Ford Foundation, into what is called the Consultative Group for International Agricultural Research (CGIAR) and includes another of Borlaug's efforts: the International Rice Research Institute, based in the Philippines.[18] This model of operation in many ways pried control of the research away from farmers and government and put it into the hands of corporations. It is the dominant model of agricultural research on university campuses around the world today. The foundation on which this system rests was the pioneering work of Norman Borlaug.

While Borlaug began as a dedicated, hard-working plant breeder, circumstances placed him at the forefront of a battle for the direction of agriculture. He placed himself squarely against people like Paul Erlich, who wrote *The Population Bomb,* claiming that there was no need to panic, that science and science-based agriculture could pull us out of this looming crisis that people ever since Malthus had described. Population can rise exponentially, but crop yields can leap past them if people will rely on three things: proven improved seed produced through plant breeding; fertilizer that reduces the limiting factors in the area of production; and credit, the ability to get loans to buy seed and fertilizers from the corporations that sell them. If these things are available, then production rises and problems are avoided. Warnings in books like *Limits to Growth*, which appeared soon after Borlaug won the Nobel Peace Prize for his agricultural work that saved lives in Mexico and India, are really valid only if we do not follow Borlaug's prescription for productivity.

The Anomalies of Conventional Agriculture

Borlaug's apologetics for the dominant form of Western agriculture, often called conventional agriculture, ignores some glaring problems with the conventional technique. In many ways this reflects the thoughts of two major philosophical thinkers of the twentieth century. Thomas Kuhn wrote about how scientific progress takes place in his seminal book, *The Structure of Scientific Revolutions*. He showed how science transforms through time, not by incremental steps constantly building on knowledge previously gathered, but in sudden shifts of theory that happen as the dominant theory of the time struggles to deal with the anomalies appearing that are not easily explained by that theoretical framework. The anomalies cause slowdown, confusion, and argument about scientific direction. When a new theory comes along that explains the anomalies easily without abandoning the knowledge that worked within the old theory, then science can readily develop and test new hypotheses based on the framework of the new theory. The transition from one theoretical framework

---

18   More on this is developed in Chapter 8, "Rice, Records and the Potential for Alternative Agriculture."

to another does not happen without a fight. Scientists, just like people in general, own their place within a theory and do not give it up easily even though their explanations of an anomaly are complex and often convoluted. Kuhn used the transition from Newtonian physics to quantum theory, developed by Albert Einstein and other physicists, as his primary example.[19] Conventional agriculture is based on a theory with deep flaws as well. In this case, the theory states that agricultural productivity is dependent upon genetics that reflect the desired traits that the market wants, inputs that overcome the limiting factors present in the fields where crops are grown, and machines that can rapidly and consistently plant, maintain, and harvest these uniform crops.

A second thinker, Jacques Ellul, who wrote in France before and after World War II, had another take on the problem. He was not writing from a scientific perspective; rather, he looked at how the economic system worked, depending primarily on the flow of communication. In *The Technological Society,* he described "technique" not so much as a method of production, but as a way to frame the process of production from the extraction of raw material to the marketing and sale of the finished product. The product did not even have to be a physical good, it could be a political system. In either case, physical product or system, propaganda built the foundation. Society is underpinned, supported, and held together by the way we explain it to ourselves and to each other. Therefore, we have to defend the system from any and all attempts to explain it differently. Sometimes all that is needed is to increase the volume or frequency of that communication. If you explain a system loud enough, long enough, and through enough media outlets, then it becomes a truth. Ellul's book *Propaganda* explains how this works throughout cultures. The propagandist's goal is to make citizens fail to see the existence of the system that derives its wealth from their compliance. Without citizen participation, the system collapses; but if you do not recognize the system's existence, it thrives. Ellul's claim is that the system defined by his concept of technique is inherently destructive. If it is not exposed, then we all fail with it.

Lest this seem like a philosophical detour and a dead end, let's bring it back to the state of agriculture right now. We have a conventional system that exhibits a number of anomalies that those who defend it would like us not to see. Soil erosion is one. Though in the early part of the twentieth century we went through a period of extreme erosion events that led to the formation of the Natural Resource Conservation Service (NRCS), the more subtle

---

19   Not everyone accepts Kuhn, but his impact on scientific thinking is widespread. There are more recent efforts in the philosophy of science to correct what some identify as problems with Kuhn's model. Nevertheless, it has value for anyone trying to come to grips with failing systems and efforts to promote change. See Kevin Laland, "Evolution Unleashed," *Aeon Newsletter,* January 17, 2018. https://aeon.co/essays/science-in-flux-is-a-revolution-brewing-in-evolutionary-theory?utm_source=Aeon+Newsletter.

versions of erosion are still happening, albeit not as fast. According to the NRCS, total erosion in the United States amounted to 1.73 billion tons,[20] which is coming from just under 260 million acres of cropland.[21] This amounts to about 6.6 tons per acre, which is approximately six times the replacement rate for mineral soils. The United States is not alone in having an erosion problem; it is simply a country that has readily available statistics. A second anomaly happening globally is nutrient pollution. It is not hard to find dead zones off the mouths of rivers that flow through agricultural areas. The most well-known in the United States is the annual dead zone in the Gulf of Mexico off the Mississippi Delta. Depending on conditions, this varies between six thousand and nine thousand square miles, and it generally peaks in August. All of it is caused by excess nitrogen, the limiting factor in the growth of algae, causing an algal bloom that exceeds the ability of organisms to consume it. When it dies, the bacterial population explodes, consuming the dissolved oxygen and killing fish, crustaceans, mollusks, and other organisms that thrive in those waters. Some experts estimate the annual death toll in the region at 100,000 tons of marine life. Dead zones like this are found in western Lake Eire, the Baltic Sea, the Black Sea, the Bay of Bengal, and off the Yangtze Delta in China, and in many other estuaries, seas, and lakes around the planet, all tracing back to excess nutrients from agriculture and municipalities. These are but two of the many cracks in the conventional paradigm, and this does not even consider what farming conventionally is doing to farmers.[22]

The third of Borlaug's pillars is credit. In the past, farmers kept their own seed and planted it the next year. They sold surplus but they kept enough to feed their families, provide seed, and cover normal storage losses. With hybrid seed that did not reproduce true to type, and with the patenting of new Green Revolution varieties produced using Borlaug's pioneering techniques, farmers could no longer keep their seed to replant. They became dependent on the annual purchase of seed from seed companies—of which there are now fewer, having become larger and more integrated corporations—that also sell the other inputs, like fertilizer and chemicals, needed to grow a successful crop. Many if not most farmers globally, not just in the Western world, do not have enough available capital to cover the inputs needed for farming in a particular year. They need credit. They get it, sometimes from banks, sometimes from the input companies like Monsanto (now owned by Bayer), Syngenta (now owned by

20   USDA. n.d. "Soil Erosion on Cropland 2007." United States Department of Agriculture. https://www.nrcs.usda.gov/wps/portal/nrcs/detail/national/technical/nra/nri/results/?cid=stelprdb1041887.

21   M. Shahbandah, "Total U.S. Cropland Area Projection from 2012 to 2028," *Statista*, March 9, 2020. https://www.statista.com/statistics/201762/projection-for-total-us-cropland-area-from-2010/.

22   A new by book by Tom Philpott, *Perilous Bounty: The Looming Collapse of American Farming and How We Can Prevent It*, explains this with more depth and detail. Bloomsbury Publishing, 2020

a Chinese conglomerate), and Pioneer (now owned by DuPont™)—which always charge to loan the money. It is in the corporation's interest to buy low and sell high. Therefore, farmers globally are finding themselves increasingly beholden to the corporate interests. They owe their souls to the company store, only this time the company store is an international corporation that does not even know the farmer's name beyond an entry on a computer ledger. In the end, whether they live in Iowa or Malawi (Wise 2019) or India (Shiva 1993), they are caught in a trap and can only act in accordance with the will of the company that holds their debt.

The "conventional paradigm"—to use the term in not quite the way Kuhn would use it, since it includes Ellul's social critique—dominates global agricultural production. No matter where you find it operating, it has similar characteristics; it all looks just the same. It is powered by fossil fuels, the inputs are created or run using fossil fuels, and its products go to corporations for refining, processing, and distributing using fossil fuels. It is not controlled by farmers; it controls farming. Conventional agriculture ignores communities of species, including communities of people. Table 3.1 shows a list of these characteristics. It would require a much longer text to explain all the details and problems associated with the conventional paradigm, and that is not the purpose of this text. Rather, this chapter is an attempt to explain how we got to the present dilemma that presents us with many problems and contributes greatly to our climate crisis.

TABLE 3.1 A comparison of the features of the dominant global conventional agriculture paradigm developed in the West, but spread throughout the world, and the emerging paradigm of agroecology.

Conventional Paradigm	Agroecology (Carbon Smart) Paradigm
Monocultures	Locally appropriate polycultures
Production focus	Health focus
Standardized systems (fossil fuels)	Ecological systems (solar)
Commodity supply	Local use
Corporate control	Farmer control
University-based research	On-farm ecosystem research
Production first	Soil first
Large-scale, uniform	Small-scale, highly variable
Chemical inputs—suppression	Biological inputs, diversity enhanced
Market-driven	Community-driven
Bank- and loan-based	Community-based
Capital-intensive	People-intensive

Column 2 of table 3.1 gives another paradigm that could have many names at the top. Agroecology is the one that I chose to put there, but others of equal merit include permaculture, perennial polyculture, agroforestry, regenerative agriculture, Holistic Management, and biodynamic agriculture. This column is the topic for the rest of this book. Agroecology is above all an agriculture developed within the bounds of the ecology of the place where it is found. It does not all look just the same. In fact, it must and should look different. The soils, plants, topography, climate, culture, and situation of every place on this planet varies. This is good. It is also the starting place for how we go about feeding ourselves. If there is one common element to agroecology, it is this: Agroecology pays attention to the soil and stores carbon. If done wisely in place, it becomes part of the solution to the climate crisis we face.

Most of the rest of the book will focus on the development of the agroecology/carbon smart paradigm. Some criticism of the conventional paradigm will arise too, but criticism is the sense of sorting out the good from the bad. Norman Borlaug's contribution to modern agriculture was praiseworthy, and he developed techniques relevant to both paradigmatic approaches. Overcoming the scourge of stem rust was a worthy achievement. What if you could apply Borlaug's technical prowess to an agriculture powered by biology and community rather than chemistry, fossil fuels, and corporations? Plant breeding has gone on for thousands of years even if it was not named as such. Borlaug showed that it is a powerful tool, especially if we use it right.

Study Questions

1. Food is essential, but most of us in the United States have very little knowledge of where our food comes from and what path it takes to get to our plate. Go to the grocery and pick out one type of food that you regularly buy. Make sure it is one with only a few ingredients, or even just one. Then trace this food from its probable origin to your plate. What did you discover? How many companies or places touched the food? Did you find out how it moves from farms to processing facilities? How many stages of processing are there? What is involved in packaging? How do the grocery stores get the food? Where do you find it on the shelves?

2. Costs are distributed in the food system. Farmers who grow the food get only a fraction of the dollar we spend purchasing the food from a store. How much goes to the farmer? How much does the food processing industry get? What is the markup in the grocery store?

3. There are many groups devoted to the study of food, and some, like the Environmental Working Group (EWG), do independent research to determine how many agrichemicals and other additives get into the food we buy and to name the potential harm.

What can you find out about the food you chose in question 1 above? What types of food are the most contaminated by our industrial food system? What types of food are the least contaminated?

4. There is a growing movement to make the food system local. How much local food is available near your home? How is it marketed? How easy is it for you, or your parents, or your neighbors, to buy this food? How do the costs compare to what you find in your grocery store?

References

Anderson, M. Kat. 2013. *Tending the Wild: Native American Knowledge and the Management of California's Natural Resources*. Berkeley: University of California Press.

Berry, Wendell. 1996. *The Unsettling of America: Culture and Agriculture*. Revised ed. Berkeley, CA: Counterpoint.

Brady, Nyle C. 1984. *The Nature and Properties of Soils*. 9th ed. New York: Macmillan.

Diamond, Jared. 2005. *Collapse: How Societies Choose to Fail or Succeed*. New York: Penguin.

Ellul, Jacques. 1964. *The Technological Society*. Translated by John Wilkinson. New York: Vintage Books.

Ellul, Jacques. 1973. *Propaganda*. New York: Vintage Books.

Howard, Albert. 1940. *An Agricultural Testament*. London: Oxford University Press.

King, F. H. 1904. *Farmers of Forty Centuries; or Permanent Agriculture in China, Korea and Japan*. Mineola, NY: Dover Publications.

Kuhn, Thomas. 1962. *The Structure of Scientific Revolutions*. Chicago: University of Chicago Press.

Mann, Charles. 2012. *1493: Uncovering the New World Columbus Created*. New York: Vintage Books.

——————. 2018. *The Wizard and the Prophet: Two Remarkable Scientists and Their Dueling Visions to Shape Tomorrow's World*. New York: Vintage Books.

Montgomery, David. 2007. *Dirt: The Erosion of Civilizations*. Berkeley: University of California Press.

Shiva, Vandana. 1993. *Monocultures of the Mind: Perspectives on Biodiversity and Biotechnology*. London: Zed Books.

Smil, Vaclav. 2001. *Enriching the Earth: Fritz Haber, Carl Bosch, and the Transformation of World Food Production*. Cambridge, MA: MIT Press.

Tuchman, Barbara. 1987. *A Distant Mirror: The Calamitous 14th Century*. New York: Ballantine Books.

Wise, Timothy. 2019. *Eating Tomorrow: Agribusiness, Family Farmers, and the Battle for the Future of Food*. New York: New Press.

Wulf, Andrea. 2011. *The Founding Gardeners: The Revolutionary Generation, Nature, and the Shaping of the American Nation*. New York: Vintage Books.

Credits

Chapter 4

From Lawns to Sustainable Perennial Agriculture
Making Permaculture Part of Your Landscape

Introduction

The suburban landscape is ripe for change, and nothing has brought that out more than the present crisis with COVID-19, the coronavirus, making us all stay home. For many of us, this has meant more time on our hands, and gardening has become a favorite pastime. In fact, the seed companies did not anticipate the demand and many have sold their inventory earlier than expected. But how do we garden? Is it a long-term commitment to the annual labor of planting vegetables? Can we take it a step further and make it into a transformation of our landscape, sequestering carbon and growing food at the same time? That is the story of this chapter, changing the ecology of place as close to home as possible, using the tested tools and guidelines of permaculture to make it work for the long term.

The Great American Yard

What can one say about America's largest irrigated monoculture? Forty million acres of lawn cover backyards, parks, ball fields, golf courses, and university campus squares across this country.[1] Lawns drink 238 gallons per acre per day during the growing season. That is 9.64 billion gallons per day, or 642 times the capacity of the Harrisonburg Water Treatment plant,[2] just to water America's grass with chlorinated water. All this says nothing about the quantities of fertilizer, weed killers, and insecticides we use on our lawns every year.

---

1   See Francie Diep, "Lawns vs. Crops in the Continental U.S," *ScienceLine*, July 3, 2011, http://scienceline.org/2011/07/lawns-vs-crops-in-the-continental-u-s/, and "More Lawns Than Irrigated Corn," *Earth Observatory*, November 8, 2005, http://earthobservatory.nasa.gov/Features/Lawn/lawn2.php.

2   A small city in the Shenandoah Valley of Virginia, with a population of just over 50,000.

FIGURE 4.1 A wasteland stretches over much of the United States. We see it every day. (a) Part of it is covered by asphalt and concrete: the highway system and parking lots, which our cars call home, and which bicyclists call the danger zone. (b) The other part is benign, even green: these are our lawns. There are many lawns in the United States. They are mowed, trimmed, fertilized, and watered to make them look, well, like a lawn.

This chapter is not intended to be an anti-lawn diatribe; there is a place for a good lawn, such as parks where children and adults can play, but too much high-quality land is now mowed weekly with no conceivable purpose. The campus at James Madison University (JMU), where I teach, is no exception. Since my arrival on campus in 1999, the lawn has intrigued me. The campus had great unused swaths of grass covering its newest section south and east of Interstate 81. Students and faculty walked through the lawn on cement pathways, but broad sections of this landscape essentially had no purpose. A strange event encouraged me to think about this in a different way. One early fall day, I was walking across this lawn on a pathway that led from the Integrated Science and Technology building to another building that has since been removed. At the bottom of the hill, near the crossing point of an ephemeral stream, a small grove of honey locust trees stood along with some scrubby bushes. Under the bushes, a squirrel was making a racket, disturbed by something I could not see. The squirrel did not flee as I approached, so I sat and looked around. In a honey locust, a juvenile red-tailed hawk sat eyeing the squirrel. If the squirrel bolted, it would become lunch. I watched. Students walked by but not a single one noticed the squirrel, the hawk, or me. Finally, I asked a passing student if she noticed anything. She said no, so I pointed out the drama taking place. She told me to throw a rock at the hawk and left. Why? At that point I realized that our landscape was teaching our students to not bother looking at the environment surrounding them. It had no life; it was just something to pass through. That is when I started to do something about it.

The first step I took, which proved to be a long and slow one, involved asking people what they thought about the lawn area and what they thought we could do about it. Most of the initial discussion focused on the stream at the bottom of the hill. In our program, we teach courses on water and hydrology, and it was quite apparent that this stream was not managed correctly. From 1999 to 2002, the Shenandoah Valley experienced a modest drought. It was hard on farmers, and the ephemeral streams, like this one on campus, which normally flow with water during springtime or after heavy rains, were continuously dry. The drought broke in August 2002, and over the next two years a series of heavy rains washed out the crossing points of the stream a number of times. JMU eventually had to build bridges and install a long stretch of riprap in wire cages called gabions to guard against erosion. The bridges worked, but the gabions only widened the erosion. They were not made with an understanding of hydrology. We began advocating for a riparian restoration project along that stream.

While this discussion continued, I thought about the hillside, eventually putting together a proposal to transform about 1.6 acres of the lawn area into a tall grass prairie filled with multiple species of herbaceous perennials native to Virginia. At the same time that I contemplated this, the Virginia Department of Conservation and Recreation and the USDA's National Resource Conservation Service were introducing native meadows as a means of conserving erosive farmland and riparian areas. People were waking up to the need for different management. An initial proposal was written and submitted in 2006, but the JMU administration and facilities management people really did not know what to do about it. Proposals from faculty concerning the lawn were not normal. This may have been the first such proposal the administration had ever seen. So it sat in a file folder for a few years. I still pushed the idea in my classes and with the administration, but it did not have traction.

Things changed in the summer of 2009 when then-president Rose changed the direction of the university, developing the idea for an office of environmental stewardship. Universities around the country were shifting, and he did not want JMU to be left behind. The creation of this office and the presence of a consultant named Michael Singer on campus opened a door that had not existed before. The proposal went to Michael Singer and to the director of the Environmental Stewardship and Sustainability office, and it received immediate attention. Mr. Singer is a well-known designer, artist, and architect, and he knew how to present a proper proposal. He took what I had done, now improved and updated by students in my Sustainability course, and with his improvements and presentation, the administration decided to implement the project. Nothing moves fast in a bureaucracy, so it took over a year before the meadow was planted. It is now thriving on the hillside. It does involve some

FIGURE 4.2   Two views of (a) a lawn converted to (b) meadow on the James Madison University campus.

maintenance. Because we are not permitted to burn the meadow, as would be the standard meadow management practice, woody perennials like *Ailanthus altissima* (tree of heaven), an exotic species from China, and weedy natives like pokeweed, carried in by cardinals, have to be thinned out annually, but these are not serious problems. The benefits far outweigh the problems—the chief of these benefits is the presence of butterflies and other pollinators and birds, especially the American goldfinch that has taken the hillside by storm.

Two additional projects soon followed. JMU's Facilities Management team worked with the stream restoration program people in the Virginia Department of Game and Inland Fisheries to redesign the stream using nature's blueprint.[3] The gabions were removed, while sinuosity, designed to slow the speed of water, was added along with a step/pool system to slow the most energetic flow rate. With the stream rerouted, a riparian buffer was planted. Instead of a mowed lawn, riparian herbaceous perennials and trees became the main tools to resist erosive forces of flood flow in the stream. This flood flow is inevitable, because a substantial portion of the upstream watershed is now impervious surface; parking lots, students' housing apartments, and the set of connecting roads have replaced the former forest. The repaired stream has nonetheless withstood the weather conditions of the last seven years without erosion, and it, too, has attracted birdlife and insects to campus.

At the same time that the stream restoration occurred, the Hillside Committee of the Office of Environmental Stewardship and Sustainability developed a plan for a demonstration

---

3   Two major influences were crucial in this process: Luna Leopold's book *A View of the River* (Cambridge, MA: Harvard University Press, 2006) changed the understanding of geomorphology and the whole understanding of riparian restoration. David Rosgen's seminal work *Applied River Morphology* (Louisville, KY: Wildland Hydrology, 1996) provided a process and a set of tools to implement Leopold's ideas in a practical way.

forest on another section of lawn. Dr. Michael Renfroe of the Department of Biology and I developed a species list for the area and marked the slope for tree planting. In the spring of 2012, facilities management planted 60 trees. These are doing well, and in 2019 they were nearing canopy closure, which will initiate change to the lawn understory. Still more changes being contemplated in the area, including the slow installation of an edible forest garden between the meadow and the riparian zone near the bottom of the hillside.

Rethinking Lawns with Permaculture

In the mid-1970s, on the island of Tasmania off the southeast coast of Australia, two men started thinking and acting on the problems they witnessed on the island. Tasmania has a moist, cool climate, originally dominated by eucalyptus forest, but the island had been perceived by European immigrants as an ideal place for raising sheep. As a result, the ecology of the island was radically altered. Exotic grasses replaced native vegetation. Native animals were shot, hounded, and driven to isolated parks or extinction. Erosion was common. Dams flooded stretches of land. Aboriginal peoples were wiped out, and even European culture was lackluster. This is the environment that Bill Mollison grew up in and David Holmgren entered as a student in the 1970s. Bill Mollison was an ecologist, forester, gardener, and fiercely independent thinker from the island. Holmgren, who grew up in Australia's Victoria Province, proved an exceptionally deep thinker with a concern for the environment. Together they contemplated the rapid environmental decline of Tasmania and what they could do to reverse it. Over a four-year stretch, the two ecologists conceived and developed the ideas that would come to serve as the foundation for *permaculture*, the new word derived from "perennial," "permanent," and "agriculture." To Mollison and Holmgren, the root of the problem of environmental degradation lay in the human conversion of native perennial ecosystems into an agricultural system based on annuals and the improper management of grazing animals. They felt strongly that all attempts to change direction must start with an understanding of local ecology, including climate, soils, rock, hydrology, native vegetation, and native wildlife. Annuals and exotic perennials have their place, they allowed, but must be rooted in the ecology of place.

Bill Mollison can be described as a man of detail who believes in strict guidelines and follows them closely. His master work, *Permaculture: A Designer's Manual* (1988), is a guidebook and map of how to turn a piece of land into a permaculture garden, orchard, and forest. His detailed work on climate, soil, cropping systems and patterns, orchard management, and forest management is a wonderful resource for those with land and time to pursue it. Holmgren, on the other hand, is more philosophical and pattern-oriented. He does not delve into details, because he recognizes that every location is a different ecosystem and each permaculture effort must necessarily adapt to its place. Instead of providing details, his primary work, *Permaculture: Principles and Pathways beyond Sustainability* (2002), develops principles that, if followed, will lead to a flourishing result. Though the two men ceased working together years ago, their two books are both rich resources. I primarily use Holmgren's text because he spends more time developing a conceptual understanding of a process; then I use Mollison's text to fill in the details when in a particular place.

The place to start is where you have land. It can be as small as a south-facing window (in the Northern Hemisphere) of an apartment, or as large as a 2,000-acre farm in Iowa. For most of us, it will simply be a yard that is in the owner's control. Like the lawn at JMU, there is a management plan already in place, though it is probably not articulated. If the lawn is like most, it is mowed once a week, or perhaps once every two weeks; there are flower beds, perhaps a decorative tree or two, and some evergreen shrubs near the front entrance of the house and perhaps near the driveway. Lawn care, spring planting, occasional weeding, and fall raking are about all the labor that goes into it. Applying permaculture to a lawn, for those who desire to do so, involves complete commitment to a total makeover, but not all at once. Following Holmgren's guidance takes effort, though it does not mean abandoning other commitments. The idea of permaculture includes people, it does not put intimacy with nature or others off-limits; on the contrary, it brings greater contact. If there is no joy in the process, then it is not being done correctly. Using Holmgren's 12 principles as a guide, let's look at what a transformation of a yard could look like.

FIGURE 4.3   A close-up of moss.

1. Observe and Interact

One of the things all of us need to practice is very simple observation. People seldom know what happens right in their own backyard, and often they cannot name what is there. David Orr, author of *Ecological Literacy*, calls this a mark of ecological illiteracy, a lack of awareness of our surroundings (Orr 1991). One sign of ecological literacy is a person's ability to identify 10 species living within 50 feet of the back door. It is amazing how few people in the United States can do this; it is an indictment of our educational system and our homes. So this is the first task: Figure out what you already have in your yard. In Kenya and in Mozambique, young children are often a great source for the local name and uses of an unknown plant. They may be unable to read a book, but they have been educated to read the land very well.

The second part of this task is similar but might take more time: Figure out what is native to your place. This may involve doing some historical sleuthing, in addition to snooping around a wide part of the neighborhood to find pockets of native vegetation. This job is especially difficult in urban or well-developed suburban settings, because developers have a habit of leaving no tree intact. For some reason they find vegetation simply in the way. But being native to a place means understanding how living systems function in a particular area; knowing what thrives provides clues about what will work in your yard. Understanding soil goes along with this. Soils are notoriously variable across even short distances, especially if there is a change in slope or in the nature of water movement. A tree that thrives in a well-drained sandy loam often succumbs in a poorly drained clay loam. Therefore, matching species to soil is critical.

Observations need not be confined to the natural environment. What works on a neighbor's plot gives clues as to what will work on yours. Building a permaculture system is easier in a community. The more heads there are working on problems, the better the solutions. That being said, there are not many people working on permaculture in urban and suburban locations because it is still a new strategy in many places. Permaculture takes people who are willing to synthesize a number of different observations and then start testing possibilities on their own land to make it work. One plant that worked on my land is pawpaw (*Asimina triloba*), a native understory fruit tree. There were previously none in my immediate area, but the tree is found elsewhere in isolated spots growing as an understory member of forested edges. That observation led me to plant a couple under the south side canopy of oak and hickory trees. The plants have flourished and now provide a surprisingly tasty fruit each October.

2. Catch and Store Energy

Modern ecological studies spend considerable time tracking energy flow in ecosystems. Tracking and changing energy flow in modern society is arguably the most critical task we face. For the past 100 years, or nearly four generations, we have relied on fossil fuels and centrally produced, distributed electricity for our household energy source. My grandfather, born in Eastern Washington in 1884, had access to neither fossil fuel nor electricity, but his people did well. Their energy came from the sun, was captured by plants, and then was used to provide power via horses and mules or to grow wood for heating. This lifestyle was normal in those days. When electricity became available, his house was a long distance from the grid, so his family used a windmill and a series of two-volt batteries to supply power for lighting and electric pumps for water. It wasn't until the Roosevelt era's rural electrification program brought power lines that my grandfather's family had regular electricity in their home. For my grandparents this was novel, but for us it is so normal that we forget that this system has vulnerabilities, such as the violent storms in the mid-Atlantic and Midwest states in the summer of 2012 that cut off power in numerous communities for up to a week. Now we face the daunting prospect of climate change and the dwindling supplies of fossil fuels. What energy source will replace these fuels and enable us to thrive? Are there sufficient sustainable sources of energy available?

Holmgren does not prompt us to look at the high-tech solutions of solar power and wind power; rather, he emphasizes passive energy capture systems and the growing of plants, which are nature's highly effective solar collectors and are freely available. Unfortunately, suburban and urban designs are predicated on the availability of cheap fossil fuels and inexpensively distributed electricity from the grid. Most of us do not have houses designed to receive high inputs of solar energy in the winter and store it passively in thermal mass inside the building. We lack overhangs and deciduous trees planted in strategic places to shield our homes and buildings from solar heat in summers. We do not have coppice woodlots to provide firewood on a rotational basis for heat. Nor have we designed our streets to promote pedestrian and bicycle-based mobility, and certainly, most everyone lacks access to a horse!

Catching and storing energy stands as the defining issue of our time. Switching to low-energy systems that depend on decentralized collection and storage is not easy. A radical redesign is needed. Perhaps the simplest and most-needed redesign is to line up all new housing with true south, not the local road (McDonough and Braungart 2002). This does not mean that a standard suburban house will be rendered useless, but it does mean that such a house will require supplemental design changes to enable it to function well in a low-energy system. Simple actions like improving insulation, caulking all cracks, modifying windows to lessen energy loss, planting strategic shade trees, and even adding a solarium will help. Observing what others have tried and adopting the best practices are a good place to start.

There is a place for higher technology as well. The two most dependent and valued uses of electricity in most homes are lighting and refrigeration.[4] Some people probably want to add electronic devices too. Having a system that generates enough electricity to power at least these basics makes some sense. Whether or not the high technology we are accustomed to

---

4   Some might argue this point, especially since the US Department of Energy ranks air conditioning as the number one user of electric power. This argument is based on replacing electricity with passive systems based on other strategies. Heating and cooling are easier to replace with other energy sources. A useful graphic on home electricity use is available here: https://www.visualcapitalist.com/what-uses-the-most-energy-home/

can survive a move to a low, decentralized energy future is difficult to say. The problems lie in the manufacture of the devices, in electricity capture and storage, and in the embodied energy they contain, not the power supply, which can come from the sun.[5]

3. Obtain a Yield

Obtaining a yield seems obvious, but at the beginning of a change process successfully implementing change is critical. When implementing change, failure is possible. Failure is also discouraging. If people do not get a return for the amount of energy put into a project, they will have less incentive to continue the process. A personal example will help. Blueberries are a favorite fruit of mine. I bought six plants, varieties known to produce well in the Shenandoah Valley, but I made two mistakes. The first was embarrassing: I failed to notice the plants' need for a low-pH soil, and my soil was basic. The second mistake was not totally my fault. There is an insect sometimes called the 17-year locust or cicada. When they emerged and found my weak blueberry plants, the result was a total loss for me. The soils in my area are far better suited for growing cane fruits like blackberries and raspberries, or serviceberries (sometimes called juneberries in the genus *Amelanchier*). If I had started with these, rather than with the more difficult-to-grow blueberries, I would have obtained a yield in the second year and probably would have increased the planting and tried other new things. Instead I dithered, eventually learning the lesson of doing better research.

The idea of picking the low-hanging fruit first is a good one. As your first stage, find what is easiest to start and most likely to give a product. Following easy ideas will give you a product and set you up to improve the land in ways that will make the next steps easier. A quick look around my area shows that black walnut and chestnut both love the soil and moisture conditions, grow quickly, and yield well with little to no maintenance. The key is to identify the best varieties of plants and grow them in places in the yard that will not interfere with other ideas. Avoid planting black walnut near an area where you might wish to grow tomatoes. This restriction does not apply to chestnuts.

Mollison and Holmgren developed a concept of zones that is important to include here. A *zone* is defined, in this case, by the distance and time needed to move from one place to another. How frequently you use a particular resource determines the zone where it should be placed. If you are a cook, for example, you probably use herbs like basil, oregano, thyme, chives, cilantro, and parsley on a daily basis. It is amazing how much better they taste when picked fresh and used immediately compared to purchasing in a store or even from

---

5   More information on this issue can be found in Chapter 5, "Reducing Your Personal and Global Carbon Footprint."

a farmer's market. The closer herbs are to the kitchen, the more readily they are available to use on short notice. If the home is zone 0, then herbs are plants for zone 1, closest to the kitchen. If they are planted further away, where they can't be seen from the house, they will eventually be ignored. Blackberries, on the other hand, are a seasonal crop; they fruit for two or three weeks once a year, so these can go further from the house in zone 3. You keep an eye on them for pruning, weeding, and harvesting, but none of these tasks are frequent. A firewood tree, or a coppice woodlot, needs little care at all. These can go in the farthest reaches of the property, as they need little attention or contact. Much less effort is needed to obtain a yield, whereas the need for basil and oregano might be daily if you like a Mediterranean diet. The success of a good herb garden located close to the house encourages the growth of other plants in their own niches on your property.

4. Apply Regulation and Accept Feedback

Probably the best example of a permaculture farm in the Shenandoah Valley is Radical Roots Farm, located about seven miles from Harrisonburg. David and Lee O'Neill started with a trailer, five acres of land, and a few tools, then slowly built their farm into an amazingly productive operation. They focused first on soil improvement and vegetables and then expanded to fruit trees, chickens, and hoop house production to extend their season. Along the way, they learned a few lessons. For example, drought is a problem. The early years on the farm were dry, making the O'Neills realize that they had to manage water and water flow. Though they used raised beds on the contour, this was not sufficient for capturing all the water, so they designed their fruit tree planting to channel water to a holding pond, where the stored water can easily be pumped back to the garden during dry spells. This is an example of nature's feedback loop, telling you what works and what improvements are needed.

Probably the biggest lesson came from deer. The George Washington National Forest is not far away on Massanutten Ridge. Low hunting pressure and ideal habitat have given deer populations a boost. David and Lee tried a number of low-cost methods to keep the deer at bay, but these did not work. The population pressure of the deer made it hard for even dogs to keep them away. Feedback led the O'Neills to accept the idea that the only way to keep out the deer was to construct a high, woven wire fence. This enabled fruit tree establishment, reduced labor previously spent on deer exclusion, and permitted greater diversity in the farm.[6]

Pests of all sizes are part of permaculture reality. They inform you of mistakes, such as an overemphasis on one species, problems with the location of particular plants, or a lack of plant health due to nutrient deficiency. By accepting these as symptoms of problems, you can act to correct system imbalances. The deer population, in the above example, indicates a system imbalance: There is a lack of predators. As Aldo Leopold has pointed out in his essay "Thinking Like a Mountain," in the absence of wolves, mountains live in fear of their deer (Leopold 1986). If we cannot tolerate predators like wolves, then we must tolerate or even celebrate the activities of hunters. This kind of hunting should not emphasize the trophy of a white tail rack; rather, it should look to regulating the population, which means taking out females as well. Failure to accept the reality that deer populations are too high leads to an increased need to build fences as well as an increased problem with erosion on mountain sides.

In the last 25 years bees have suffered from a number of causes but the most troubling is the sudden disappearance of entire hives. Called colony collapse disorder (CCD)[7], it is a problem that remains undefined and unsolved, and is a type of feedback. Though there is tremendous debate about the cause of CCD, a number of clues indicate that our use of chemicals may lie at the root of it. Bees are vulnerable to a variety of problems, including parasites like the varroa mite and a tracheal mite. High parasite pressure keeps colonies weak by killing off bees early in their productive life. Although parasites can wipe out a colony, they are more likely to merely weaken it. Scientists looking at the problem have identified neonicotinoids and chlorpyrifos (an organophosphate commonly used in agriculture) insecticides used on crops, along with a number of antifungal chemicals, which can kill weakened bee colonies. Groups like the Pesticide Action Network and Friends of the Earth are actively campaigning to have these chemicals regulated, and recently the European Union mandated a two-year moratorium on neonicotinoids to assess whether they are the problem. Unfortunately, chemical companies in the United States and Europe (the specific pesticide is made by Bayer) refuse to accept feedback about this problem, and they use all the lobbying pressure they can apply in order to block regulation. Since bees pollinate about a third of all US crops, the issue is very serious. Applying a cure that creates a more severe problem is an extreme example of ignoring feedback, this time on a very broad scale.[8]

---

6 For more detail on Radical Roots, see http://radicalrootsfarm.com/.

7 https://www.epa.gov/pollinator-protection/colony-collapse-disorder

8 Tom Philpott, a blogger and reporter for *Mother Jones*, has written a number of articles on CCD. See "First We Fed Bees High-Fructose Corn Syrup, Now We've Given Them a Killer Virus?" February 5, 2014, http://www.motherjones.com/tom-philpott/2014/02/whats-killing-bees-plot-thickens.

5. Use and Value Renewable Resources and Services

Every year a resource falls into our yards that we mostly regard as annoying. Raking leaves gives us a task every fall, and depending upon the sheer number of trees we have, the chore can be daunting. Leaves on grass smother the lawn and, if thick enough, kill it completely; oak leaves and lawns do not mix. Yet what are leaves for? In a stream, they are the source of energy for a vibrant, healthy ecosystem. Species in the family of crane flies, some mayfly groups, and others have larvae in the water that shred leaves, enabling an entire system of filter feeders, rock scrappers, and small predators to flourish, in turn providing fish with an abundant supply of food. In a forest, leaves blanket the ground, deaden the energy of falling rain that can loosen soil particles, stop erosion, feed worms, and create a humus layer rich with nutrients. Bagging leaves and sending them to a landfill makes absolutely no sense ecologically. In fall leaves we have an annual gift that enriches the system. Carbon captured over the course of the summer becomes the soil nutrients of next spring's growth and even years down the path. They lose value only because they fall on a lawn that is not native to the place.

On the other hand, in a garden they are a blessing. My neighbor lives in a forested setting, and he uses every leaf he can get. His other neighbors have woodland with widely spaced trees; they mow the land, and every fall they pile up the leaves and burn them. Jason volunteered to take the piles instead. He brings them to his garden and piles them up to eight inches thick on his raised beds. This is so thick that the ground stays insulated, allowing saprophytic fungi, worms, and other critters to stay active for most if not all of the winter. They come up through the soil and chomp on the dead leaves from underneath. As spring commences, the pile of leaves is thinner; the soil is well aerated and moist, with improved structure, better water-holding capacity, and more nutrients available for capture by the plants. Jason plants seedlings of his vegetables through the remaining leaf mulch. No fertilizer is required. The nutrients from the leaves, even though small in relation to their carbon, are processed by the soil organisms. These organisms use the leaves as an energy source—thus using up excess carbon. Since he does not mix the leaves into the soil, the carbon-to-nitrogen ratio after worm processing is just about right in the soil itself. The remaining leaves prevent weed seed from reaching the soil, while those already in the soil cannot find the sun, so die before they capture solar energy. Leaves, when used this way, are a free and valuable resource instead of an annual nuisance.

Another resource is the praying mantis. When we initially decided to have a meadow with perennial shrubs in our front yard instead of a lawn, we did not fully understand the life cycle of this predator. The mantis prefers a shrub habitat for reproduction. Every fall, females with large abdomens look for shrub branches located about one to three feet off the ground, hidden by remaining leaves, to lay their eggs in a frothy, sticky substance that adheres to the branch and then hardens into a ball that resembles blown-in foam insulation. These eggs stay dormant until spring, when the nymphs hatch and eat through the protective and hardened froth. These little mantises prowl for the eggs of a variety of insects. They are not particularly picky eaters, although they especially like the eggs of cabbage worms. We found that planting brassicas like kale, broccoli, collards, and cabbage close to bushes where praying mantises laid eggs the previous fall leads to a reduction in cabbage worm problems. Here was nature's service coming to our aid,

FIGURE 4.5   Praying mantis egg sack on a privet stem.

all because we unintentionally provided the right habitat. Now that we know that fact, we deliberately plant these crops close to the shrubs that provide the free service.

Services come from a number of places. Goats provide many of them. There is a service in Portland, Oregon, called Goat Rentals Northwest that uses goats to assist in clearing brush from properties.[9] Goats enjoy blackberry leaves and don't mind the thorns. They will strip unwanted English ivy to bare stems, making it easy for humans to complete the removal task. Goats don't ask for additional compensation. The owner charges by the acre, not by the hour, and goats require only a portable electric fence to keep them contained and a decent water source. Goats can even be used to mow lawns if you set up the fencing correctly. Milk goats will continue to produce in these conditions; owners use portable milking stands and visit the working animals on-site. Along the way, the goats also fertilize the soil, reproduce, and provide meat if their population gets too high. All these benefits come with minimal use of fossil fuels. The goats that I had provided a benefit I did not expect; they liked eating poison ivy.

The examples of nature's services are many. The specific actors change from ecosystem to ecosystem, but the pattern of interactions is a constant in healthy systems. Our tendency to reduce components to a minimum in our lawns creates a desert of interactions. By opening the door for biological diversity, nature gradually will heal the land. We can choose the core species for our own benefit, yet nature will determine the set of mutualistic relationships that let that system thrive. Every component has its role, whether it is thriving bacteria in

<hr />

9   "Goats Get to Work Clearing Land in Portland," *Oregon Business*, September 15, 2011, https://www.oregonbusiness.com/article/item/3105-goats-get-to-work-clearing-land-in-portland.

soil, endomycorrhizal fungi, native bee pollinators, flycatchers, assassin beetles, or a pile of leaves from the fruit trees and nearby oaks. The key is to recognize the value of these services and let them happen.

6. Produce No Waste

There is a phrase used by botanists, gardeners, and others that says a weed is simply a plant in the wrong place. A similar statement applies to waste; waste is a potential resource in the wrong place. Waste is really a symptom of a system that does not work properly. When you have a feedlot with thousands of cattle living on a few hundred acres, manure begins piling up and must be moved away. Manure is a valuable resource, but like anything, too much of a good thing is a waste. Centralized feedlots produce waste; therefore they have a design flaw. Likewise, if your lawn produces waste in the form of grass clippings with nowhere to go, you have a design flaw. Permaculture systems ideally produce no waste. Nature has a cyclical pattern, where the excess growth and waste from one species become food energy for another. Ultimately a nutrient used by a tree comes back again to be part of another tree when the design is right.

Think about this in the context of a lawn: What produces waste? Have you ever purchased inputs for your yard like fertilizer, compost, or potting soil that comes in a plastic bag? What happens to the bag? Why do we sell these inputs in a bag in the first place? The system produces waste, so it is flawed. When a local Shenandoah Valley composting company like Black Bear Composting of Crimora, Virginia, sells compost, they do it in bulk from a truck, delivering the amount needed directly to the user.[10] This works for large buyers, but it is inconvenient and expensive to supply small producers this way. Having customers come to purchase small amounts at the production site means constant disruptions for the few workers on-site, many of whom do not work every day. This argues for a different system. Why not have someone bring a truckload of compost to a farmer's market and sell it by volume to customers who bring their own containers? Could compost be sold using the same means as selling tomatoes? In this way, customers get what they want, Black Bear reaches consumers they presently can't reach, and there is no plastic involved. Waste in this case is measured by emissions from the exhaust pipe of the truck, though this is far less than individual home delivery or having customers drive all the way to the production site.

Permaculture systems follow a guideline stating that nothing should come into the home, yard, or farm that will have to leave to be disposed of elsewhere. Plastic is the easiest item to identify as problematic, because plastic is so ubiquitous in our society and has limited

---

10   The address for Black Bear Composting's website is www.blackbearcomposting.com/.

usefulness once it has finished performing its first job as packaging. So are pizza boxes, though at least pizza boxes are paper, and as a natural organic polymer, nature has a way to eat it. Pizza boxes cannot be recycled because grease from the pizza spoils the reprocessing system. Using pizza boxes as mulch between rows of garden crops actually works. I used them to keep weeds down in patches of sweet potatoes and green beans. They worked well until they disappeared into the guts of very healthy worms. So pizza boxes are allowed into a properly functioning permaculture system, but the little three-legged tables used to keep the pizza boxes from collapsing on the food are not.

Water is another issue. We pipe it into our houses clean and send it off the premises dirty. Any water used in a sink, washing machine, dishwasher, or shower is considered gray water after use. In our present systems, it typically travels through the same pipes as black water from the toilet. But we do not need to design our water systems this way. Gray water is useful for irrigation. Instead of using clean, purified water from a treatment plant to water our lawns, why not use the nutrient-enriched gray water on our garden and fruit trees? Black water is a separate issue, because the parasites in human waste should not be used on a garden. However, there are ways to turn even this waste into a resource, as elaborated in Chapter 7, "Managing Manure: Following Nature's Nutrient Cycles." The moral of this story: Produce no waste. And don't forget to take your own cotton, canvas, hemp, or even plastic reusable bags to every store you happen to use.

7. Design From Patterns to Details

Nature is replete with patterns. A pattern may be as basic as the mosaic of soil types across the topography of your land, or as complex and confusing as the global climate. Sorting out the patterns in a place is a work of observation, a discussion with a community, and an examination of historic evidence. The details are worked into the underlying patterns. If the details do not fit well in the existing patterns, the pattern will fail. Some patterns we understand easily because they give us daily clues. We know, for example, that in the month of March the amount of daylight gradually increases, but at latitude 38° north we also know to wear a jacket, or to at least have one handy, something we would not bother about in July.

Annual patterns are comprehensible. Succession as a pattern is less so. Part of this is due to timing. An oak/hickory ecosystem, for example, may allow for the oak and hickory species to dominate for centuries. Our human life spans, on the other hand, are shorter. The entire pattern of succession may not show itself on one piece of land within the scope of our lifetimes of observation. Even old oak forests may change over time. Fire, flood, disease, or a freak windstorm will stimulate natural change, sometimes back to bare soil, or sometimes wiping out the canopy and opening up the understory to increased light. When any of these things happens, the species that thrive in other phases of succession come to the fore. Exposed soil gives rise to rapidly reproducing and easily spreading annuals like dandelions, lamb's-quarter (an edible relative of amaranth), bedstraw (a sticky plant that climbs other plants), chickweed, and many more. Most of our annual crops are in this category, requiring an opening in bare soil to thrive. What we do in a garden mimics the early succession patterns in nature, and the closer we are to native early succession species, the better our garden performs.

But there is no requirement to stay in early succession over an entire yard. A lawn is really an attempt to keep a yard in an early stage of succession—when the herbaceous perennials have moved in, but before the woody perennials take hold. It takes continuous energy to combat a succession process. Permaculture's premise is that we should mimic as nearly as possible the ecosystem's natural succession process in our place. This means that gardens will eventually yield to perennial shrubs and pioneer trees, and these will, in turn, yield to closed canopy species. Yet the closed canopy stage of succession is not necessarily the most productive phase in terms of food for human beings, so a good permaculture garden manages its succession in a way that maintains high productivity and minimizes losses. Getting to a point where the lawn is transformed into a mixture of species and phases of succession is often best. The point is to *remember nature's pattern of succession so that you can control it with low-energy input.*

8. Integrate Rather Than Segregate

Much of modern agriculture is predicated on the idea of separation of species. The origin of this characteristic is a function of mechanization. You can't use the same setup on a combine to harvest corn as you use to harvest soybeans. The mechanics are different, so the equipment adjustments must be different. The mechanization of agriculture led to monocultures. It also resulted in a highly energy-intensive agricultural system. Nature, though, does not work that way. Monocultures in nature are rare, usually occurring only on badly degraded sites that are overwhelmed by invasive species not subject to local control systems, such as kudzu on degraded land in the American Southeast. Nature's way prefers diversity. Native prairies, for example, mix grasses, legumes, composites, and other species in complex and shifting ways. After a fire, the balance shifts in favor of nitrogen-fixing legumes in order to address the now nitrogen-limited soils. As the legumes grow, their decaying tissues and soil exudates add nitrogen to the mix, allowing composites and grasses to come back. These plants eventually suppress the legumes, until fire resets the system again. Grazing animals also serve to shift things, preventing the taller grasses from overwhelming the commonly shorter legumes and other forbs. The integrated complexity makes for a highly productive system.

The same principle is true in forest ecosystems. The only time you find monoculture is when humans plant one type of tree exclusively, such as Douglas fir in the Pacific Northwest after a clear-cut, or loblolly pine in the Southeast. Our own oak/hickory forest, however, naturally has numerous other members, including multiple species of both oak and hickory. My own backyard forest has northern red oak, white oak, chestnut oak, mockernut hickory, pignut hickory, bitternut hickory, black walnut, sycamore, basswood, tulip poplar, white ash, red maple, black locust, autumn olive, tree of heaven, and ironwood. There aren't many members of this group I would want in a permaculture-based edible forest garden, but the mix models what a healthy garden should mimic. Having a mixture of species integrated in the yard stimulates health. Perhaps no one demonstrates this mixing better than Mark Shepard on his farm in Wisconsin (Shepard 2013). He takes the concept of edible forest gardens far beyond the backyard, but his model of mixing fruits, nuts, firewood trees, timber trees, good forage systems, animal production, bees, and water management exemplifies what a well-designed and functioning permaculture system can be. A person cannot and should not mimic this exactly in a backyard, even one in Wisconsin, but the integration is replicable at a smaller scale. In a small yard, having a raised bed garden surrounded by cane fruits and hazelnuts, with another layer of fruit and nut trees, is perfectly plausible. The numbers of each and, perhaps, the total diversity possible is, of course, restricted by space.

9. Use Small, Slow Solutions

Roland Bunch, in his book *Two Ears of Corn*, says, "Start slowly, start small." The idea is not to jump quickly into a new idea with both feet and a large percentage of your resources, because the likelihood of failure is always present. Sometimes it may not be a complete failure, but insufficient success. Consider Polyface Farm, a complex grass-based farm in Virginia. Polyface thrives on innovation, but its people have failures more frequently than they have successes. Yet the failures do not set them back, because they design many of the "failures" in such a way that the resources can serve another purpose. One example is sheep. The Polyface staff developed a mobile sheep pen and shelter to rotate the sheep across a pasture, as they already had done for cattle. The shelter specifically provided shade in the summer, when the sheep are most sensitive to heat. The sheep did well, but at the same time they occupied the same niche on the farm as the cattle, which cut the amount of grazing available for the farm's primary animal. Having two animals in the same niche proved unviable, so the sheep shelter was modified to become a home for turkeys, which do not occupy the same niche as cows and proved more able to generate income without creating a loss in other areas. The experiment lasted only two years, and Polyface started the trial on a small scale, so no one on the farm regretted the attempt. It was just a lesson learned through trial and error.[11]

---

11   This paragraph is based on personal communication with Joel Salatin during frequent visits to Polyface Farm.

Yards and plants are fickle. You might know everything about your backyard, but you won't know what will happen when you add a new species to the mix until you try. Planting raspberries is a fine place to start, but if your suburban area is prone to inundations by Japanese beetles, you may find that raspberries are not viable. By beginning with just a few plants as a test, you can discover whether the soil suits, whether there are unidentified pests in the area, and whether the timing of harvest fits the family routine.

Part of my research work in graduate school involved a slow, small trial. In Mozambique, near the city of Nampula, I noticed that farmers grew sweet potatoes in ridges elevated above the surrounding soil by 15–30 centimeters. As the farmers built the ridge, they integrated any nearby vegetation into the pile. That gave me an idea. I redesigned the ridges, which are about a meter wide, and built them perpendicular to the slope, along the contour, to stop erosion and to capture more rainfall on the sandy soils. My four Mozambican helpers and I did an experiment, using three different construction methods on one ridge. On the first part of the ridge, we used the traditional method; on the middle part we put a control section, with no vegetation incorporated with the sweet potato planting; and on the third part, we tried my idea of using leaves from leguminous trees and shrubs as the incorporated vegetation. It was a small trial; it took the five of us just one day to build, and it was easy to guard from pests. At harvest time, we found that the leguminous third of the ridge produced 50% more sweet potatoes than the ridge that used the traditional method, but both methods out-produced the control area. What I found out later was that my four helpers reproduced the experiment on their own plots, and the idea started spreading. I did it with another farmer in another area with the same results, and it spread from him to others without my doing anything to promote it. The small experiment addressed the problem of lacking nutrients in the sweet potato planting, and because it required using only locally available, essentially free resources (excluding labor), it succeeded (Teel 1994).

Roland Bunch (1982) gets credit for promoting the idea of small-scale farmer experimentation. The idea is simple: Develop side-by-side experiments on farms that farmers themselves plan, manage, and measure. The development advisor provided them with only a process for testing, and perhaps the idea to test. Many times, the farmers already have something they wish to try, but either the scale or the design of the test is wrong. By making small adjustments and giving clues about how to do proper measurements using local resources, workable ideas can proceed with low risk and potentially high returns.

10. Use and Value Diversity

Much of what constitutes sustainability is found in the concept of diversity. There are a number of forms of diversity. One that intrigues evolutionary biologists is *genetic diversity*, the range of characteristics within a single species that permits the species to survive changes in conditions. The classic example used to illustrate this involves the pepper moth of England, which has two forms, light and dark. When Londoners burned coal as their primary heat source, the dark form thrived on the darkened bark of the city's plane trees. When coal was replaced by oil and natural gas, the soot disappeared and the white form became dominant again. Genetic diversity allowed the species to survive in differing local conditions over time. Species diversity was given focus in the section above entitled "8. Integrate rather than segregate." Its importance is central to ecosystem health, but there are more levels of diversity. Consider *spatial diversity*, the number of niches that exist in a given location that provide spaces for different species preferring slightly different conditions. These appear in small yards and across large landscapes. Or *cultural diversity*, the differences between people, their histories, learning, experiences, and knowledge that all have value in contributing to design. All of these are related to the conditions of the place they are found.

A yard can illustrate some forms of diversity easily. Conditions vary on the north, south, east, and west sides of a house due to shade impacts, differing forms of shelter modifying temperatures, and light levels. For example, the time of peak use of cooling is often mid-afternoon, between 2:00 p.m. and 4:00 p.m. Temperatures reach their zenith at this time, so air-conditioning use maximizes. In the past, these hours marked a time for siestas—afternoon naps. A shade tree on the southwest corner of the yard has a powerful cooling effect, reducing the need for cooling. Alternatively, if the goal was to produce electricity, aiming solar collectors slightly to the southwest for fixed panels changes the profile of electric production slightly, maximizing it when peak demand hits without reducing overall production—if the panels are mounted correctly. Shade trees on the north side don't help with that problem, but having evergreens on the north side reduces heat loss in the winter. Shade trees to the south might eliminate the need for air conditioning altogether, but there you use deciduous trees so winter sun can warm the house, though you might reduce the solar photovoltaic or hot water potential. Understanding the diversity of niches influences sustainable design that works to meet particular needs at a particular time using a diverse set of organisms.

Think of a yard as a complex set of nested niches, each one suited for a different type of plant or a different set of uses. The house in relation to the sun comprises one set of niches. The same is true for a tree, and as it grows over time, the set of surrounding niches determined by shade and moisture conditions change as well. Many times, when only a small space is available, the tendency is to squeeze plants closer together. This does not increase production, and it may negatively impact the plants (Jacke and Toensmeier 2005). It is better to think vertically. Niches are defined by location across the vertical dimension of the tree. So instead of growing just one species tightly, you grow more species arranged by their natural niche. For example, on the south side of a large pecan tree, a serviceberry or hazelnut will do well. On the north side in deeper shade and cooler conditions, plants like ginseng or goldenseal will slowly grow, giving a very valuable product over time. Another set of my neighbors choose a different solution for deep shade: Whenever they find some freshly felled oak trees, they gather the larger branch wood, too small for timber processing, and after impregnating the wood with shitake mushroom spawn, stack the pieces loosely in an open square beneath the dense shade of living oak trees. All they really need to do is wet the wood occasionally, and large quantities of mushrooms bloom twice a year.

Mushrooms and fungi, in general, are a category of diversity we do not make use of enough. No one pushes this harder than Paul Stamets. His book *Mycelium Running: How Mushrooms Can Help Save the World* is worth a good, slow read. Shitake is just one of thousands of species in the fungi pantheon that we can tap. In the setting of an edible landscape in your yard, there are a few species that could provide both a service and food. My personal favorite is the oyster mushroom, of which there are a number of species. These are saprophytic mushrooms, sometimes called white rot mushrooms, which prefer humid environments of various temperatures, depending on the species. They thrive on yard waste that is freshly trimmed and somewhat packed. You can purchase spawn from a company like Fungi Perfecti®, owned by Paul Stamets, and place it in a new pile of yard trimmings including straw, hedge cuttings, pruned branches, and even dry grass. The fungi spread a thin white mat of mycelia through the pile, and in six to ten weeks you just might have a batch of delicious, sauté-ready mushrooms. In the meantime, the mycelia mat turns your pile of sticks and straw into a rich brown pile of compost ready for the garden. All this happens in the "useless," shadiest part of your yard, mostly out of sight and with little labor.

A final note on mushrooms as a highly overlooked natural resource: Stamets's work has shown that mushrooms could serve as key players in environmental cleanup. The oyster mushroom is an example. Stamets's early work showed that oyster mushrooms could consume hydrocarbons from oil spills, though the initial work was slow. He did a selection process, eventually isolating a strain of the mushroom that ate oil readily. The initial development of the mycelia takes place on wood chips, which can then be transferred to a pile of contaminated soil. The study, reported in *Discover Magazine* (Miller 2013), showed that oyster mushrooms cleaned up the oil better than other trials, yielding both a fresh, clean earthy-smelling soil and edible mushrooms. Whether the mushrooms are really edible is a good question. The oyster mushroom is capable of completely breaking down organic molecules from petroleum products, but it does not break down polychlorinated hydrocarbons like dieldrin or polychlorinated biphenyls (PCBs), which are known to be carcinogens. Nor do the mushrooms eliminate the threat from heavy metals like lead, mercury, or cadmium. It is best to know what the waste is before eating a mushroom raised this way.

11. Use The Edges and Value the Marginal

When it comes to providing habitat for a variety of creatures, there is nothing like a hedge. Unfortunately, there are many fewer hedges today than existed a hundred years ago. Mechanization again takes the blame for this. Hedges once marked the boundaries of fields, making a living fence to keep animals in or out, according to what was needed. Hedges provided spaces for wildflowers with abundant niches related to temperature, shade, and moisture. A good thorny hedge even works to secure goats, while at the same time providing a food source. Birds love hedges; they provide protection, nesting sites, and nightly roosts. Many of these birds are insectivores that help keep various insect populations in check. In former times, when fields were bordered by hedges and horses worked the fields, both farmer and horse would rest in the shade of the hedge taking needed breaks, and the horses often ate some hedge while waiting for the trip back across the field. Tractors don't need a break, however, nor are they fueled by a hedge, so farmers took the hedges out. The more turns a tractor must make in a field, the greater the fuel costs per unit of land covered. Unfortunately, the demise of the hedges correlates with the decline in wildflowers and bird populations, especially bush-loving species like the bobwhite quail and the loggerhead shrike.

The loggerhead shrike is a small predatory bird native to the plains of North America, though it is widespread across the southern United States. The bird is about eight to ten inches long with gray above and white below, especially the throat, and a distinctive black eye mask and black outer wing feathers. It thrives on a diet of larger insects, like grasshoppers and crickets, though it also consumes small lizards, mice, and voles.[12] Shrikes often impale their prey on thorns as a way of storing food for later consumption. Though most of their predatory activity takes place in open fields, they store food, nest, and rest in hedges, bushes, and trees. As farming became mechanized, many hedges and windbreaks were removed, reducing habitat for the

FIGURE 4.6   Loggerhead shrike on a hedge.

---

12   My favorite bird website is the Cornell Lab of Ornithology. Their description of the loggerhead shrike is available here: https://www.allaboutbirds.org/guide/Loggerhead_Shrike/

shrikes. Numbers have dropped steadily since World War II. Pesticides have played a role as well, since many insecticides bioaccumulate and loggerheads eat higher on the food chain than some other birds. Reestablishing hedges is one way to encourage reproductive success of the bird.

Hedges are more highly valued in Africa than in the United States. There they still serve as field boundaries, animal fences, forage, and even as sources of fruit and firewood. Even more important is the expansion of available niches they provide. A tall hedge provides a housing development for numerous bird species that keep insects down. If a farmer is lucky, a hedgehog family will take up residence in the base of a hedge, especially if there are rocky cracks and crevasses. These little mammals consume grubs that damage crop roots, but they do not travel far from their daytime hedge hideouts. Hedges also serve as a food source for bees. By having a hedge of multiple species, the range of flowering expands available bee forage, keeping bees nearer the hive and increasing honey production.

Almost any ecology text will discuss the benefits of edge effects. The boundaries between environment types, or *ecotones*, like that between a woodlot and a pasture, a windbreak and a crop, or a riparian buffer and its surroundings, will provide combination habitats that suit a number of species. Though the productivity of a pasture may yield more food than a woodlot or a hedge, the presence of the wood, buffer, or hedge will noticeably improve that productivity in the transition zone, the area in each system of mutual habitation. Nutrients flow across the boundaries, enabling better growth. Simplification of a system to make a landscape more workable requires replacement of these nutrients and services provided by the neighboring environment, often at high cost. Again, as long as energy in the form of fossil fuel is cheap, we tend to undervalue the services of edges, but as energy costs climb, these edges will come back—out of necessity.

12. Creatively Use and Respond to Change

Change happens all the time. Succession is the natural process of change on a landscape across time. Catastrophes happen even in the absence of human-induced climate change. What we have done with climate change is to increase the speed and nature of the change, but change is inevitable. We humans have induced change wherever we settled. The way we choose to respond to inevitable change is what matters. This is not to say we should not fight to stop climate change. Barbara Kingsolver's novel *Flight Behavior*, a fictional account of the impact of global warming on monarch butterflies and a family in Appalachia, uses fever as an analogy for climate change. If you have a 1°F fever, 99.6°F, you rest and wait. If you have a temperature of 101.6°F, you go to the doctor and get medicine. That is where the world stands now, according to the fifth report of the Intergovernmental Panel on Climate

Change, the IPCC.[13] The IPCC's report shows that a 2°C (3.6°F) rise in temperature is nearly unavoidable. If you have a 5°F (2.8°C) rise in body temperature for a long time, you go to the hospital, and the IPCC says we are heading that direction unless we change course now. Unfortunately, the IPCC has long erred in its predictions; change has happened faster than the organization thought. Here is the challenge we face: How do we creatively respond to this change? Doing nothing is no longer a viable option, because the fever is rising. We are now to the point where we have to respond, or the planet will force us to. How we respond remains to be seen. We have yet to identify the best planetary medicine.

There are three obvious invasive species on my property: tree of heaven (*Ailanthus altissima*), autumn olive (*Elaeagnus umbellata*),[14] and multiflora rose (*Rosa multiflora*), introduced originally for combating erosion or aesthetic value. These species, which have spread to unoccupied niches in our damaged environment, have little immediate value in these new places and they crowd out more useful natives. They are now ubiquitous and difficult to remove. So how do we respond to this change in the environment? One idea is simple: Use these species as the main components of making biochar. By keeping them in check through frequent pruning and by making something useful for the garden out of their woody biomass, we move them from the weed category to the resource category. Since biochar is also a method of sequestering carbon, we fight climate change at the same time (Bates and Draper 2019). There is a similar response to invasive weeds like garlic mustard and Japanese honeysuckle, though instead of being used to make biochar, these go in the compost pile. These minor changes, if repeated widely, can add to big differences. The trick is finding the creative way to respond.

Climate change is bigger than any one response. It will require significant changes, especially in terms of energy use and land use. The planet cannot afford the further burning of fossil fuels, nor the continual sacrifice of farm land and forest land to pavement that serves our cars better than it serves us. Changing our attitude to travel will provide a huge challenge to most of us. I am not exempt, for I go to Kenya and Malta on a regular basis. My carbon footprint for these trips is perhaps my greatest contribution to the global problem. Are my trips really worth the environmental cost? How would this be measured? What is the best way to change my behavior without sacrificing the good that the trips accomplish? What choices do we need to make as individuals and as a society in order to prevent the fever of global warming from changing global habitat so radically that humans cannot survive?

---

13   http://www.ipcc.ch/report/ar5/

14   http://www.dcr.virginia.gov/natural_heritage/documents/fselum.pdf

Perhaps the greatest change must come in our notion of security. The human community, as a whole, lacks security right now. We think of security as freedom from threats, but we define these primarily as outside forces impinging on our way of life. There is another threat that is deeper, though, and we do not as readily acknowledge this. Our infrastructure—from our agricultural production to our waste water treatment systems and almost everything in between—depends on inexpensive fossil fuels. Most Western nations, and indeed most of the planet, operate on a fragile network of corporate-controlled energy distribution. We have nearly lost our ability to meet our own needs locally. This is the ultimate form of insecurity: the inability to meet our own needs and a failure to secure the ability of future generations to meet their needs. Ultimately, change must move in the direction of meeting our own needs locally. Until we do this, the insecurities of resource supply, the insecurities of poverty and distribution of wealth, and the insecurities on international relations will plague us all.

As environments change and ecosystems suffer, the pressure grows to invade those few places that remain intact. We need more oil, more trees, more fish, and more soil in order to satisfy an insatiable demand for profit in every corner of the globe. Our inability to sustain growth makes entire systems insecure. But the capacity for continuous growth is a myth that our finite planet cannot afford (Meadows, Randers, and Meadows 2004). At all levels, we need to develop a concept of limits at the personal level as well as at the levels of local community, national, and global. We cannot have or do everything we want. The biggest change that we must incorporate is the knowledge and understanding of planetary carrying capacity at all scales; from there, we must redesign our household management (the real meaning of economics) to reflect those ecological boundaries. Nature sets the limits. We are responsible to act within those boundaries lest we destroy our own house.

True security will come only when we comply with the energy and natural resource limits provided by our "pale blue dot" of a planet. We do not lack for examples of how to do things well locally. The farms mentioned earlier in this chapter, Radical Roots and Polyface, are but two examples local to the Shenandoah Valley. Eric Toensmeier and a neighbor, Jonathan Bates, both of whom live near Boston, have turned a plot of less than one-quarter of an acre into a permacultural dream. Their tiny lot now has over 200 species of edible plants in complementary arrangements. This is documented in a book entitled *Paradise Lot* (Toensmeier and Bates 2013). This is not a blueprint for everyone's yard; rather, it serves as prime example of how we can rethink the lawn. There are many more examples in other niches that will be profiled in other chapters in this book. The task we have for the rest of our lives is to discover and implement systems that thrive within these limits.

Study Questions

1. What is the most interesting or attractive item in your lawn? What does the lawn look like overall, and how do you and your family manage it? Can you name 10 species of plants within 50 feet of your front door?

2. Imagine a transformation. What would you like to see in that lawn that is not there now? Can you envision a way, and a place, where you can grow some of your own food on land that is presently growing mowed grass? What would your neighbors think if you did?

3. What plant in your yard captures and stores the most energy? Is there room for more? What should those additional plants be? If you can, think of the place closest to your home that has the highest biodiversity? Is it a natural space? Who owns it? What species are found there? Could any of these occupy a niche is your yard?

4. What marks the boundary of your landscape? Is this boundary productive, or is it static? Is your yard a place that attracts a wide variety of birds, bees, butterflies, and beetles? Or is it a place where you are trying to keep them away? What are the keys to attracting a healthy diversity? What are the limiting factors keeping that diversity at bay?

5. How has your yard, your neighborhood, your town, suburb, or city changed in the last decade? Do you see positive aspects of this change? What do you identify as negative? What type of intervention might you pursue to move the negative toward the positive at each of the places identified above? How can you move the needle of your community toward a permaculture perspective?

References

Bates, Albert, and Kathleen Draper. 2019. *Burn: Using Fire to Cool the Earth*. White River Junction, VT: Chelsea Green Publishing.

Bunch, Roland. 1982. *Two Ears of Corn: A Guide to People-Centered Agricultural Improvement*. Oklahoma City, OK: World Neighbors.

Holmgren, David. 2002. *Permaculture: Principles and Pathways beyond Sustainability*. Hepburn, Victoria, Australia: Holmgren Design Services.

Jacke, Dave, and Eric Toensmeier. 2005. *Edible Forest Garden: Ecological Vision and Theory for Temperate Climate Permaculture*. White River Junction, VT: Chelsea Green Publishing.

Kingsolver, Barbara. 2012. *Flight Behavior*. New York: Harper Perennial.

Leopold, Aldo. 1986. "Thinking Like a Mountain." In *A Sand County Almanac*. New York: Ballantine Books.

Leopold, Luna. 2006. *A View of the River*. Cambridge, MA: Harvard University Press.

McDonough, Williams, and Michael Braungart. 2002. *Cradle to Cradle: Remaking the Way We Make Things*. New York: North Point Press.

Meadows, Donella, Jorgen Randers, and Dennis Meadows. 2004. *Limits to Growth: The 30-Year Update*. White River Junction, VT: Chelsea Green Publishing Company.

Miller, Kenneth. 2013. "How Mushrooms Can Save the World." *Discover* Magazine, May 30, 2013. http://discovermagazine.com/2013/julyaug/13-mushrooms-clean-up-oil-spills-nuclear-meltdowns-and-human-health#.UqtC-dJDvag

Mollison, Bill. 1988. *Permaculture: A Designer's Manual*. Stanley, Tasmania, Australia: Tagari Publications.

Orr, David. 1991. *Ecological Literacy*. Albany: State University of New York Press.

Rosgen, David. 1996. *Applied River Morphology*. Louisville, KY: Wildland Hydrology.

Shepard, Mark. 2013. *Restoration Agriculture*. Austin, TX: Acres USA.

Stamets, Paul. 2005. *Mycelium Running: How Mushrooms Can Help Save the World*. Berkeley, CA: Ten Speed Press.

Teel, Wayne. 1994. "Catching the Rain: Agroforestry and Soil Conservation in Nampula, Mozambique." Diss., Cornell University.

Toensmeier, Eric, and Jonathan Bates. 2013. *Paradise Lot: Two Plant Geeks, One-Tenth of an Acre, and the Making of an Edible Garden Oasis in a City*. White River Junction, VT: Chelsea Green Publishing.

Credits

Chapter 5

Reducing Your Personal
and Global Carbon Footprint

Introduction

In the end individuals cannot solve the climate crisis or ecological degradation by purely personal action. It takes a village, yes, but it also takes a city, a county, a country and a planet acting in concert to really get the job done. At the same time our personal carbon footprint counts against the total carbon footprint of humanity, so we cannot pass the buck to someone else either. Understanding our own use of energy, and society's use of energy is paramount. While there is no study that provides a definitive reduction that must take place, in general citizens of the US, one of the highest per capita energy using countries, will have to reduce consumption far more than citizens of Costa Rica, who might sit at the per capita sweet spot, while citizens of the Central Africa Republic do not have any obligation to reduce energy at all. And citizens of every country should seek to source their energy use much more wisely than done at present. This chapter is designed to help you do that.

Defining Ecological Footprint

The ecological footprint of most North Americans is huge. An ecological footprint is equal to the quantity of resources we use to sustain ourselves and our lifestyles. This includes the food we eat, the amount we move, the wood, cement, steel and other metals we extract and plastics we mold, the paper we read, the water in which we bathe, the landscape we mow, and much more. Every one of these actions has an underlying energy cost, and that cost directly relates to the amount of fossil fuels used to provide that energy. While there are other energy sources, fossil fuels in the form of coal, petroleum, and natural gas has supplied most of the energy powering our planet since the beginning of the industrial revolution. Look at any item in your home and behind it you will see a pool of oil, a pile of coal, or a cloud of methane.

One way to measure an ecological footprint is to calculate the amount of land it takes to support a person's lifestyle based on energy extraction and resource use.[1] Mine, when roughly calculated using my responses to the variables listed above on the myfootprint.org website was 7 hectares (17 acres), way more than it should be, and I am aware that I have a footprint and should be able to reduce it. The size of my footprint was expanded greatly by flying to Kenya, which is a highly energy and land-use intensive activity. Most of us, in the United States anyway, operate in ignorance of our impact on the planet. We continue to drive everywhere, live too far from work and shopping locations, overcool our buildings in summer, overheat them in winter, and use too many appliances all requiring material input and energy to build and run. All this despite the overwhelming evidence that humans are causing catastrophic changes to the planet. In fact, many Americans deliberately deny they have any impact at all, claiming that climate change lacks credibility and is nothing less than the biggest hoax ever foisted on society.[2] Part of the problem is that climate change is so all encompassing, and at such a long-term time scale, that many have trouble seeing it as something that needs immediate attention.[3] The other problem is that fossil fuels permit centralization of production and generate large profits for many corporations. It is not in their self-interest to promote or encourage change.

There are numerous resources that describe in detail the nature and problems of our fossil fuel use. James Hanson and Bill McKibben are two writers who deserve special attention. Dr. Hanson of NASA was one of the earliest and most consistent voices stating the reality of climate change. He worked as a systems modeler of climate, focusing on paleoclimatic data as the base for making projections of future climatic patterns. While there is no perfect model, the increasing accuracy of the models since Dr. Hanson's first statement of his fears has made him a powerful advocate for fossil fuel reduction and for fossil fuels' eventual elimination. Without a radical reduction of carbon dioxide in the atmosphere, and a corresponding shrinkage in other greenhouse gasses, which he calls climate-forcing gasses, we face catastrophic changes to our planet that will affect our grandchildren[4], though recent publications and reports indicate that climate change already affects us to a substantial degree.[5]

---

1   See myfootprint.org and other similar websites.

2   See *The Greatest Hoax*, by Senator James Inhofe as one example of the denial party.

3   See "Our House in on Fire: The Reality of Our Climate Change." Rebecca Solnit, The Nation: http://www.thenation.com/article/176520/our-house-fire-reality-our-changing-climate

4   See *Storms of our Grandchildren*, by James Hanson, 2012

5   National Climate Assessment and Development Advisory Committee, Third National Climate Assessment Report, May 6, 2014 http://www.globalchange.gov/ncadac

Bill McKibben was arguably the first person to grasp the enormity of Hanson's initial statement about climate change in 1988 and translate it into a popular format for non-scientists. His 1989 book, *The End of Nature*, argued that human action on the planet was changing environments in radical ways that nature was not able to handle. The result, if the pattern continued, would be a planet unrecognizable by people alive today. Even environmentalists at the time found it hard to swallow the message McKibben gave. Today, though, it is broadly accepted by environmentalists and environmental scientists and even an ever-widening public. Nothing symbolized this more than the gathering on a freezing February 17, 2013, in Washington, DC, to protest the Keystone XL pipeline, led by 350.org, the Sierra Club, the Hip Hop Caucus, and First Nations groups from Canada. Over 40,000 people showed up and marched. McKibben continues to push, to march, to write and to speak, but unlike in 1989, he is no longer alone.[6]

These two men, among many others, have pushed us all to recognize that our ecological footprint is really our carbon footprint.[7] Carbon in the right place is the key element of life. Carbon as carbon dioxide in too high an atmospheric concentration, however, does a great deal of harm. According to the recently released fifth report of the Intergovernmental Panel on Climate Change (IPCC), glaciers are melting at a fast rate, the oceans are acidifying rapidly due to dissolving CO_2 in the water, temperatures are climbing in the deep ocean, the arctic ocean is melting, opening up the fabled northwest passage, and animals and plants are moving their ranges north or uphill every year.[8] This evidence is overwhelming yet invisible during the daily activities of most people. Despite the evidence, there is a lack of urgency because there are more immediate problems that demand attention. That means it is up to those who are aware to push for actions that reverse the present planetary direction. This effort must be directed toward reducing carbon output and increasing carbon capture. These actions are essential to keeping us as a society moving toward sustainable systems.

---

6   Another gathering on September 21, 2014 in New York City dwarfed the Keystone protest. The People's Climate March was organized by 350.org, the Sierra Club and over 1500 other environmental, social justice, union and other organizations and attended by over 310,000 people in New York, and 570,000 worldwide in similar events. http://peoplesclimate.org/wrap-up/

7   Though I note the influence of two white males here, women and people of color and other cultures have had a great influence on my thinking, Vandana Shiva, Wangari Mathai, Terry Tempest Williams, Sandra Steingraber, Van Jones, Will Allen and Rachel Carson are among them.

8   The IPCC http://www.climatechange2013.org/images/uploads/WGIAR5-SPM_Approved27Sep2013.pdf Working Group I Contribution to the IPCC Fifth Assessment Report, Climate Change 2013: The Physical Science Basis Summary for Policymakers.

The previous paragraph was written in 2013. It is now 2020. Since then the IPCC has come out with two new reports with further grim news, stating that we must reduce carbon emissions by 55% by 2030 if we hope to keep global temperatures from rising more than 2°C. Events like Hurricanes Harvey and Michael in the United States, drought along the Pacific coast of Nicaragua, Honduras, El Salvador and Guatemala, civil war in Syria, fires in California and Australia, and methane emissions from the permafrost regions of Siberia, Alaska and Northern Canada have prompted even more dire predictions. At the same time youth have responded. Greta Thunberg of Sweden is symbolic of many who will no longer keep quiet. The Extinction Rebellion and the Sunrise Movement are camping at the doors of politicians preventing them from pursuing business as usual, even though they were elected by those who deny the reality of the climate emergency. Their message is the same. We can no longer ignore the facts, climate is changing, fossil fuels stimulate the change, and we have to reduce their use, now, not later, and we should act to force that reduction on the unwilling.

Thankfully there are many actions that can be done from the personal level to the community, regional and national levels. This chapter will look at actions in the energy reduction and production area. Later chapters will look at how we can capture carbon in ways that produce goods and improve ecosystems simultaneously. We will start with systems that directly reduce our carbon footprint, reducing the amount of fossil fuels we use to power our daily lives.

Reducing Home Energy Use

As I wrote this initially while on sabbatical in Florida, sitting in a one-bedroom condominium, a heat pump air-conditioning system was whirling, pushing cool, dehumidified air into the room. We set the temperature relatively high, 76°F (24.4°C) but the pump still frequently operated. The windows were single pane and the amount of insulation above the ceiling was quite thin. The place where I wrote was relatively dark, but thankfully the condo had a Solatube® that captures sunlight on the roof and feeds it to the room, thus reducing the need for electric lighting. Increasing the number of Solatubes® would eliminate the need for electric lighting during the day.

Living in Florida, albeit temporarily, reinforced awareness that good design is key to reducing energy use. If you want to eliminate fossil fuel use at the household level, then you have to design the house correctly first. Retrofitting is possible, but it is extremely difficult to get a fully passive house, one requiring no fossil fuel inputs at all, when you start with a pre-existing structure. However, there are ways available to significantly cut your carbon footprint in any structure. Since it is always easier to do this where you are as opposed to where one is not, my abode in Florida will serve as an example.

Without doubt, the biggest users of energy in this condo are the air-conditioning system, the refrigerator, the lighting, and the hot water heater—in that order. This is Florida, along the south gulf coast, so it is hot, humid, and mostly windless. Sitting in the heat is decidedly unpleasant and promotes lethargy, so air-conditioning promotes productivity. The system in this condo is an air-to-air heat pump that moves calories from inside to outside air. It is modestly efficient and we keep the temperature higher than local restaurants and businesses do. Yet it struggles against the heat gains coming through the single-pane windows and the thin ceiling insulation. Improving insulation is the least expensive and most effective thing that could be done immediately. The present insulation is one to three inches thick. Increasing it to 6 or even 8 inches could be easily done since the attic space is open and blowing in cellulose fiber insulation would be simple. This would greatly reduce heat gain in summer and correspondingly shrink the power needed to condition the air. Changing the windows to double or triple pane is possible but more expensive, though I would consider that a reasonable possibility.[9]

Another effective strategy would be to change the heat pump itself. A newer, improved heat pump would work better than the older model operating outside, but one has to include the resource cost of metals when considering a change like this. There is a high environmental and energy cost to the making of a heat pump. Here is where a life-cycle analysis (LCA) is important. LCA involves looking at all the materials and the extraction processes for getting those minerals as part of the cost of the device. (Ecologists use the term *emergy analysis* for the same evaluation, described below.) Cost alone is not a complete measure because there are commonly externalized costs of production, especially water and air-pollution costs of mining, smelting, and manufacturing metals, which are not reflected in the final product cost. The LCA will tell you if the replacement of a heat pump is beneficial. Since the present heat pump will eventually wear out, perhaps the best option for major energy savings is a ground-sourced heat pump, which involves exchanging heat with the ground or groundwater rather than air. Coastal Florida has high ground water. It is not expensive to drill, and one does not have to go deep. It is far more efficient to exchange heat with groundwater than with air, and the year-round temperature differential is not significant. Switching to

---

9   There is a resource on building envelopes (exterior walls and ceiling) values, managed by Oak Ridge National Laboratory at https://www.ornl.gov/news/buildings-pushing-envelope/. According to this website increasing ceiling insulation alone, from 3 to 6 inches, would increase the R-value (resistance to heat loss) from 7.5 to 15, and this accounts for the lower R-value of the ceiling joists. The energy saving is more difficult to determine, but a lowering of electricity use by the heat pump by 20% is predicted by the calculator.

a ground-sourced heat pump will cost, but the savings in this case could amount to 60% of the electric bill thereafter.[10]

The refrigerator in this house is loud and runs frequently. The noise creates an odd and deeply frustrating situation. Refrigeration requires moving heat from inside the box to outside the box. The process is a physical chemistry/thermodynamics puzzle that has generated many useful solutions but also has led to many unintended consequences. The ability to use the physical change from a liquid to a gas at differential pressures using the latent heat of vaporization makes the refrigerator, freezer, and air conditioner all amazing engineering feats. At the same time, the refrigerator dumps the heat pumped out of the box directly into the room we are trying to cool in the Florida heat, making the air conditioner run even more. This is a design flaw that is not correctable in an existing domicile or with existing refrigerator designs. The only choice here is to have a more efficient and effective refrigerator/freezer. Luckily there are many now on the market. The US Department of Energy labels certain products with an Energy Star rating. Energy star labels provide the annual energy cost for refrigerators and other appliances, granting a star to those with the highest ratings. Preferred newer models have thicker insulation, better door seals, and move the compressor and heated coils to the top of the box (as opposed to locating them behind and underneath), are smaller (under 18 cubic feet), and have improved options for the freezer. The best option for the latter is to locate the freezer on the top and keep it relatively small. For long-term storage of frozen vegetables, fruits, and meats, use a well-insulated chest freezer. This takes advantage of the cold air sinking and lowers heat loss when you open it. Newer models of refrigerators use less than half the energy of the best models from fifteen years ago, with the best models arguably coming from Sun Frost®.[11] Before making a change, once again it is important to consider the material cost and life cycle assessment of the switch.

Perhaps the greatest transformation of energy use in the home comes through new lighting technologies. Vast improvements in lighting have occurred over the last three decades. The advent of the compact florescent light (CFL) bulb started the transformation. This house has a free-standing light for reading that uses five small 25-watt incandescent bulbs. This carbon spewing use of electricity could be easily avoided. If the mounting screw were larger, we could replace the bulbs with CFL bulbs, probably the 9-watt variety, and get more total lumens as well. Light emitting diodes (LED) lights are another option that have now

10   See the website of the International Ground Sourced Heat Pump Association for more information: https://igshpa.org/

11   Musings of an Energy Nerd, by Martin Holladay. http://www.greenbuildingadvisor.com/blogs/dept/musings/choosing-energy-efficient-refrigerator

entered the mainstream. LEDs save slightly more electricity than CFL bulbs, cost more, though that is dropping fast, and last a lot longer, up to 22 years if used an average of three hours per day.[12] LEDs use a more adaptable system for generating light than CFLs, enabling them to take on a wider variety of shapes. LED bulbs are available at most big box stores that could replace the reading lamp bulbs in this room. The type of LED bulbs available in 2020 has expanded greatly, so it is now possible to find bulbs to fit almost any lamp, eliminating the need for less efficient and more polluting on disposal CFL bulbs.[13]

The next issue to consider is the water heater. It does not make any sense to use fossil fuels to heat water in Florida. The sun was shining as I looked out the window, the temperature was about 85°F; why did I need to heat water with energy from a coal-fired power plant? There is no frost danger in this part of Florida. It would be simple to mount a passive solar hot water system on the roof.[14] In fact there is already one outside on the roof of the carport, and another on the roof of one of the community centers on the compound. Spain, Greece, and Israel make solar hot water systems mandatory for all new construction and these countries have the lead in design of these systems as well. Energy.gov estimates that a solar hot water system will save $240 per year over a standard electric hot water heater and about $175 per year over a natural gas system. Though the initial system cost is higher, they also estimate a payback period of approximately 5 years for a lower cost system.[15]

On my home in Virginia, the roof holds six glazed flat-plate collectors that back-drain water to a storage tank when temperatures are not hot enough. This also prevents any possibility of damage from freezing in winter. These require a pump to operate, and the pump is activated when the temperature under the glazing of the flat panel is 15°F (6.5°C) higher than the water temperature in the 500-gallon insulated storage tank in the cellar. When the sun shines on the panels they heat up, which triggers the pump that drives water through the copper tubing embedded in the black metal of the panel, heating it up. This in turn heats the 500-gallon reservoir that contains two lengths of coiled copper tubing. This tubing is part of the pipe feeding our hot water tank, so it reaches the tank at a temperature higher than the setting on the tank. We keep ours at 120°F. When our system is operating properly, we are able to heat our water without reliance on fossil fuels. In the winter, when there is less sunlight and we use the water for floor heat, the liquid propane hot water tank kicks in to help, but in 20 years of use we have not reached $3500 for our entire house's heat and

---

12 This information comes straight off the label of Phillips LED lights for sale in local stores.

13 The US Department of Energy is a great source for a lot of information about home energy source. Here is the link to lighting. http://energy.gov/energysaver/articles/lighting-choices-save-you-money

14 http://energy.gov/energysaver/articles/solar-water-heaters

15 http://energy.gov/energysaver/articles/estimating-cost-and-energy-efficiency-solar-water-heater

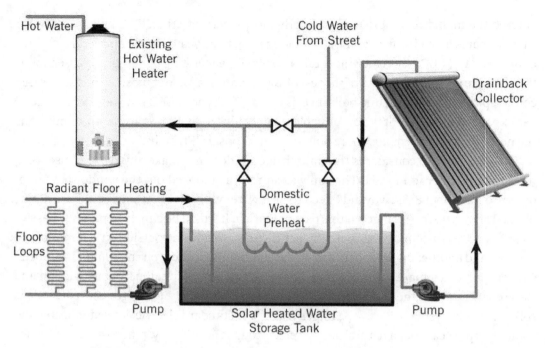

Hot Water

Existing
Hot Water
Heater

Cold Water
From Street

Drainback
Collector

Radiant Floor Heating

Domestic
Water
Preheat

Floor
Loops

Pump

Solar Heated Water
Storage Tank

Pump

FIGURE 5.1   Solar hot water system using a collector to heat a storage tank which is used to preheat water for the household hot water and radiant floor heating. The storage tank is closed and well-insulated, often located in a basement or cellar. Water flowing through the collector drains back to the storage tank when there is insufficient solar to warm the panel, preventing any danger of frost damage to the system.

Source: https://www.motherearthnews.com/diy/home/solar-water-heater-zmoz12fmzphe

hot water costs. Given that the initial cost of the system was high due to using hot water for floor heat as well as household use, it took approximately 12 years to pay back the entire initial cost with the energy savings. (Figure 5.1)

In Florida, a similar system could be even simpler because a pump is not needed. Passive systems work very well when the hot water storage tank sits above the heat capture system. This process takes advantage of the physical property of liquid water expanding when heated above 4°C. Cool water at the bottom of the tank sinks through the pipe to the bottom of a solar thermal collector, then this water heats and rises through the collector and into the top of the storage tanks (See Figure 5.2). Cold water feeds into the storage tank at the bottom while hot water leaves from the top to service the hot water faucets. Heating takes place continually throughout the day and the storage tank is insulated and covers nighttime use. It is an elegant solution, costing a bit more up front, but in this system there are no running costs.

Residents of southern Florida, the sub-tropics, and the tropics do not worry about heating costs. For those in the rest of the USA, however, heating costs come into play. In many ways the same techniques used to keep a house cool perform the same function when keeping it warm, only the direction of heat flow is reversed. Insulation, along with the orientation of the house, remain the key variables. Bill McDonough, architect and co-author of *Cradle to Cradle*, claims that the first thing any new architect should learn is how to find due south. Nothing irked him more than seeing a new development designed with houses facing the roads rather than aligned with the

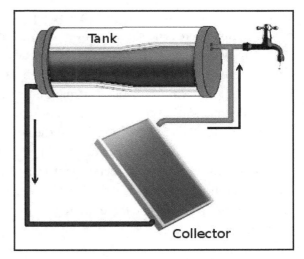

FIGURE 5.2 This system is driven by solar energy alone. It works well in a climate where freezing is not an issue. These systems are common in the tropics and the Mediterranean region. https://en.wikipedia.org/wiki/Solar_water_heating

sun. We should have enough intelligence by now to realize that the simple act of facing the widest roof expanse south provides the best chance of capturing energy from the sun.[16] It is a crime against the planet to not orient a house, or any building, in such a way as to capture solar energy in cooler climates.[17] This enables the home owner to capture the low rays of the sun through glass on the south side of the house in winter and heat the house with no other energy source. My house is designed this way. We have straw bale insulation on the east, north, and west outer walls and R-50 blown in cellulose insulation in the attic. The south wall contains four eight-foot-wide sliding glass doors and complementary windows. When the sun shines, we do not need additional heat. When it does not shine, we have hot water floor heat and a Tulikivi wood fireplace as a backup. A cord and a half of wood lasted us three years, and in those same three years, we used under $400 worth of liquid propane[18]. On clear

---

16   There is some debate about this. Peak demand for electricity in the US is usually in the early afternoon, between 1:00 and 3:00pm. If a house is directed about 10 degrees off true south to the west, this aligns peak energy from photovoltaic panels with peak energy use in most households with air conditioning. It does not greatly diminish overall production but arguably makes it easier for utility companies to meet demand.

17   This advice is given by William McDonough and Michael Brungart in their book *Cradle to Cradle* (2002).

18   If I could do the house over again I would not use liquid propane for energy. Photovoltaic is now inexpensive and an electric hot water system makes more sense, perhaps using a ground source heat pump.

cold days in January, we sometimes have to open a window in the late afternoon to cool one of our rooms. There is no shame in overheating for free when there is snow on the ground.

In July, we use the high solar angle to our advantage. In January, the sun is low in the northern hemisphere. Our house sits at 38°N latitude. At the solar minimum angle on December 21, the winter solstice, the maximum height of the sun is equal to 90°-38°-23.5°, or 28.5° degrees above the horizon at noon. To calculate the angle for June 21, the summer solstice, change the -23.5° to + 23.5° and the sun is at 75.5°. You can stop any direct solar input to the house with an overhang. If your south wall is 20 feet (6 meters) high, the overhang need only be 4 feet (1.2 meters). Planting deciduous trees, shrubs, and vines at strategic locations around the house can shield the east and west walls from solar input as well. The bare branches in winter allow the sun to warm these walls, supplementing the heat during the cold season. [19]

Generating Electricity

To this point, the emphasis has focused on conservation of energy and using less in our appliances and lighting as well as capturing direct solar input. These are our best options for reducing dependence on fossil fuels and we should continually strive to use less and, at the appropriate time, purchase less energy-demanding goods. Nevertheless, we still need to use energy since our modern systems of communication, information sharing, information storage, and computing are energy drains. Just look around your house. How many little LED lights in red, green, blue, and white are glowing or flashing everywhere you look? From my Florida condo, I see a cordless telephone, a Wi-Fi tower, a digital clock on a microwave, a bluish shine from a clock radio, a red light from the cable TV connection and, of course, this computer screen–all within my line of sight. I have two cell phones and a tablet charger ready to plug in when their batteries run down. How many more energy vampires hide in this small apartment? How many do you see in yours? How many coal, nuclear, and natural gas power plants are operating just to keep all our little lights glowing all the time? Why aren't these easy to turn off? I cannot answer these questions, but I do see that the sun is shining outside and the Solatube is giving me all the light I need to operate at the moment. Can we escape this energy trap?

---

19   For more complete instructions on passive solar input control using overhangs and thermal mass Borst Engineering has a Calculator with complete instructions to work out the details. http://www.borstengineeringconstruction.com/Calculator_Instructions.pdf Copyright © 2015 Borst Engineering & Construction LLC

Solar Photovoltaic

The answer is yes, but the process is not simple and would require policy changes that may not be forthcoming from our current dysfunctional government.[20] The technologies needed to diversify and decentralize our energy system are available and constantly improving. We already have solar and wind technologies, of course, while hints about ocean wave and ocean current technologies peer from the horizon. The best technologies are those appropriate in your present living situation and the natural resources available. Whether one is in Florida or Virginia and the sun is shining, solar photovoltaic (PV) electricity generation looks like a good possibility. In fact, solar power is probably the best option for a majority of Americans. The only exceptions would be those who live within canyons or dense forest where direct sunlight is rare, or in far northern regions where the sun disappears for months at a time. Ten years ago, this answer was not so obvious.

To explain why requires the introduction of another word from ecology, *emergy*. It was coined by an ecologist named Howard T. Odum from the University of Georgia. His basic work was on the energy flow in ecosystems by which he monitored the different forms of energy—sunlight, wind, ocean currents, etc.—and the means by which living organisms captured this energy and used it for their sustenance. But energy has different qualities. Solar energy, for instance, is abundant and very diffuse. A plant captures only a thousandth of the solar energy that falls on its surface in its own tissues, on average, though some plants are more efficient than others. This energy, when transferred to the next trophic level, is further concentrated. Odum eventually coined the term *emergy* to represent the embodied energy in the organism. Thus a plant may embody 1,000 parts of solar energy per 1 part chemical energy of its tissues. An herbivore eating the plant may embody 10,000 units of solar energy per unit of energy in the form of body mass. To Odum, this move from one trophic level to the next represents an energy cost. The higher an organism resides on the food pyramid, the greater the embodied energy in that organism.

The same principle is true for goods. Every good we own has an embodied energy cost, some parts of which are reflected in its price while others are not. So, for example, the heat pump's price reflects the monetary cost of the extraction and processing of its metals, lubricants and gasses, but may not represent the environmental costs or passive energy costs that were involved. Solar panels should be evaluated to take these things into account. The biggest single cost of a panel is the crystallized silicon used as the semi-conductor that allows

---

20 At this edit, in December 2015, the US passed a budget that continues the solar and wind energy incentives for the next 5 years. This is good, but perversely balanced by the odd gift to oil companies of the right to export US crude.

solar radiation to drive an electron through the crystal to generate useful power in the form of electricity. Energy is required to make the silicon crystal, more energy to cut it to the right thickness and shape, more energy for the metal on each side of the crystal that then carries the power to more wiring, additional energy to mount it properly, energy to seal it, energy to make the sealant, the glass cover and the aluminum trim around the panel, and finally, more energy is needed to package, store, transport, sell, and mount the product on a person's roof. All these are costs embodied in the panel. When ecologists like Odum looked at a panel in the 1990s and saw these embodied energy costs, they equaled enough that the energy the panel produced over its lifetime of operation exceeded its monetary energy cost, but not its emergy cost.[21] This meant that the perception of the cost-to-value ratio was dramatically different from its actual cost-to-value ratio.

Things have changed in the last decade. The energy used to make the silicon crystals has dropped, new techniques have helped to shrink the amount of silicon needed to make the same amount of power, the quantity of glazing has shrunk, along with the trim, and as a result, the costs of the panels, both in terms of energy and emergy, have plummeted. Instead of costing $5.00 per watt, panels now cost under a $1.00 per watt.[22] Panel systems over the 25-year guaranteed life of the unit produce electricity at the same price or even less than that of coal, which has all kinds of externalized emergy costs. The objection that the emergy costs of solar are too high are no longer true. At the same time, emergy calculations make us aware that photovoltaic panels are not entirely without costs, so energy use reduction remains the single most important action.[23]

The question of whether or not to have a solar PV system on your home or business is an economic and ecological question. How much will it cost you? How much will it save on an electric bill? How long will it take to pay for itself? How much will you have to change

---

21 See David Holmgren 2002 *Permaculture: Principles and Pathways beyond Sustainability*, and H.T. Odum, 1996 *Environmental Accounting: Emergy and Environmental Policy Making*. John Wiley and Sons, New York.

22 These costs continue to plummet. Reports read at Clean Technica (www.cleantechnica.org) show that the per watt cost of a panel has dropped to under $0.60 and will no doubt be lower when you read this. Part of this drop is, of course, due to externalizing environmental costs in China, but US and German factories also have much lower prices with much lower externalized costs. Another factor is the rise in efficiency of amorphous solar panels with lower material inputs and costs. The technology is rapidly improving.

23 A word of warning is needed here. Kris De Decker of Low Technology Magazine makes a strong argument that not all solar panels are equal. Solar panels made in China cost less because they are made with low cost labor and highly subsidized and high externalized cost coal. These panels then have much higher emergy than panels made in countries with higher cost labor and more diversified energy portfolio. Ultimately solar panels should be made using the energy from solar panels and wind turbines from the energy produced by the turbines.

the present structure of your home or business in order to install the panels? What kind of deal will your electric company give you if you do this? In answering these questions for myself, I had to look at our household energy use over the last year. Dominion Virginia Power Company is essentially a regulated monopoly enterprise that supplies our electric power. From October 2012 to September 2013, a 12-month period, we used 5300 kWh of electricity and paid $724.80 to the company for this supply. This bill is determined based on a flat distribution service fee, calculated at $8.40 per month, which is charged independently of any energy use. The rest of the bill is a charge for use, which in August of 2013 was 12.1 cents/kWh.

In order to figure out how large a photovoltaic (PV) system is needed to produce all the electricity a person would use in a year, the best place to start is the National Renewable Energy Laboratory (NREL) website PV Watts Viewer (https://pvwatts.nrel.gov/). This link takes you to page where you can put in your address and enter, taking you to a series of pages giving you information about the potential of a solar system. The table presented gives the amount of solar energy falling upon a square meter of ground in an average year. In the case of Harrisonburg, Virginia, it is 4.79 kWh per day.[24] This number ranges from 3.17 kWh/day in December to 6.3 kWh/day in June. The page also provides an estimate of how much energy is supplied by a fixed array with 4.0 kW of PV. In Harrisonburg, this PV system would generate 5474 kWh/year, or approximately the amount that is used by my household. In my case, I would need slightly more than 4.0 kWh of production capacity to guarantee that we could cover all our annual energy cost from home production.

The cost of a solar PV installation is highly variable, depending on a variety of factors at the local, state, and federal levels. If we ignore subsidies, which are volatile and dependent upon legislative decisions mostly beyond our control except from the voting booth, we can get an approximate idea of cost. First, note that we need to produce 5300 kWh of alternating current (AC) power. Solar energy produces direct current (DC) power and there is a cost to changing the form of electric power. NREL estimates that there is a 23% loss in converting from DC to AC, so the system must be oversized by that amount. Second, an inverter and wiring system is needed to convert and move the power into our present household system. Third, we have to pay labor to mount and install the system, unless we do most of the work ourselves (which would require specialized knowledge, skills, and tools). All these factors are incorporated into the final cost of the system. In adding all this together, taking into consideration all the variables above, the total cost would be between $14,000 and $16,000

---

24   There are a number of abbreviations involved in discussing electricity. A kilowatt hour, or kWh means using 1000 watts of energy for one hour. When you see 4.0 kW of PV, it means 4000 watts of photovoltaic production capacity.

FIGURE 5.3   The author's household photovoltaic system with 14, 315-watt panels, 4410 watts of production capacity in ideal conditions. The average productivity of the system over a 3-year period is 13.04 kwh/day. Maximum production happens on cool, bright sunny days in April. Production tends to drop with high temperatures.

to have a company install a system adequate to cover 100% of our electric use given the present pattern.[25] Given the present price of electricity, not accounting for inflation, and only considering the actual cost per kilowatt hour (excluding the distribution service fee), we could pay off the system in 25 years based on current costs at the high end. If the distribution fee were included in the per kilowatt hour charge, which would raise the price of electricity to the more realistic level of 13.67 cents per kilowatt hour, it would take 22 years to cover the cost of the system at the higher cost above, which is better. With present government subsidies at 30% of total cost in tax incentives, then the system pays for itself in 15.4 years.[26] All in all, as of 2013, solar PV at the household level is competitive, but still costly up front. If the true cost of electricity, with no externalized costs and no government subsidies for any power supply system, is considered, then a solar system as described above is competitive, but not sufficient.

Other factors that we must consider are diurnal variation and seasonality. PV systems produce power very well during the time of day, and season of the year, when it is most needed for air conditioning, but it does nothing at night. Decentralized solar power cannot light up the night unless that energy is stored. This makes costs prohibitive for a lot of people because

---

25   This installation cost estimate was provided by a local installer of solar PV systems in Harrisonburg for a 4kW system. He gives a range because of price fluctuations for materials in the system. However, this was based on 2013 prices. We completed installation of a 4.4 kW PV system on our house in February 2015 for $12,700, a 20% price drop in one year. Costs have continued to drop and this same system would cost 20% less now. From 2016 to 2019 we did not pay anything to Dominion for electricity. At present we have a $430 credit on our electric bill.

26   For these calculations I used my own electric bills and the Solar-Estimate website: http://www.solar-estimate.org/index.php. All the numbers used were based on prices as of November 2013. Given that it cost only $12,700 in 2015 and there is also a $3000 subsidy, the system will be paid off in 13.2 years if electric prices do not rise and without receiving any payment for surplus electricity produced.

battery systems are expensive. If your house is off the electric power grid by a kilometer or more, then a battery system makes sense cost-wise. However, most of us are not off the grid. It is better to grid-tie the system, feeding surplus to the grid when we produce more than we consume, and take from the grid when the opposite situation occurs. This creates a dilemma for power companies since grid-tying requires smart grid management systems and more sophisticated monitoring. Some power companies, like Dominion VA Power, put roadblocks in the way of homeowners, while others, like Harrisonburg Electric Cooperative, have been more welcoming to solar innovations. [27] Other states are far ahead of Virginia at prompting power companies to cooperate with household, grid-tied PV. Unless government assists in breaking the barriers to the broad adoption of decentralized solar power production, adoption lags. Virginia, as a rule, is very friendly to power companies like Dominion while states like New Jersey and California have policies to promote solar energy. Cooperation is critical in overcoming the problem of intermittency inherent in integrating solar power.[28]

Wind Power

Wind power has grown by leaps and bounds over the last decade, becoming the number one source of added power in the US in 2011 and continuously growing every year since. Costs have come down and government subsidies have helped financially. Wind pays for itself, so subsidies are not needed over the life of the units, but subsidies remain important for tying wind power to the grid. Like solar, wind power is intermittent, but it is not tied so tightly to the diurnal cycle. In that sense, wind power compliments solar, with production peaking in the morning and the evening, before and after solar comes on or goes off. Yet not all places have wind, but there are some wonderful map resources that give clear indications where the best wind sites are. A map for the US is shown in Figure 5.4.

---

27 There is a question about why the difference in philosophy between the states and the power companies. At the state level, it all depends on whom we elect to make the laws. In conservative Arizona, there was an attempt by the power companies to attach a service fee to grid-tied PV systems to cover costs, but conservative politicians like Barry Goldwater, Jr. nixed that idea in the legislature, supporting the idea of homeowners having the right to grid-tie their household electricity production without additional expense. Dominion VA Power has a strong lobbying presence in Richmond and essentially controls energy policy. Harrisonburg Electric Cooperative, on the other hand, operates locally and is therefore more responsive to local demand. They are constrained because they buy power from Dominion, but they do include the distribution service fee in the per kWh charge for electricity, thereby making a grid-tied system more competitive.

28 A book is a fixed report. Solar PV is a dynamic industry and costs are changing constantly, too fast to keep up. Use the numbers given in this chapter with healthy skepticism. Prices of PV panels, PV systems, and battery storage options are dropping.

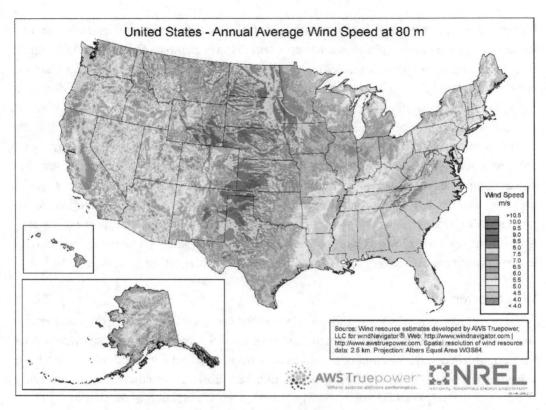

FIGURE 5.4   This map is produced by the National Renewable Energy Laboratory (NREL) showing the best places for wind installation at 80 meters hub height. As indicated, most of the land mass east of the Mississippi, with the exception of small isolated points in the Appalachians up to Maine, do not have much to offer. On land, the belt from the Texas panhandle to North Dakota is rich in wind resources with notably superb wind in SE Wyoming and South Dakota. (https://www.nrel.gov/gis/images/80m_wind/USwind300dpe4-11.jpg)[29]

Wind has the same emergy problem as solar power in that its production involves a substantial embodied energy cost in materials and installation, but it has a lower environmental cost than that of coal or even natural gas, so in the end, it is a better choice than fossil fuels. At the same time, it is important to note the ecological costs. Early turbines, especially in the Altamont Pass in California, had a deserved reputation as bird killers, especially of predator species like hawks and the golden eagle. Their nickname "aerial Cuisenarts" says it all. This reputation is undeserved for the new monopole, large, three-bladed turbines that now dominate the market; however, the lesson of Altamont shows that care in site selection is

---

29   For a beautiful real time map of present wind speeds in the US, go to: http://hint.fm/wind/

important. Putting a wind farm on a migration route for predatory birds, like offshore at Cape May, New Jersey, would be a mistake. However, 10 kilometers offshore in Virginia is not nearly as risky. The problems of wind are not technological, they are social (concerned birders) and political (competition to pre-existing power companies), and so careful planning is needed to overcome the obstacles.

The major problem with wind in the US, which separates it from solar, relates to the map again. The wind does not blow where the majority of people live because people prefer gentler and commonly wetter environments. South Dakota and Southeast Wyoming are not population centers. So how do we get the power from those locations to where it can connect with the existing grid and major population centers? This is where the federal government comes in because the power lines to carry the electricity will have to cross state lines. In Wyoming's case, many companies are taking advantage of the wind power there[30], but they also are expanding power lines to carry it to where it can be used.[31] Recently rapid expansion of wind power in S. Dakota began. Decreasing costs per kilowatt of production capacity, dropping from $3500 to less than $2000 over the last 8 years[32] and the completion of the "Green Power Express Project" that will open up major areas of the state for development by 2020[33]. In 2017 South Dakota got over 30.2% of its electrical power from wind.[34] When the present construction of turbines and transmission lines is complete the state will become a net power exporter from wind alone. Another question ecologists must ask concerns the costs of these power lines. These, too, affect birds and use substantial amounts of non-renewable resources, mostly aluminum, and are considered by some to be an eyesore. The "not in my back yard" (NIMBY) objection is common with wind turbines and power lines; people think wind is a good idea, but do not want their local region to be impacted. Again, the problem is both political and social and will take time to resolve.

---

30 For an excellent analysis of the Wyoming situation see "Wind Power in Wyoming: Doing it Smart from the Start." by a coalition of environmental groups in November 2008 and prepared by the Biodiversity Conservation Alliance. Nothing like this was done for coal or hydraulic fracturing for natural gas. Available on-line at: http://www.voiceforthewild.org/WindPowerReport.pdf

31 3 Gigawatt Wind Power Project In Wyoming Moves Closer To Approval. Jake Richardson, November 15,2019. https://cleantechnica.com/2019/11/15/3-gigawatt-wind-power-project-in-wyoming-moves-closer-to-approval/

32 https://www.argusleader.com/story/news/2019/09/06/wind-energy-expansion-south-dakota-bring-888-more-turbines-3-3-billion-investment/2236210001/

33 https://www.cfra.org/green-power-express

34 US Energy Information Administration in wikipedia: https://en.wikipedia.org/wiki/List_of_U.S._states_by_electricity_production_from_renewable_sources

Europe faces a similar problem with power transmission. Even though Germany leads the world in producing solar power and developing policies to promote it at the local level, they are a northern country and, therefore, limited in their solar input.[35] Mediterranean countries like Spain, Italy, and Greece are better placed in terms of available solar power, but the real solar resource lies in the Sahara desert of North Africa, a politically unstable region, with transmission requiring crossing the Mediterranean at a narrow point. The EU is considering a project that would stretch a power line from Morocco to Spain, and another that would take power from Tunisia and cross to Sicily on DC power lines. The costs of such a venture are enormous, but so is the potential amount of energy that could be captured. The price to the planet compared to the continued use of coal, oil, and natural gas might well make it worthwhile. On the other hand, recent political instability in the region makes the prospects more difficult.[36]

Even with wind, technology is addressing some of the problems identified above. The data used above was based on a turbine hub height of 50 to 80 meters. As hub heights climb the available wind energy increases. The most recent turbines are designed with hub height of 100 to 140 meters. Yes, there is substantially more emergy involved in construction, but there is also significantly more consistent production at these higher levels. Not only does this increase productivity per turbine, it increases the area available for wind power in the US substantially. In Figure 5.4 the southeastern portion of the US has almost no wind production potential. With these new turbines these states can now join the harvest of wind energy (Chabot 2015).

Other Alternative Power Sources

Solving the dilemma of our electricity generation will require a combination of diverse, decentralized, and centralized solutions in a variety of contexts. There is no one answer. Decentralized solar will cover much of the demand. Wind covers another fraction. In some areas, centralized solar will have value, as is shown in new solar thermal plants in California and Spain.[37] PV and solar thermal systems in the Sahara will provide a lot of power.

---

35   Though true, German solar PV provided one-third of the country's entire electric demand on Friday May 25, 2014 and half the 40-gigawatt demand on Saturday May 26. "Germany sets new solar power record, institute says." By Erik Kirschbaum. http://www.reuters.com/article/2012/05/26/us-climate-germany-solar-idUSBRE84P0FI20120526

36   "Quagmire in the Sahara: Desertec's promise of solar power for Europe fades." By Joel Stonington. Der Speigel online November 13, 2012. http://www.spiegel.de/international/europe/the-desertec-solar-energy-project-has-run-into-trouble-a-867077.html

37   Grist magazine, John Upton, September 25, 2013: http://grist.org/news/worlds-biggest-solar-thermal-power-plant-fired-up-in-california/

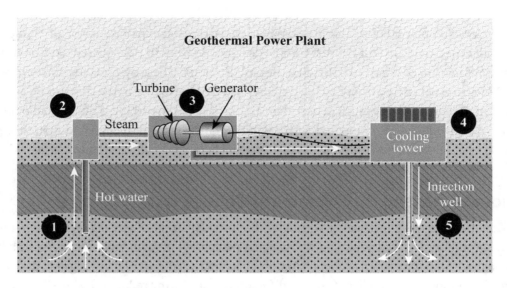

FIGURE 5.5   A schematic of a geothermal power plant.

Hydroelectric power has long dominated the alternative energy scene. While there is still some slow expansion of hydroelectric generation in China and Brazil, the developed world has basically exhausted the easily tapped hydroelectric sources, which depend on appropriate geographic locations, the ability to achieve a significant head height in relation to the volume of water and the ability to transmit that power to population centers. Big dams also carry large environmental costs. The loss of salmon runs in the Pacific Northwest and British Columbia are just one example of environmental losses attributed to dams.

In the Rift Valley of East Africa, geothermal systems are under construction. There, like in Iceland and New Zealand, power from underground will involve the extraction of heat, not the extraction of molecules. The basic idea is to take advantage of the internal heat of the planet where it rises closest to the surface. By drilling holes to this superheated rock and forcing water down one hole where the rock can heat the water, then having the water rise back to the surface under pressure, producing steam (see Figure 5.5). The cost of these systems are dependent on depth drilling, availability of water and the presence of existing power lines, aside from the turbines and generators involved. Kenya has enough potential geothermal energy to meet its present electricity demand, all coming from a string of sites located in the Rift Valley. In the US geothermal potential is strong primarily in the western US, with California having the most production.[38]

---

38   See http://www.nrel.gov/geothermal/; see also https://en.wikipedia.org/wiki/Geothermal_power_in_Kenya

Underwater power is also another possibility worth greater exploration. For an example, consider the Davidson Hill Venturi turbine designed to work in tidal currents or the near constant motion of ocean currents like the Gulf Stream.[39] These systems use underwater turbines to exact energy from flowing water with little disturbance to the surrounding ecosystem. Because water is much denser than air, the size of the turbine is much smaller per unit of captured energy compared with a wind turbine. However technical difficulties of working in saltwater have limited installation of all but experimental systems so far.

Liquid Fuels and the Dilemma of Transportation Energy

As a nation, we use more energy within our buildings than we use on transportation, but transportation runs a close second, and a higher percentage of fossil fuels is used, especially oil. Liquid fuels have a dense energy content, between 44 and 48 kilojoules/gram, and are excellent mobile fuel supplies. They are difficult to replace. Any reduction of fossil fuel use in a mobility-addicted society must use multiple strategies, including the redesign of our communities so that liquid fuel use is less necessary, at least at the personal level, combined with developing mass transit systems for longer distances, and finding alternative forms of fuel that have lower environmental impacts than those we presently rely upon.[40]

Redesigning Communities

In 2012, Alex Steffen published a small book in an alternative way. It came out as a series of articles in the on-line environmental magazine/website, *Grist Magazine*, www.grist.org. Steffen's book, *Carbon Zero,* is a look at the way American cities are designed and how we can change that design to reduce our personal transportation carbon footprint to zero. Our present cities in the United States are designed for cars, not for walkers or bicyclists. Even from my writing perch in a Florida condo designed with a strong environmental appeal, I still saw the dominance of the personal car. Though an aerial look from the perch of Google Earth shows mainly roofs and trees, the reality on the ground is that parking areas and roads dominate the surface; in fact, in the condo 50% of the total landscape is impervious surface, much of which is geared to getting us very close to our doors in a private car. That is 729 condo units with at least one car slot designated to each household. There is a sidewalk

---

39 Tidal Energy, Ltd Australia. http://www.youtube.com/watch?v=4Iq-h4ShZ8s

40 Tesla is revolutionizing the electric car and making rapid strides to replace fossil fuel powered transportation using batteries. This change is happening so quickly that most I would say here will be dated in a year's time. It is better to keep up with these changes on sites like www.cleantechnica.org.

leaving the property, but none on the main highway nearby; as a result, travel by vehicle is mandated by design.

It is Steffen's hypothesis that in order to fix our car dominant culture, we have to redesign our cities, suburbs, and even our small towns to make walking, biking, and public transit the easiest types of transport. The implications of this are many and complex. Our main development model at present is highway sprawl. When a major road is built, it creates a corridor for business growth. Side roads become avenues for the building of individual homes, and developers take the larger spaces between major highways to construct housing tracts; often these are well over a mile from any stores, schools or public services and have no sidewalks or bike lanes to facilitate non-car movement.

European development took a different direction than that of the United States. Their history is longer and well before the invention of the automobile, they were built as a system of dense villages, each protected by a "lord" and knights, commonly tied with other lords under another leader. When the industrial revolution and the nation state finally dominated, the already existing system determined the type of development that took place, essentially leaving the villages intact, although in industrial areas, like the Ruhr Valley, around Paris, London, and Milan, megacities did form. The villages had shops and businesses in their centers that were a walkable distance from most houses. In some villages, navigation by car remains problematic. The need for a car is far less great than in the US. Steffen uses this as a starting point for thinking about American redesign.[41]

The US expansion westward coincided with the industrial revolution. In the 19th century, especially on the east coast, we did have a village system, but this was not feudal. We had a much more individually-oriented structure. We did not live in a center and move back and forth to our farmland, as was the common practice in European villages. Instead, we lived on the farmland and only went to the village for supplies. A sense of community did grow, but in a looser fashion, devoid of a continuous sense of outside threat. What little real outside threat existed in the form of Native Americans or predators like wolves, was effectively eliminated by the 1890s, so we felt free to spread out. Then came the automobile, invented in Europe, but mass produced in the USA. Our love affair began with the Model T Ford in 1909 when Henry Ford reduced the price and profit margin for each vehicle and efficiently produced a lot more of them. Following World War I, the automobile displaced the horse as the dominant means of transportation throughout the country, so all subsequent development was done with the needs of the car firmly in mind. In the period from 1920 to 1950, developmental activities focused on people but included cars as faster versions of the horse

---

41   *Carbon Zero*, Alex Steffan. August 2012. http://grist.org/carbon-zero/

and buggy. After 1950, a subtle but profound shift took place; development continued but this time, people were in the cars. This was intentional, as designers perceived the automobile as a symbol of progress.

This was the situation when Dwight Eisenhower became President in 1953. Historians look back on his administration and see two dominant strains: a sense of American exceptionalism in foreign policy in a period of cold war with the Soviet Union, and the interstate highway system. Early in Eisenhower's administration, he toyed with the idea of an improved passenger rail system connecting cities throughout the US. By that time, the corporate lobbying partnership of Automobile Companies led by General Motors, oil companies led by Standard Oil in its various forms, and chemical companies led by DuPont pushed Congress and the President toward an automobile-centered society. Thus, the interstate highway system was born. Sixty years later, the battle over transport rages between these companies (though DuPont is no longer a major player) and environmental groups pushing for "green" alternatives.

This battleground is where Steffen's book starts. The infrastructure of the US is centered on the car. This is a fossil fuel-dependent system. To reduce our dependence on the car, we have to develop in ways that promote other forms of movement. The keys are: housing density, proximity of resources and supplies, good social spaces, and connection to locally-produced food. At this point in time, the dominant form of housing in this country is the single-family unit with a yard. From the 1950s to the present, the size of the house and the yard grew, but the model was essentially the same. All facets of development centered on fossil fuel use: driving, mowing the lawn, and using electricity from centralized sources, commonly coal-fired power plants. People drove to the grocery store, drove to a hardware store, and finally drove to a mall to buy everything else, and sometimes people saw their neighbors more at the mall than in their own backyards. To Steffen, the fix is to change the distances between these places and then create new spaces to play.

Americans need to build up rather than out. We need to pull our housing closer together. By creating greater housing density, business moves toward that density as a way of capturing a market. Shops can even be on the ground floor of an apartment building, as was once traditional. As this happens, people see the convenience of walking increase relative to driving the car. The distance people easily choose to walk is about a half a mile, or up to two miles for a bicycle. The key to increasing foot traffic and bicycles is promoting safety, keeping some separation between the car and foot or bicycle traffic.

Here we need to jump back to Europe, especially to Copenhagen, Denmark, and Amsterdam, The Netherlands. These two cities are bike-centered. This is not the American bike culture of Lycra and shiny helmets with high-tech, 18-speed racing bicycles that cost thousands of dollars; this is the bike culture of Copenhagen with baskets on the front, a cushioned rack on the back for a passenger, all dressed in work clothes. The bike becomes a tool for the commuter, not an exercise machine. Bike lanes are crucial. These are not just painted lines on an improved shoulder, but real lanes that cars cannot touch or accidentally encroach. That separation reduces the need for a helmet and promotes the five-year-old child accompanying his or her parents on his or her own wheels. Sidewalks are built for people, too. The cities have wide walkways and places where cars are excluded completely. Once the comfort level is high enough, use expands until bikes and walking become dominant. A number of locations in the US have started developing a bike and walk culture. Among the best are Davis, California; Portland, Oregon; and Boulder, Colorado. Also in the mix are the larger cities of Minneapolis, Minnesota; San Francisco, California; and Seattle, Washington. Even New York City is doing better in this respect, but backlash hampers a rapid transition.

Density of housing does not necessarily mean everything is built in high-rises like some futuristic super city. People need open space and garden space, too. A limited amount of this green space could happen on the top of the building with an intensive green roof, but realistically, most garden space must sit on the ground. The same is true for recreational space. Kids and adults need open areas to play, for sports, or simply to enjoy a connection with life. Nature, of which we are a part, requires less-managed places to thrive. Providing habitat for squirrels and cardinals, hawks and tanagers, even voles, rabbits and raccoons, opens our own sense of opportunity and connection. Suburban sprawl, strip malls and parking lots do nothing to promote this connection with nature. Density and open space must go hand in hand.

Not all movement will happen within a one-mile or even a four-mile radius. Some provision for movement over longer distances is needed as well. Some cities already have subways or light rail systems filling this development niche, but others do not. Such was the situation in Curitiba, Brazil, when the architect, Jaime Lerner, became mayor in 1978. Curitiba is a large city in southern Brazil's Parana State on the Atlantic coast. Within it dwell over one million people, with over half of them living below the poverty line in sprawling favelas, the urban slums of Brazil, occupying the land between upper-class enclaves. Lerner perceived a problem with transportation; the dominance of the car among the elite prevented full participation in city life by the poor. He developed a plan in full recognition that the elite would not let him implement it. So he did not tell them his plan; he just did it. One morning, the mayor's office closed an eight by eight block area of downtown to all cars; in fact, the city tore the streets up, except for those having bus access. Then Lerner and his team quickly remade them into a walking plaza. The process took eight days. The businesses were furious for about a month, and then their tunes changed. Business grew instead of shrinking. Traffic congestion had previously clogged the downtown restricting access. Without the cars, more people came, and with less stress, they spent more time in the shops. Lerner suddenly had new allies in the change process.

He did not stop there. People needed transportation from suburbs and the favelas (poorer areas) to make this new model of transportation work. Lerner's team recognized that subways were beyond the city's budgetary constraints. Instead they focused on the bus system and what would entice people to use it more frequently. Routes needed to become more straightforward and with a faster pace. The city planners created a spoke system that brought people into the city center, the area where cars were not allowed. They also saw that having people pay on the bus for tickets slowed the loading process. Instead, they created loading stations where passengers paid before they got on the bus and the stations were elevated so people walked straight onto the bus instead of climbing stairs. This reduced stopping time while the designated bus lanes increased the speed between stops. They made routes that went into the favelas and kept the pricing low so that the poor could use the transport system as needed. Ridership rose significantly, so Lerner could shift his focus toward solving other city problems.

Models for improved bus systems are under development in a number of American cities, notably among those cities improving bike transport. Recognizing the importance of convenient access and rapidity of movement is crucial to the success of a transport system. High technology systems, like a subway, elevated train, light rail, or even magnetic levitation may have a romantic appeal, but might not effectively address the broader need just to move from one location to the next economically and simply.

Alternative Fuel Vehicles

We still have a romance with the car, and nothing has addressed this romance like Elon Musk's Tesla Model S, an all-electric sedan. It does 0 to 60 mph in less than four seconds, seats five comfortably and seven in a pinch, has a low center of gravity because of the location of the batteries and, therefore, has outstanding handling. The car's range is nothing to sneeze at either, 258 miles in optimum conditions, dropping some in cold weather. Its running cost is low, under 8 dollars for the electricity to charge it in many locations, and, even with the electricity coming from coal fired power plants, it has a lower carbon footprint than most cars.[42] However, Model S does have a very high sticker price of over $70,000, so it remains a car for the elite.[43] The Model 3, introduced widely in 2017 and now one of the

---

42   This cost is based on charging from home using energy from the grid. Electric vehicles get a rough average of 4 miles per kilowatt of power. It takes 64 kilowatts to go 258 miles.

43   Elon Musk and Tesla have a goal that is worthy of note. This quote is from a 2006 speech by Musk on his plan for Tesla Motors. "As you know, the initial product of Tesla Motors is a high-performance electric sports car called the Tesla Roadster. However, some readers may not be aware of the fact that our long-term plan is to build a wide range of models, including affordably priced family cars. This is because the

best selling cars around the world of any make, is much more affordable at under $50,000, lighter weight, with a range over 300 miles.

Electric cars have a high ecological footprint not only in terms of the metal they are made of (like most cars), but even more because the lithium-ion batteries increase that footprint substantially. Lithium is not a common atom like sodium or even nickel. Only three countries have substantial deposits, with 90% of the world's known reserves in Bolivia, Chile and Argentina in the dry altiplano of the Andes Mountain range. Developing these reserves while maintaining an eye for justice for the people and ecological sensitivity presents a challenge to the rising generation of transport pioneers.

Tesla was not alone in pursuing electric vehicles. In addition to the fact that electric vehicles were around at the beginning of the automobile era, a number of modern efforts have been made to build newer versions of them. General Motors was most famous with its surprisingly good EV1, which for some odd reason, it destroyed in 2002. Regretting that error, they designed and built another alternative called the Chevy Volt, a plug-in hybrid with an electric only range of about 47 miles, again in optimum conditions. If you go beyond 40 miles it has an on-board gasoline engine tuned specifically to keep the batteries charged, recognizing that gasoline engines have an optimum operational RPM, while electric is much more efficient at variable speeds. This offers an attractive option for a commuter car for total round trips of less than 40 miles.

The Nissan Leaf is an all-electric model, but much less expensive than the Tesla, less powerful, and more utility-shaped. Originally pricey, the cost in 2019 is $29,900 for the no frills model. and serves a broader market niche. It uses advanced Lithium-ion batteries to get a 226-mile range and the equivalent of 129 mpg.[44] Of course, if you charge your car with solar or wind power then this number is irrelevant. Other companies are stepping gingerly into the electric car fray including Ford, Mitsubishi, Volkswagen, BMW and Honda. Toyota has held to its hybrid model Prius, with good gas mileage and electric assist. It does not have much range in all-electric mode and neither does its newly introduced plug-in descendent, but the latter has increased gas mileage. It is too early to tell how much electric cars will reduce the carbon footprint of cars, but they cannot hurt.

The ecological footprint is a different story. Here the emergy of the automobile is highly significant. The modern electric vehicles do not decrease the footprint of mining, synthetic

---

overarching purpose of Tesla Motors (and the reason I am funding the company) is to help expedite the move from a mine-and-burn hydrocarbon economy towards a solar electric economy, which I believe to be the primary, but not exclusive, sustainable solution." It does look like he is doing this. Source: Zachary Shahan, http://cleantechnica.com/2015/12/23/secret-tesla-master-plan-coming-to-life/

44 From the Nissan Leaf website: https://www.nissanusa.com/electric-cars/leaf-2019/?pth=6

fiber use, or the overuse of other materials. They remain one to two metric ton machines hauling around 40-140kg people, most often traveling alone. As global supplies of minerals, including rare earth metals like columbite-tantalite (coltan)[45], neodymium, lithium, and copper drop, prices rise and the impact per unit mined increases. We have failed to fully appreciate the insight of Amory Lovins, cofounder and director of the Rocky Mountain Institute who, over 40 years ago talked about the need to lighten and build down our cars (Lovins, 1979). By learning to build smaller, less weighty vehicles we can substantially decrease their ecological footprint. This was done by the makers of Edison II, a conventional internal combustion engine in a very light car that got over 100 mpg and was a co-winner of Progressive Insurance's X-prize.[46] In order to keep sales high and risks low, car-makers use presently existing tastes as their starting point instead of looking toward innovative designs that make cars smaller with far less impact. Reducing a car's carbon footprint is one thing, but reducing its ecological footprint is quite another. Overall, the most sustainable mode of transportation is still a bicycle or a good walk because even for electric cars, the emergy factor is significant.

Batteries vs. Liquid Fuels

The transportation industry uses a phrase that sums up the battle between batteries and liquid fuels—fuel density. Fuel density is essentially the amount of power contained in a unit, measured by volume or mass, of fuel. Electricity itself has no mass, but it has to be stored chemically, and the batteries used to do this are bulky. The dominant battery in the automobile industry is the lead-acid type, which is effective but massive, usually weighing over 25 kg, and sometimes over 50kg for the deep cycle type used for storage or in golf carts and forklifts. These heavy batteries are not practical for longer range vehicles. The focus is now on lithium-ion batteries which have a much better fuel density than lead-acid batteries, especially by mass, but not better on a per volume basis than gasoline, diesel, or compressed natural gas. Research is progressing on this issue, with many engineers using nanotechnology to attack the battery problem, but as Boeing found with the fires started by the lithium ion batteries on it new 787 airplanes in 2013, the more energy-dense you make a battery, the more you have to worry about over-heating in the event of a problem or during high discharge.[47]

---

45 Columbite is the name of the ore of niobium, a metal used in magnets for electric motors and generators and tantalum is used in capacitors in a wide variety of electronic equipment. http://en.wikipedia.org/wiki/Coltan

46 "# 42 X Prize Shows the Easy Path to a 100 MPG Car." By Michael Lemonick, December 16, 2010 http://discovermagazine.com/2011/jan-feb/42#.Ul1NxdK-rFo

47 For more on Li-ion batteries, options and potential problems see http://batteryuniversity.com/learn/article/possible_solutions_for_the_battery_problem_on_the_boeing_787

For these reasons, some have concluded that, ultimately, the battery cannot compete against liquid fuels. The problem then becomes finding better sources for those liquid fuels. Richard Branson is out front on this issue in his capacity as head of Virgin Atlantic and other airlines. Finding a biological source for jet fuel is his goal. At first, Virgin Atlantic's engineers tried using coconut oil and other vegetable oils on a jet between London and Amsterdam.[48] Environmentalists were not kind in their responses to this attempt since coconut oil, oil palm, and other plant-based oils commonly require either sacrificing existing agricultural land to grow fuel crops, or even worse, sacrificing habitat of charismatic megafauna like orangutans to grow the oil palm, the most productive of the tropical biofuels.[49] Used cooking oils were more welcome as a source for biofuels, specifically as biodiesel, but this is and will remain a niche market because the overall demand for diesel is far higher than the existing production of seed oils. Ultimately, seed oils and tropical biofuels cannot meet the demand for aviation fuel, let alone the larger demand for transportation fuel in general. Companies are therefore pursuing other options.

One source they are pursuing is algae, the one-celled type that contains a large amount of oil to keep it buoyant in water, whether salt or fresh. The key is finding the right algae, where production is high, extraction of oil is easy and environmental risks are low. It is possible that scientists will need to breed a new one. The Algal Biomass Organization is one group pursuing fuel uses for algae.[50] Although they are making progress, they are a long way from having a large scale, mass-producible product that will cut the use of fossil fuels. Pursuit of this fuel is happening in labs across the US and in other countries, but the verdict on its use remains inconclusive.

The major biofuel now in use is ethanol. It is not without controversy. In fact, ethanol is probably loathed by environmentalists even more than oil palm. Ethanol is a natural byproduct of the anaerobic digestion process of yeast that people have used since the beginning of agriculture to make alcoholic beverages. Any starchy food can serve as a source for alcohol with some preparation. The higher the simple sugar content, the easier alcohol can be made from it. Grapes, apples, and the malts of various grains have historically dominated the trade. Perhaps the single greatest source of ethanol is sugar cane. Sugar is squeezed from the stalk of the plant and, when heated to about 35°C (95°F), rapidly ferments to make the ethanol, which is then distilled to purify it; this distillation process is the primary energy cost. Distillation produces a mixture of 95% ethanol and 5% water, which is fine as a fuel, but not

---

48   Wired magazine: *www.wired.com/autopia/2008/02/virgin-atlantic/*

49   See Rainforest Action Networks oil palm campaign: http://ran.org/conflict-palm-oil

50   http://www.algaebiomass.org/

when mixed with gasoline because the water interferes. Anhydrous ("without water") ethanol is made a number of ways, with the most common involving a bed of molecular sieves that absorb water but exclude ethanol. [51] Overall, this process is energy-intensive and the argument against ethanol fuel is that it takes so much energy to produce that it does not have a positive impact on reducing atmospheric carbon dioxide from fossil fuel (Pimentel, 2003).

At present, the energy argument against ethanol fuel holds up very well when field corn grown in the American Midwest is used as the primary feedstock. It does not hold up as well when using sugar cane as the primary feedstock, which is done in Brazil. David Blume has argued quite persuasively that the key in all this is really the feedstock (Blume, 2007). By starting with monoculture field corn, with its high energy cost in the form of tractor fuel, fertilizer, herbicides, and other inputs, and high environmental cost through soil erosion and degradation, it cannot be made in an environmentally friendly or cost-effective way. However, he names a number of other possible feed stocks that do pass the energy balance and environmental impact tests. These include seaweed algae, cane sorghum, cattails, lawn clippings, miscanthus grass, mesquite pods and many more.[52] The beauty of these alternative feed stocks is that they require very little energy to produce and many are perennials, so once they are growing, there is no need to replant them. The major expense is the fermentation and distillation process. Blume and his company have developed techniques to incorporate solar energy to reduce this cost. The rest of the energy comes from the byproducts and leftovers of the fermentation process.

While it is still too early to say which alternative fuel will be the winner—and it could be a combination of electric power with improved batteries, ethanol, biodiesel and others not yet known—it is fair to say that our present system requires an extreme makeover. As of this final edit, it looks like batteries are winning, especially under the leadership of Elon Musk and Tesla, with their recent introduction of the 4680 tabless lithium ion battery which have been laboratory tested to more than 2 million miles of range.[53] But changing our power source alone does not solve the deeper problem. This will involve a combination of redesigning the way we live, reducing the energy we need, and finding alternative systems to provide that energy. Meanwhile, we can always walk or ride a bike.

I walked a lot in Florida. The development we lived in had a walking path along the water of Little Sarasota Bay. A daily view of cormorants, leaping stripped mullet and manatees in

---

51 http://en.wikipedia.org/wiki/Ethanol_fuel

52 Replacing alcohol for gas would lower prices and create 26 million jobs. By Kenneth Shortgen Jr. October 11, 2012. http://www.permaculture.com/node/1507

53 Electrek: Tesla battery researcher shows new test results point to batteries lasting over 2 million miles. Fred Lambert, October 18, 2020. https://electrek.co/2020/10/18/tesla-battery-test-results-over-2-million-miles/

the harbor made the walks interesting and helped to purify the thinking process. Always in the background was a distant rumbling of traffic. Was that traffic the very thing that was slowly destroying the land and the walk that I enjoyed daily? What would happen if we refused to change, and sea levels consequently rose to cover this beautiful coastal habitat? How we use energy may determine what we are left with in our own habitats. It is time to reduce our footprint so our grandchildren can follow ours in a healthy place.

Study Questions:

1. What about your own energy/carbon footprint? Go to the Global Footprint Network website (https://www.footprintnetwork.org/), find your ecological footprint and your personal overshoot day. What is your leading contributor to your footprint? What do you think you can do to cut that cost to the planet?

2. How much energy do you use in your home or apartment? See if you can figure out how many kilowatt hours of power you use in an average day over the course of a year. What contributes the most to your power use? How can you cut that back?

3. Transportation is commonly the second largest or largest contributor to our carbon footprint. How do you move from place to place? How many miles is your average daily drive? Is there a way you can change the way you move on a daily basis? What means of alternative transport works best for you?

4. Given what you have discovered from the previous three questions, what are the low hanging fruits available in your energy saving strategy? How much do you think you can save now? In the long term, what do you think will reduce your energy consumption the most?

References

Blume, David. 2007. *Alcohol Can Be a Gas*. Santa Cruz, CA: International Institute for Ecological Agriculture.

Chabot, Bernard. 2015. "The fast shift towards the « silent wind power revolution » in USA and the related huge energy and economic benefits." *Renewables International* - www.renewablesinternatonal. net http://cf01.erneuerbareenergien.schluetersche.de/files/smfiledata/4/7/8/6/3/2/114bSWRcase-USA.pdf

Holmgren, David. 2002. *Permaculture: Principles and Pathways Beyond Sustainability*. Hepburn, Victoria, Australia: Holmgren Design Services.

Lovins, Amory B. 1979. *Soft Energy Paths: Towards a Durable Peace*. New York: Harper Colophon Books Cn653

Odum, Howard T. 1996. *Environmental Accounting: Emergy and Environmental Decision Making.* Hoboken, NJ: Wiley

Pimentel, David. 2003. *Ethanol Fuels: Energy Balance, Economics, and Environmental Impacts are Negative.* Natural Resources Research, Vol. 12, No. 2, June 2003

Steffen, Alex. 2012. *Carbon Zero: Imagining Cities that can Save the Planet.* August 2012 digital only http://grist.org/carbon-zero/.

Credits

Fig. 5.1: Gary Reysa, "A Double-Duty Solar Solution: How to Build a Solar Water Heater," *Mother Earth News*. Copyright © by Gary Reysa.

Fig. 5.2: Source: https://en.wikipedia.org/wiki/File:DirectSolarSystems.jpg.

Fig. 5.4: Source: https://www.nrel.gov/gis/images/80m_wind/USwind300dpe4-11.jpg.

Fig. 5.5: Adapted from: https://ris.utwente.nl/ws/portalfiles/portal/136102524/2019_Madirisha_et_al_ ICEAS2019_POSTER_MMM_1_.pdf_final_final.pdf.

Chapter 6

Water
A Global Issue with Local Solutions

Introduction

Water is the medium of life. All living organisms contain water. While water is chemically neutral, it is active in its relationships with other molecules. All of this is due to the unique character of the molecule itself, called polarity. A molecule of water has a neutral charge overall, but it is bent into a triangle with a bend of 104°, not linear like carbon dioxide, which is much heavier but is a gas at temperatures when water is a liquid. This bend creates an unbalanced charge, where the hydrogen at each of two of the angles is slightly positive and the oxygen at the other angle is slightly negative. This positive–negative charge is analogous to the poles of a magnet. This water becomes an excellent solvent, allowing things such as sugar and salt— two white, crystalline solids at room temperature—to dissolve in water and move with water wherever it goes. Water then acts as the carrier of vital nutrients like simple sugars and proteins and of even larger things like blood in the bodies of plants and animals. It does the same outside bodies.

Water is everywhere, but not equally. Some areas of the planet, like the Amazon basin in South America or the Congo basin in Africa, have vast amounts of it. Other areas are very dry, and the water in those areas is both rare and treasured. This chapter will look at a broad range of issues surrounding water: how it is distributed, how it is used and treated, and what local issues it faces. To cover the full range of issues on water is not possible, so instead this chapter will examine the standard ways we collect, treat, and distribute water in localities in the United States; the issues with water in drier parts of this country; examples from areas in other parts of the world dealing with water storage; and water issues in another country, Kenya. Finally, we'll zoom in on a water resource–poor area of Kenya that has learned lessons about water that are relevant to all of us.

A Quick Global Look at Water Issues

It is easy to forget, when we rise in the morning and wash our faces, take a shower, or flush a toilet, that water holds a central place in our lives. It is just there. We have it at our fingertips, on demand: cool, clear, and clean. We do not worry that the next drink will cause us harm, nor worry that one flush too many will prevent us from doing the dishes. We take our water for granted, forgetting that there is a massive infrastructure in place to get us that easy tap water.

Though there is much speculation about the causes of the present six-year civil war in Syria, it is seldom mentioned that an underlying cause is a shortage of water. The conflict followed a five-year drought that affected the interior of the country to the east of the Mediterranean highlands. Most of Syria is dry normally, but this drought proved exceptional, driving many people from their homes in the Euphrates River valley, effectively turning them into wards of the state in the western regions. Displacement builds tensions, and tensions about water in Syria are constantly high.[1]

FIGURE 6.1   The Emosson hydroelectric dam in the Swiss village of Chatelard.

---

1   This tension is not only in Syria, but throughout the region. Tensions are presently very high between Turkey and its Kurdish minority population in the southwest, mostly in the Tigris River watershed where Turkey is nearing completion of a new dam. See Joris Leverink, "Water: Source of Life and Conflict in the Land of Rivers," *Roar Magazine*, August 1, 2015, http://roarmag.org/2015/08/water-conflict-turkey-middle-east/.

The Euphrates headwaters lie in the eastern Turkish highlands—the home of Kurdish peoples, and one of the underdeveloped regions of that country. The Turks hoped to revitalize the economy of that region by building massive dams on the river for irrigation, but this has had an adverse effect on the downstream countries of Syria and Iraq, so delicate negotiations took place related to water retention and release to minimize conflict. These water usage rates are often based on years of normal flow, but in drought years all parties suffer, though Turkey controls the tap. The result of drought and Turkish water control is the Syrian civil war.

A glance around the world shows that water conflicts lie at the heart of many violent outbreaks. Wars in Iraq and Afghanistan and troubles in Israel/Palestine are regional examples. A survey of countries around the Sahara desert read like a set of impending or actual disasters, with water as a core theme; Egypt, Libya, Tunisia, Algeria, Morocco/Western Sahara, Mali, Niger, Northern Nigeria, Chad, Sudan (Darfur), and Eritrea all have water shortages as a core issue.

Anytime water is an issue, so is food. An Ethiopian proverb sums up the water- and food-based problems: *Starving people eat their leaders.* Frighteningly, climate change is altering the profile of rainfall on the planet in ways that could kick off a series of water wars that no amount of UN activity or US and European intervention could prevent. Yet, if we really seek to understand the nature of the hydrologic cycle in most of these places, there are things that can be done to improve the supply of water and therefore food. This is the theme of this chapter: How do we understand local hydrologic cycles and work with them to come up with locally appropriate solutions? The best solutions for water problems are derived from local realities of climate, topography, vegetation, soil conditions, and community needs.

Where Does Your Water Come From?

My home sits a short distance from the headwaters of Cub Run, a creek that flows into the South Fork of the Shenandoah River, which flows north to eventually join with the North Fork at Front Royal, where they flow together with the Potomac at Harper's Ferry, eventually reaching the Chesapeake Bay. I teach at James Madison University in the city of Harrisonburg, which has a slightly different address lying in the Blacks Run watershed, which flows into Cooks Creek, and then merges with the North River, which becomes the South Fork of the Shenandoah. The Shenandoah Valley lies between the Blue Ridge Mountains to the east and the Shenandoah Mountains to the west. These two ridges act as barriers to moist air from the Great Plains, the Mississippi Valley, and the Gulf of Mexico, raising clouds and promoting rain right outside of the valley. The valley itself is actually rather dry, getting 34 inches a year, only two-thirds of the rainfall that normally falls on either side of the mountains. It is

FIGURE 6.2   Reservoir behind Switzer Dam near Harrisonburg, Virginia, during low water in 2002.

prone to occasional droughts—not as severe as the ones in the American Southwest or the Sahel of Africa, but troubling nonetheless.

Water for the city of Harrisonburg is captured in the Shenandoah Mountains along the West Virginia border in the George Washington National Forest. The forest serves as a natural sponge, capturing, filtering, and protecting the water until it arrives in Switzer Dam and a smaller reservoir on the Dry River just to the north.

The dams buffer seasonal fluctuations in the water flow of the Dry River. The Dry River serves as a natural pipe from these dams downstream to a location near Blue Hole where a human-made pipe captures a portion of the flow and takes it to the city of Harrisonburg. The city treats the water to ensure that no disease organisms reach the tap, and then pumps it to high points in the town. Every town has a local water tower or towers that allow a gravity-feed system to reach houses, businesses, industries, and fire hydrants. Although much of it will never come in contact with people, the water going to toilets, sprinklers, sinks, and drinking fountains is all treated water from the Harrisonburg water treatment plant. It takes a lot of pipes, tanks, and pumps to get that water to you for your morning shower. And what happens to the water once it's been used? It goes into another pipe and disappears.

FIGURE 6.3   Primary treatment tank, Harrisonburg/Rockingham Wastewater Treatment Plant. Photo by Robert Brent.

For the most part, we do not give that disappearing water a second thought, but as with any item on the planet, there really is no "going away."

The water has to go someplace, and in this case it is the Harrisonburg/Rockingham Wastewater Treatment Plant near Mount Crawford. This facility is nearly new. Harrisonburg and the surrounding development area have grown substantially during the last two decades—the expansion of James Madison University has played a large part in that growth—and more people require more water. The treatment plant that was in place to meet the criteria set up by the 1972 Clean Water Act had a daily treatment average of 8 million gallons per day, with a peak of 12 million gallons. Agreements between the states in the Chesapeake Bay Watershed mandated a lowering of nitrogen and phosphorus reaching the bay by 40% by 2010. So with the population growth and the need to reduce these two nutrients, the plant required an upgrade, which was completed in 2012. It can now more effectively remove nitrogen and phosphorus from an average of 12 million gallons per day, with up to 20 million gallons per day in peak flow. All the water we put in the pipes from our showers, dishwashers, clothes washers, toilets, poultry processing plants, and other industries is treated in the same facility, and then the water flows into the North River and downstream, providing a supply for other cities and a backup supply for Harrisonburg itself. The infrastructure of supply, treatment, disposal piping, and sewage treatment is significant, energy-intensive, and expensive.

In rural Rockingham County, on the other hand, most households are not connected to the city's system. Rather, people in that area depend on groundwater. The depth to groundwater, and the consistency of groundwater supply, vary greatly depending on location. My own situation illustrates this well. Our farm, which is co-owned by six families, has a single well drilled to a depth of 450 feet. The short uppermost part of the well is lined with a 6-inch PVC liner until rock is reached. A 2-inch-diameter steel pipe with a submersible pump lies within the well at a depth of 380 feet. Although the water table is about 260 feet deep, this depth fluctuates with annual rainfall levels, which explains why the pump is placed so deep, and why the well goes even deeper in order to provide a buffer against drought. This pump moves water from the well to a pump house containing two pressure tanks that each hold about 50 gallons of water. The pressure tanks buffer flows so that the pump can work at its ideal speed and not switch on and off as the water is demanded. From the pressure tanks, the water flows through distribution pipes to the six houses and the outside standpipes that are used to irrigate gardens and water the cattle.

Unlike the city, we do not treat our wastewater. Instead, we let nature do the work for us. Wastewater goes into a septic tank buried outside each house; most of the tanks hold around 1,500 gallons. The water stays in these tanks for three to seven days depending on use, during which time organic matter is broken down and partially consumed by bacteria. From there, water flows or is pumped to a drain field dug below the winter frost line and distributed through porous pipes into a rock aggregate surrounded by soil. Underground bacteria and soil fauna take over from there. If water rises from the drain field, as it does in some places on the farm, the grass takes on a deep, green, lush color indicative of high nutrient availability. The water infrastructure in a system like ours probably costs the same or slightly more than the household cost of Harrisonburg's water supply and treatment. The infrastructure cost in terms of energy and materials involved should not be ignored when this system is compared to city water supplies. We do have one additional disadvantage: We are completely dependent on electricity, without which we have no water.

In many ways, as a society, we are spoiled by our water systems. We do not have to think about water as a requirement for daily life, because we can get as much as we need whenever we want. The harsh reality is that this convenience is not available for over half the world's population, and that for much of the planet, water is both a concern and a daily cost in terms of personal labor and finances. This is the reality for Syria, Iraq, Turkey, Afghanistan, the rural poor in Kenya, and even the western United States.

Lessons from the Western United States

The change resulting from small and slow adjustments to water catchments is incremental, but a series of slow, small, locally controlled and implemented steps can ultimately restore an ecosystem. It is time that we in the West recognize that the dramatic changes often promoted in the past ultimately do more harm than good. However, we do not need to travel as far away as Kenya to see this. Just look at the Colorado River basin in the United States. We had a water problem in Los Angeles, Las Vegas, and Phoenix, so the US government (more specifically, the Army Corps of Engineers) built Hoover Dam, Glen Canyon Dam, and a series of slightly smaller dams. What was the result? The entire Colorado River delta in Mexico died; Mono Lake in California nearly dried up; the ranches in the Owens River valley nearly collapsed. This large-scale watershed change altered the entire ecosystem, making it more vulnerable to natural changes in climate, to say nothing of the long-term effects of anthropogenic climate change on this region. There is no large-scale solution to the problem of the Colorado River basin that will not result in unintended consequences doing more harm than good. However, small changes repeated in multiple locations might just work.

To solve the problem of the Colorado River, we have to start at the top of the watershed. The headwaters of the river lie in the Rocky Mountains of Colorado, Wyoming, Utah, and Arizona. These lands were once dominated by multispecies pine and fir forests, extensive grassland meadows, and forested rivers. The land was never as rich or deep-soiled as the Midwest, nor was it teaming with wildlife like the shortgrass prairies, but it did have American bison, elk, mule deer, pronghorn antelope, wolves, mountain lion, and, perhaps above all, beavers. Beavers are the water engineers of the animal kingdom. They are the kings of local, small-scale water solutions and a pain in the neck to those who want things to always stay the same. Beavers eat trees, build dams, spread out water, promote fish habitat, and encourage the growth of new species of trees and shrubs. Above all, they slow the rush of water downhill, making it do more work as it goes: filling water tables, promoting springs, and creating more niches for other life. We no longer manage land that allows for beavers or really for any of the other animals that are listed above. In fact, humans really do not like bison or wolves, we tolerate elk and deer, and beavers we would just like to go away.[2] But what would the Colorado look like if we decided to accept beavers again?

It is highly unlikely that we will let the beavers back. It is also highly unlikely that we will let the bison dominate the Great Basin again, because our cattle are too important. What

---

2   For an excellent discussion of the beaver, see the first two chapters of *Water: A Natural History*, by Alice Outwater (New York: Basic Books, 1996).

is more likely is that we will change our management of the Rocky Mountain highlands. The work of Allan Savory and Holistic Management play the central role in this process. Savory's work focuses on the ecologically appropriate use of livestock to restore vegetation, to limit water runoff and erosion, and to change local productivity. The system does not try to restore a watershed; instead it provides a set of guidelines implemented on a single ranch that can improve the environment as it improves finances. The environment and the economy do not have to operate as oppositional forces. They can operate in concert. One example of Holistic Management was recorded by Scott Daggett in his book *Beyond the Rangeland Conflict*. A ranch in Colorado, west of Denver, experienced flash floods and erosion on a regular basis. After implementing Holistic Management—rotationally grazing their animals for intense short periods separated by long periods of rest, allowing the prairie to recover— they reduced flash flooding and eliminated erosion on the land while their income from the cattle and fishing-centered ecotourism climbed (Daggett 1995). The many similar examples provided in Holistic Management are analogous to the examples of success found on the farms that now rely on sand dams for their water: Small, slow, local solutions work, and when the number of small, slow, and local solutions spread across a watershed at any scale, the ecosystem of that watershed heals (Savory 1998).[3]

Capturing Water in Australia, Austria, and Jordan

A few more examples will help to explain the ecosystem impacts of restoring hydrologic cycles. In the twentieth century, Australia set the record for the most rapid human demolition of a continent; in the nineteenth century, it was the United States that held the record. This shameful legacy was illustrated graphically in a documentary showing two large bulldozers tied together with a thick chain dragging it across a landscape and tearing out eucalyptus and acacia trees by the roots to prepare the land for grasses and ranches. Needless to say, the results were not pretty. Massive erosion, degraded streams, failed grasses, and desertification were the result. Australia has some of the oldest, most weathered soils on the planet. They are nutrient-poor, often acidic, and commonly low in organic matter. Tearing out the tree roots did not help with that problem. With the trees gone, water flowed directly downslope, perpendicular to contour lines, creating gullies as it went. When the rains stopped, the unprotected soil formed a nearly impermeable cap, preventing infiltration of water—so the next time it rained, the runoff was even worse. It was nearly impossible to get grasses established in these conditions.

---

3   More information on Holistic Management is found in Chapter 12, "The Problem of Brittle Landscapes: A Deeply Rooted Solution."

The problem did not go unnoticed. P. A. Yeomans first acknowledged these issues and developed a solution during the 1950s (Yeomans and Yeomans 2008). The answer lay in addressing water flow and soil permeability simultaneously. To accomplish this, Yeomans created a new style of plow that had a deep chisel. When we think of plows, we often picture the smooth, elegant curve of the moldboard plow, which turns over 15 to 30 cm of soil at a pass and flips the sod upside down. The Yeomans plow is different. It is designed to go much deeper—50 to 75 cm—creating a slot, opening the soil and allowing water to penetrate, but minimizing overall disturbance. Yeomans saw that surface exposure of soil allowed the formation of a clay cap that limited water penetration. In addition, the regular use of heavy machinery had compacted the soil, reducing channels for water to deeply penetrate the soil. This capping and compaction were the chief problems preventing water penetration. Yeomans also realized that to combat these issues, he had to plow nearly perpendicular to the direction of flow, while directing any surface flow away from gullies.

He called this "keyline plowing." A "keyline" is the contour line that passes through the steepest slope on a gully or a stream on a hillside (see Figure 6.4). Above this point the percent slope declines; and below it, all slopes decline as well. All plow lines on the slope should be

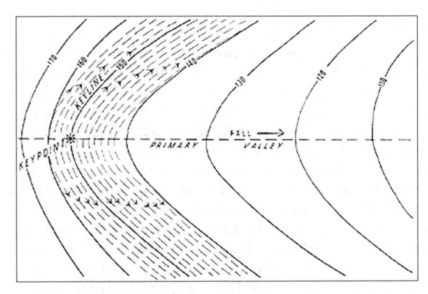

FIGURE 6.4   A diagram of a keyline plowing pattern. The steepest point is on the 150-meter contour line in the center of the valley. The first plow line follows that contour line in both directions. All other plow lines are parallel to the keyline, not on the contour line. This forces water to move away from the valley and on to drier parts of the slope.

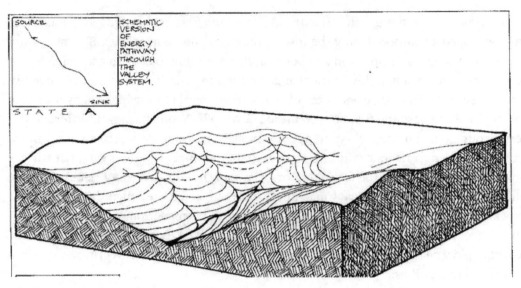

FIGURE 6.5   The contour lines in a valley drawn to depict the flow of water off the slope and the ridges between the valleys. The contour lines are used to determine the steepest points of flow at inflection points, where the slope decreases as you travel either upstream or downstream.

made parallel to the keyline.[4] This helps to discourage water from concentrating in a low valley, and moves the water toward the drier soils of a convex slope on a ridge. Water constantly soaks in along these plow lines, but any surplus moves away from, rather than toward, the points of maximum erosion. The length and variability of a slope determine the number of keylines required. A series of keylines on a long slope with low permeability will create a pattern that encourages spreading and penetration of water into the soil. Any remaining surface water can then be directed to a series of ponds on a hillside to store the water and release it slowly to another keyline, as illustrated in Figures 6.5 and 6.6. Like beavers and Holistic Management, these changes in system conditions can change the nature of a watershed when they are implemented repeatedly by farmers and ranchers in an area.

When keyline systems work, they increase available water throughout a farm. Increased moisture encourages increased vegetative growth and meets the goal of keyline plowing: to enhance soil fertility through increases in soil organic matter via the roots of plants and surface organic deposition and subsequent reduction in soil bulk density. The soil becomes the main water-holding agent on the landscape. The longer the soil retains water, the better the land produces grass and other plants, and ultimately, the more evenly the flow in a stream

---

4   For more detail on this, see http://yeomansplow.com.au/5-creating-fertility-locating-keylines/.

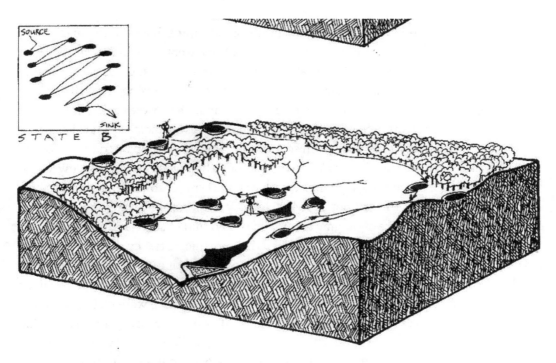

FIGURE 6.6 Once the inflection points in streams are identified (Figure 6.5), then keylines are drawn (Figure 6.4) and water is directed away from the valley bottom along the keyline to the ridges. Small dams or check dams are then dug on the ridge to use as a water source for animals or crops.

is distributed throughout the year. The main way that water enters a stream should be not by surface runoff but through subsurface flow and springs. Keyline plowing was developed to make this the case.

Sepp Holzer had a similar idea, with a completely different implementation method, in the foothills of the Alps in Austria. Holzer farms steep, naturally forested slopes between 1,100 and 1,500 meters in elevation. In this ecosystem, rainfall is not a problem, but the uneven distribution of moisture across the landscape can cause difficulties. Steep, south-facing slopes are hotter and drier, while valleys and north-facing slopes are cooler and sometimes overly moist. By moving water slowly downhill across the slope to a series of ponds and small wetlands, Holzer increases the moisture available to his perennial and annual crops without having a negative effect on the natural streams throughout his property. In fact, the ponds and wetlands help moderate the microclimate where they are found in such a way that plants normally incapable of surviving at this altitude find a niche where they can thrive (Holzer 2010). Holzer's work deserves more attention than this brief mention, because it is an integrated, systems approach to farming on a hillside landscape in a way that improves the quality of the land rather than extracting from the land, but it is outside the scope of this chapter.

One last example helps explain this ecologically based approach to water management: Geoff Lawton, a permaculture practitioner from Australia, went to an area near the Dead Sea in Jordan to advise on an agricultural project. The land at this site was relatively flat, very dry, hot, and with salty soils. It was not a place that would be anyone's first choice for a farm. The group Lawton worked with had 10 hectares of land. There were some nearby farms where most of the land was used for grazing goats. The animals ate most of the available vegetation, and erosion was a problem. Even so, Lawton came up with a plan to revitalize the watershed. He started by making swales on the contour. His goal was to prevent any loss of water on the property and even, if possible, catch water flowing onto the land from upslope. He also recognized that the dry, hot air would quickly evaporate any water that fell, so he began collecting any source of organic material he could find to serve as mulch to hold in moisture. Surrounding farms commonly burned their organic matter every year to prepare fields, so Lawton bought the organic matter from them and used it on his soil, covering it to a depth of 6 inches. Then he planted trees: Date palms formed the high canopy, figs and citrus made a lower canopy, and other crops were placed underneath. All were planted through the mulch into what was relatively humid soil protected by the surface organic matter. The humidity and organic matter produced something people did not expect: mushrooms. Saprophytic mushrooms require organic material for food and humidity for moisture, and the mulch met both needs. The fungal mycelium provided an unexpected benefit for the crops: They absorbed salt and limited its impact on the plants, causing them to grow faster than expected. Figs started producing in their first year.[5]

The whole project created something of an internet phenomenon when the video "Greening the Desert" was put on YouTube. It turns out that while the permaculture ideas practiced there really do work, the cultural aspects of the project made it much harder than expected to maintain and replicate. Unlike the Kamba in Kenya,[6] Yeomans in Australia, or Sepp Holzer in Austria, the Bedouin culture in this area of Jordan was not ready for an agricultural project. Without the continuous input of outside energy from Geoff Lawton, the project could not sustain itself. This story teaches us that conditions have to be right for innovation to catch on. In this case, the cultural conditions were wrong. Although people can change over time, this is a tale that illustrates the human factor involved in any such project. We are, after all, a part of the ecosystem. We need to be willing to change ourselves before anything else can change in an environment.

---

5   Material from this paragraph came from a well-known YouTube video called "Greening the Desert." The two
     video links provided here are updates to that original effort. https://www.youtube.com/watch?v=W69kRsC_
     CgQ and https://www.youtube.com/watch?v=6fjo0eyREeM
6   The Kamba will be discussed later in this chapter.

Water as a Primary Resource: Lessons from Kenya, Part 1

Earth, air, water, and fire—the four basic elements of the Greeks—are the four primary divisions of ecosystems. Imperiling any one of these resources endangers the entire system. Water in liquid form is the major identifying characteristic of living systems. When astronomers look for conditions where life can exist, they look for the fingerprint of water first. Earth is blessed with an ideal climate for life in that water is found in all three of its forms: solid ice, gaseous vapor, and dominantly liquid. However, water is not distributed equally across the planet. Some countries, like Canada and Brazil, are blessed with abundance. Others, like Kenya, are perched on the edge of water deficits on a regular basis. Learning how to handle water in areas of scarcity holds lessons for the entire planet, especially in this age of anthropogenic climate change.

Kenya is a country of extremes. It has harsh deserts, along with extensive arid and semi-arid bushland, where getting water and forage for animals involves constantly moving across the landscape to isolated watering points. It also has smaller patches of wet tropical forest, and high-altitude cold forest with tundra-like conditions, where water volume is not an issue but sanitation is a major problem. In all locations, water issues are apparent. Often it is a question of supply, sometimes it is a question of sanitation, and in cities it is a question of an equitable distribution network. There is no possibility of finding a single answer to the question of water. The answers are always local, and so locally is where we will look.

High-Rainfall Areas

In western Kenya lies Kakamega County, just north and east of Lake Victoria, the largest surface-area lake in Africa. A land of fertile farms and dense population, it is home to the Abaluhya people, a mixed group of Bantu language speakers who were thrown into a single ethnolinguistic category during the colonial era. The 11 dialect groups (a number that varies depending by whom and how it is determined) share land that is made up of the best soil types on the continent and is also supplied with abundant rainfall. However, this abundance of rain does not mean that water is readily available to all members of the population. Availability depends on the relative wealth and situation of a household.

The population in Kakamega has exploded since Kenya's independence in 1963, changing the water dynamic. Only two generations before, the location of a household and farm was determined by access to water and there was space for people to build accordingly. People set up their grass-roofed huts as close to the water supply as they could while still keeping dry during a rain or flood. Fetching water was not an issue, wastewater was thrown onto nearby gardens and fields, and sanitation was simply a short trip to the woods, which were never that far away.

As population grew, things changed. People occupied land that had been converted from forest or grassland, and houses changed from round thatch huts to rectangular mud brick and cement plaster homes with metal roofs. Homes were farther from water; therefore, getting water to the house became an issue. Some people with enough means have addressed this by building roof catchment systems where gutters catch the runoff and channel it to a pipe that transfers the water to a tank. Poorer households just find an old oil drum or shipping barrel and let it fill with rain, along with any other containers on hand. Wealthier households either build a ferro-cement tank or purchase the now-common black plastic water tanks that contain from 100 to 10,000 liters each, depending on the availability of skilled labor and resources. For poorer households, however, limited access to storage means that during periods with little rainfall, people must carry water from natural water sources to their houses. Women bear the bulk of this burden, hiking from the local stream or spring with 20 liters strapped on their back. Occasionally they have access to covered springs, which have a cement cap and tank around the outlet to protect the water from contamination by continuous use and by animals. These springs also make it easier to channel the water into a jerry can, usually using a steel pipe (Figure 6.7). Although the journey to water may be short, even a 15-minute walk three to four times a day is an energy-sapping activity to accompany the similarly taxing farm work, cooking, cleaning, and childcare.

Sanitation issues arise as well. Although wastewater is not an issue, because it is easy to pour onto nearby crops (a fact that makes the land closest to the house the most fertile), contamination by human feces is a significant problem. Population growth has converted much of the wooded area to farms, and the woodland per household is now small, if there is any at all, so privacy is an issue. Again, relative wealth determines how people take care of their needs. Long drop toilets with a cement platform, walls, a metal door, and a roof are found in high-income households. Shorter mud and wattle drop toilets with a cloth draped across for privacy are all you find in poorer households. In the countryside there is at least space for these; this is not the case in major cities.

Nairobi

Cities have a different problem: the need for a significant water infrastructure. Nairobi is the largest city in Kenya. Its water system was designed during the colonial era and was realistically

FIGURE 6.7   Covered spring near Eregi, Kakamega County, Kenya.

intended to supply a half million people. According to the Kenya Bureau of Statistics, in 2019 there were over 4.4 million people in the city, and much of the population growth happened without a strategic development plan.[7] While many people have tap water in their homes, there are no reliable statistics on how many do not. It is easy to find people carrying water in the city's slums and poor areas, and these people do not have accessible tap water. It is also easy to spot the nearly ubiquitous water trucks that ply the city streets, delivering water to the homes of both wealthy and poor. The city's overall plumbing is technically functional, and sources of water from reservoirs in the southern slopes of the Aberdare Range are adequate, but it is far from reliable at the neighborhood level. As a result, households buy water in batches and have it pumped to storage tanks, which they keep on their roofs or in spaces in their attics. Some households have their own pumps, and they fill larger tanks on the ground hidden discretely near the house. The majority of the poor cannot afford a tank, nor the security to keep other poor people from stealing their water, so they buy it in 20-liter jerry cans. These go for about 3 Kenyan shillings per container if the seller is honest, which is not always the case.

The marketing of water is a major source of corruption in Nairobi. The government has a legal monopoly on the movement of water, but while they do own the pipeline and treatment system, they cannot police the pipes everywhere, all the time. Water-selling companies, some licensed and others not, tap the main lines to fill their trucks and then sell the water to people who should be getting water through the piping system. Demand from wealthier families is high enough to force up the price of water, meaning that these companies can defy the government price control and sell water for more than 3 Kenyan shillings for 20 liters. This system thrives as long as they do not get caught, and bribes usually keep the police and other city officials from enforcing the rules. This dual system for getting water to houses works reasonably well as long as the supply is high, but in a drought year the situation can become chaotic, especially in the city's vast slums that house at least half of its population. To date, the government has kept the situation somewhat under control, but controlling the distribution of the available water supply will always be a concern.

Another issue is sanitation. Kibera, which straddles the main railway line running west of Nairobi, is one of the largest slums in Africa. A stream flows right through the slum, and people live precariously on either side of the stream and railway. The population of the slum is highly debated, but it is a small area of just over 200 hectares and is very crowded. The minimum population reported by the government is about 350,000, but could be as

---

7   In my original text, written in 2013 and based upon a 2009 census, Nairobi had a population of 3.1 million. Both sets of data were found on Wikipedia, sourced from the Kenya Bureau of Statistics.

high as 500,000. There are no roads through the slum, just alleys, and in the heart of the slum the alleys are simply ditches that are narrow enough for a person to straddle. When it rains, the area is muddy and dangerous to walk through, not because of thieves, but because a combination of plastic and a frictionless red clay makes passage treacherous. Toilets are rare, and are more common around the edges of the slum than in the center. Kibera has a reputation as the "house of flying toilets," a reference to the habit residents have of defecating into a plastic bag and throwing the bag out the window. When it rains, the sewage is washed down the ditches and into the stream. Kibera is a place where it is hard to stay clean, meaning it is hard to stay healthy; yet people manage.[8] An NGO called Carolina for Kibera established a health center called the Tabitha Clinic in the heart of the slum. It deals with AIDS, malaria, and a variety of tropical diseases, but the most common problems all relate to sanitation. Diarrheal diseases like amoebic dysentery, giardia, typhus, typhoid fever, and even cholera, which thankfully is very rare, are a constant concern. Prevention is the primary goal, but the poor water supply and lack of good toilet facilities make this very difficult.

The Water Problems of Pastoralism as Population Grows

Outside the cities and the area with high potential for agricultural production, water supply becomes the main concern; sanitation, while still important, recedes. Three-quarters of Kenya is populated by pastoral peoples. Their lives are dominated by the need to seek water and fodder. This is a complex dance with a fickle environment. In northern Kenya, around the southern end of Lake Turkana, the Rendille people have herded their cattle, sheep, goats, donkeys, and camels across the harsh, windy landscape for centuries. The landscape in this region is harsh and rocky, with volcanic hills and isolated mountains, like the Ndoto Mountains and Mount Nyiru, which provide places to see across wide distances. Memory is one of the most important resources these people possess. To successfully traverse this landscape, it is essential to know where the isolated, reliable sources of water can be found. A Rendille elder interviewed by an anthropologist on a hilltop with a detailed map was able to trace over 50 years of migration across this land. The old man kept in his mind a journal of the grass and shrub growth, water levels, length of each stay in a particular location, the distance of each move, and the time it took. It was a diary of life—good years and bad years—all defined by rainfall and fodder. The hills enabled the old man to see rain in the distance, assess the amount, anticipate the resultant feed supply

---

8   See Kel Otsuki. "What Sanitation Means in Nairobi Slums," *Solutions* 4 (5): 38–41, http://www.thesolutionsjournal.com/node/24010.

for the animals, and then time the movement for the extended family group.[9] The length of stay between movements depended upon the needs of the animals and their ability to provide food for the family.

These migrations still happen, but increased population, the immigration of people to the highlands of the Ndoto Mountains, and the restrictions of government policy have all changed the people's way of life. Portions of the family, especially mothers and younger children and the very old, now stay sedentary in villages with a permanent water source. The animals still move with the men and younger women, because this is the only way to keep them fed. This new pattern has led to overgrazing around village water sources and to dependence on food from outside. No place in Kenya has remained immune from these changes, though the changes are more extreme closer to the higher-population areas.

In southern Kenya, the Maasai are the major pastoral group. Their lands straddle the Kenya–Tanzania border from the Serengeti and Maasai Mara in the west to Mount Kilimanjaro in the east. To the north, their range formerly extended to what is now Nairobi, whose name derives from the Maasai word for a "cold, wet place." The Nilotic-speaking Maasai people interacted with the Bantu-speaking Kikuyu and Kamba groups to their north on a regular basis. They overlapped every dry season when the Maasai brought their animals into the Kamba and Kikuyu lands to graze. This was not historically an antagonistic relationship; certainly there were tensions between young men at crucial dry season watering spots, but intermarriages, friendships, and economic exchanges were also happening all the time. Then came the colonial era and the creation of fixed borders; instead of relationships determined by rainfall in any given year, suddenly there were antagonisms established by fences and railways. The seminomadic Maasai were cut off from their full dry season grazing area, confined now to the fewer permanent watering sites in their drier region. As a result, overgrazing and erosion became more common. To address this issue, the government, first colonial and then national, in cooperation with international donor agencies, established new watering places using boreholes and diesel-powered pumps. At the same time, the Kenyan government, run primarily by agricultural peoples from high-potential areas, decided that pastoral peoples like the Maasai needed to have fixed boundaries—so the government came up with the idea of group ranches. This essentially overlaid a "private property" system on top of a pastoral system that required constant movement. As this movement stopped, new problems surfaced.

---

9   This is based on an article I read while living in Kenya in the 1980s, but I have not located the exact reference. I did use the article by Eric Abella Roth and Elliot Fratkin, "Composition of Household Herds and Rendille Settlement Patterns," *Nomadic Peoples* no. 28 (1991): 83–92.

Maasai normally live in camps with relatively simple, rapidly constructed huts made of sticks, mud, and cattle manure. These huts are made inside a *boma*—a thorn branch fence made of locally cut bushes and trees. The people stay in these settlements seasonally, protecting their animals at night and then moving out daily to graze the animals. The bomas are usually close to a water source, and the people change bomas when the forage declines. With the group ranch system, however, they don't change bomas, or at least not as often. They build within easy walking distance of a borehole or other water source, and sometimes they stay there for years. This has a number of negative impacts on the environment. First, manure becomes a problem: It builds up day by day in the boma, getting thicker through time, sometimes thick enough that some sell it as fertilizer to wealthier farmers in highland areas. This means that Maasai land exports nutrients from its dry landscape. It also means that when rains arrive, the number of parasites in the boma that build up over time have a field day with the animals and people. Second, deforestation of the thorn tree bushland and savanna becomes an issue, and people have to go farther to fetch firewood. Finally, their animals, especially the sheep and goats now confined to a smaller grazing area, consume everything in a slowly expanding ring around the borehole, and so the boma becomes an area of circular desertification centering on the water source.

The long history of the Maasai and other pastoral groups included development of a complex and deep understanding of local and regional ecology. One major reason why modernized cultures fail is their loss of an ecological foundation: the knowledge of rainfall patterns, vegetation response, and nutrient cycles. The Maasai, Samburu, Rendille, and other pastoral groups had an innate, though unwritten, understanding of these systems and they developed a sustainable culture within these ecological boundaries. Tragically, the new political reality has forced a transformation and most of that is negative. There is one surprising bright spot in this gloomy picture, however: the positive social role that the cell phone has begun to play in empowering these cultures. Political control, especially centralized political control, often requires citizen ignorance; if you cannot access the right information, then you cannot control your own destiny. In fact, some politicians organize their entire careers around capitalizing on the ignorance of their citizens. Because pastoral people live in a diffuse landscape, accessing information was difficult and the people were easy to manipulate ... and then came the cell phone.

Cell phone towers are common in Kenya. In fact, in many ways the coverage is better there than in the United States; it is certainly better than in low-population areas in the western United States. Kenya never had a good landline phone system, because such systems are too expensive and too resource-intensive to establish. Cell phone systems, on the other hand, have a distinct advantage relative to landlines; if you can get cell phone towers established on high points approximately 10 kilometers apart, then you can cover the country. Solar power and batteries can supplement or replace diesel generators to supply electricity for the towers, making the systems independent of an electrical grid or fossil fuel supply chain as well. Once in place, the system is accessible by everyone. A Samburu herder on the slopes of Mount Sabachi can contact the elders in his area from miles away simply by touching a few buttons, and if he needs help, it will come (Figure 6.8).

So what does this mean for water?

FIGURE 6.8　Mount Sabachi, Samburu County, Kenya, with a boma fence in the foreground. Photo by Mike Deaton.

In pastoral areas of Africa, conflict often revolves around water sources and grazing territory, especially if the rains have not been good. Young men from different groups cross paths at water holes, conversations get heated, and sometime violence erupts. Politicians can easily manipulate the situation to their advantage. In the past, they have often made a substantial profit by stealing cattle and using misdirection to deflect the blame from themselves. Now, however, the young men have cell phones. Rather than waiting for the politicians to settle disputes between groups, they now call their elders. The elders have the cell phone numbers of the elders of the other group; they talk, they argue, and then they come to an understanding and call the young men back with a resolution. While highly effective, this is not a perfect system: It does not always work cleanly and quickly or stop all the violence. However, it is locally controlled and the ability of politicians to manipulate the system is minimized. As these new relationships mature, the potential to resolve long-term water-based conflict grows, and better management systems are developed. The centralized control diminishes, and local systems come to the fore with better ecological and cultural understanding. Even if flawed, this use of the cell phone has added a new dimension to pastoral life that could lead to better systems in the near future.[10]

10　Based on conversations around campfires with Mike Rainy and Samburu elders north of Archer's Post at Mount Sabachi, Samburu County, Kenya in June 2013.

Water in Semiarid Lands: Lessons from Kenya, Part 2

Development in Kenya of a Locally Appropriate Water Supply

Semiarid land is defined as regions with low and highly variable rainfall and correspondingly high-risk agriculture. In many cases, the historic land use was pastoralism, but as the population grew, agriculture spread to marginal landscapes that were capable of producing crops only in above-average rainfall years. The potential for failure is always high, and risks are great. At the same time, creative solutions to water problems arise locally in unexpected and highly creative ways. The land of the Kamba-speaking people lies in the counties of Machakos, Makueni, and Kitui. Here the landscape is hilly, with the highest points reaching nearly 2,000 meters. It is often steep, and commonly dry. This region lies between latitude 0 and 3 degrees south and longitude 37 and 39 degrees east, and rainfall patterns are complex and often insufficient to produce crops. The intertropical convergence zone, the equatorial phenomenon that produces weather in the tropics, passes over the region twice a year, giving it two rainy seasons. The long rains occur in March and April and into May. The short rains last from October to early December. However, these two 60-day periods of rain are inconsistent, occasionally fail completely, and sometimes do not last long enough to allow a crop to complete its growth cycle. As a result, the region has a chronic food deficit, broken only in the rare good season when rains permit growth of maize.

In order to paint an accurate picture of this region's rain profile, it is important to take into account the rainfall variation across the region's geography.

The topography slopes from high points in Machakos and northwestern Makueni, lowers toward Kitui to the north, and gradually drops in elevation and gets correspondingly drier as you move south and east toward Kenya's Indian Ocean coast. These areas are to the east and southeast of Nairobi, as shown in Figure 6.9. The upper regions receive 800 to 1,200 mm of rainfall per year on average, while the lowest areas of Kitui and Makueni receive less than 500 mm annually. Generally, maize requires 600 mm of rainfall in one season to guarantee a crop. Only on the hilltops of the upper region during normal or above-average seasons are rainfalls consistently sufficient. Yet every year, the Kamba people persist in planting maize in the hope that they will catch a good rainy season.

In the 1970s, Joshua Mukusya, working with the National Council of Churches of Kenya (NCCK), was very aware of the dual problems of erratic rainfall and poor supply systems. Mukusya grew up near Kola, a town not far from the present border between Machakos County and Makueni County. As a young boy, he was often sent down the hill to fetch water in whatever container he could find and then carry it back uphill to his mother. If he spilled a drop on the way, he received a sharp verbal or physical reminder of why he should be careful.

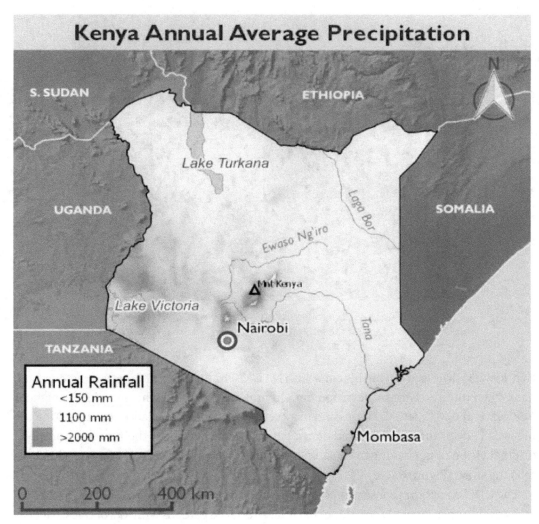

Kenya Annual Average Precipitation

S. SUDAN

ETHIOPIA

N

Lake Turkana

UGANDA

Laga Bor

SOMALIA

Ewaso Ng'iro

Lake Victoria

Mt Kenya

Tana

Nairobi

TANZANIA

Annual Rainfall
- <150 mm
- 1100 mm
- >2000 mm

Mombasa

0   200   400 km

FIGURE 6.9 Average rainfall in Kenya.

As he grew, he wondered why it is that rain falls on his house and runs off downhill, then later he has to run downhill to fetch it. Why not catch it before it runs away?[11]

In 1978, Joshua and his wife Rhoda joined with five other families and founded a self-help group (SHG) they called the Utooni SHG. They wanted to work on issues related to water, agriculture, firewood, trees, and local economic development, including housing. The fundamental importance of water kept them focused, as did the lessons from development failures

11   Personal communication with Joshua Mukusya, July 2011.

FIGURE 6.10 The UDO compound's main water storage, which holds 220,000 liters. The square tank on the left holds 60,000 liters. The main office building is on the right.

that Joshua witnessed during his time with NCCK. The SHG is still functioning today and has grown into the Utooni Development Organization (UDO), which works throughout Machakos and Makueni Counties and has even expanded into Kajiado County among the Maasai. They primarily build sand dams, but they have never lost their focus on Joshua's original vision of not having to chase water downhill. One look at their compound in Kola tells the story (Figure 6.10).

The UDO compound consists of four large buildings made of rock and cement, and a covered parking area. It stands on a slope that is now terraced gardens with lots of trees, which is somewhat unusual for the area. All the buildings have metal roofs, and every roof has gutters to collect water. Hardly a drop of rain landing on the roof ever hits the ground; instead, water is channeled to a number of water tanks. Five of these tanks are the large black plastic variety: three holding 10,000 liters each and two of 5,000 liters each. These, however, are dwarfed by the 220,000-liter capacity large cement tank that holds nearly all the runoff from the office building, the covered parking area, and two ends of the long, narrow buildings where guests stay. A smaller cement tank next to it holds an additional 60,000 liters. Joshua calculated that the 320,000 liters of water storage would be completely filled only during a heavy rainy season, but he wanted to catch all possible water, and this storage system does. UDO seldom has to buy water, nor do they need to expend extra energy to fetch it. UDO models its own philosophy through example: Make the best use of the resources close to home.

UDO has taken this philosophy to the field. A self-help group near the town of Mtito Andei built a catchment system on a large rock outcropping. These rocky outcroppings are primarily hunks of granitic rock, very resistant to erosion, that were remaining after the surrounding plain eroded. It is impossible to know if the barren nature of these slopes is natural or if it's a result of past overgrazing, but to UDO they became a resource. The Miamba Mitamboni SHG and UDO designed a catchment on the rock face, outlined by a low rock-and-cement wall that ranges between 15 and 30 cm high, depending on the slope (see Figure 6.11).

The wall channels rainfall to an outlet pipe at the lowest section of the approximately 3,500-m² catchment. This water flows to two 150,000-liter storage tanks. Because there is no forage on the catchment rock, for the most part animals stay away and the resulting captured water is quite clean and much lower in salt compared with the water found in nearby streams or wells. In fact, it is the preferred water supply for all the families within donkey cart distance of the storage tanks (Figure 6.12).

FIGURE 6.11 Catchment area of the Miamba Mitamboni SHG. The low cement and rock walls converge at a point behind the shrub in the lower left and feed into a pipe leading to the storage tanks.

FIGURE 6.12 Miamba Mitamboni water storage tanks, with the native acacia bushland in the background.

The members of Miamba Mitamboni SHG sell the water for 3 Kenyan shillings per 20-liter jerry can. This money goes into a group fund to finance group projects like their community garden, which is irrigated by catchment water, as well as a revolving microloan fund available to SHG members.

Though the catchment system is impressive, the available rock required for their creation is relatively rare, so most of UDO's energy is focused on building sand dams. The idea of the sand dam arose from work that Joshua Mukusya did with a man named Ndunda who had built dams with the British in the 1950s. Joshua visited some of these dams with Ndunda and saw that many were filled with sediment, primarily sand. When he dug in the sand behind the dam, there was water even in the driest of seasons. The thought came to him, "Why not build dams intentionally to capture the sand?" During his work with NCCK, he had seen literature about subsurface dams that slowed the flow of underground water and allowed pastoralists to water their animals without the need to dig deeply and lift the water to the animal. Instead, the subsurface dams enabled the animals to drink the water directly without additional human labor. Mukusya knew that a subsurface dam like this one would not work very well in Machakos, since the rivers had too steep a slope and the amount of sand trapped would be minimal. However, by constructing a dam between one and three meters high, they could capture more sand and therefore more water in the pore space between the sand grains. Joshua and the Utooni Development Organization SHG built their first trial dam in 1978, and it worked.

FIGURE 6.13   This sand dam was built in 2009 by the Kitandi Fruit Tree Growers SHG on the Kaiti River in Makueni County. It was extended one year later to reach its present height. It has a 17.9-meter spillway and holds nearly 11,000 cubic meters of sand and 4,000 cubic meters of water when saturated. Note the strong stand of napier grass on the right stream bank. It is also planted as cuttings on the left bank.

Sand dams are of necessity bulky structures, like the one seen in Figure 6.13. They stand across a stream and hold a considerable volume of water and sand that varies depending on the height of the dam and the degree of slope in the stream. In order to hold fast, they must anchor to the bedrock of the stream. Across the entire width of the stream, loose bedding material, including sand, must be cleared all the way to the bedrock. This can involve digging through a lot of soil to anchor the wings of the dam. Most dams measure between one and four meters in height above bedrock and are highly variable in width. Figure 6.14 shows a typical dam, this one built by the Kitito SHG. In general, the dams are just under two meters thick at their base, and they slope inward on their downstream side until they narrow to just one meter of thickness at the top. The upstream side is vertical and straight. The dam in Figure 6.13 contains approximately 85 cubic meters of cement, sand, water, and rock. These materials are anchored to bedrock using 18-mm rebar that extends from the rock to just below the top of the dam. Forms for the cement are made after the rebar is secured and the process of building the dam begins.

The sand in the dam, seen in Figure 6.14, builds up naturally from the bed of the stream. Natural erosion moves sand as the water flows every rainy season. The dam slows the movement of water, and the sand particles, heavier than silt or clay, drop out rather quickly. Each time it rains, more sand moves downstream and the dam fills up in consecutive layers.

FIGURE 6.14   A sand dam constructed by the Kitito Self Help Group, finished in June 2013. The dam has a 17.5-meter spillway. The 1.4-meter-high left wing adds an additional 7.7 meters and the right wing another 6 meters. It stands 2.8 meters above bedrock, and it is 1.8 meters thick at the base, 1.0 meter thick at the top of the spillway, and 0.68 meter thick at the top of each wing. The completed dam has a volume of approximately 85 cubic meters. The entire structure was built by hand.

According to UDO field officers, this takes between one and three years. Early in the process, the sand dam will have some clay and silt, most of which concentrates on the surface of the sand, but this is flushed over the dam in the next rainy season. When fully mature, the dam fill is primarily sand. When the dam shown in Figure 6.13 was measured in July 2013, it was found to contain nearly 11,000 cubic meters of sand. Since sand has a porosity of between 35% and 42%, this means it contains a minimum of 3,800 cubic meters of water at full capacity. Moreover, this does not include the elevated water levels in the natural water table on both sides of stored sand. The total amount of water available for extraction from this dam could potentially be greater than 10 million liters.

The water newly available from these dams has transformative effects, even if they are not immediately visible. UDO has documented a number of these changes—as has Sahelian Solutions (SASOL), another NGO working on sand dams in the neighboring county of Kitui. The first impact is felt by women, since they are normally the ones who fetch water for their households. It is not unusual for a woman to cut the time they used to spend fetching water by three hours a day, though the average used by UDO is between one and two hours per day. The shortened distance can also allow women to transfer the job of fetching water to other family members, increasing the time available to work on the farm, cook, care for children, and participate in community activities. Additionally, since the water is cleaner, instances of diarrheal disease drop. SASOL has documented an increase in school attendance after sand dams are fully functional (Ertsen et al. 2002) primarily because illness drops and nutrition improves.[12] These immediate benefits lead to longer-term gains.

When water is available, opportunities change for the entire household. The general pattern in rural Kenya is for women to manage household activities and for men to seek work for cash. Income from farming in semiarid areas is minimal and highly inconsistent across seasons, so many men seek work in the cities. Having water changes local employment prospects. This is especially true for households that have land a short distance from a sand dam. When walking and measuring sand dams in July of 2013, a number of farmers were seen in close proximity to the stream: Men and women were preparing and planting vegetable gardens in small terraced plots. Their primary crops were sukuma wiki (a vegetable related to collards and kale), tomatoes, onions, and Swiss chard (which they call "spinach" when translating from Kamba). These vegetables are all highly marketable and are often sold in the early morning and taken to local cities like Wote and Machakos. In these smaller gardens, the farmers carry 20-liter jerry cans (also called jerricans) of water from the sand dam to their plots and water the vegetables, which they grow in shallow depressions. Though I

---

12   Gideon Mutiso, personal communication, July 2013.

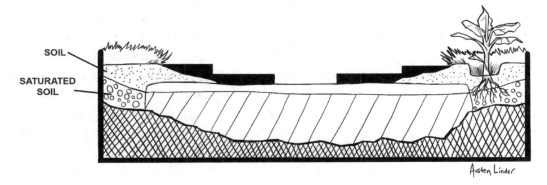

FIGURE 6.15 The upper illustration demonstrates how animals and people get their water from the sand dams. Generally, community members protect the holes that provide household water by placing thorny branches around to prevent animal entry. The lower illustration shows how water is held upstream from the dam and raises the water table along the side, allowing crops like bananas and napier grass to thrive without additional irrigation.

did not see this personally, the UDO field officers said that a number of households, as far as half a kilometer uphill from the dam, plant similar gardens around their houses. They often use a donkey to carry up to four jerry cans of water per load from the sand dam, with children between 8 and 14 years of age leading the donkey.

Also observed in July of 2013 were farmers who had installed pumps, although these were less common since level land near the streams is rare. For instance, Justin, chair of the Mkuta Mwea SHG, has a diesel-powered pump at the base of a dam in an enhanced natural depression in the river. He pumps to a garden where he raises tomatoes, French beans, Swiss chard, green peppers, sikuma wiki, maize, and green gram (an Indian legume also called mung beans). Though he uses some to feed his family, most of his product is sold. However, he does not have to take the crop to market himself. His reputation as a quality farmer is high, and those who sell his goods in Wote come to him to get their produce. The loan he took out for the pump was paid off completely in his first year of operation.

Another farmer, chair of the Kitandi Fruit Tree Growers SHG, has a large farm adjacent to a stream that is irrigated with a pump and tank system. True to the name, he has planted a lot of fruit trees. When asked if other members also plant fruit trees, he said yes, but most grow them near their homes and bring water from the dams to get them started. All of these other farmers were using the large nursery on the chair's property to grow the seedling trees for their farms. The species grown include avocado, citrus, mango, guava, papaya, banana, and even macadamia nut. Most of the trees are young and haven't reached their primary production years, but despite this, the avocado production was impressive. Also impressive was the quantity of vegetables growing on the farm. The vegetables are watered by gravity from two 1,000-liter tanks that are filled by the pump. These serve as a reservoir for the water and help conserve fuel. The chair had hired a woman who had no land of her own to water and weed the vegetables. Most of his product was sold in nearby towns.

While the number of vegetables and fruit trees generally appearing around sand dams is significant, the most common plant grown near the dams is napier grass (Figure 6.13 on the right of the dam), or *Pennisetum purpureum*.[13] This very deeply rooted fodder grass is able to spread slowly via rhizomes and stolons, but mostly it is planted through root cuttings. When established, it can stabilize the steep banks of terraces, and it also does very well on stream banks, but its primary purpose is as a fodder grass. The chair of Kitandi Fruit Tree Growers SHG explained that the grass provides cut-and-carry fodder for lactating cows and goats, extending the milking periods and improving the health of goat calves and kids, especially— and people as well. This otherwise unavailable protein supply is one of the most important benefits of the sand dams. When combined with its erosion control qualities, napier grass is arguably the most important sand dam crop.

Another important long-term benefit of the sand dams is trees. No one has done more than Patrick Musyimi of the Makuta Mwea SHG, who has planted over 10,000 trees and is still working on his forest. Other than fruit trees, the most commonly planted species in the higher-elevation areas of Machakos and Makueni are *Eucalyptus camaldulensis*, *Grevillea robusta*, *Croton megalocarpus*, *Warburgia ugandensis*, and *Prunus africanum*.[14] The last three of these are Kenyan native plants and the last two have medicinal properties. In lower, drier areas, *Melia volkensii* and *Azadirachta indica* are more important. Most trees need little or no supplemental water after they are established. The trick is getting them started, and then the sand dam will provide the water to enable them to thrive. Over time, this will promote a reforestation of the region, a trend that is already visible in satellite data (Ryan 2012).

---

13   Elephant Grass (Pennisetum purpureum): https://www.feedipedia.org/node/395

14   Eucalyptus and Grevillea are both Australian imports used for firewood. Grevillea does well when close to crops, as it does not compete for nutrients and its shade is light. *Croton megalocarpus* is a favorite native shade tree whose leaves make good mulch.

As UDO helps communities to build sand dams, other communities both inside and outside the country have expressed interest, including the Maasai in neighboring Kajiado. The Maasai primarily want to improve available water for their animals, and sand dams have distinct advantages over boreholes. First, sand dams provide water over a long area, not just at one distinct point, so the damage to the landscape is reduced. One Maasai made a very simple comment to Arnold, the UDO field officer for Kajiado, which illustrates this point: "At our sand dam, there is no need to queue." Second, they are far cheaper than a borehole and are built using primarily local resources. An average sand dam costs around $15,000, excluding labor, sand, and rock, all of which are provided by the community SHG doing the building. A borehole, on the other hand, costs an average of $75,000. Most local communities can afford neither, so outside assistance is required, but since communities participate in building a sand dam, the sense of local ownership is much higher and therefore the sense of responsibility for the outcome is higher as well. Third, sand dams have no running costs and rarely need repairs. Since starting construction of sand dams in 1978, UDO has built nearly 1,500, of which only four have failed. Perhaps the greatest advantage, though, is the impact that the higher water table near seasonally dry streams has on nearby vegetation. Over time, this causes riparian vegetation to improve and this becomes an important source of dry season fodder for the Maasai. Since the Maasai are almost entirely dependent on milk for sustenance, any improvement in cattle, goat, and sheep production results in significant improvements for them.

Thinking Big By Thinking Small

A question almost always asked by people new to sand dams and the idea of catching water at high points in a watershed is this: What about the people downstream? Don't they have less water available because the people upstream are keeping their water? This is a good question, and it deserves a solid answer. SASOL and UDO have started sorting this out. The starting point is the ecosystem: What does the watershed, the entire area that drains water to the dam or series of dams in a stream, really look like? How does water move across this landscape? What did the natural system look like before humans altered the landscape? How did the flow patterns of water change in the altered landscape? Historical information is difficult to find in this region of Kenya, and what we do know is contained in the memories of the oldest community members. Dr. Gideon Mutiso, a cofounder of SASOL and a long-time development consultant and academic, interviewed many of the old farmers in Machakos and Kitui, his home area, and captured a piece of this lost information.

The Kitui, Machakos, and Makueni region has always been dry—specifically, subhumid to semiarid. What has changed is the number of trees. Previously, it was a near-continuous deciduous tropical forest in its higher regions and savanna woodland in the lower regions. These lower reaches were the home of large mammals like elephant, black and white rhinoceros, and numerous antelopes from eland to dik-dik, Cape buffalo, giraffe, lions, and leopards. Stream flow throughout the region was low, but continuous. Rainfall did not rush off the landscape when it fell; instead it hit a vegetated surface, slowed, and flowed through the soil and in the water table. Springs were common, still existing in much of the region even to the end of the 1940s. That is when the dramatic changes really hit. The local population expanded rapidly. The big game was almost entirely wiped out and confined to newly created parks by the colonial administration and then the new Kenya government. The highlands were deforested and then converted to agriculture. The lowlands changed with the loss of browsing game like black rhinos, and acacia/*Commiphora* scrub took over. Rainfall more commonly hit bare soil in the highlands and ran off quickly, carrying soil with it, and failed to reach the water table at all. The water table lowered, springs dried up or became ephemeral, and streams widened, with an increased bed load of sand, silt, and clay.

The renewed landscape promoted by UDO, SASOL, and others seeks to restore a modified original ecology while maintaining a productive agriculture for people. They recognize the need to supply water as a first step, thus the sand dams. They also see the loss of perennial vegetation as a key aspect of degradation, so they promote tree planting and the growing of grasses. They also know that people have to grow crops in a way that reduces or eliminates further damage to the soil. So they promote terraces, advocate no-till and no-burn agriculture, and push for drought-tolerant crops. These changes capture more rainfall and put it back in the ground. In fact, a dam captures only a tiny fraction of the water flowing off the landscape: researchers from Vrije University, Amsterdam, studied this in a watershed south of Kitui town and calculated a capture of 1%–3% of seasonal flow by the dams (Borst and de Haas 2006; Hut et al. 2008). However, this water is not lost; it is merely slowed and stored for more controlled release. As the sand dams rise and groundwater begins to swell, the dams raise the stream level. This rising water level combines with the terraces and trees, which slow surface runoff and allow more water to enter the soil, and eventually the water reaches the spring outlet points. The total amount of water flowing down the river does not change; what really changes is the timing of the flow. Instead of rushing in quick, energetic, and damaging bursts, water flows more gently over a longer period both on the surface and underground. When the original underground water profile is restored, the amount of water available downstream at any given time goes up, not down. The most significant change is that the size of the flood flow drops, while the base flow is restored.

Climate Change, Water Supply, and Our Response

As the reality of climate change stares us in the face, there is only one thing that we know: We really do not know that much. What we have are models—very complex models that are able to crunch a seemingly impossible amount of information and come up with projections. As climate scientists like the paleoclimatologist James Hanson (Hanson, Sato, and Ruedy 2010) explain, what they are doing is taking actual data from the past and building a model that accurately matches the actual data as far back as possible, and then using that system to project what will happen in the future as conditions change with increased CO_2 and other carbon-forcing gases in the atmosphere. The outlook is particularly bleak if we continue burning fossil fuels at the present rate for 25 years. We still have a good shot to reduce the level of damage to the planet if we act now with urgency.

Much of the problem lies with water. Water is our major store and mover of energy on the planet. As oceans slowly warm to greater depths, and air temperature warms as well, the air holds more water vapor. In the heated air, the vapor begins to follow slightly different patterns than what the world's ecosystems have evolved to expect: In many places rains become less frequent but heavier.[15] More rarely, in other places rains become more frequent. These changes provide temporary advantages to pests like the pine beetles in the western United States, which are not killed during warm winters in the way they were in the past, making ecosystems more vulnerable to collapse. The results are major fires like the ones recently seen in Arizona, California, and Colorado and in New South Wales in Australia, typhoons like Haiyan in the Philippines, hurricanes like Harvey and Floyd in the United States, drought in Zimbabwe, and the list could go on. We do not really know what is going to happen, yet we do know that the planet sits on a precipice. So how do we respond?

The answer does not lie in the projections of the scientists, nor in the denial of reality among global and local politicians. The answer is not one global strategy. The first step is simple: We have to recognize the reality of the problem we face and then develop strategies to respond locally. While all of these strategies may have similar components, they must be modified to complement the ecological conditions of a particular place. Questions must be taken into account, such as the following: What are the abiotic factors of the place where you live? What is the present climate? How has that climate shifted in the last decades? How does rainfall come? Has this changed over time? What are the runoff patterns on your landscape? Where are the most vulnerable places? What needs to happen to slow water down? What type of water supply do you have? Do you control the water supply to your household? What makes the supply vulnerable? How are crops grown in your area? If rainfall decreases,

---

15   As I edited these pages, a rare 3.75-inch rainfall occurred on our farm.

what needs to be done to still get a crop to grow? If rainfall increases, what needs to happen to reduce erosion and keep fields moist but not waterlogged? The list may keep growing, but regardless, the questions must be asked. We have to stop contributing climate-forcing gases to the atmosphere, and we have to adapt to the changes that are already inevitable.

Changes to the hydrologic cycle are arguably the most important aspect of climate change. The centrality of water to the productivity of the planet is unarguable, and the way in which we respond to climate change must deal with the changes coming in the hydrologic cycle. Moreover, we cannot be sustainable if we don't figure out how to make these changes. The examples given in this chapter are just a few of the many possibilities. Now we must adapt these solutions or find new ways to respond in whatever ecosystem we happen to find ourselves living.

Study Questions

1. Where does you water come from? Where does it flow? How much do you use in a day?
2. In some areas, water is abundant and people use it without a lot of thought. In others, such as semiarid Kenya, every drop is carried from source to point of use. How would you conserve water if you had to carry it even a short distance before using it?
3. What contaminants are most likely to get into your water? How could this be avoided? Are the contaminants in the water potentially used as a resource for some other species?
4. Take these study questions and the ones asked in the penultimate paragraph above and ponder them. How would you go about changing the water system that supplies you and your neighbor in the time of climate change?

References

Borst, L. and de Haas, S. A. 2006. "Hydrology of Sand Storage Dams: A Case Study in the Kiindu Catchment, Kitui District, Kenya." Senior thesis, Hydrogeology (Code 450122, 27 ECTS), Faculty of Earth and Life Sciences, Vrije University, Amsterdam.

Daggett, Scott. 1995. *Beyond the Rangeland Conflict: Towards a West That Works. Kaysville, UT: Gibbs Smith.*

Ertsen, W. Maurits, Bernard Biesbrouck, Leonie Postma, and Maartje van Westerop. 2002. "Kitui Sand Dams: Social and Economic Impacts." *Muticon.* Nairobi, Kenya. https://ocw.tudelft.nl/wp-content/uploads/Background-Paper.pdf

Hansen, James, Makiko Sato, and Reto Ruedy. 2010. "Perception of Climate Change." *Proceedings of the National Academy of Sciences of the United States* 109 (37): E2415–E2423. https://doi.org/10.1073/pnas.1205276109.

Holzer, S. 2010. *Sepp Holzer's Permaculture: A Practical Guide to Small-Scale, Integrative Farming and Gardening*. White River Junction, VT: Chelsea Green Publishing.

Hut, R., M. Ertsen, N. Joeman, N. Vergeer, H. Winsemius, and N. van de Giesen. 2008. "Effects of Sand Storage Dams on Groundwater Levels with Examples from Kenya." *Physics and Chemistry of the Earth* 33 (1–2): 56–66. https://doi.org/10.1016/j.pce.2007.04.006.

Mollison, Bill. 1988. *Permaculture: A Designer's Manual*. Stanley, Tasmania, Australia: Tagari Publications.

Neufeld, D., B. Muendo, J. Muli, and J. Kanyari. 2020." Coliform Bacteria and Salt Content as Drinking Water Challenges at Sand Dams in Kenya." *Journal of Water Health* 18 (4): 602–612. https://doi.org/10.2166/wh.2020.192.

Outwater, Alice. 1996. *Water: A Natural History*. New York: Basic Books.

Ryan, Cate. 2012. "The Potential for Sand Dams to Increase the Adaptive Capacity of Drylands to Climate Change." Senior thesis, Climate Change Management, Birkbeck College, University of London.

Savory, Allan. 1998. *Holistic Management*: *A New Framework for Decision Making*. Rev. ed. Washington, DC: Island Press.

Teel, W. 2019. "Catching Rain: Sand Dams and Other Strategies to Develop Locally Resilient Water Supplies in Semi-Arid Areas of Kenya." In *Agriculture and Ecosystem Resilience in Sub Saharan Africa*, edited by Yazidhi Bamutaze, Samuel Kyamanywa, Bal Ram Singh, Gorettie Nabanoga, and Rattan Lal (pp. 327–42). London/Berlin/New York: Springer Nature.

Yeomans, P. A., and K. B. Yeomans. 2008. *Water for Every Farm: Yeomans Keyline Plan*. Self-published, CreateSpace Independent Publishing Platform.

Credits

Chapter 7

Managing Manure
Following Nature's Nutrient Cycles

Introduction

Nutrients were the major issue driving the thinking of Duncan Brown (2003) when he wrote his book *Feed or Feedback*, about the impacts of human waste entering Sydney Harbor in Australia. In many ways, having too many nutrients is more destructive than having too few. Our modern systems are full of nutrient flows that are linear, from point of origin mainly to the ocean, instead of being circular as natural systems often are. This chapter explores nutrient flow, looking specifically at manure, the biological waste of all animals, which is a resource in natural systems and a detriment in ours. Examining how we change these linear systems into circular ones is the task of this chapter.

The Problem of Nitrogen Again

Tom Philpott, a journalist who handles the agricultural beat for *Mother Jones Magazine*, wrote a story on China.[1] In it he looked at six worrying trends in Chinese agriculture. People have worried about China for a long time, and not just because of its centralized Communist structure and potential military might. China has the world's largest population, burns more fossil fuel than any other nation (though still substantially less than Americans per capita), most of which is coal, and is rapidly converting its comparatively small amount of farmland to industrial sites. *Who Will Feed China?* is the title of a small book by Lester Brown from 1995 that gives us the details on many of these changes. In 2012, a Chinese firm bought Smithfield Farms, the largest pork-producing company in the United States. China still feeds itself, chiefly by pouring

---

[1]   Tom Philpott, "6 Mind-Boggling Facts about Farms in China," *MotherJones*, August 21, 2013, http://www.motherjones.com/tom-philpott/2013/08/why-china-wants-us-grown-pork-chops-part-2-land-edition.

on masses of fertilizer, especially nitrogen made using an energy-intensive synthetic nitrogen manufacturing process called the Haber–Bosch process (explained in more detail in Chapter 3), powered by coal. Philpott has reawakened readers to Brown's point: If China cannot feed itself because of deteriorating environmental conditions, the impact on the global agricultural market will be huge.[2] To understand this, we have to consider the history of nutrients with respect to agriculture.

In 1904, the agricultural historian F. H. King took a trip to the Far East, visiting Japan, Korea, and China. His intent was to understand the agricultural system in those countries that had fed their high populations for four millennia. His book *Farmers of Forty Centuries* (1904) is one of the classics of agricultural literature. King tells one especially striking story from his observations in Shanghai. At that time, Shanghai was the center of foreign influence in the country, the operational base for the "spheres of influence" exerted by European and American economic sectors. Britain, France, Germany, and the United States vied for economic benefits derived from the vast labor market of the country, manipulating leaders with well-placed bribes and even opium-powered deals. Shanghai thrived amid the corruption, feeding a large population from surrounding small farms. The city had no sewer system. Instead it had night runners with honey buckets, men who collected the human waste of the city at night and took it to the surrounding farms to serve as the primary nutrient input. The farmers paid for the privilege of collecting poop. Certain areas of the city had more valuable human manure production, with the German sector having the highest value. Because they ate the most meat, their urine and feces had the highest nitrogen content. While the system was not flawless, as the odiferous streets proved, there was a constant movement of nutrients from the farm to the city and from the city back to the farm; it was at least a partially closed loop.

At almost the same time that King made his journey to China, an intense search had started in Europe for a way to capture nitrogen from the air. Even though Justus von Liebig had developed the concept of limiting factors in agriculture some decades before and showed that nitrogen was a critical limiting factor, the quest for nitrogen was more about explosives than nutrients. Saltpeter and gunpowder are nitrogen-based explosives that were used to fire cannons and guns. The wars of the nineteenth century exposed a military weakness related to the availability of nitrogenous chemicals for explosives. Alfred Nobel was a student of

---

2   Some of this impact expanded in 2019 when African swine flu attacked the hog farms of China. Even in the face of President Trump's tariff policy, China was forced to import more pork from the United States. Agriculture is the United States' main leverage in trade negotiations with China, but only if China is having a poor year and cannot get the soybean imports they need from Brazil and Argentina.

Ascanio Sobrero, the Italian chemist who invented nitroglycerine, an unstable, volatile liquid explosive. A few years after that 1846 invention Nobel, working in Sweden, needed a better way to blow up rocks during construction.[3] He combined nitroglycerine with silica to make a stable paste he called dynamite, which could easily be formed into tubes and placed safely into blasting holes. He then invented a detonator, or blasting cap, to ignite the explosion. It did not take long for this invention to get into the hands of the military, much to Nobel's chagrin. The military demand for nitrogen compounds exceeded the readily available supply, much of which came from isolated islands and mainland sites, inhabited by birds, on the western coast of South America in southern Peru and northern Chile. The United States and the United Kingdom controlled access to this resource.

Nitrogen was one of the last of the light elements identified by chemists. Its naturally abundant state in the atmosphere occurs because it is nonreactive, having a triple bond between two nitrogen atoms. Breaking this bond to get nitrogen to react with hydrogen or oxygen proved a major challenge. Scientists tried using electricity, with some success, but the energy cost was very high and the resultant products were difficult to control (Smil, 2001).[4] A chemist in Germany named Fritz Haber had a different strategy. He started experimenting with different combinations of heat and pressure to force a reaction between three parts hydrogen obtained from coal and one part nitrogen, making ammonia. Eventually he found a catalyst, osmium, which worked well. The problem was that the chemical reaction is reversible, since the energy of the reaction between hydrogen and nitrogen is only slightly exothermic, so the ammonia produced has to be continuously removed or else the reaction moves to a balanced state and no further ammonia is produced. Carl Bosch, cofounder of the German chemical and pharmaceutical conglomerate IG Farben, took Haber's invention and worked with him to extract the ammonia and improve the process, eventually coming up with the industrial techniques that allowed continuous production of synthetic ammonia and powered the German army during World War II. Without the Haber–Bosch process, World War I and World War II could not have happened. Smil claims that without this same process the population explosion, pun intended, of the twentieth century could not have occurred either.

The initial manufacture of nitrogen-based chemicals like ammonia was very energy-dependent, taking about 100 GJ (gigajoules, or billion joules) to produce one ton of ammonia.

---

3   Nils Ringertz, "Alfred Nobel—His Life and Work," *The Nobel Prize*, http://www.nobelprize.org/alfred_nobel/biographical/articles/life-work/.

4   Vaclav Smil's book *Enriching the Earth: Fritz Haber, Carl Bosch, and the Transformation of World Food Production* (Cambridge, MA: MIT Press, 2001) is the source for this paragraph. He is one of the most prolific science writers today and is worth reading across a broad spectrum of subjects.

Over time, with better catalysts and a switch to methane as the source of energy and hydrogen, manufacturing a ton of ammonia now takes only 20 GJ, enough energy to power a 2,000-square-foot American house for a year if the house does not use electric heat. This is a large energy savings and monetary cost savings for farmers, who since WWII have become increasingly dependent on nitrogenous fertilizers. The United States started its move to chemical agriculture after World War I, but the big switch took place after World War II, since the nitrogen fixation capability that developed during the war to supply munitions was no longer needed for that purpose. By the 1980s, use in the United States leveled off; globally, though, synthetic nitrogen use continued to climb, especially in China after 1978 when Deng Xiaoping liberated the agricultural sector. Unfortunately, China still relies on coal as its primary energy source in manufacturing fertilizer, and this coal use is polluting the air, land, and water in a variety of ways. The details of this make the evening news in the United States when air pollution gets so bad in Beijing that it requires school closures and restrictions on commuters.

While the manufacture of fertilizer is not the only source of pollution in China, it is a matter of grave concern. The problems caused by its use, including dead zones in the China Sea, eutrophication of major lakes in central China, and acidification of soils, has led to speculation about the ultimate fate of China's agriculture. Both Smil (2001) and Lester Brown (1995) have speculated that tensions in Asia will rise in relation to China's ability to feed itself. When we see reports in the media about tensions rising over small, barely occupied islands in the North China Sea, underlying issues of food and natural resource scarcity are often to blame. China partly responds to this dilemma by looking for land elsewhere on the planet, primarily from neighboring countries like Myanmar (Burma), but also farther away—for instance, in Africa.[5] China is not alone in neocolonial exploitation. India, Saudi Arabia, the United Arab Emirates, and other nations have entered the leasing market, signing long-term agreements for land in many countries (Klare 2012). It is all in a quest for food stability and recognition that internal demand for agricultural products exceeds the projected ability to supply that amount of food. Simply pumping fertilizer on fields is not enough to increase production.

The problem with fertilizer was addressed in Chapter 1, "Ecology: The Language of the Planet." In the use of fertilizers, we have created a linear system with relation to nitrogen

---

5   "New International Land Deals Database Reveals Rush to Buy Up Africa," *The Guardian*, April 27, 2012, http://www.theguardian.com/global-development/2012/apr/27/international-land-deals-database-africa. Also see Timothy Wise, *Eating Tomorrow: Agribusiness, Family Farmers and the Battle for the Future of Food* (New York: New Press, 2019).

and phosphorus that creates a positive feedback loop rather than a stable, cyclical loop. If the energy fed into this type of system is not shut down, eventually the system destroys itself (Brown 2003). Shutting the system off is one of the major challenges of our time. What now exists in the United States, and is replicated elsewhere, is a highly efficient way of producing food, especially animal products that embody a high energy cost and externalize an environmental cost that is not yet paid. The way in which we address the problem and maintain the high productivity of the present system is the challenge of this generation. At present, most politicians are not even aware of the problem. In any case, the problem will not be solved by politicians (see the text box entitled "Vertical Integration and Corporate Control"). The solution to our present global agricultural dilemma must start at the bottom, on farmers' fields, with farm management using integrated ecological solutions. In the end, the solutions identified and implemented will all involve managing manure.

Box 7.1 Vertical Integration and Corporate Control

The rise of conventional agriculture explained in Chapter 3, "The rise and pending fall of conventional agriculture"—with its emphasis on heavy mechanization, chemical use, and genetics, all powered by fossil fuels—simultaneously gave rise to corporate control. Over the last few decades, that control has consolidated to fewer and fewer corporations controlling production, especially of meat, from the growing and processing of feed to the sale of the final product to retail outlets. The biggest of these corporations are Tyson Foods™ (poultry and beef), Archer Daniels Midland or ADM® (grain, alcohol production, high fructose corn syrup, and more), Cargill® (grain, poultry, beef), JBS (Brazil—beef, pork, and poultry), WH Group of China (Smithfield Foods—pork), Dean Foods® (dairy and meat processing), Bayer-Monsanto (seeds and agrichemicals), and ChemChina-Syngenta (seeds and agrichemicals). These companies and others commonly provide inputs that they move and process; they also enter into exclusive contracts with farmers for the animals raised, slaughter and process all the meat, and sell directly to retail companies like Walmart, Kroger®, and Costco® and food contractors like Aramark® and Sysco®.

Poultry farmers under contract are commonly paid based on the weight gain of the animals, but the farmers never own the birds and are told exactly how to raise them, right down to the details of the water and food delivery systems found in the poultry houses. Farmers do not determine the food ration or content of the feed they use; all of that is company-controlled. However, these companies take no responsibility for the manure the animals produce. That is the responsibility of the farmers, who also must supply the bedding needed in the houses.

(Continued)

Governments do have a role in regulating these large companies, but they seldom exercise much control, commonly approving any mergers and acquisitions that led to a company's present consolidation. Instead, many countries subsidize the farmers so that they do not go bankrupt—like the crop insurance program in the United States, which in the end turns out to allow corporations to supply the market with cheap meat. Meanwhile, they completely externalize any cost of dealing with the waste produced by this system, resulting in dead zones off the coast of nearly every river that exits into a lake, sea, or ocean. Getting governments to exert some control of corporate behavior when the corporations can directly or indirectly choose their own politicians is a trick most countries have failed to master.

Dairy Farms

I start with dairy farms because this is one area of concentrated animal feeding operations (CAFO)[6] in which I have some personal experience. In the 1960s in the Pacific Northwest, dairy farms dotted the valleys of major streams coming out of the Cascade Mountains and flowing toward Puget Sound. Farmers grew grass for the animals, and cows grazed daily and then were brought into the barn for milking twice a day. Production was limited, because Western Washington has sandy, relatively infertile soils and a cool climate that is not conducive to growing alfalfa hay or corn. Most farmers could not increase production unless they could get additional land or find another source of feed. The trend toward increasing the size of individual farms had begun, but conditions blocked easy expansion. Then new land opened up in Eastern Washington in the dry desert in the middle of the state. The Columbia Basin Project, part of the original purpose behind the building of Grand Coulee Dam in the 1930s, brought water from Roosevelt Lake via giant electric-powered pumps, opening up a couple of million acres of fertile soils where water rather than land or fertility was the limiting factor. My family bought some of this land and hired people to farm it. I spent a number of summers moving irrigation lines and mowing alfalfa on that land. Trucks loaded with hay then fed the dairy cattle of Western Washington, and production climbed.

Here was where the problems concerning manure begin. Production climbed in Western Washington, but the amount of acreage on which that production took place did not climb.

---

6   The acronym CAFO, for confined animal feeding operation, is commonly used in discussing the mega-farms now dominating the American agricultural landscape. It is difficult to know whether these should even be called farms; they are really industrial operations involving animals, and they defy any notion or understanding of ecology.

Cheap hay and corn silage from the other side of the mountains increased manure production as well as milk production on the west side. Manure piles started growing on dairy farms, and farmers needed to do something with it. Every farmer knows the nutrient value of manure, but it takes more labor and energy to spread it back on the fields, adding a cost to production not necessarily tied to the price of milk. Most of the farmers were highly responsible and took care of their manure well, but a few were not so diligent. Some cut corners, and thus nutrient pollution started becoming an issue in rural areas. Since Western Washington streams are salmon streams, damage occurred to salmon runs and the habitat of other cold-water fish. This stimulated legislation at the state and federal levels.[7] Because of the soils, even the good farmers had trouble with all the manure; since the land now had more cows than grass, the manure spread exceeded the holding capacity of the soil, and leaching became an issue. At the same time, the human population of Western Washington climbed, squeezing farmers off their land. Higher milk demand and a reduced number of larger farms, combined with lower quantities of affordable, available farmland, pushed farmers to move east to the land of alfalfa.

My family's land sits on the western edge of the Columbia Basin, about five miles from the Columbia River. About eight miles east, toward Royal City, a dairy farm bought land and started production. This was not the small 40-cow herds of my youth, or even the 200-cow herds of the late 1970s when I drove a milk tanker as a summer replacement driver. This was a different monster: an 8,000-cow operation with no pasture involved at all. It is basically a giant feedlot for dairy cattle eating alfalfa, timothy hay, and corn supplied by surrounding farms in the basin. That there are 8,000 cattle here, each producing around 36 kg of manure per day, means this operation produces 288 tons of manure per day.[8] Most of this moves to surrounding farms and is spread on that land. However, 105,000 tons of manure per year is a lot of manure and a lot of spreading. This amounts to three tons per acre of available farmland in a ten-mile radius around the dairy operation. Ten miles is the maximum distance a farmer can move manure with a net positive economic value, assuming cheap fuel prices. You can apply up to 20 tons of manure per acre in a single year if you incorporate it in the soil. In no-till situations, where manure is not incorporated into topsoil immediately, the limit is 25 tons over a period of five years.[9] The assumption that farmers can collect and distribute 100% of the manure produced by the cows, however, is problematic. Leaching

---

7   Dairy herds larger than 250 head must acquire a permit as a point source from the EPA, a provision of the Clean Water Act.

8   http://www.nrcs.usda.gov/wps/portal/nrcs/detail/national/technical/?cid=nrcs143_014211#collected.

9   Fred Madison, Keith Kelling, Leonard Massie, and Laura Ward Good, *Guidelines for Applying Manure to Cropland and Pasture in Wisconsin*, http://learningstore.uwex.edu/assets/pdfs/A3392.pdf.

inevitably occurs. Manure leaching from the dairy reaches the irrigation-enhanced groundwater of the basalt and moves toward Crab Creek, a long stream that is the main drainage of the Columbia Basin, about eight miles south. Though there is a threat of pollution reaching Lenice Lake and Sand Hollow Lake, nearby, groundwater movement is very slow and there is no available evidence that this has occurred.

Though cattle produce manure daily, spreading it cannot occur daily. There are restrictions on manure use. The EPA, the National Resources Conservation Service (NRCS), and state agencies do not allow the spreading of manure when the ground is frozen. This eliminates any spreading between late November and mid-March in the Columbia Basin. Also, most state agricultural departments do not allow spreading of manure within 90 days of harvest for crops like corn or alfalfa, and within 120 days of harvest for any directly edible crops like vegetables, potatoes, or other root crops. This means that manure must be stored until spreading can occur. Storage causes problems. Any pile of manure can leak across the surface or leach into groundwater. This particular dairy in our example has a large holding pond for cattle waste, the combination of manure, urine, and water produced by the animals. Two things almost inevitably happen when you hold manure this way: both urine and manure have a lot of nitrogenous material that volatilizes ammonia compounds, causing the bad odors common to any CAFO, while anaerobic conditions lead to the production of methane and nitrous oxide, both greenhouse gases more powerful than carbon dioxide.

A study published in the *Proceedings of the National Science Foundation USA* indicates that the United States is releasing far more methane than the EPA and the global methane inventory previously thought (Miller et al. 2013). The study relies on higher altitude measurements of the gas above the known release points rather than on ground-level site measurements. The organization claims that total concentrations over Texas, Oklahoma, and Kansas are 2.7 times as great as the amount counted by the EPA, and that the sources are gas and petroleum drilling operations with subsequent leaks and cattle feedlots found in all three states. It is probably unnecessary to say that fuel companies are less careful than they claim about pollution. We knew this already from numerous accidents and reports. What is less well known is the extent to which cattle operations, CAFOs, contribute to these emissions.

It is not that farms or feedlots do not know about these emissions. Some actually turn this into a major farm resource—none more spectacularly than Fair Oaks Farm®, an hour south of Chicago.[10] This is a farm on a scale heretofore unknown: 32,000 animals on 25,000 acres of prime agricultural land. The farm produces 2.5 million pounds of milk every day, just over 78 pounds per cow, and about 80 pounds of manure per cow, to say nothing of all

---

10   Fair Oaks Farm website: https://fofarms.com/about-us/

the urine. Each cow eats 40 pounds of grain and 30 pounds of silage and drinks 30 gallons of water daily. The operators do not milk the cows all in one place. There are 10 milking parlors that each handle 3,200 cows on a 72-cow carousel that circles every 8.5 minutes. Though the milk is sucked out in only 5 minutes, the cows need more time to eat the allotment of grain and silage given to them based on their daily milk yield, which is recorded on a computer chip in each cow's collar. Everything is automated, including the vacuuming of manure and urine into a slurry mixer and then an anaerobic digestion tank where methane is produced, captured, and sent to a generator to produce electricity for the farm.[11] Not all dairies have anaerobic digestion systems in their operations, though these are far more common in dairies than in beef feedlots, which are far less technologically developed. But even when manure is handled in this way, is it really handled effectively?[12]

What does the effective handling of manure really mean? To understand the impact of a dairy like Fair Oaks Farm, or the operations in the Columbia Basin, you have to understand the ecological context and the embodied energy cost of the entire operation, including the handling of manure. Would anything resembling these farms even be possible without cheap fossil fuels? The manure requires daily vacuuming, mixing, and loading into giant concrete and steel anaerobic digestion tanks. It is usually inside the tank for three weeks, a normal retention time for anaerobic systems. Then it requires storage in a leak-proof lagoon until spreading time, which usually takes place in spring and fall. Thankfully, digested effluent is relatively stable and less stinky, but although the methane production is low at this point, there is still some possibility of nitrogen volatilization and loss as nitrogen (N_2) or nitrous oxide (N_2O) gas, the latter of which is a potent greenhouse gas with over 200 times as much ability as carbon dioxide (CO_2) to increase atmospheric temperature.[13] The loss of N_2O occurs more commonly in fields that use ammonia-based fertilizers—such as those used for growing corn, the main source of feed for the dairy cattle. Spreading requires energy too, this time in the form of tractor use pulling a tank and sprayer. The equipment has a lot of embodied energy. Fair Oaks Farm produces about 1.5 million tons of manure/urine slurry per year that it must spread on its 25,000 acres, which is more manure than the Wisconsin Department of Agriculture recommends spreading over a five-year period. There is an obvious ecological

---

11   All of this information is derived from Fair Oaks Farm publicity video embedded in the article in footnote 8.

12   Fair Oaks Farm has come under attack recently due to an undercover operation to record how the farm really works. The revelations are hard to stomach and obviously emphasize the worst of the dairy, just as their own publicity emphasizes the best. It is best to make your own judgement by looking at both. Here is the undercover video: https://www.youtube.com/watch?v=rUN3jox2rIY

13   Climate scientists refer to this as "global warming forcing," the relative power of each molecule to absorb infrared radiation and therefore increase temperatures.

problem here; there are too many cows living on too small a land base to handle the manure/urine in an environmentally sensitive way. There is no report available on how Fair Oaks Farm handles their abundant slurry.

Though dairy serves as an example of CAFOs, it is not the most egregious example of mishandling manure. Beef cattle feedlots, industrial pork producers, and giant poultry houses all concentrate animal waste to a degree that would have been unfathomable half a century ago. It is done in the name of efficient meat production, and all attempts to point out obvious environmental contradictions are beaten off with the evidence of high demand from Kentucky Fried Chicken™, Wendy's®, Burger King®, McDonald's®, and the ubiquitous bacon cheeseburger. If cheap food is demanded, this is the way we get it, with Fair Oaks, Indiana, Clovis, New Mexico, Falling Creek, North Carolina, and Marshall County, Alabama, serving as sacrifice zones for meat production. These are certainly not alone. According to the EPA, 15% of all counties in the country have a surplus of phosphorus.[14] When you add more nutrients than the land can hold, it has to go somewhere, and that is usually the nearest water body. This surplus of nutrients explains the dead zones of the Gulf of Mexico, Chesapeake Bay, Pamlico Sound, eastern Lake Erie, and the mouths of smaller rivers throughout the country. This is all because of our making nutrient flow on farms a linear system instead of a complete loop.

One important note to add to this discussion concerns pork: In 2013, Smithfield Foods®, the largest pork producer in the United States, was purchased by the Shanghai-based conglomerate Shuanghui International. China is the largest consumer of pork in the world, yet China's land base for agriculture is significantly smaller than that of the United States. Producing meat takes a lot of land, since it involves so much grain. Production also necessitates a lot of water use in the United States for growing the grain, processing the meat, and disposing of waste. One need look no further than North Carolina to see the results of problems associated with disposing of that waste.[15] China has waste disposal problems too—for example, a bout of flooding that brought 6,000 dead pigs to Shanghai.[16] Author Kai Olsen-Sawyer calls this a meat-for-manure swap; China gets the pork and we get the shit.[17]

---

14 http://www.epa.gov/oecaagct/ag101/printpoultry.html

15 http://www.themeatrix.com

16 "Dead Pigs in Shanghai River: More than 6,000 Carcasses Found," *The Guardian*, March 13, 2013, http://www.theguardian.com/world/2013/mar/13/dead-pigs-shanghai-huangpu-river

17 "Shuanghui-Smithfield Deal: Water for Waste," Food Tank, December 2013, http://foodtank.org/news/2013/12/shuanghui-smithfield-deal-water-for-waste?utm_source=Food+Tank%3A+The+Food+Think+Tank&utm_campa

Unless we figure out a way to grow the pigs without creating the manure problem, China will essentially be transferring its pollution to our land. Of course, this is the type of deal that our corporations have done to developing economies for decades. The deforestation of the forests in coastal West Africa, from Cameroon to Liberia, for the production of oil palm, cocoa, coffee, and rubber is just one example.

While normally a hog CAFO will look clean from an overhead view, the manure lagoon next to the confinement sheds has a peculiar maroon hue caused by a type of bacteria that thrives in the nutrient rich soup. The stench of these places is unmistakable, having a mixed ammonia smell consisting of methylated amines reminiscent of putrefied onions. At the same time these lagoons are off-gassing methane and nitrous oxide, both powerful climate forcing gasses. Even more severe is the episodic and inevitable flooding that washes the lagoon and the contents of the confinement sheds into nearby rivers as seen in Figure 7.1. This event, documented by Tom Philpott in *Mother Jones* in 2016, happens every time a major hurricane hits North Carolina. This makes the waters of Albemarle and Pamlico Sounds unusable until tides and rivers at normal flow push the nutrient and bacterial load into the Atlantic. The manure load is also implicated in outbreaks of *Pfiesteria piscicida*,

FIGURE 7.1   Hog confined-animal feeding operation in North Carolina overwhelmed by flooding from Hurricane Matthew in 2016. From an article by Tom Philpott (http://www.motherjones.com/environment/2016/10/hurricane-matthew-killed-animals-hog-poop).

a type of dinoflagellate, normally benign, but under polluted conditions becomes highly toxic to fish and can cause illness in humans in close contact.[18]

Reconstructing Nutrient Cycles

Justus von Liebig identified nitrogen in the form of ammonia and nitrates as a key limiting factor in European agriculture. Until the nineteenth century, farmers did not know about nitrogen or fertilizer, but they did know about soils and they knew the value of good soil enriched with manure from their animals. In fact, many of the soils in the plains of northern Europe, from England to Russia, had a layer of topsoil that soil scientists call plaggen. This is a thick horizon of mineral soil continuously enhanced by the addition of manures, mainly from cattle and horses. In England, for example, animals on these farms were grazed in areas called commons, the forests and meadows that were part of every village. The cattle, horses, sheep, and goats brought nutrients from these areas back to the farm, where the animals were kept at night to prevent theft but also to supply the nutrients gleaned from the commons. Spreading this manure by horse- or ox-drawn cart, or even from baskets carried on their backs, was a constant part of farmers' lives. Most production on small farms was consumed by the farm or was used as barter for goods like cloth or for the services of blacksmiths, carpenters, ferriers, and other artisans. Nutrient loss from the vicinity of the village where most farmers lived was minimal.

Historically and globally, farmers have known about the benefits of crop rotation. While they may not have known the role of root nodules and rhizobium bacteria in fixing nitrogen in legumes, they did rotate or intercrop these nitrogen-fixing crops with grains. In European agriculture, it was primarily small grains like wheat, barley, oats, and rye mixed with lentils and peas. In Asia, similar complementary mixes of millet and mung beans were planted in drier areas, or rice was followed by soybeans. China and Southeast Asia had some particularly complex mixes of rice with a nitrogen-fixing, mutualistic coupling of azolla, an aquatic fern, and *Anabeana azollea* cyanobacteria.[19] This arrangement worked particularly well if the system had sufficient phosphorus. It was also common in the irrigated paddies for farmers to add a small fish, which helps to keep the weeds at bay, fertilizes the rice, and provides a protein source when the time comes to harvest the rice. Likewise, Africans commonly mixed

---

18   *Pfiesteria* is not contagious, it gives off a toxin that causes the illness. More information can be found from the EPA, "What you should know about *Pfiesteria piscicida*", 1998. https://nepis.epa.gov/Exe/ZyNET.exe

19   http://en.wikipedia.org/wiki/Azolla. Also see Yatazawa, Michihiko, Naoki Tomomatsu, Noriyo Hosoda, and Katsunori Nunome, "Nitrogen Fixation in *Azolla-Anabaena* Symbiosis as Affected by Mineral Nutrient Status," *Soil Science and Plant Nutrition* 26 (3): 415–426, https://doi.org/10.1080/00380768.1980.10431227.

sorghum with cowpeas, or followed millets with chickpeas, to get the complementary action of the two crops. In addition, African farmers often permitted or encouraged the grazing of livestock on their fields during the dry season. This happened in West Africa as cattle herders brought their animals south during the dry season and moved back north during the rains. In Kenya, the Maasai would graze their cattle in the farm country of the Kamba and Kikuyu after crops were harvested. In both cases, the exchange of milk and goats for grazing access was common, and farmers would trade surplus crops for the animal products as well, creating a beneficial cycle for all participants.

Cultural knowledge like that found in Kenya is commonly rooted in some sound science even if the practitioners do not know these details. The science is centered on an understanding of biogeochemical cycles, which is the study of nutrient flow in ecosystems. One of these is the nitrogen cycle, which is quite complex and highly fluid since nearly all forms of nitrogen outside of biological molecules are soluble in water. The element can move, and the nature of its bonding shifts according to the biotic and abiotic conditions of its place; such conditions include the availability of oxygen, the movement of water, the amount of organic matter in the soil, and the temperature. Figure 7.2 provides a glimpse of a simplified

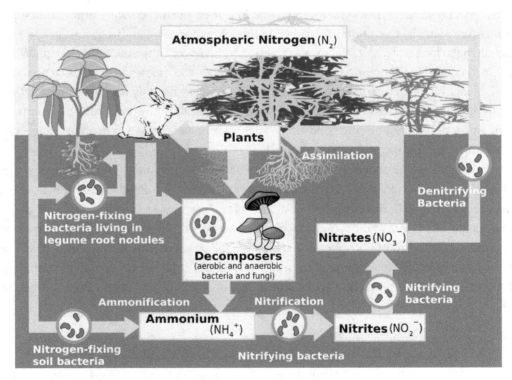

FIGURE 7.2   A simplified nitrogen cycle.

nitrogen cycle.[20] The main depository of nitrogen in the environment is the atmosphere in the form of nitrogen gas (N_2). From there, nature moves it to the soil via lightning strikes, which provide about 4% of natural soil nitrogen, or through nitrogen fixation involving free or symbiotic bacteria, as will be explained in a moment. In the latter case, usually the plants use the nitrogen fixed in their roots, so its availability to other plants occurs when the plant dies and rots or when an animal eats and defecates nitrogenous waste. Some free-living soil bacteria are able to turn atmospheric nitrogen into nutrient and then are consumed by single-celled predators like amoeba or larger bacterial feeders such as nematodes. The movement of nitrogen in soil can get very complex (Coleman, Crossley, and Hendrix 2004). If a mycorrhizal mycelia or a root hair captures free nitrogen in the form of ammonium or nitrate, it can then be incorporated into plant tissue, normally as an amino acid. Ammonium in higher concentrations is toxic to most organisms, so nature has designated nitrifying or *nitrosomonas* bacteria to convert the NH_4^- ions to NO_3^- ions that are equally mobile in water but less toxic. If there are pockets of anaerobic conditions in the soil, such as saturated soil horizons, denitrifying bacteria will sometimes strip the oxygen from the nitrate and convert it to N_2 gas. A surplus of nitrate even in near anaerobic conditions can lead to conversion to nitrous oxide, N_2O, the potent greenhouse gas. Detrivores, such as bacteria, nematodes, springtails, and a host of worms, convert organic waste to humus-like material that contain nitrogen in their structures where fungi can get them, or hold nitrogen ions on their surface for extraction by plants or fungi, including lichen. Water plays a crucial role in moving the nitrogen around, but too much water leads to nitrogen loss by leaching or denitrification. Leaching losses are commonly larger in soils that are low in organic matter. The complexity of the cycle should not be ignored, since management shifts of biotic or abiotic conditions, such as removal of a cover crop or tillage, can change nitrogen balance in soil dramatically.

Another crucially important nutrient is phosphorus. Unlike nitrogen, phosphorus does not have a gaseous state involved in its movement through the environment. Phosphorus tends to get trapped in soil particles because it is far less soluble as an ion, PO_4^{3-}, and therefore less mobile. It is also far rarer, with global resources of phosphorus rapidly becoming depleted. A linear flow of phosphorus is unsustainable, even within our lifetime.[21] The flow of phosphorus is also less complex than nitrogen, since it has fewer chemical forms and phases. The ion bonds powerfully with aluminum, iron, calcium, and magnesium and quickly

20   Biology Dictionary: Nitrogen Cycle. https://biologydictionary.net/nitrogen-cycle/
21   Stuart White and Dana Cordell, "Peak Phosphorus: The Sequel to Peak Oil," *Phosphorus Futures*, after 2014. http://phosphorusfutures.net/the-phosphorus-challenge/peak-phosphorus-the-sequel-to-peak-oil/.

goes into a solid, immobile phase as long as there are free metals to bind it. Most plants are incapable of breaking these bonds and sucking up the nutrient phosphorus, which is why farmers have relied on frequent additions of fertilizer even on soils that have the nutrient. Nature has another way of releasing phosphorus, however, through the action of mycorrhizal fungi. These fungi thrive in undisturbed soils where they can establish linkages with the root systems of most plants. The fungi exude powerful enzymes that can break phosphorus loose from its bonds with metals and exchange it with plants, often in the form of organic molecules, in return for sugars. Unfortunately, the thin, nearly microscopic mycelia of the fungi are easily destroyed by soil disturbance, especially by the action of moldboard plows or deep disk plows. Even chisel plows and deep hoeing cause damage, though this type is reversible. A typical phosphorus cycle in a farmer's field would look something like that shown in Figure 7.3.

That farmers understood the importance of nutrient cycling long before they even knew what the nutrients were is not surprising. Farmers interacted daily with their

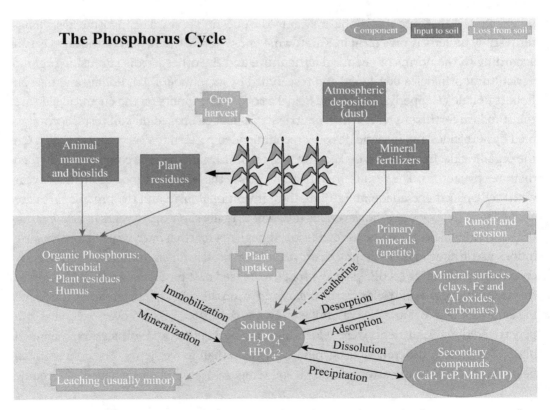

FIGURE 7.3   An example phosphorus cycle that is missing the crucial mycorrhizal component as well as the role of soil bacteria and organic matter.

land, observing closely what happened to yield in relation to what they added or took away from a particular plot. Their knowledge was ecological and biological, as opposed to chemical. The irony is that as we developed the ability to peer into the smallest particles of matter, we somehow lost our connection with the visible and tangible. There are reasons for this. Though the ecological knowledge of past farmers was profound, their ability to correct problems in fields was limited by resource availability and cost. They lacked both the mechanical and energy resources that we presently take for granted. We overwhelm the productivity of the past through application of mechanical and chemical energy, with the complement of understanding genetics. However, as our mechanical complexity expanded, our biological complexity decreased, and as a result, the cyclical nature of nutrient flows on farms was lost. Now, as our awareness of the damage that linear nutrient flows have done increases, we must ask ourselves whether or not a cyclical nutrient flow in agriculture with minimal energy subsidies can actually feed the planet's expanded population. Top-notch agricultural thinkers like Vaclav Smil (2001) think the answer is no.

The Rodale Institute thinks the answer to the question is yes. The institute has a long-term study underway on a farm in Kutztown, Pennsylvania, where part of the farm is run according to the norms of chemical agriculture and the other part is run using organic agricultural principles developed and researched by its founders, J. I. Rodale and his son Robert Rodale (Hepperly, Douds, and Seidel 2006).[22] The inputs on the chemical side are the standard fertilizer (NPK + micronutrients as needed) based on soil tests, accompanied by herbicides and insecticides on a recommended pattern to keep pests in check. On the organic side, inputs focus on keeping the soil healthy and include composts and green manure cover crops. The results are intriguing, to say the least. In a good agricultural year with well-spaced and adequate rainfall, the conventional farm and the organic farm are about equal. In poor years, however, the differences really show up. In years of heavy rains, the conventional fields show signs of erosion, though not like that of 40 years before because it does use limited and no-till practices; yields drop mostly due to difficulties in the early crop stages, drowning seedlings in low spots, increased pest problems, and nutrient losses from leaching or runoff. Yields on the organic farm, on the other hand, remained high even in years with heavy rain, since rainfall energy was dissipated by soil cover, excessive rain penetrated the soil, nutrients were held by high organic content, and soil aeration remained high. Even greater differences occurred in dry years than in wet years. The conventional fields showed high water stress, had high soil temperatures, and yields dropped. Organic

---

22   https://rodaleinstitute.org/

fields had much better moisture-holding capacity, so water stress was much less and soil temperatures stayed low because of the organic cover.

Composting

Compost was the major input on the organic side of the Rodale Farm and is a major component of many farms. Most compost is made from a combination of manures of various types, green material from plants and kitchen waste, and brown materials such as fallen leaves, old hay or straw, woodchips, or sawdust. Ideal compost has a ratio of carbon to nitrogen between 25:1 and 30:1. If the carbon content is lower than 25 times the amount of the nitrogen, the resulting balance allows microbial activity to free the nitrogen through volatilization, which is what causes the bad smell of manure, or conversion to N_2 or N_2O, both gases that escape to the atmosphere. If the carbon content is much higher than 30:1, then the carbon will tie up nitrogen for a time and plants will not have access to it until microbial activity reduces the overall carbon through respiration.

Compost is made a number of ways and does not require manure. Most urban or suburban gardeners do not have access to barnyard production, so they use a mixture of green materials. including kitchen waste and green lawn clipping or pruned leaves, mixed with dried leaves, wood chips, and straw. These are combined in piles, often in layers like lasagna and allowed to mature through consumption by bacteria. Fresh grass clippings are rapid stimulants for bacterial activity since they have a full complement of nutrients in the leaves and active bacteria on the leaf surface. Materials in the center of piles are processed faster. Sometimes, in larger piles of approximately 3 cubic feet, temperatures rise very quickly, reaching as high as 150°F (66°C), warm enough to cook rice in a pressure cooker if you leave it inside the pile for two hours. I have done this myself with good results. Mixing a hot compost pile after two weeks reignites the process, and complete compost is ready in less than three months. Most piles are not hot because it takes ideal mixing, size, and ingredients to do them well, so most gardeners rely on longer composting time and less frequent mixing. In general, good compost is obtained by either fast or slow methods as long as the C:N ratios are right. Manures add more green material, lowering the C:N ratio, thereby enabling use of more brown materials in the pile and often resulting in a hot compost pile more quickly. Table 7.1 gives a list of compost ingredients types and their C:N ratio. Note that poultry litter and pig manure are very high in nitrogen and therefore require good mixing with high-carbon material.

Composting has become a business. Two such operations in the Shenandoah Valley are worthy of note. Dennis Stoneburner is a poultry and cattle farmer north of Harrisonburg in Rockingham County, Virginia. He has six poultry houses, each producing seven batches per year of 25,000 chickens, giving an annual bird total of 1,050,000. Since each bird weighs

TABLE 7.1 A list of compost materials and approximate C:N ratios.

Material	Carbon Nitrogen Ratio*
Fresh cut grass	12–20:1
Vegetable kitchen waste	12–20:1
Coffee grounds	20:1
Green leaves	30:1
Bark mulch	100–130:1
Sawdust and wood chips	200–400:1
Pizza boxes, cardboard	200:1
Brown fall leaves	80:1
Cow manure	15–20:1
Chicken litter (no bedding)	7–10:1
Chicken litter (industrial bedding)	12–18:1
Pig manure	5–7:1
Horse manure	30:1

*The C:N ratios are compiled from a variety of web-based sources and are considered approximations.

an average of 4.5 pounds at full growth, that means producing 4.7 million pounds of birds every year. The poultry industry estimates that there are 1.5 pounds of fresh poultry litter for every pound of bird, for a total of 7 million pounds, or 3,200 metric tons of poultry litter, per year. Since this poultry litter has previously had some bedding mixed into it, the C:N ratio is approximately 12:1. Stoneburner uses wood chips made by the companies that clean under power lines and on roadsides as his brown material, a high carbon source at 200:1. In this case, he needs 1.2 parts wood chips and 1 part poultry litter to get to the ideal windrow ratio of 25–30:1 for compost. He mixes these ingredients in windrows that are easily turned by a tractor-pulled stirrer every one to three weeks, depending on outdoor temperatures, and he keeps the piles moist with a sprinkler system. This good-quality compost is purchased and used by a number of local farmers.

The second example is Black Bear Composting,[23] located in Augusta County, Virginia, near Parnassus. It is not associated with a farm; instead, it gets its green materials from restaurants and schools, including the James Madison University (JMU) dining halls. JMU processes all its kitchen waste using a pulper and ships the pulped material weekly to Black Bear. Black Bear then mixes the kitchen waste with a variety of woody debris that is ground into chips on-site, mixing at around a 1:1 ratio. This ratio varies according to the type of material available when the Black Bear team make their windrow piles. When they mix the piles, they also add water from a tank that is connected to the mixer in order to get the piles evenly moist, which is a key variable in making compost. Compost piles are aged for six months before they are ready for sale, ensuring that any potential pathogens in the original material are killed by the process.

---

23 http://www.blackbearcomposting.com/

Perhaps the most creative and elegant composting system comes from Polyface Farms, researched, developed, and designed specifically by Joel Salatin for his farm operation.[24] The farm does not sell the compost; it is entirely used on the farm, which is located in Swoope, Virginia. Every winter when the grass no longer grows in the pastures, Polyface brings the cattle back to two open-sided barns on the property, located within easy walking distance of those living on the farm. Each barn holds about 150 animals that feed from mangers on either side of centrally stacked, rectangular bales. These bales are dropped into the mangers held on a pulley system that allows them to be raised as needed throughout the winter. The cattle start off the season standing on a four-inch layer of bedding made from wood chips. The wood chips come either from the roadside and from power line cleaning crews or from the farm's own chipper-shredder. As the cattle eat, urinate, and defecate on the wood chips, more are added to keep the bedding fresh. Now here is the main innovation: Polyface adds shelled corn to the pile just before adding the wood chips. Though cattle will eat corn, they dislike smelling or touching their own manure, so the corn remains safe, buried in the rising pile of wood chips and manure. At this point the pile is compressed and anaerobic, so decomposition is by anaerobic bacteria and yeast. Composting temperatures are low, so the process is slow and the corn ferments. By early spring when the grass starts growing in the nearby pasture, the cows leave the barn to graze and the anaerobic mix, now about three to four feet thick, is ready for turning. Here come the pigs. Pigs do not mind cattle manure, and the parasites the manure contains do not harm hogs. The hogs love fermented corn, though, and they have the noses to smell and dig for it. They thrive on burrowing into the composting pile and feasting on the corn. This turns the mix over, making it aerobic, and now it warms from bacterial activity. Contented hogs stay on the warm piles from March until May; then they move out to pasture as well, and the fully composted manure and wood chips smell like excellent soil, ready for spreading on the pasture, all parasites having been consumed. The pasture on which this compost is spread also produces hay for the next round of winter feeding. Although there is some input of new nutrients into the system via the corn,

---

24   Joel Salatin's Polyface Farm is a large operation now primarily managed by his son, Daniel. Joel is an unapologetic Libertarian capitalist and has some controversial economic and political ideas, nicely summarized recently by Tom Philpot of *Mother Jones*; https://www.motherjones.com/food/2020/11/joel-salatin-chris-newman-farming-rotational-grazing-agriculture/. My reference to Joel in no way endorses his economic or socio-political views particularly those with negative racial and gender-based implications. I do recognize that Joel gets the ecology right on his farm, and as a result has developed a highly productive operation with few externalized costs. The externalized costs that Polyface does have are mostly related to fossil fuel use, and Polyface uses far fewer fossil fuel inputs per dollar of production than the average American farm.

FIGURE 7.4   A pig at Polyface Farm atop the pile of manure, wood chips, waste hay, and fermented corn performing its aerobic composting job.

replacing the amount lost through the sale of meat, the majority of nutrient is recycled on the farm. This serves as a best-practice example of how farms can revive systems of onsite nutrient cycling.[25]

Vermicomposting

Most homeowners do not have access to composting facilities, and many do not have space in their yards to do composting properly on their own property. There is another option, though, that works almost everywhere, and it involves the use of worms—in particular, red wigglers, *Eisenia foetida*, a worm that lives horizontally, thrives in dense populations, and will eat its way through a broad range of kitchen waste in small containers.[26] The normal method for using worms in household composting involves a set of stackable bins with holes or a screened bottom that allows water to drain and the worms to pass through but holds the composting material. Kitchen waste includes almost everything except meat products and citrus peels. Meat waste tends to get stinky too fast, and citrus peels are too acidic so the worms avoid them. Having a bit of high-carbon, organic material at the bottom of the lowest bin when you start provides a base for the worms. A water catchment is normally found below the bottom bin, because the surplus water serves as a nutrient-rich compost tea and excellent plant food. The kitchen waste is added as you need to, and the worms will hide out in the dark under the waste and eat their way up into it as they need food. Most kits start off with a thousand worms or so, and these are easily available online. You can build your own worm bin using wood and wire screen. As you add kitchen waste, the bottom bin will fill with worm castings (the term used for worm manure), and new waste can be added to the bin above (See Figure 7.5). The worms will finish off the lower bin and move up as long as there is no light visible to them. Once all the worms have moved up a layer, the bottom bin

25   Information here comes from numerous visits by the author to Polyface Farms and from Joel Salatin's book *You Can Farm* (Brattleboro, VT: Echo Point Books & Media, 1998).

26   Instructions for building bins are available here: http://home.howstuffworks.com/vermicomposting2.htm

can be removed and used as compost for your house-plants or vegetable garden. Normally, you start filling the fourth bin up the stack before the bottom bin is done. If you have a stack of four or five bins, then you can keep rotating the pile as the worms eat. The worms do not need any special care other than keeping the bins moist but not saturated and maintaining temperatures between 40°F and 80°F (5°C and 27°C).

Worm composting is used on much larger scales as well. Will Allen of Growing Power in Milwaukee used vermicomposting as the primary agricultural input in urban gardens. Growing Power's system, which was well described on their website,[27] relied on a raised bed of compostable materials where the worms feed. It takes about 12 weeks for the worms to eat through the material. When complete, a screen is added to the top of the pile with a fresh food source for the worms, which will then squeeze through the screen and start eating the next layer. After a few days, over 80% of the worms have moved up and the underlying worm compost is ready for use. When space permitted, Growing Power also used an adapted windrow system for the worms, processing even more kitchen waste for their gardens and greenhouses.

The importance of worms should not be underestimated. Darwin praised them, as has been noted earlier (Montgomery 2007). Municipal governments interested in reducing the amount of waste entering landfills have started separating organic waste and either com-posting or using vermicomposting. A major review by Rajiv Sinha et al. (2010) identifies companies and municipalities in the United States, Canada, France, the United Kingdom,

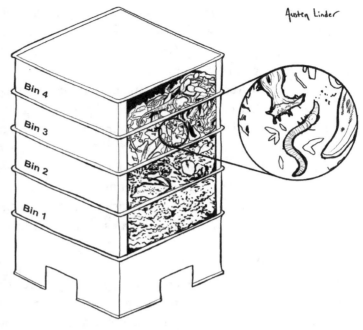

FIGURE 7.5   A worm composting bin.

---

27   The Growing Power organization ceased in 2016 due to personnel and structural issues not connected to their use of worms. https://civileats.com/2018/03/13/behind-the-rise-and-fall-of-growing-power/

New Zealand, Australia, India, the Philippines, Argentina, China, and Russia that are investing in vermicomposting operations. Studies in a variety of places globally indicate that worm composting is superior to regular composting when it comes to processing food waste, and vermicomposting can incorporate animal manures as well. In general, worm composts are ready in six to eight weeks—far sooner than regular composting, which can take six months— with more complete elimination of potential parasites (Sinha 2009). The major drawback of vermicomposting is that the worms cannot handle woody material well and are sensitive to pH and temperature problems, though these are easily avoided by restricting inputs. A small amount of citrus is fine as long as it is not a large percentage of the biomass used. On the plus side, the value of vermicompost more than compensates for the inputs needed to make it, since it replaces the constantly rising expense of synthetic fertilizers as long as the farms using it are within a reasonable transportation distance.

Green Manure and Mulch

Wheat farms in much of Eastern Washington rely on relatively sparse rain: 8–12 inches per year. This is not sufficient to get a good wheat crop. Farmers in this rolling hill country that once was shortgrass prairie adopted a style of fallow farming that left half their field devoid of any growth for a full year while they farmed the other half. The pattern from the time of my grandfather, who farmed from 1900 to 1955, until the 1970s was to plow under this year's stubble in the fall, then carefully harrow the land to keep it weed-free with a dirt clod mulch on top to reduce evaporation. Then patterns began to shift. Farmers and researchers realized that stubble on the surface had value for reducing erosion, so plowing ended. Instead, a shallow disk was used to kill weeds but keep the stubble on the surface. Then along came Monsanto's Roundup®, enabling farmers to kill weeds with a spray, reducing soil disturbance and keeping even more stubble intact to protect soil. This no-till system works well for stopping erosion, but the continuous monoculture of wheat still slowly degrades the soil. It does not add enough organic material to promote a healthy, stable soil ecosystem.[28]

Farmers in North Dakota, another dry agricultural area—though with slightly more rain than Eastern Washington: some 12–20 inches depending on the farm location—realized through a long learning process that plants do not necessarily use all soil moisture even in these dry environments. In fact, with the right management, a healthy mixture of cover crops can increase the moisture-holding capacity of soils and increase the amount

---

28   Though Roundup has its value, the full understanding of its side effects is under study. I do not endorse using this chemical, and in general I avoid all synthetic chemical use.

of moisture available for the cash crop. A champion of this thinking, Ray Archuleta along with David Brandt, has developed four rules for using cover crops, sometimes called "green manure crops":[29]

1. Limit disturbance of the soil, thus keeping the soil ecosystem intact.
2. Keep the soil continuously covered, mostly with living plants.
3. Increase the diversity of that cover; there is no ideal single species—mixtures are best.
4. Keep a live root system.

His basic point is to feed the soil. The primary feeders and shapers of soil structure are plants. Without plants, there is no energy available for ecosystem function in the soil. The diversity of the below-ground biomass is enhanced by the diversity of the above-ground biomass. The more diversity you have, the better the soil-forming organisms below ground will operate. Living plants provide energy through decaying plant materials on the surface and through the continuous sloughing and exuding actions of a living roots system. The main purpose of these plants is to enhance the soil, and in doing so they reduce the need for chemical inputs. A good mix of intentionally planted cover crops reduces or eliminates places for weeds to establish, captures any loose nutrients in organic form, fully protects the soil surface, reduces soil temperature, reduces soil evaporation even as they increase transpiration, and provides food for organisms that reduce bulk density and increase the moisture-holding capacity of soils. The four rules are counterintuitive to the prevailing paradigms of agriculture, but as farmers begin implementing them, they will start seeing positive results.

Probably the best articulation of the rules that Archuleta gave above comes from Gabe Brown, a farmer in North Dakota who started farming in 1993, following the conventional paradigm, but slowly switched to an agroecological model. The first step was a switch to no-till, basically foregoing use of the plow in any form. Instead, he left crop residues in place and planted right through them. Next, he added cover crops, at first single species like rye grass, slowly increasing the number as he gained experience. He saw organic matter levels rise on his farm, from a low of 1.5% to near 5% as he made these changes. While he increased his number of cover crops, keeping a living root system in his fields year-round, he also increased the diversity and rotation of the crops he was growing. This further bumped up his soil organic matter to 5.5%, where it stabilized. Yet he knew that the shortgrass prairie mollisols, the USDA name for prairie-derived soils, was originally above 8%. That was when

---

29 A YouTube video featuring Ray Archuleta and David Brandt: https://www.youtube.com/watch?v=nNMdWnfjs8s

bison roamed the Great Plains. Brown learned from others that incorporating grazing animals appropriately in short intense bursts, followed by long periods of rest, stimulated more growth and increased soil organic matter, so he tried it. It worked, and organic matter began climbing to 8%. He describes this process in his book *Dirt to Soil* (2018).

There is no fixed cover crop recipe. As in all ecological approaches, the present combination of abiotic and biotic factors of a place determines what mix is best for a given farm. As a general guide, there are categories of plants that should be included. Using a very broad brush, Archuleta mentions warm-season and cool-season grasses and warm-season and cool-season broadleaf annuals. Kristen Ohlson describes farmers in the Red River Valley of the Dakotas using over 20 different species in combination as cover crops. As the farmers explain it in her book, the more species above ground, the greater the biodiversity below ground—and the net result is better soil (Ohlson 2014). Plant categories include grasses, legumes, composites, and other leafy annuals. Wild rye grass is probably the most common grass used, but wild wheat, oats, and millet are also common. Legumes fix nitrogen, so they are key players in any cover strategy. Some common types are clovers, birdsfoot trefoil, and lupines. Composites are a very large group of plants that includes annual and perennial sunflowers. Other plants commonly used as cover crops include buckwheat, daikon radish, and other deep-rooted tuberous plants that are great for opening soil and adding organic matter. When it comes time to plant the main crop, farmers can prepare the ground in a number of ways, remembering to limit any soil disturbance. A technique that is gaining acceptance is the roll and crimp method, developed by the Rodale Institute.[30] This uses a heavy roller with sharp ridges to bend and break plant stems. It does not kill the plant immediately, so a living root system is still working when the crop seeding takes place. The crimped and rolled plants protect the soil surface as the new crops get established, preventing erosion, lowering soil temperature, and conserving moisture, while at the same time starting to rot as plant parts touch the soil surface, releasing nutrients to the new crops. The result, even for new adopters is an increase in crop productivity and a decrease in input application. There is no magic to this process; it is simply recognition that nature has good tools for agriculture.

Green manure cover crops do not eliminate or even reduce the role of animal manures in agriculture. They are simply another tool in a farmer's kit. It does not matter if the field is a small backyard garden, or a 1,200-acre stretch of Red River Valley floodplain; the tool works the same even if the species used are different.

---

30   Mark Misar, "Roller-Crimper Helps Combat Herbicide Resistant Weeds," Rodale Institute, October 4, 2016, .https://rodaleinstitute.org/science/articles/roller-crimper-helps-combat-herbicide-resistant-weeds/

Humans

One of my favorite humans, though I never met him in person, is Gene Logsdon, a farmer and writer from southwest Ohio. His book *The Contrary Farmer* (1994) is a great read about the way to farm corn without the industrial agriculture trend to believe that "bigger is better." Logsdon wrote another book recently with a more earthy title, *Holy Shit: Managing Manure to Save Mankind*. That book was the inspiration for this chapter. Logsdon is concerned that for too long we have ignored a crucial resource, and that resource includes more than only farm animal manure, for we are animals, too. Every time we flush our toilets, we are taking nature's nutrient cycles, putting them in a pipe, and sending them in a linear wash to the sea. We do this to our peril.

We have a natural fear of our own shit, so much so that this earthy word from the Anglo-Saxons has become a swear word that you used to not be able to say on television. Sitting on a toilet is more forbidden in the movies than sex in a bedroom. There is good reason to have some reticence about shit, or as Joseph Jenkins calls it, humanure (Jenkins 2005). All animals have a reticence about their own excrement because of the risk of contracting disease and parasites. It is a self-protection mechanism. Cows kept in one field for a long time will still avoid eating near old manure piles even though the grass is green right next to them. Pigs kept in a spacious area will always poop in the same corner and avoid that corner the rest of the time. Dogs will eat human excrement, but not the excrement of another dog. The thing that made the Industrial Revolution so vile to writers like Charles Dickens was the concentration of humans in degrading conditions that include living in or near their own shit. London had no sewage system. The stench in the Thames River got so bad one year that Parliament had to close. That event prompted the development of the London sewers, the flushing of excrement away. At that same time, on the other side of the world's largest landmass, farmers in Shanghai were collecting the same type of shit in honey buckets and putting it on their crops. They connected the nutrient dots; we did not.

Ultimately, we cannot solve the problem of nutrient loss in agricultural systems until we reconnect all human waste back to the farm. This is less difficult in rural areas, but there are many roadblocks to making this happen, not the least of which comes from the various Departments of Health around the United States. For example, in Virginia you cannot get an occupancy permit for a house if you do not have a flush toilet and are not connected to a sewer system or septic tank with an approved leach field that will not affect groundwater. The mere idea of keeping humanure as a resource is unacceptable. After you spend all that money investing in a toilet and septic system, it is rather difficult to spend the resources needed to construct an alternative system. So we get locked into the societal norm on farms even though we know it is wrong. Nevertheless, there are alternatives, and Logsdon and Jenkins point the way.

The first task in dealing with humanure is getting past the stink. This is not as hard as you might think. Humanure comes in two different forms: feces and urine. The stink is a result of the waste's high nitrogen content. For our feces, the C:N ratio is similar to pig feces, about 7:1, but this varies according to diet. Meat-eaters have feces richer in nitrogen and generally stinkier than that of vegans. Urine is also high in nitrogen, being a mix of water and urea, $CO(NH_2)_2$.[31] The concentration of urea in urine varies according to the consumption of fluids. Keeping urine and feces separate is one way to deal with the odor. Liquid slurries of urine and feces get smelly fast because anaerobic conditions quickly result. However, if the two waste streams are kept separate, the sterile urine makes good fertilizer for perennials immediately, while its use on annuals, especially leafy vegetables, should be considered only if it is diluted and used at least three weeks before harvest. Feces contains a lot of water, though it still remains in a semisolid form most of the time. It is not sterile. Over a trillion microbes live in the gut at any given time, and some of them are dangerous outside that context, so treatment is a must before use. The initial smell of feces is easily neutralized by adding a high-carbon source to raise the C:N ratio. Shredded leaves, saw dust, finely shredded paper, toilet paper,[32] and fine wood chips work well.

A neighbor of mine has made a simple system to accomplish the separation task. He built a square box large enough to go over the top of a five-gallon plastic bucket to hold feces. The top of the box holds an extended-length toilet seat, and near the front of the seat is a funnel into which both women and men can pee when seated. The funnel then channels the pee to another, smaller bucket. The small bucket is emptied outside daily on his fruit trees and vines. The five-gallon bucket starts out with a thin layer of organic carbon source material at the bottom, and then every time someone defecates in the bucket you add a scoop of organic material to cover the feces. This makes it easier to empty the bucket when it gets nearly full, and it also prevents odor. Outside, there is a designated compost pile for the bucket. It is a layered compost system, so that every time a bucket of feces is added, more green and brown organics are added as well. Keeping the pile actively processing the compost is important.

---

31 Urea is not the only chemical in urine. Urine also includes creatinine, uric acid, traces of enzymes, carbohydrates, and fats, and inorganic ions like sodium, potassium, chloride, magnesium, calcium, and phosphate (PO_4^{3-}). These are also valuable in agricultural systems. See Anne Marie Helmenstine, "What Is the Chemical Composition of Urine?" ThoughtCo, January 28, 2020, https://www.thoughtco.com/the-chemical-composition-of-urine-603883.

32 Toilet paper is a problem. It is a refined and energy-intensive paper product. Do we really need to clean ourselves with a dry piece of paper cut from a virgin Canadian forest? Does having toilet paper come from a monoculture of yellow pine in the American Southeast feel any better ethically? Perhaps we need to rethink the sustainability of toilet paper.

You want the pile moist but never saturated, so that there is no leakage. It may take a year to build the pile to full height. Mixing the pile will speed composting, but mixing is not required. After the pile is full-size, mixing is necessary to make sure all the pile is adequately treated. After one or two mixings, the pile is kept moist while it ages. At the end of another year, all pathogens are gone and the pile can be used as fertilizer. Though it is safe to use on any crop at this point, most people prefer using it on perennials and use non-humanure compost for vegetable production. The system is effective, inexpensive—especially when compared to commercial composting toilet systems—and easy to implement in rural areas, or even in suburbia if a large backyard with isolated areas for the compost pile is available.

This still does not solve the rural-to-urban nutrient leak, which our global economic system has created. Farms are not located close to urban areas anymore. The question of how we get our urban waste back to the farm or forest is one that still needs an answer. At present, the most advanced wastewater treatment facilities remove most of the nitrogen through the sludge or by alternating aerobic and anaerobic biological nutrient reduction tanks. The aerobic tanks convert ammonium ions into nitrate ions, and the anaerobic tanks reduce the nitrate to N_2 gas. Phosphorus that is not removed in the sludge is captured and precipitated by combining it with metals like aluminum or calcium, which enables it to settle and then join the sludge at the bottom of the settlement tank. These methods are efficient, but the remaining sludge is not easy to handle and may have contaminant metals or chemicals mixed in with the flush or other household wastewater or even industrial wastewater. In the Shenandoah Valley, some farmers have allowed sludge-spreading on pastureland. The verdict is still out on the long-term impact of the sludge.

Decentralization as a Solution

The way we handle human waste is not that different from the way we handle animal waste. Cattle feedlots, and pig and poultry houses, are centralized production facilities for animals with in-house manure handling. A wastewater treatment plant is a centralized way to treat human waste. Both systems result in the same problem: a heap of nutrients with nowhere to go. Transporting the manure to places where it can be used is cost-effective only up to a certain distance, and this distance declines as the cost of fuel rises. Any solution that relies on fossil fuels is fated to be short-term.

Gene Logsdon, Wendell Berry, David Orr, Jim Hightower, and others have suggested a partial solution that is usually rejected out of hand—that people need to move back to the farm. This is not a flippant idea. We have concentrated agricultural production in the hands of a small number of farmers as a percentage of our population. Only 1% of Americans make their living growing food. In most of Africa, the number of farmers is more than 50% of the population. The only reason this has happened in America is due to cheap, high-density energy, in the form of fossil fuels. There is as yet no viable substitute, though some are hopeful about electric tractors and other equipment.[33] As fossil fuels increase in price, either agricultural produce has to rise in cost as well, or we have to farm using less fuel. If there is reduced fossil fuel input, then human energy input must increase to replace it. Farming is not easy work. It is hard, physically demanding work. The less fuel you use, the more you have to use your brain to figure out how nature can work with you to grow successful crops. We have unfairly relegated farmers to the back of the room when it comes to intellectual endeavors, but extremely bright people farm. We need to encourage a lot more people to do so.

Manure need not be a problem if there is a correct balance between animals, people, and land. Our problem is that we have let things get way out of balance. Nature cannot correct our over-centralization. This is not to say that cities cannot exist, but it does mean that cities must shrink and must fit with their surrounding rural areas in a way that allows nutrients to cycle once again. Allowing a linear nutrient flow to continue will only lead to collapse.

Study Questions

1. Going for a walk in nearly every major city in the United States means interacting with dogs. Where there are dogs there is also dog poop. The present method of dealing with this is a stark reminder of the flying toilets of Kibera: get a plastic bag from one of the dispensers in the park, turn it inside out around your hand, then pick up the poop through the bag, tie it off, and throw it into a nearby garbage can (or not, in some cases). What would be a better way to handle the dog poop problem in the parks?

2. Every day you use water. You rise in the morning and wash your face, maybe your hands, you flush the toilet, you run water to get a drink or make coffee, and the use continues through the day. What you use eventually goes down a drain. Where does it go? Can you follow your water from its source to its ultimate destination, the sea? Where in this system do you see places ripe for change? What is the quality of water along the way?

3. Dirty water is often nutrient-rich water. How can we stop putting nutrients in the water in the first place, and how can we get them out once they are there? Find a nutrient source where the flow is presently linear, source-to-sea, and turn it into circle. How close can we get to the nutrient going back to where it started?

---

33 Electric tractors can revolutionize agriculture. https://cleantechnica.com/2020/11/13/electric-tractors-can-revolutionize-agriculture/

4. How much of our nutrient problem is related to the centralized, factory-style production of meat, dairy, and poultry products? What would an alternative system look like? How close to your current residence could this type of operation locate?

5. Whenever we talk about human waste, especially feces, there is a ick factor that arises and the conversation quickly turns to another subject. How can we talk about human manure and the need to get it back into a active part in nature's cycles?

References

Brown, A. Duncan. 2003. *Feed or Feedback: Agriculture, Population Dynamics and the State of the Planet.* Utrecht, the Netherlands: International Books.

Brown, Gabe. 2018. *Dirt to Soil: One Family's Journey into Regenerative Agriculture.* White River Junction, VT: Chelsea Green Publishing.

Brown, Lester. 1995. *Who Will Feed China?* New York: W.W. Norton.

Coleman, D. C., D. A Crossley Jr., and P. F. Hendrix, 2004. *Fundamentals of Soil Ecology.* 2nd ed. London: Elsevier/Academic Press.

Hepperly, P., D. Douds, and R. Seidel. 2006. "The Rodale Institute Farming Systems Trial 1981 to 2005: Long Term Analysis of Organic and Conventional Maize and Soybean Cropping Systems." In *Long-Term Field Experiments in Organic Farming*, edited by Joachim Raupp, Carola Pekrun, Meike Oltmanns, and Ulrich Köpke. *International Society of Organic Agriculture Research* (ISOFAR) Scientific Series 1. Verlag Dr Köster, Berlin 204:15–31.

Jenkins, Joseph. 2005. *The Humanure Handbook*, 3rd ed. Grove City, PA: Joseph Jenkins.

King, F. H., 1904. *Farmers of Forty Centuries.* Mineola, NY: Dover Publications.

Klare, Michael T. 2012. *The Race for What's Left: The Global Scramble for the World's Last Resources.* New York: Picador.

Logsdon, Gene. 1994. *The Contrary Farmer.* White River Junction, VT: Chelsea Green Publishing.

Logsdon, G., and B. Budner. 2010. *Holy Shit: Managing Manure to Save Mankind.* White River Junction, VT: Chelsea Green Publishing.

Madison, Fred, Keith Kelling, Leonard Massie, and Laura Wood Good. (n.d.). "Guidelines for Applying Manure to Cropland and Pasture in Wisconsin." Madison: University of Wisconsin—Extension. http://learningstore.uwex.edu/assets/pdfs/A3392.pdf.

Miller, Scot M., Steven C. Wofsy, Anna M. Michalak, Eric A. Kort, Arlyn E. Andrews, Sebastien C. Biraud, Edward J. Dlugokencky, Janusz Eluszkiewicz, Marc L. Fischer, Greet Janssens-Maenhout, Ben R. Miller, John B. Miller, Stephen A. Montzka, Thomas Nehrkorn, and Colm Sweeney. 2013. "Anthropogenic Emissions of Methane in the United States." *Proceedings of the National Academy of Sciences USA* 110 (50): 20018–20022. https://doi.org/10.1073/pnas.1314392110.

Montgomery, David. 2007. *Dirt: The Erosion of Civilization.* Berkeley: University of California Press.

Ohlsen, Kristin. 2014. *The Soil Will Save Us.* New York: Rodale Books.

Salatin, J. 1998. *You Can Farm: The Entrepreneur's Guide to Start & Succeed in a Farming Enterprise.* Brattleboro, VT: Echo Point Books & Media.

Sinha, Rajiv. 2009. "Earthworms Vermicompost: A Powerful Crop Nutrient over the Conventional Compost & Protective Soil Conditioner against the Destructive Chemical Fertilizers for Food Safety and Security." *American-Eurasian Journal of Agricultural and Environmental Sciences* 5 (S): 1–55.

Sinha, R. K., S. Agarwal, K. Chauhan, V. Chandran, and B. Kiranbhai. 2010. "Vermiculture Technology: Reviving the Dreams of Sir Charles Darwin for Scientific Use of Earthworms in Sustainable Development Programs." *Technology and Investment* 1:155–172. https://doi.org/10.4236/ti.2010.13019.

Smil, Vaclav. 2001. *Enriching the Earth: Fritz Haber, Carl Bosch and the Transformation of World Food Production.* Cambridge, MA: MIT Press.

Credits

Chapter 8

Rice, Records, and the Potential for Alternative Agriculture

Introduction

While no one knows the exact date of the first intentional cultivation of crops, it is quite recent in terms of the span of human history. Where it began is also a question, but a lot of people with more knowledge of this than me now think it may have started independently in many places. The patterns of cultivation developed with culture, and patterns of growing crops became culturally normative. People grew a crop in a particular way because that is what they grew up with, not because it was the only or best way to grow that crop. More recently, changes to cultivation practices took place due to the application of science, laboratory discoveries about chemistry, and replicated field trials with specific chemical inputs. This permeated much of global agriculture through the Green Revolution described in Chapter 3, "The Rise and Pending Fall of Conventional Agriculture." Yet traditional agriculture and modern conventional agriculture did not include ecological understanding in cultivation practices or the use of inputs. What could happen if this were done, whether intentionally or by accident? This chapter is the story of one crop and the successful adaptation of centuries-old cultivation practices that are derived from watching crop performance in conditions that are not culturally normal. Rice is the most widely eaten food crop on the planet, and the lessons learned may apply far beyond this one species.

The Recent History of Rice

World records attract attention. Nothing proves this more than the continued success of the *Guinness Book of World Records* and our global obsession with who is best, what is biggest, what is tallest, or how many people can do a backflip while holding hands and skiing at the same time. So we look for, pursue, and "wax eloquent" about the latest world records.

Farming is not immune to these obsessions either. The continuous pursuit of the world's largest pumpkin is a case in point. The immensity of a 2,009-pound (910-kg) pumpkin shown at a county fair in Topsfield, Massachusetts, is genuinely impressive, even if the pumpkin is inedible.[1] We keep track of more than just incredible giants. We also pay attention to yield per acre for a number of crops, continually pushing the boundaries of what can be grown on a single acre or hectare of cropland. Who grows the most corn per acre in the United States? Francis Childs of Manchester, Iowa, is one claimant at 442 bushels to the acre (27.2 metric tons per hectare).[2] There is a striking similarity among the yield kings, at least in the United States: they commonly trumpet the use of insecticides, herbicides, fungicides, and fertilizer, and news of their triumphs is accompanied by publicity and advertising by agro-chemical companies. The big exception to all the fanfare is rice.

Rice is the most widely produced grain on the planet, and unlike corn, most of it is directly consumed by people. Rice is a tropical annual grass that grows well in seasonally wet climates, probably evolving as a crop in the monsoonal climates of Southeast Asia, from Pakistan in the west, Indonesia in the south, and southern China in the east. It is now a global crop, from the tropics to warm temperate regions. More people are dependent on rice as their primary subsistence grain than any other crop, and therefore attempts to improve the yield of rice are constant. For most of history, these attempts have been local, with farmers choosing rice for seed from the best-producing plants in their own fields. The types of rice that people developed were appropriate in the context of the soils and conditions of their specific place. These varieties were traded and used in villages, eventually evolving into the myriad of cultivars recognized as varieties, or landraces, by the International Rice Research Institute (IRRI) in the Philippines.

IRRI is part of a group of food research institutions set up after World War II to research methods of improving crop production around the planet. Its parent organization, the Consultative Group for International Agricultural Research (CGIAR), was first financed by large, private, philanthropic organizations like the Rockefeller Foundation and the Ford Foundation, but soon grew, through the financing of bilateral and multilateral government agencies. The first of these groups was the International Maize and Wheat Improvement Center (Centro International Mejoramiento de Maiz y Trigo, or CIMMYT[MR]), located in

---

1   Amy Marturana, "Ron Wallace Grows the Largest Pumpkin, Breaking World Record," *Huffington Post*, October 8, 2012, http://www.huffingtonpost.com/2012/10/05/the-largest-pumpkin-world-record_n_1939922.html.

2   Matthew Wilde, "Iowa's Corn Yield Champ to Sell Equipment," *The Courier*, April 7, 2004, http://wcfcourier.com/business/local/iowa-s-corn-yield-champ-to-sell-equipment/article_0ca6a1d1-d8d1-54c5-a62c-d70792f00095.html.

Mexico, and founded and led by Norman Borlaug, the most famous and decorated plant breeder in history for his work with wheat and, later, with rice.[3]

Realignment after World War II into two main protagonist camps, the capitalists and the communists, created both fear and competition for influence and control. Though the war between the United States and the Soviet Union was, to say the least, cold, their battle over influence in key countries was very real. One of these countries was India. India became independent in 1947 and desperately wanted to develop industrially. At the same time, its population grew at a rate that exceeded its ability to produce food and manage its distribution. From the mid-1950s to the late 1960s, India suffered episodes of famine. The United States supplied grain, sometimes up to one-fifth of the entire US yield, but India's desired goal was food independence. Into this breach came the CGIAR system and Norman Borlaug.

The first thing Borlaug noticed was that India and neighboring Pakistan, in the area known as the Punjab, had the perfect conditions for growing the wheat varieties his team had developed in Mexico. These two countries were locked in tense relations that occasionally resulted in war, so conditions for agricultural research were not ideal. They lacked three things: a seed supply, fertilizer, and a credit system for the farmers so they could purchase the required inputs. Borlaug hounded the Indian government about this, and he even brought in his new seed variety secretly, without proper papers, to test in situ. Eventually the government relented and gave permission for import of the various inputs, paid for, at least in part, by substantial aid from the United States. This led to rapid success, since the Punjab was gifted with excellent farmers and good irrigation from the Himalayan-sourced rivers that crossed the region.[4] However, India is not just the Punjab; the dominant crop in the country is rice, not wheat. You can't solve the food problem in the country without focusing on the rice crop, which Borlaug subsequently did.

India was not the best country, politically speaking, to set up a research institute like the one existing in Mexico. The Philippines, a close ally of the United States and relatively stable, was much more suitable, so the CGIAR set up the IRRI at Los Baños in 1959. The team that Borlaug helped to assemble followed many the same research protocols that he

---

3   For further information on Norman Borlaug, see Chapter 3, "The Rise and Pending Fall of Conventional Agriculture."

4   It should be noted here that many references to Borlaug omit an important feature of his work: breeding the plants to respond to fertilizer and irrigation. This is probably not deliberate, but it is important now that fertilizer prices are rising, water tables are dropping, and the land on which the wheat (and later rice) is grown is depleted of organic matter and is increasing in salinity. Most articles about Borlaug are celebrations of a great plant breeder, not critiques of the Green Revolution that emphasize the downsides of boosting production with energy-intensive inputs (Mann 2018).

had pursued in Mexico. Their first task was to collect varieties of rice from around the world and grow them on the Los Baños research site. Borlaug's team recognized that rice had the same problem as wheat when it came to adding nitrogen; instead of producing more grain, plants produced more leaves and elongated stems. So the researchers began crossing different varieties, hoping to hit the right combination. It took some time, but eventually they did, finding that a short-stemmed rice variety from Japan crossed with another variety worked. This variety was dubbed IR8, and soon was shipped out for trial beyond the Philippines. It achieved massive initial success in Indonesia and India. Yields increased dramatically, and by 1974, the cycle of famine that previously dominated India had ceased. Norman Borlaug won the 1970 Nobel Peace Prize for his work. It was, by any standard, a great success, and Borlaug's work was dubbed "The Green Revolution." Yet it is not without problems and detractors. Nor does Green Revolution rice hold the world record for productivity. That story takes a different direction.

Rice began its move to becoming a domesticated crop over 10,000 years ago. It is likely that hunter-gatherer peoples of south Asia knew of the plant and collected seeds on a regular basis from ones growing naturally. Though no one really understands why or how people began settling in permanent locations and becoming farmers, that they did so independently in a number of places is a reality. The dominant domestic crop throughout the region, from the Indus Valley in Pakistan to the flat lands of the lower Yangtze River in China, was rice. It was probably domesticated independently in multiple locations, though most sources pin its origins to the valleys of the Indus, Ganges, Mekong, and Yangtze Rivers. Cultures developed around rice in multiple areas and cultivation spread beyond its native region long before Europeans began trading and exploiting the region in the 1500s.

Ecologically speaking, rice is much like wheat and other small grains. It is an annual pioneer plant with large seeds that flourish on soils exposed to sunlight. It pours much of the energy it captures into root production and growth at the outset, but it turns that energy into seed production once it produces a specific number of leaves per stem. Like all annuals, once the seed has matured, the plant dies. Humans selected specific traits when growing the plant domestically. They preferred plants with large seeds, good flavor, and good cooking qualities; plants that did not shatter in high winds or when picked, losing seed; plants that did not lodge, but stayed upright, making the seed easy to harvest; and finally, plants that thrived in local conditions. For rice, these local conditions included episodic flooding that also reduced competition with invasive weedy plants.

Though rice is grown in numerous places, the pattern of planting and cultivating the crops is similar almost everywhere the crop is found. Rice fields are usually dead level and surrounded by a bund or small dike to enable flooding. This is done even on steep hillsides, giving rise to beautiful terraced landscapes as found in the Philippines, Indonesia, and Nepal,

FIGURE 8.1   Rice fields near Higashihiroshima, just east of Hiroshima, Japan.

among others. Fields are plowed—often using water buffalo, which are much more tolerant of wet conditions than cattle—in order to create a low-permeability soil to hold water. Seeds are first sown very densely in smaller seed beds and allowed to grow for 20 to 30 days until each plant has three to five leaves. These are then carefully pricked out and transplanted to mounds in the broader field, usually with three to five seedlings per mound, with mounds about 20 cm apart. Fields are then flooded to a depth of 5 to 20 cm, depending on the variety and stage of growth, and are kept flooded until just a few weeks before harvest, when they are allowed to dry and the rice crop matures. Though variations to this pattern exist in different places, this system is so ancient and common that it can be considered normative.

Observations and Discovery in Madagascar

Somewhere between AD 300 and AD 500, a group of Malaysian people moved from Peninsular Malaysia across the Indian Ocean and landed on the island of Madagascar. As far as is known, no humans had settled the island before that time. The Malay brought their rice culture with them. They also succeeded in transforming one of the few places on the planet untouched by humans into a human-dominated agricultural area in a very short time. Madagascar is a very old landscape. It has few fresh geological features such as volcanoes or basalt flows. The soils are very old and nutrient-poor, and at that time they were covered by thick tropical vegetation. The climate on the island is not uniform. The north and east are wet tropical rainforests, while the south and west are drier with savanna woodland vegetation. Soils are best in the central highlands of the country, the mountainous backbone extending the full length of the island. Here temperatures are cooler, and the climate gentler and conducive to agriculture. The Malay immigrants thrived here, further developing their rice culture in the high country.

The Malagasy did not remain isolated. They too were caught up in the scramble for Africa of the nineteenth century, landing in the colonial net of the French. Trade links were established, and Madagascar became known for its exports of vanilla, black pepper, and litchi fruit, among other things. It also later became known negatively as the Great Red Island. This name was coined by astronauts during the early Space Shuttle flights. Looking out their windows as they circled the planet, the astronauts noted that the sea around Madagascar was colored a deep red from all the erosion of the iron-rich soils, especially on the western side of the island's mountainous backbone.

On the ground, the story was a familiar one. European influence and colonial occupation triggered a change in land-use, combined with a population explosion that spilled out from the central highlands to the more vulnerable landscapes of the island. These more recently settled lands had different soils and conditions than those highland areas, thereby requiring a different approach to agriculture that had not yet developed. Application of highland methods to soils that could not withstand cultivation led to massive land wasting, sheet erosion, gully formation, and then further expansion to lands even more vulnerable when those eroded landscapes ceased producing. Madagascar became, in a few short decades, one of the most eroded landscapes on the planet and vulnerable to cycles of hunger not seen on the island since the arrival of humans.

Around the time that Madagascar moved to independence from France, in 1960, a Jesuit priest named Henri de Laulanié arrived on the island. He had a strong interest in agriculture and proved to be a keen observer of the systems used by local farmers. From 1961 until the mid-1980s, Father Laulanié spent his time learning and making notes on the farming system and trying his own hand at growing crops, including the dominantly cultivated rice. He was concerned that the continued expansion of rice cultivation into the tropical forest and savanna areas was unsustainable and that the only answer to the problem was to increase the productivity of rice on existing farms.

As an observer, Father Laulanié noted that not everyone grew rice in the same way. While the dominant pattern was to plant rice in clumps on small mounds, a few farmers planted rice individually and claimed a higher overall yield. He tried this on his own plot at 25 × 25 cm spacing and confirmed their claim. In another place, he noticed that some farmers did not keep their rice continuously flooded, but alternated between wet and dry conditions, irrigating only when the soil began cracking. He tried this too, and found the rice doing better. He now had two innovations: wider-spaced individual seedlings and moist but not flooded conditions. This enabled him to use a Madagascar government–introduced rotating hoe in his plot. The wider spacing allowed him to weed in two directions, reducing competition with less effort. The hoe drove weed seeds and plants into the soil to rot, simultaneously providing organic matter.

At this point, Father Laulaniè and some of his students had a "fortuitous accident."[5] In 1983, preparing to plant seedlings in a field, they realized they did not have enough, so they sowed more seeds. When transplanted later, the first group of seedlings was 30 days old, while the second group had only two leaves and was just 15 days old. To the students' surprise, the smaller seedlings outgrew their larger companions in the field and produced a larger crop per plant. This prompted the growers to try transplanting all their seedlings at an earlier stage in the next season, which again worked successfully. So a fourth innovation—adapted timing—was adopted, and the System of Rice Intensification (SRI) was born.

All during this period of SRI development, the rice planted according to these innovations was fed using fertilizers. Madagascar's soils are notoriously low in nutrients, and in the tropical rainforest, areas of the country are prone to acidification upon conversion to agriculture. It was thought that chemical inputs were essential. However, in the mid-1980s the government program that was subsidizing fertilizer ended, and it was decided to try compost as an alternative. Yields of SRI rice did not drop after this change, and in some cases, they actually rose. The four innovations can be done with or without fertilizer, which is helpful since in many places fertilizer is either unavailable or unaffordable.

In the mid-1980s, Father Laulanié and his team realized they had found a set of innovations that could increase rice production quite dramatically. These are the four (or five) innovations:

1. Planting rice seedlings individually and spacing them 25 × 25 cm or wider
2. Changing irrigation patterns from continuously flooded to alternating moist and dry conditions, avoiding the anaerobic conditions of normal rice production systems

---

5   The story of Henri de Laulanié is found in "Development of the System of Rice Intensification (SRI) in Madagascar" by Norman Uphoff of the Cornell International Institute for Food and Agricultural Development (CIIFAD). See https://thenaturalfarmer.org/article/development-of-the-system-of-rice-intensification-sri-in-madagascar/.

3. Weeding in both directions using a rotary hoe developed in Madagascar
4. Transplanting seedlings much earlier, with only two leaves rather than three to five leaves
5. Using compost instead of fertilizer, or using less fertilizer depending on availability

These became the basis for the work of a new nongovernment organization (NGO) the team founded called Tefy Saina. They set up a number of demonstration farms in Madagascar and began spreading information about their techniques around the country with considerable success.

In 1994, Tefy Saina crossed paths with a team from Cornell University led by Dr. Norman Uphoff, who was working on agricultural problems around Ranomafana National Park in southeastern Madagascar. The park was newly founded to protect the rare golden bamboo lemur but was under threat from expanded agriculture in the rainforest. Soils in this area are nutrient-poor and vulnerable to acidification, making rice production nearly impossible and causing people to move into virgin forest land. Dr. Uphoff connected Tefy Saina with the project to protect the park, recognizing that increasing production of rice on land neighboring the park would reduce pressure to expand agriculture within the park's boundaries. The SRI process worked, and pressure on the park diminished. At that time,

FIGURE 8.2   Rice production using flood irrigation near Ranomafana National Park, Madagascar, in 1994.

Dr. Uphoff also headed the Cornell International Institute for Food, Agriculture and Development (CIIFAD), which works in a number of developing countries. They took the SRI techniques developed in Madagascar and spread them to Sri Lanka, Cambodia, Viet Nam, India, and elsewhere.[6]

Setting the Record

The province of Bihar in Northern India, bordering Nepal, is one of the most crowded agricultural areas on the planet, and also the poorest province in that country based on per capita income, under $250 per year.[7] On the other hand, it is blessed with good rainfall and continuously renewed soils, the result of flooding from the rivers coming out of the Himalayas in Nepal. Yields in this area seldom exceed 8 tons per hectare, and most yields are lower. CIIFAD brought SRI to this region, training farmers in the new methods with amazing success. In 2012 Sumant Kumar, who has a farm of just two hectares in Darveshpura village, produced a rice crop with a yield of 22.4 tons per hectare, breaking the previous world record set in China of 19 tons per hectare, which had used more conventional techniques and high fertilizer and other chemical inputs. Sumant Kumar used some fertilizer, but well below the normally recommended amount, and he used no pesticides or herbicides, though there was some use of a low-toxicity fungicide.[8] He was not alone in his success. Other farmers in the village, using SRI techniques, also had yields exceeding the Chinese record.[9]

Although Sumant Kumar and his neighbors used an improved variety of rice developed by IRRI, they relied on a different set of inputs than was normal for this variety. It was not a GMO variety. Dr. Vandana Shiva, an internationally renowned supporter of traditional agriculture, a critic of the Green Revolution and GMOs, and the developer of seed banks for local varieties of crops, has long held that traditional seed is not as low-yield as claimed by the Green Revolution.[10] Other factors have conspired to keep yields

---

6   The details of Cornell's CIIFAD efforts with SRI are found at http://sri.ciifad.cornell.edu/.

7   Based on data from 2009–2010 found at http://www.mapsofindia.com/maps/india/percapitaincome.htm.

8   Jonathan Latham, "The Next Green Revolution (This Time Without Fossil Fuels)." *The Solutions Journal*, 4, no. 2, June 2013 (http://thesolutionsjournal.com/node/22521).

9   Norman Uphoff, "Empowerment of Farmers through ICT," Cornell University. Draft paper for *ECOSOC Expert Group Meeting on Promoting Empowerment of People in Advancing Poverty Eradication, Social Integration, and Decent Work for All*, UN HQ, NYC, September 10–12, 2012.

10   *Monocultures of the Mind*, *Stolen Harvest*, and *Soil Not Oil* are among the many books by Vandana Shiva that address the issue of corporate injustice versus sustainable agriculture.

low—including, but not limited to, economic systems that suppress rural economies, the poor quality of land possessed by the poor, the tendency of the state to favor resource-rich farmers, and agricultural extension systems that are designed to promote corporations rather than to develop appropriate agriculture for the poor in the context of their own ecosystems. The success of SRI using the SRI methods supports the contention that it is not the genotype (genetics of the seed) that is wrong in local agriculture; rather, it is the condition of local impoverished farmers. Trials of local rice varieties using SRI techniques may show that these local varieties are competitive and that they may provide more of other needed farm inputs, like straw for water buffalo feed and thatch for use on traditional housing. When these conditions are improved, as addressed by SRI, then local farmers thrive.

This is not to say that plant breeding is not important. Ecosystems are dynamic places. Climates, conditions, diseases, pests, and plant varieties are engaged in a constant dance. Sometimes, diseases develop the ability to overcome a variety's resistance and cause dieback. Thankfully, they do not kill off all of the existing variety or varieties, and farmers take the surviving plants to grow the next year. These remaining plants have higher levels of genetic resistance to the new disease traits, and eventually the local varieties adapt, until the disease shifts and the plants have to adapt again. This dance depends upon a broad range of genotypes in the population of local varieties that contain the characteristics necessary to resist disease which are not necessarily expressed in the phenotype. The problem with Green Revolution varieties is that they were not developed locally, they are genetically narrow in terms of genotype, and they require inputs that sometimes are not easily available, including pesticides and herbicides. Therefore, they are inherently vulnerable to pests and diseases, which are easily resisted by local varieties. Local varieties are not perfect, but they do have greater genetic diversity, and they provide a broader base to maintain productivity over the long term.

This discussion brings up another question related to ecology: Did humans get the ecology of rice right when they originally designed the agricultural system that is widely dominant with rice now? The answer might be no. Rice may work in swampy areas naturally, but this does not mean that that environment is ideal for the plant. Norman Uphoff cites a 1974 article by S. S. Kar which states that rice grown in anaerobic conditions suffers root loss and subsequent retarded growth, compared with rice grown in episodically wet soil remaining aerobic (Kar et al. 1974). Essentially, the ideal conditions for rice are not continuously flooded fields, but rather the irrigation strategies developed by Tefy Saina in SRI. Looking at plants as they grow naturally may tell us a great deal about how they will grow best under cultivation. This is a lesson we are still learning.

Observing the Ecosystem

Another keen observer of human and natural systems made an important observation about rice in Japan. Masanobu Fukuoka was a young plant pathologist in a PhD program in Japan when a life-threatening bout of pneumonia made him rethink his life. He turned away from mainstream agriculture and started "doing nothing" (Fukuoka 1978). This is not meant to be a recipe for laziness; rather it was a recognition that humans did not necessarily know best what to do. By suppressing the urge to think that humanity knows best and by looking instead to natural systems for understanding, Fukuoka turned himself into a keen thinker and developer of an amazing agricultural system relevant to his island in southern Japan.

While working in a government agricultural office during World War II, as a wartime assignment, Fukuoka was walking home and spotted a rice plant growing in a ditch downstream from a conventional rice field. The rice was not in the water, but at the side of the ditch. Perhaps it was a stray seed washed out of the field by rains and deposited high on the ditch bank as the water receded. He noted that the plant was very healthy. It was stronger and had more tillers than the rice in the adjacent field. It received no inputs, no irrigation other than rainfall and ditch flow, yet it thrived. So what had happened? This gave Fukuoka an idea. What if he could plant a field not by transplanting rice the way all farmers do, but by simply broadcasting the seed and letting nature do the work of supplying water and nutrients? He tried this, and of course it failed miserably.

Fukuoka then rethought the problem of the ditch-side rice. The problem was with birds. Birds could see his seed and gobble it before it had a chance to grow. The ditch rice must have been covered in order to prevent the birds seeing the seed. So he set about covering his seed and found that a mixture of clay and humus, combined with a light spray of water, made a paste into which he rolled the seed in order to form a coated seed ball. When he broadcast this coated seed and let the field go, it germinated well, but the field did not yield well because of weed competition and a lack of nutrients. So he rethought this process further.

His next insight was that the ditch-side rice plant did have nutrients in the occasional excess water from storm flow, and it was free from competition because the road and ditch ecosystem kept weeds down. Fukuoka realized that his field lacked organic material because the field was frequently burned before the rice was planted. So he did not burn the field, instead letting the straw from the barley grown as a winter crop lie in the fields. Ducks were allowed to patrol the field, eating the broadleaf weeds that they prefer to rice and gobbling down any slugs and insect larvae they saw in the field. As Fukuoka developed his system, the rice yields improved while labor requirements dropped. He moved closer to his ideal of "do-nothing" agriculture. Yet his insights were not finished.

Rice and barley straw can protect soil, restrict weed growth, and improve organic matter in the soil, but they cannot be laid down parallel to one another. When they are laid down in neat rows, they suppress the growth of the rice and the subsequent barley crop. Better results occur when they are scattered randomly and when some of the straw stalks are upright rather than laid down evenly with the soil. This helps the stalks to last longer, restricting broadleaf weed growth, while benefiting the grasses. The straw also provides a home for beneficial arthropods. This lesson came when there was an outbreak in Japan of the brown leafhopper insect. This pest has the ability to suck juices from rice plant stems, killing bits of the plant. If enough leafhoppers are present in sufficient numbers, they can kill the plant outright. Fukuoka's neighbors sprayed their fields to stem the outbreak, and they begged him to do the same. He refused and just waited. When the hoppers came, Fukuoka experienced an outbreak of his own: the rapid growth and reproduction of spiders in his ecologically friendly rice field. The leafhoppers did some damage, but it was limited and did not affect yield. Instead, the spiders reproduced better than ever. This became the basis for Fukuoka's book called *The One-Straw Revolution*, which influenced an entire generation of alternative farmers from Bill Mollison to Roland Bunch and beyond (Korn 2015).

The Fukuoka system and SRI provide two excellent examples of developing agriculture using lessons from the direct observation of local ecosystems and a willingness to experiment to get the system working correctly. Things do not always work well the first time. When we observe natural systems and make adjustments related to soil, water, pests, and weeds, high-productivity and low-labor systems emerge that are appropriate to the places where they are developed. Just as local ecosystems are diverse, local agricultural systems will ultimately be diverse as well. Agroecology, the study of ecological interactions that benefit agricultural systems, is establishing itself as a mechanism for developing new methods of crop production specific to place. The high degree of variation around the planet requires that we seek agricultural systems that reflect this diversity. Our present tendency to use a one-size-fits-all mechanization and a chemically dominated approach with a limited number of varieties endangers both the agricultural system and human health. True reform in agriculture will develop based on an agroecology of place—which, at present, is still in its infancy.

Study Questions

1. Every crop is rooted in a place, and the place has particular characteristics of soil, climate, surrounding ecosystem, and human impact. If you were to improve a crop in relation to a particular place, how would you go about doing that? What are the variables you would need to consider?

2. What do you want from a plant? Most of the time that answer is yield, something that you eat. But is there more than that? How were crops used historically, beyond just food for humans? What are the needs we have that are met through growing plants?

What are the needs of plants that humans can provide? Our crop plants have evolved in relationship with us, and our diet has evolved in relationship with the plants.

3. What were the factors that made Father Laulanié and his team successful observers of rice? What are the lessons for us if we are to embark on a similar process? How does Masanobu Fukuoka help us in this effort?

4. How can these lessons from Tefy Saina and Fukuoka penetrate the mindset of conventional agriculture in the US? Where do you think these lessons will have an impact first? How might they spread?

References

Fukuoka, Masanobu. 1978. *The One-Straw Revolution: An Introduction to Natural Farming*. Emmaus, PA: Rodale Press.

Kar, S., S. Varade, T. Subramanyam, and B. P. Ghildyal. 1974. "Nature and Growth Pattern of Rice Root System under Submerged and Unsaturated Conditions." *Il Riso* (Italy) 23:173–179.

Korn, Larry. 2015. *One-Straw Revolutionary: The Philosophy and Work of Masanobu Fukuoka*. White River Junction, VT: Chelsea Green Publishing.

Mann, Charles. 2018. *The Wizard and the Prophet: Two Remarkable Scientists and Their Dueling Visions to Shape Tomorrow's World*. New York: Vintage Books.

Chapter 9

Why Say No to Genetically Modified Organisms?

Introduction

Genetically modified organisms, or GMOs, have risen to front and center of debates around agriculture, whether it be the insertion of genes from bacteria into plants, the transfer of genes from one plant to another, or even the manipulation of genes in people to provide resistance to disease. There is a lack of debate about the ethics involved. It is good to remember that this is not the plant-breeding work of scientists like Norman Borlaug, which involved finding genes from within the existing genome of a crop species. Instead, this involves moving genes from one species to another, completely different one. Like many technologies, it is a tool that cuts both ways. There is tremendous potential to blunt the impact of plant diseases. At the same time, it has allowed the use of toxic herbicides and other chemicals that normally would kill a plant. What we do about this technology in the long run is still under acrimonious debate.

The Case of Bovine Growth Hormone

Back in 1986, I started a graduate program at Cornell University in the Department of Natural Resources. We were a small department—no huge grants were coming in for large scale research—but plenty of interesting things were going on, and many debates raged around campus that had environmental ramifications. We were not idle.

The first debate I bumped into, quite by accident, involved the Animal Science Department and the School of Veterinary Medicine. The issue was productivity of dairy cattle. In my youth in Washington state, I had frequent contact with dairy farmers, since my uncle owned and operated a milk-processing plant in Seattle and my family co-owned a piece of land in the Columbia Basin irrigation project that grew alfalfa hay for dairies on the western side of the mountains. Back in the 1960s, a good cow produced 40–60 pounds of milk a day and could go through 10 lactations in her productive lifetime.

This figure changed in the 1970s through techniques like artificial insemination from improved, high-quality bulls and through the increased feeding of grains and silage. Animals spent correspondingly less time in the pastures, and milk production increased to herd averages of 70 pounds per animal, with some of the best cows going over 100 pounds with the new, three-times-a-day milking regime. Small herds still existed, but the herd size on farms grew through time as well. The family farm was pushed by science, corporations, and extension agencies to become bigger and more productive or to get out of the business. At the same time, the number of lactations per productive cow was dropping. It seemed that the increase in daily milk production had an adverse effect on lifetime milk production, but the hard-boiled agricultural economics of the time favored faster turnover of animals to promote higher daily yield.

Then the bovine growth hormone (BGH) came on the scene. BGH, or bovine somato-trophin (bST), was identified as being able to increase milk production in cows. The two acronyms were used by the two sides in the argument: BGH was the choice of the anti-use party, common among students in the Department of Veterinary Medicine; and bST was the choice of those who favored its use in milk production, mostly in the Department of Animal Science. The hormone bST was developed following the pattern used for insulin in the 1970s. The genetic code for insulin is relatively short and simple. When the insulin code was found, the gene was isolated and cut from DNA and then placed in *Escherichia coli* bacteria, a process called recombinant DNA technology. Human insulin extracted from the bacterial soup could replace the pig-produced hormone in the treatment of diabetes. This success prolonged the life of people with diabetes as it helped them manage their blood sugar much more accurately. The compound bST is similar, and its code was isolated from cattle. When bST was placed in *E coli* bacteria, it could be extracted and used on cows. It had the desired effect, which was to help slow-growing cows come into lactation sooner, but it also prolonged and increased milk production during the lactation cycle.[1] Farmers usually started using bST after the first two months of milking, when the cow's milk production begins to drop—as it naturally does when calves begin eating grass. Holstein cattle became efficient milk-producing machines. Since this was the goal of breeders in the Department of Animal Science, they started intensive studies on the hormone and its use in dairies, pushing for its adoption by agricultural agencies.

---

1   US FDA. Bovine Somatotropin (bST). https://www.fda.gov/animal-veterinary/product-safety-information/bovine-somatotropin-bst#:~:text=Bovine%20somatotropin%20(bST)%2C%20also,somatotropin%20naturally%20produced%20in%20cattle.

The BGH crowd was not enthralled by use of the hormone. They were concerned for the health of the cows. Already the genetic and feeding regimes in modern dairying had shortened the life of the cows, increasing the chances of mastitis infections and other maladies. They felt that the additional stress on the animals would further decrease the animals' quality of life and also increase stress on the dairy farmers managing the animals. The controversy over the use of this hormone did not abate for two decades.

The company that originally developed bST was bought out in the early 1990s by an increasingly aggressive company named Monsanto. Monsanto had deep pockets, a strong team of research scientists, and an even stronger team of lawyers. In fact, in the 1990s Monsanto became the big, bad wolf of anything having to do with genetic engineering, which is the process of moving genetic material from one organism to another. This company sits at the center of the story about genetically modified organisms, or GMOs. The story of bST/BGH is a subset of the larger story, and the BGH saga quieted in 2009. By then, Monsanto had tired of the continual attacks on its product and sold it to Eli Lilly and Company. The number of farmers using bST declined because of the controversy, and though it is still used in some places, many dairies and milk processors around the country, such as Stonyfield Farm, refuse to accept milk from producers who use it. But the GMO controversy, a broader issue than dairy, still sits front and center.

Transferring Genes to Crops

The most confusing thing about the GMO debate is trying to make clear exactly what a GMO is and is not. Plant breeding, as done by Norman Borlaug and the global cast of plant breeders, is not genetic engineering and plant breeders do not produce GMOs as a product. They specialize in crossing varieties of a single species of plant to isolate traits that will increase productivity. So, for example, an apple that is resistant to cedar apple rust will be crossed with a good-tasting variety that lacks such a resistance, with the goal of combining the good taste and the rust resistance in one variety. Apples may be a bad choice for an example, because they are notoriously fickle when it comes to breeding, but this is the thinking process. Genetic engineering, however, is different. Here a scientist finds a trait in one species that is desirable—say, resistance to papaya ringspot virus, which could come from another plant, an algae, or even a bacteria—and takes that genetic sequence from that species and puts it into a papaya. Presto!—the grower now has a genetically modified papaya that is resistant to ringspot virus. The process avoids the fickle nature of plant breeding, and though the process is time-consuming and expensive, it is also effective (Luis 1997).[2]

Monsanto has two highly successful GMO genes that it has transferred to a number of high-profile crops like corn, soybeans, cotton, canola, and alfalfa. The first gene comes from bacteria called *Bacillus thuringiensis,* or Bt for short. Bt bacteria are natural in the environment, and they produce a toxin that kills Lepidoptera larva (the larva of butterflies and moths). Back in the 1990s, this bacterium was sprayed from airplanes above East Coast oak–hickory forests to kill the larva of the gypsy moth, an invasive insect pest with no natural predators in North America. The bacteria worked very well for this task. Organic farmers have long used it in powder form to kill such things as the cabbage worm, a moth larva quite fond of all *Brassica* species. It is not effective against borer-type worms as topically applied, because the bacteria cannot reach the hidden larva of the corn stem borer and similar insect larva. A company that Monsanto eventually bought isolated the gene of the Bt toxin and inserted it into corn, transferring the production of the toxin into the plant itself, thus reducing the necessity of spraying the crops with insecticides (Bessin n.d.).[3] This GMO became available to farmers in 1996. While the transferred gene has proven effective at reducing the corn rootworm and stem borer problems, it is not without controversy and its long-term effectiveness is questionable.

Monsanto was first a chemical company. One of its antecedents that it would like to forget is that it made the chemical Agent Orange for the Vietnam War. Agent Orange is really not one chemical, but a combination of 2,4 D and 2,4,5 T, both herbicides, used to defoliate forests and expose the Viet Cong guerillas hiding among the vegetation. In 1969, a third unintentional component was found in 2,4,5 T: dioxin, one of the most toxic chemicals ever produced.[4] After the war, Monsanto looked for other products and discovered and patented a novel chemical called glyphosate, or N-(Phosphonomethyl)glycine. When this chemical is dissolved in a solution as a salt with isopropylamine, water, and a surfactant called polyoxyethalene-alkylamine, it is able to penetrate the leaves of plants. It is packaged as Roundup®.[5] By the standards of chemical applicants, glyphosate has a low number of known side effects, though some question the wisdom of using the chemical

---

2   Pathogen-derived resistance provides papaya with effective protection against papaya ringspot virus. June 1997. http://link.springer.com/article/10.1023/A:1009614508659#page-1

3   http://www2.ca.uky.edu/entomology/entfacts/ef130.asp

4   https://www.aspeninstitute.org/programs/agent-orange-in-vietnam-program/what-is-agent-orange/#:~:text=Agent%20Orange%20was%20a%20herbicide,dangerous%20chemical%20contaminant%20called%20dioxin.&text=As%20many%20U.S.Vietnam%2Dera,birth%20defects%20and%20other%20disabilities.

5   https://en.wikipedia.org/wiki/Glyphosate

repeatedly on the same piece of land. It does bind with soil particles and is essentially immobile in soil. It is not absorbed by the roots of plants, but only through the leaves. This process blocks an enzyme called EPSP synthase, preventing the plant from assembling proteins thereby killing it.[6]

The problem with Roundup, unlike atrazine or many other herbicides, is that it kills all plants. Spraying it on a crop after the young plants have emerged from the ground would kill them. So, not long after the chemical was introduced in 1974, people in Monsanto began looking for a way to make certain plants resistant to the herbicide. They did not find natural resistance in plants, but they did find natural resistance in bacteria. (The claim that glyphosate does not kill other organisms is contradicted by this bacterial connection; many types of bacteria are killed by the chemical or its breakdown products, as is stated in Monsanto's own literature.) During tests in Los Angeles where they attempted to kill weeds in waste ponds, scientists found a bacteria strain that was highly resistant to the herbicide. The trick was to find the gene that was responsible for this resistance and insert the gene into a crop. They attempted this but lacked the technology to get the gene into a crop.

Three companies teamed up to figure this out: Asgrow® was a major soybean seed company; Agracetus had developed a gene gun capable of putting genes into the nucleus of a plant cell; and Monsanto had the glyphosate-resistant gene and the financial ability to put the three things together. Monsanto eventually bought out Agracetus. The company worked on the gene insertion for three years, from 1989 to 1992, but development was slow and Monsanto was losing money. In stepped Pioneer Seed Company (founded by Henry Wallace), which made a one-time payment to Monsanto for the right to use the genetically engineered seed in perpetuity. Monsanto's gain was that the notice "Roundup Ready" was placed on all the seed packages. This money enabled Monsanto to complete the gene insertion in soybeans, and they were finally ready for farm distribution in 1996. Asgrow made a deal with Monsanto to sell seed that prevented farmers planting seed from their own Roundup Ready crops. Monsanto made its money by charging every farmer a technology fee of $5.00 per acre.

---

6   Glyphosate was not regarded as toxic or a carcinogen until recently. The company Monsanto, now owned by Bayer, the German chemical and seed giant, has lost three lawsuits to people claiming their cancers were caused by Roundup. Which specific chemical in the formula is responsible is not known. There are well over 1,000 other cases regarding the chemical, and Bayer is suffering a strong case of buyer's remorse. See Kurt Cobb, "Bayer Suffering Buyer's Remorse for Monsanto Acquisition," *Resilience*, December 2, 2018, https://www.resilience.org/stories/2018-12-02/bayer-suffering-buyers-remorse-for-monsanto-acquisition/. Another source relevant to this discussion is, https://geneticliteracyproject.org/2019/02/12/deep-dive-into-the-science-and-history-of-monsantos-glyphosate-based-weed-killer/

This fee later grew to $6.50 per acre.[7] Other crops soon followed: in 1997, Canola™ and cotton; in 1998, Pioneer® corn; in 2005, sugar beets and alfalfa.[8]

Monsanto makes considerable money from its technology fee. By 2012, over 420 million acres of GMO crops were planted worldwide from all sources. This provides $2.73 billion of income at the $6.50 per acre fee. The total value of the market for biotech seeds and fees is over $14 billion, or about 23% of the global seed market.[9] In 2012, Monsanto-provided seeds were sown on 282 million of these acres, giving the company a 67% share of the market.[10] Monsanto jealously guards this territory, policing the farmers who buy the seed to make sure that no one replants the crops from the farm-grown crop. The policing came to a head with the prosecution, or some would say persecution, of Percy Schmeiser, a long-time Canadian Canola farmer from Saskatchewan. Mr. Schmeiser sprayed Roundup around some poles on the edge of his property, and some drifted onto his Canola crop. He noted that the plants did not die. There had been a windstorm on the day when his neighbor had used Roundup Ready seed for the first time, so Schmeiser believed that the seed had blown into his field from an open-bed truck. He and an employee then sprayed three acres with Roundup and found that a number of plants survived. They harvested this portion of the crop separately and then planted it on 420 hectares the next year, in 1998. Replanting the seed was his mistake.

Monsanto actually acknowledged that Schmeiser did not buy or intentionally plant any of the patented seed on his property in 1997, nor had he signed a contract with the company. Monsanto went after him for bulking the seed and planting it in 1998, an action that violates their patent rights. Schmeiser did not argue that point; rather, he argued that seed grown by the farmer, from plant material not purchased by the farmer, but rather continuously grown by the farmer, was not subject to patent obligations. He did not deliberately plant the original seed, but it is his right to do so after it had grown on his land. Monsanto countered that he had known the deals that his neighbors made in purchasing the seed and he should not have violated the patent in this way. In 2004, the Canadian Court in Saskatchewan, in a 5–4 decision, ruled in favor of Monsanto. Monsanto

---

7   Information in this paragraph comes from SourceWatch.org: History of Roundup Ready Crops. http://www.sourcewatch.org/index.php/History_of_Roundup_Ready_Crops

8   Pioneer is no longer an independent company, it was bought out by DuPont, like Monsanto a chemical company.

9   http://www.isaaa.org/resources/publications/pocketk/16/

10 The web is filled with information on this case, including documents from the Canadian Supreme Court. Perhaps the most accessible source on Percy Schmeiser and his case is the Wikipedia page: https://en.wikipedia.org/wiki/Percy_Schmeiser

publicized this on its own website.[11] However, the case did not end there. Schmeiser took the case from the Provincial Court to the National Court, where in 2009 he won, and Monsanto was forced to clean up its contamination of Schmeiser's property. While it is true that Monsanto did have a right to complain about Schmeiser's unauthorized use of the seeds, Schmeiser also had a right to complain about Monsanto's contamination of the genetic stock he had developed during his years of farming. After all, the genetics of Monsanto's seed were not developed after long years of farming on a particular soil in a specific climate. They were determined in a lab with the successful shooting of a gene into a variety that Monsanto owned from an entirely different ecosystem. So who is really "right" in the long term?

The Problem of Gene Control

Monsanto now faces another problem that is far more daunting to them and to the planet than Percy Schmeiser. The whole intent of Bt corn or Roundup Ready soybeans is to give the crop an advantage in relation to pests, whether a stem borer or a weed. However, many geneticists recognize that any genetic advantage given to a crop over a pest will eventually be matched by the pest's ability to adapt to this new reality. This is simply the first law of ecological bloody-mindedness rearing its head again. The unintended consequence of developing a Roundup Ready soybean is that eventually we will get a Roundup Ready weed; such weeds have shown up with a vengeance in the American Southeast and have since spread toward the Midwest and the North. The biggest problem is giant pigweed, a thick-stemmed monster that, if not removed early in its growth, becomes a major headache at harvest time by plugging combines and damaging equipment. The largest plants require hand removal—not a pleasant prospect in one-square-mile fields. An irony in this situation is that giant pigweed is actually a species of amaranth with edible leaves. Other members of this very adaptable and resilient plant genus produce edible seeds, which can be ground and used as flour, popped like popcorn, or simply cooked like quinoa.[12] You can easily purchase similar seed from companies like Johnny's Selected Seeds. So far, Roundup-resistance is documented in 15 common weed species, and the list is likely to expand. For more about the consequences of this gene insertion practice, see the text box entitled "The Transfer of Inserted Genetics from One Species to Another."

---

11 Most of the Monsanto based information on this case available on the web in 2013 has disappeared.

12 Willem Malten, "Rethinking a Weed: The Truth about Amaranth," *Our World*, November 10, 2010, http://ourworld.unu.edu/en/rethinking-a-weed-the-truth-about-amaranth/.

Box 9.1 The Transfer of Inserted Genetics from One Species to Another

A trait like resistance to glyphosate was originally not found in plants. It came from bacteria, and the excised genes were inserted into the crop using a variety of insertion technologies. The latest and most effective of these is called CRISPR (for "clustered regularly interspaced short palindromic repeats"), which I will not describe in this text. How does a trait move from the crop to a weed, since no one is deliberately inserting these novel genes into nontarget species? The answer is perhaps more complex than the one I give here, but it is worth attempting in order to understand the process.

Justus von Liebig (introduced in Chapter 3) sent most of the agricultural world off on a false tangent about nutrients. His idea was that most nutrient compounds, like nitrate and phosphate, or elements, like calcium, magnesium, and potassium come into the plant in the form of inorganic salts. These are the end result of the decomposition process in soils, where bacteria and fungi break down the cells of organisms to their basic components. Plant roots then absorb these salts and reincorporate them into living tissues. However, this hypothesis has not proven true. A series of scholars, many of them from Liebig's home country of Germany, had a different take (Pommeresche 2019). They say that plant roots, especially the cells in the tiny root hairs, are capable of endocytosis, the ability of a cell to surround large molecular structures or even bacterial cells and bring them to the cellular organelles for processing (see Figure 1.12). These molecules come in all forms: carbohydrates, fatty acids, proteins, enzymes, RNA, and DNA. These would then get broken down for energy, or broken into their component parts and used to promote the growth of the plant—never really becoming salts, which are often toxic, inside the cell.

DNA is the main center of the genetic code of all organisms. The extremely long chains of codes that guide the formation of cell and organism structures are all made of up of four nitrogenous bases—adenine, cytosine, guanine, and thymine—and all are connected in sequence by deoxyribose and phosphate bridges. In most cases, cells break these compounds apart and then sequence them for the plant's growth. However, evolution is both opportunistic and pragmatic. We don't fully understand its methods, but mutations do occur, and mutations that lead to reproductive success enter the gene pool on a more or less permanent basis. A trait like glyphosate resistance is in this genetic code. If the gene is intact when it is transferred by a bacteria into the root hairs of a giant pigweed via endocytosis, or perhaps it's a mycorrhizal fungi and it gets incorporated into the genetic code of the plants, leading to the plant's successful resistance to glyphosate, then there is a natural selection success story. It is a long shot, probably less than one in a billion—but it does not take much to have a primary succession annual plant's population take an unexpected turn.

How have Monsanto and other seed companies responded to the weeds' new resistance? Basically, they have upped the ante in this chemical warfare; now they want to market plants that are resistant to 2,4 D (and they are already marketing a dangerous, drifting herbicide called dicamba). Unfortunately, this herbicide is more toxic, affecting humans, other mammals, birds, and reptiles. People in Vietnam and the American soldiers who returned from that war are still suffering from its use. Adding this chemical to the agricultural arsenal (the warfare analogy is entirely apt) makes farming more dangerous for farmers and perhaps for consumers and certainly to wildlife.

Roundup causes another problem as well. This involves the iconic monarch butterfly. This creature defies logic in that it migrates from Canada to Mexico and back in an annual trek that involves multiple generations. The insect that flies north is not the one that starts back south, and that southern traveler is not the one arriving in the pine forest in the central Mexican highlands. Along the way, migrating monarchs that stop and lay eggs on their favorite food species, the milkweed genus, become larvae, pupate, and emerge as the next generation of monarchs. The problem is that Roundup kills off the milkweed. Since farmers are growing corn and soybeans on 90% of the land in the Midwest, especially Iowa and surrounding states, and most of these are now Roundup Ready crops, the farmers blanket-spray the herbicide, killing off milkweed in ditches, road medians, and even small patches of unused land where the butterfly could find food. Thus, the annual migration to Mexico has shrunk to historic lows with a majority of losses in the largest migration route for the butterflies.

Nor is Roundup-Ready the only GMO in trouble. Resistance to Bt has appeared in the western corn rootworm. This internal GMO insecticide was quite effective at inhibiting damage from the bug for 15 years, just about the amount of time entomologists had predicted it would be, when the GMO seeds were introduced. Now it is losing its punch and farmers are spreading more insecticides again (Gassman et al. 2011). Other insects are sure to follow suit. How long will farmers put up with paying higher prices for seed and paying a technology fee to a corporation whose product no longer functions as advertised?

The Bt gene, at one point, was implicated in the killing of monarch butterflies as well. Pollen from Bt corn has a tendency to fly long distances. The sticky and hairy leaves of some milkweed species catch this pollen, and then larvae of monarchs eat the leaves. Studies at Cornell University showed that this pollen could kill the butterfly larvae, but subsequent research showed that this effect was minimal as encountered in the field. But another insect, far less charismatic or known, is more vulnerable. This is the net-spinning caddisfly, whose larvae attach themselves to rocks in streams, especially on riffles, areas where water runs over cobbles. These macroinvertebrates spin a net and send it into the water to collect small particles of plant debris, including pollen. Scientists at Iowa State University found that caddisfly death during the pollen season on streams near Roundup-Ready cornfields was significant (Rosi-Marshall et al. 2007).

Even though the problems of resistance are major and could doom the GMOs concerned, underneath this problem lies an even larger concern, one involving an evolutionary times-cale. All crops that humans grow are derived from natural systems. Humans selected the crops for certain key characteristics like flavor, nonshattering seed to ease collection, non-lodging stalks so rot is not a problem, and the ability to thrive on a particular soil or in particular moisture conditions. A study done by Arnoud Budelman along the Tana River in Kenya in the early 1980s found 33 varieties of rice grown in the fields of the Pokomo people. Each type had particular characteristics in relation to soil conditions and the depth of the floods in the river. These varieties undoubtedly came originally from Asia but evolved in the conditions of the Tana River delta (Budelman and Eisses 1983). Vandana Shiva (1993) documented the same phenomenon in India, but there the wider range of soils and climate conditions has produced over seven thousand known varieties and possibly many more. Dr. Ronald Coffman of Cornell University and the International Rice Research Institute had information on 33,000 varieties of rice available to IRRI for their research.[13] No crop is a single entity. It may crossbreed widely with varieties globally, but each variety is unique to a place and a set of conditions.

Monsanto (now merged with Bayer) and its competitors like Pioneer (DuPont), Syngenta (now ChinaChem), are in the business of making money through the selling of seed and associated agrochemical inputs. These inputs include things like fertilizers, insecticides, herbicides, and fungicides. Like Norman Borlaug, who bred wheat and rice to respond to fertilizer, they engineer their crops to respond to the inputs that they sell. They do not have the capacity for their seed to develop over time in specific locations and contexts. They ignore the ecology of place. Thus, over time, with more and more energy poured into the development of crops bred to require inputs, the crop's genetic diversity drops, and its resilience in many locations is diminished. Perhaps there will no longer be an ability to find a gene that resists Ug99 if the traditional and local varieties are not grown but are instead replaced by a GMO or Green Revolution wheat.[14] The unintended consequence of lowered genetic diversity due to the centralization of corporate genetic control could eventually result in

13   Personal communication from Ronald Coffman, Cornell University, 1989.
14   See the subsection on Genetic Diversity in Chapter 1, "Ecology: The Language of the Planet," in this volume.

the complete loss of the crop, unless we cease pouring our energies into that system and reawaken an awareness of the need for genetic diversity.

The biotech industry likes to counter the argument of varietal narrowing and its own obsession with profits with the story of Golden Rice. This rice was developed to solve a specific human problem: the lack of vitamin A in the diets of the poor in places like Indonesia and the Philippines, which are rice-growing societies. Rice does not produce vitamin A or its precursors like β-carotene. Two scientists identified this as a problem: Ingo Potrkus, formerly of ETH Zurich, and Peter Beyer of the University of Freiburg. They found that if researchers take two genes from other plants and insert them into rice, the pathway that turns off the production of the β-carotene is blocked and the plant will produce β-carotene in its seeds, giving the rice a golden color. An excellent website, http://www.goldenrice.org/, describes both the problem its team is are addressing and the means to reach their ends. They state very clearly that there will be no restrictions on replanting this rice and no technology fees attached to the crop. It is all very altruistic and humanitarian in its motives and agenda. Yet the ecological and environmental assumptions made by the project lack field reality. The proponents of golden rice addressed the symptom of a problem without addressing the problem itself.

In Chapter 3, "The Rise and Pending Fall of Conventional Agriculture," the work of Dr. Norman Borlaug, who developed "green revolution" varieties, was described. These varieties were not developed in the context of the places where they were eventually to be grown; they were developed at international research stations, pulling different varieties together from around the planet to maximize production in response to inputs like fertilizer. It worked. Production spread and the food crisis was temporarily abated. But even Dr. Borlaug admitted during his Nobel Prize acceptance speech that this work was not sufficient to solve the problem over the long term, because his solution does not deal with the increasing population in the affected countries. These rice varieties are dependent not only on fertilizer, but also on inputs, precise irrigation, application of herbicides or labor-intensive weeding, and application of pesticides to fight insects like the brown leafhopper. The use of herbicides is especially problematic, because they are used to spray fields to kill broadleaf (dicots) weeds. Such herbicides also killed the green leafy vegetables (dicots) growing on the rice bunds— vegetables that provided many of the nutrients that are now deficient in local diets. Simply inserting a gene to make rice golden does not address the larger problems of diet diversity, overpopulation, soil depletion, and other factors. It is a "monoculture of the mind" approach: attempting to find a simple solution to an extremely complex problem. The green revolution and the GMO thinking neglects the first law of ecological bloody-mindedness, which states that the negative effects of any intervention often show up later than the positive effects and potentially overwhelm them. When we ignore ecology and evolution, we do so at our own peril.

Mutualism Theory and the Ecology of Place

Organisms evolve over time in a particular place in conjunction with communities of other organisms dwelling both above and below ground. Mutualisms are a regular feature of these systems. Crops therefore achieve their greatest health, highest nutritional content, and highest yield when grown in systems that best reflect their natural habitat and their association with organisms that are native to a particular place. It is only through the deliberate selection of parent stock growing in a particular location and community context over a long period of time that crops achieve their maximum potential. Geneticists call this process the development of landraces. It is how humans developed the wide variety of crops and animal breeds that dominated agriculture until the twentieth century.

Consider cattle again. Today we basically have a vision of a black and white cow grazing in some bucolic field, providing us with milk (or advertising for a fast-food chain.) The Holstein name comes from the Holstein region of Germany, along its northwest coast between Denmark and the Netherlands. The Holstein is actually a nineteenth-century cross with another breed called the Friesian, named after the northern region of the Netherlands and the major milk breed of the Schleswig-Holstein area. These were, at one time, local breeds.[15] There are many others. Two other dairy cattle, the Guernsey and the Jersey, are named after islands that are off the coast of France but governed by England. Jersey cows are especially known for their milk, with high butterfat content. The Brown Swiss is yet another breed that dominates the milking parlors of Switzerland. These breeds and many others, now lesser-known or gone, were all developed in particular climates depending on different combinations of pasture plants, different soils, and even different management practices. Through long periods of interaction with farmers, these breeds became emblematic of an ecology of place. The Holstein we know is no longer a breed of a place; it is a breed designed to maximize yield anywhere it is placed. Its genetics are no longer locally controlled, but selected from catalogs of breeding companies based on the milk yield of the offspring of selected bulls.

Corporate attempts to bypass this long-term, locally developed approach will eventually produce animals that succumb to unanticipated disease or pests, or that become chronic underachievers if they do not receive energy-intensive outside inputs. This is what we see in our agriculture today. The systems we have in place depend upon the use of chemicals, mechanical interventions, and above all, high inputs of energy in the form of fossil fuels. If the supply of energy dries up, this type of agriculture will fail. If we keep insisting that this is the only type of agriculture that will feed the planet, the resulting collapse will be catastrophic. So a different way is required.

---

15   Personal communication from Dr. Arnoud Budelman.

Our starting point for this new agriculture is not entirely new. On a small scale, more and more people are doing it. Over time, on small farms, people are beginning to develop new landraces appropriate to the conditions of their local ecosystem. Daniel Salatin, son of Joel Salatin of Polyface Farm, has developed a landrace of rabbits. They are unique to the farm. It took time, a willingness to accept risk, and yes, the death of many rabbits, before a healthy breeding stock emerged. Today the beautiful, light brown meat-producers thrive at Polyface with very few problems.[16] The importance of these local breeds is now widely recognized. It is easy to find information on breeds of chickens, ducks, pigs, and cattle all now used on small farms by farmers who are rediscovering old ways and blending them with more recently gained knowledge of genetics, pasture management, no-till farming with cover crops, and ecology.

Our crop plants are now developed in the context of a mechanized, chemically doused, and genetically narrow environment. The new agriculture will develop in an entirely different environment, where soil and the soil ecosystem are enhanced by management that encourages subsurface diversity. This involves a rethinking of our above-the-surface actions. We need to reimagine farming as an ecological activity involving numerous plant partnerships. Instead of thinking that we maximize yield through exclusion to produce one product, we need to think of maximizing health through the inclusion of multiple products, including some to feed the soil, some to attract beneficial partners for the crops, and some to feed us. Kristin Ohlson's book *The Soil Will Save Us* documents efforts to do exactly this. She highlights efforts by farmers in the United States, Australia, and Zimbabwe who think first about the soil and find that their productivity rises with diversity on the surface and a healthy ecosystem underground (Ohlson 2014). Plants that thrive in this environment become the seed sources for the farm. Over time, farmers develop their own landraces of plants that are appropriate to their climate, their soils, and the nuances of their management style. Instead of genetics yielding a narrower product of corporate control, it becomes a local product of ecological health. This does not happen all at once, but if given time, a healthy agriculture evolves in an ecology of place.

Study Questions

1. Know your food. Where does your food come from? Is it genetically modified in any way? Does your dairy say its products are hormone-free, or do they say nothing if you ask the question? You are almost certainly eating a GMO if your processed food

---

16   Personal communication from Daniel Salatin, 2013.

product has "high fructose corn syrup" in the list of ingredients. How many of these do you have in your cupboard?

2. Recently the Monsanto Corporation, now owned by Bayer of Germany, has lost a number of suits related to cancers blamed on its glyphosate products. While they claim that glyphosate is not the cause, the courts disagree, saying that the preponderance of the evidence indicates that Roundup is to blame. Now this is not to say that the GMO food we eat is carcinogenic, but how much glyphosate residue is in our food? Is there a way that a consumer can find out? How should we, as consumers, respond to this dilemma?

3. The alternative to GMOs is non-GMO varieties of crops. How available are these in your area? Does your grocery store have a spot labeled for GMO-free food? How many alternative food markets are available in your home area or where you attend school?

References

Aspen Institute. What is Agent Orange? nd https://www.aspeninstitute.org/programs/agent-orange-in-vietnam-program/what-is-agent-orange/#:~:text=Agent%20Orange%20was%20a%20herbicide,dangerous%20chemical%20contaminant%20called%20dioxin.&text=As%20many%20U.S.Vietnam%2Dera,birth%20defects%20and%20other%20disabilities.

Bessin, Ric. (n.d.). "Bt-Corn—What It Is and How It Works." ENTFACT-1q30: University of Kentucky. https://entomology.ca.uky.edu/ef130.

Biotechnology Information Series (Bio-3). 1993. "Bovine Somatotropin (bST)." North Central Regional Extension Publication, Iowa State University—University Extension. http://www.biotech.iastate.edu/publications/biotech_info_series/Bovine_Somatotropin.html.

Budelman, A., and J. A. Eisses. (1983). "The Pokomo Farming System, Lower Tana, East Africa." *Tropical Crops Communication (Wageningen)* 3:1–9.

Charles, Daniel. 2002. *Lords of the Harvest: Biotech, Big Money and the Future of Food*. New York: Basic Books.

Gassmann A. J., J. L. Petzold-Maxwell, R. S. Keweshan, and M. W. Dunbar. (2011). "Field-Evolved Resistance to Bt Maize by Western Corn Rootworm." *PLoS ONE* 6 (7): e22629. https://doi.org/10.1371/journal.pone.0022629.

Lius, Suwenza, Richard M. Manshardt, Maureen M. M. Fitch, Jerry L. Slightom, John C. Sanford, and Dennis Gonsalves. 1997. "Pathogen-Derived Resistance Provides Papaya with Effective Protection Against Papaya Ringspot Virus." *Molecular Breeding*, no. 3, 161–168. http://link.springer.com/article/10.1023/A:1009614508659#page-1.

Ohlson, Kristin. 2014. *The Soil Will Save Us: How Scientists, Farmers and Foodies Are Healing the Soil to Save the Planet*. New York: Rodale Press.

Pommeresche, Herwig. 2019. *Humusphere: Humus, A Substance or a Living System?* Translated by Paul Lehmann. Greeley, CO: Acres USA.

Rosi-Marshall, E. J., J. L. Tank, T. V. Royer, M. R. Whiles, M. Evans-White, C. Chambers, N. A. Griffiths, J. Pokelsek, and M. L. Stephen . 2007. "Toxins in Transgenic Crop Byproducts May Affect Headwater Stream Ecosystems." *Proceedings of the National Academy of Science USA*, 104(41): 16204–16208. https://doi.org/10.1073/pnas.0707177104.

Shiva, Vandana. 1993. *Monocultures of the Mind: Perspectives on Biodiversity and Biotechnology*. London: Zed Books.

Chapter 10

Putting Carbon Where It Belongs
An Introduction to Soil

Introduction

Soils are central to agricultural productivity—and beyond that, they are also central to solving climate change. Yet most people know less about soil than we know about the solar system. In this chapter, the nature of soils is introduced, first in terms of their mineral content, particle size, and characteristics. These characteristics vary greatly depending on the rock from which they are formed, the climate of the area where they are found, the vegetation that grows on their surface, the topography of the landscape, and time. Students will learn some of the variables in soil that they can see, feel, and even smell. The key variable humans can influence via management is organic matter. The amount, formation, and properties of this organic matter is determined by the vegetation in the biome where the soil is located. The chapter takes a look at the planet's land biomes and the types of soils they contain, giving special attention to the organic material in the soil.

If we are going to reduce the emergency caused by climate change, then soils will be key. But each soil type is a function of the place in which it is found. This chapter provides broader insight into how you can look at a specific soil and the vegetation growing there and move management toward methods to increase soil organic matter, productivity, and health. No one-size-fits-all solution exists. Every effective action on soils will take on the characteristics of the place you find yourself working.

Mineral Soil: The Matrix of Plant Life

Earth, air, fire, and water are the four elements of the ancients; from these come all forms of life, and yet we still do not understand them well or use them wisely. Fire—energy—we receive freely from the sun, but we primarily use the less accessible energy that we extract from deep underground. We pull out coal, oil, and natural gas, and then transform them into carbon dioxide, water, and a variety of harmful chemicals, letting them fly into our air and our water. In air, the carbon dioxide becomes a heat trap, warming the planet. In water, the same molecule becomes an acid, lowering pH and endangering a host of marine life. In soil, however, carbon becomes quite different. It smells good, it grabs nutrients, it supports plants, it belongs. When someone asks, "Where do we put all the CO_2 when we take it out of the air?" The answer is simple: Put it in the dirt.

Earth, or soil, is deceptively complex and misunderstood. It is an abundant natural resource, and at the same time it is vulnerable, abused, and neglected at our peril. It's at the center of Jared Diamond's book *Collapse* (Diamond 2005), which describes his version of how some civilizations in the past have declined and how a large number of of our present ones are endangered because of the way we treat soil. *Dirt: The Erosion of Civilizations*, by David R. Montgomery (2007), takes much the same tack but with better depth on what people did to their soil. Both books use the isolated incidents of the past to depict what could happen more broadly if we do not respond properly to evidence in the present. Soil can move, shrink, and even disappear if we do not take care of it. In too many places around the planet, we have not taken care of the land. The consequence: its all-too-rapid march to the sea.

To really come to grips with the problem of soil erosion, the rapid displacement of soil due to the action of water and wind on soil particles, it is crucial that we understand what makes up soil. It does not have uniform physical characteristics. Soil varies from place to place for reasons having to do with the circumstances where the soil is found. Soil scientists call these *soil forming factors*. There are five of them.

The first factor is parent material. Essentially that material is rock; but *rock* is a generic word that to a geologist encompasses thousands of different varieties of solids, from soft, white talc to green, nearly diamond-hard jade. All rock is made up of different combinations of elements that are variably abundant in the earth's crust. Included among these elements, in order of abundance, are oxygen, silicon, aluminum, iron, sodium, calcium, magnesium, potassium, titanium, hydrogen, phosphorus, and manganese. All other elements are found in the crust as well, but only these have more than 1,000 parts per million (ppm) by weight.[1] By far the most common combination of elements in rock is silicon dioxide (SiO_2), which is the primary composition of quartz. Quartz is a hard, erosion-resistant material that makes up a significant portion of granite, white beach sand, and the translucent stones called agates. Quartz in granite is found in combination with smaller amounts of colored crystals

---

[1]   Parts per million (ppm) is a measure that scientists use to establish relative abundance. Commonly it is measured as the weight of a substance in milligrams found in one kilogram of a particular material. It can also be a count, as in the number of molecules of carbon dioxide in a million molecules (or atoms) of air.

like feldspar (pinkish brown), hornblende (black), and mica (shiny black). Another common silicate rock is basalt. Unlike granite, which hardens and crystallizes deep underground and then appears after the rock above erodes away, basalts flow through volcanic vents and cool much faster on the surface. Most basalt is found on the bottom of the ocean, though near formerly active volcanic vents, such as the Rift Valley in Africa or the plains of eastern Oregon and Washington in the United States, it appears on the surface. Basalt has a lot more iron, titanium, magnesium, and manganese in its silicate structure than granite has, so it is heavier.

But not all rock on the surface of the earth is volcanic. Some rock forms from sedimentary materials in the ocean that consolidated under pressure to form various types of material. Examples include limestone formed from calcium carbonate, dolomite composed from calcium and magnesium carbonates, sandstone formed from quartz-based sand, and shale made from clay deposits. This material is heated and pressurized, but not to the point of completely melting, in order to form sedimentary rock that appears on continents when the movement of continental plates lifts them from the sea. If these sedimentary rocks or igneous rocks actually melt, they are referred to as metamorphic rock, a category that includes marble, slate, gneiss, and schist. Each of these has its own chemical combinations, hardness value, and susceptibility to the other soil-forming factors.

Climate is the second major factor driving soil formation. Air, with its oxygen supply, and water, with its ability to carry chemicals, act together to weather the rock. Sometimes this is a chemical process involving oxidation or the action of acids. Sometimes this is a physical process such as the freezing and melting of water, or a mechanical process as when water flowing on the surface bangs rocks together, breaking off little bits. With this action, rocks fracture, crack, crumble, or flake, forming smaller and smaller pieces that eventually make soil. The process is not only a physical transformation; also, the smaller particle size opens the door for additional chemical transformations, changing the crystalline structure of the original material.

Climate does not act alone. Vegetation is the third soil-forming factor. Lichen is really a combination of algae and fungi in a mutualistic relationship. The algae make food from water and carbon dioxide, while the fungi attach them to a rock and extract nutrient elements. It is an amazingly tenacious combination, surviving even on the rock that makes up the fireplace in my house. In this process, the lichens slowly break down the rock while trying to extract nutrients, leaving small pieces behind that eventually form a soil. In this new environment, other plants take hold, forming associations with more organisms and creating a more active chemical soup than lichens do, further acting to break down rock. Each vegetation type produces a different combination of chemicals, and each in turn leads to a different type of soil. As the soil thickens over time, plant size, diversity, and abundance also expand, depending on climatic factors, and the process continues.

Topography is the fourth factor in soil formation. The degree of slope in a landscape changes the availability of water and hence the type of vegetation that can thrive there. Steeper slopes also permit greater movement of particles due to the actions of wind and water in combination with gravity. Slope also influences climate. In the Northern Hemisphere, a north-facing slope is cooler than a south-facing slope; this orientation lowers temperature and evaporation rates, which, in turn, slows the rate of chemical reactions. The changed evaporation rate also changes species composition and influences the impact of freeze–thaw cycles. For example, in the Shenandoah Mountains along the border between Virginia and West Virginia, the southern slopes of the mountains are dominated by oak and hickory, tolerant of heat and drought, having a longer growing season and fewer frosts. The north-facing slopes often have red maple, cold-tolerant oaks, and hemlock, with moister soils and a shorter growing season. The soil type on a slope is determined by its incline, its compass orientation, and its adjustment of climate.

The last factor, but certainly not the least, is time. How long has the particular type of rock been in contact with the soil-forming factors on the surface? Some soils have been in position for only a short time. Much of the Northern Hemisphere was affected by glaciation as recently as 14,000 years ago, an eye blink in geologic time. The soils of Canada and Siberia are early in the soil-forming process. Soils in the state of Georgia in the United States or the country of Georgia in the Caucasus Mountains, however, have a longer history. They have seen more action of climate and vegetation and thus have different characteristics than those in the north. Equatorial soils are even older; or, at least because of climate, they have seen a lot more chemical activity and have further developed characteristics. The exceptions to this rule are the mountain areas of the tropics. The relatively recent volcanic activities of the Indonesian Islands, the Andes Mountains, and the Rift Valley of Africa produce younger rock and more recent soil formation. These newer soils have different characteristics than the soils of the Amazon basin, for example, or the Congo. The amount of time over which surfaces are exposed to climate and biological life makes for different soils.

The age of a soil depends upon the conditions of its place. Near the bottom of steep-sided valleys, it is not uncommon to see a debris fan where the water runoff slows down. This deposition is often younger soil than that in the main portion of the valley, or the top of the surrounding ridges and hills. Streams and rivers continuously shift material, primarily during flood events. In larger rivers, the floodplains are continuously renewed by the inflow of eroded particles from higher elevation. Even old landscapes can have young, less weathered soils. Overall soil is formed in place slowly. Estimates vary, of course, but the general consensus in the literature is that about 1 cm of mineral soil forms every 200 years, or 1 inch every 500 years. Thus, losing an inch of soil requires a 500-year recovery process (Brady 2007).

Soil is a tactile substance. Each soil type has its own feel. A scene from the movie *Dirt: The Movie* shows this very well.[2] In it, children from India are playing in the dirt, grabbing fists full of soil and tossing them into the air. Aside from the fact that the children squeal in obvious delight as the particles drop on their heads and dust swirls in the air, obscuring the view, the scene shows a complexity to dirt that is not found in the word itself. The dirt in this case separates into component parts based on particle size as it rises and falls through the air. Soil scientists have precise measures of particle size for the three parts of soil: sand, silt, and clay. Sand is the largest of the three and falls first. Particles are considered sand if their largest diameter is greater than 0.05 mm. The most common type of sand is primarily made of SiO_2 (silicon dioxide) and is the most recalcitrant to physical breakdown or chemical weathering. Sand is usually considered chemically inert, has a grain density around 2.65 g/cm³ and, if found in pure form as on a beach, has a porosity between 35% and 43% (Brady 2007).[3] *Porosity* is a measure of the air space found between the grains. It is measured as the volume of air space over the total bulk volume of the soil. Because sand is relatively large, water moves through it freely, making sandy soils well-drained.

Silt is smaller, drifting down more slowly when the kids toss it into the air, making up the majority of the dust seen in the film. Silt's largest diameter is sand's smallest, going from 0.05 mm to 0.002 mm. Many of the world's best soils are derived from a parent material of silt picked up by wind and deposited away from their point of origin. The Palouse Hills of Washington and Idaho, much of the soil in Iowa, and the yellow loess soils of north central China along the Huang Ho (Yellow) River, are derived from silt originally made by glacier activity during the last ice age. Silt is also relatively inert chemically, but it is harder to classify a dominant chemical makeup for it. Certainly SiO_2 is there, but so are pieces of other types of rock, depending on what the glaciers have ground up. While silt's porosity is slightly higher on average than that of sand, the sizes of the air spaces or voids are smaller; therefore, drainage is slower. Rainfall will penetrate silty soil, but heavier rain will cause massive erosion on soils that are not protected by plants.

Clay size is anything less than 0.002 mm. It is likely that, when they're tossed in the air, the clay particles are not even seen. They tend toward stickiness, latching onto sand and silt or each other and falling as a group, not as individual particles. In general, clays have a lower bulk density, 1.3 to 1.5 g/cm³, and a higher porosity than sand or silt, about 51%–58%,

---

2   *Dirt: The Movie* is based on the book by William Bryant Logan entitled *Dirt: The Ecstatic Skin of the Earth*, originally published by W. W. Norton & Company in 1995.

3   Nyle C. Brady published the first edition of *The Nature and Properties of Soils* in 1947. The edition I've drawn from is the 14th, published in 2007. It is perhaps the most widely used introductory text in soil science. The fifteenth edition was revised by Ray R. Weil in 2017.

but because the pore size is very small, water movement is restricted. Clay is far more complex than sand or silt. It is usually placed into two broad categories based on the ratio of silicate-based and aluminum oxide (AlO_6)–based layers. The 1:1 layered clays are quite stable, have less chemical activity, which is referred to as cation exchange capacity (CEC), and are mechanically useful. Kaolinite is a type of 1:1 clay that is often white, though it can be red if there is some iron oxide in the mix, and is very useful for making pottery or for sealing the bottom of a human-made pond. It drains poorly if at all.

Shrink–swell clays, or 2:1 clays, have much higher chemical activity or CEC, measured either as centimoles per kilogram or as mmoles per 100 grams, and are therefore not as good mechanically. These clays are much harder to work agriculturally because of their stickiness. They swell when wet, then shrink as they dry, making those cracks seen on the bottom of puddles after drying, or the cracks in fields during droughts. The most spectacular cracking is seen on soils called vertisols, so called because of their tendency to crack deeply, allowing the top layers of soil to fall into the cracks, and inverting the soil over time. In Southern Sudan, where these soils are common, I have measured cracks over two meters deep. Some names used in association with 2:1 clays, depending on their parent material, are illite, smectite, and montmorillinite.

Soils in general are not purely sand, silt, or clay; rather, they are mixtures of all three particle sizes. These are often discussed in terms of texture classification. The USDA developed a useful way to assign a texture class to soils based on the relative proportions of sand, silt, and clay, called the texture triangle, reproduced in Figure 10.1 below. Soil texture is one of the first items soil scientists assess when coming into contact with a new soil. There are a number of different ways to do this, and most are relatively simple. A method I use is to make a moist ball of soil in your hand. If it is nearly impossible to make a ball that holds together, the soil is likely to be very high in sand. But if you can form a ball, throw it on a piece of paper held against a wall or a tree. If most of the ball sticks, then you have a high-clay soil. If it messily shatters, leaving some stuck to the paper and the rest in small clumps, it is likely a loam. Silty soils tend to fall off the paper, leaving only a thin film behind but still staying together. Another way to discern a soil's texture is to rub the soil between your fingers. This will tell you a lot. Sandy soils are very gritty and easy to rub off. They do not form a ribbon when squeezed. Silty soil feels very smooth, but it also does not stick in a ribbon well, instead falling apart after a few millimeters are made. Clay soils will stick together, with 1:1 clays easily forming a long ribbon. The 2:1 clays form a ribbon, but they tend to stick to your skin and are less easy to work. With practice, you can learn to assess the texture of a soil quite quickly, gaining a lot of information about the mechanical workability of the soil, its porosity, its susceptibility to erosion, and its potential to retain nutrients.

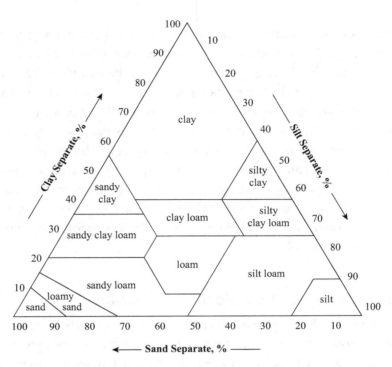

FIGURE 10.1 USDA texture triangle. Each category of soil in the triangle is based on the range of sand, silt, and clay found in the soil type. The web source cited here explains a technique for assessing the texture of a soil using just your hands and some water. (nrcs.usda.gov/wps/portal/nrcs/detail/soils/edu/?cid=nrcs142p2_054311)

The soil triangle shown in Figure 10.1 provides soil texture names according to the relative abundance of different particle sizes. The size of the geometric shape in the figure is not a measure of relative abundance; rather, it indicates how the particle size dominates the characteristics of the soil. Note that clay has a strong presence in the triangle because the physical and chemical properties of clay tend to overwhelm those of both sand and silt. However, high clay soils are not the best for agriculture. Farmers prefer loams for workability, sometimes called tilth, though they want some clay for its chemical properties. Note also that the texture triangle does not account for organic material, which will receive more attention later.

One aspect of soil particles not mentioned yet is their relative surface area. In general, particle size is inversely proportional to surface area, and surface area in part indicates relative chemical activity. Surface area is given in the literature as area per gram. Sand is coarse and has a low surface area. Silt is silky and has a higher surface area, but still not enough to have a significant amount of chemical activity. Clay is different from either sand or silt. If you assume the largest clay particle is a cube that measures 0.002 mm on each side, there would be 125 billion particles in a cubic centimeter of clay, with a cumulative surface area of 30,000 cm^3. This is a vast underestimation of the total surface area of clay, because the particles are not cubes; they are mostly flat plates and normally much less than 0.002 mm on a side. In general, average clay has 90 billion particles per gram (remember there is a lot of air space) and 8 million cm^3 of surface area per gram. This surface area in some types of clay is highly charged, usually with negative ions, attracting and holding positive ions on its surface. This is where the CEC comes from: the ability to attract and hold positive ions like calcium, magnesium, potassium, and ammonium, all important ions in healthy soils.

Soil Organic Matter: The Role of Soil Carbon

So far, the discussion in this chapter has been limited to the mineral composition of the soil and its three size fractions: sand, silt, and clay. Humans have manipulated, used, abused, and eroded mineral soils with our actions, but we can do next to nothing to make or change them on a large scale. Nature makes mineral soils slowly over long periods of time; we get this key act of nature's services for free, but it has immense value (Costanza et al. 1987). The fourth component of soil—the organic matter—is far more amenable to change via human activity. All the damage we can do to mineral soils is done to soil organic matter (SOM), but we can also do a lot to increase the quantity of SOM, and therein lies the hope. SOM is an amazingly diverse organic chemical stew, made and mixed by a complex and highly diverse soil ecosystem. Just getting a handle on the numbers of living organisms in soil boggles the mind. A single teaspoon (5 ml) of healthy soil from a temperate deciduous forest contains 5 billion bacteria (Nardi 2007). Before the "ick" factor kicks in, keep in mind that the vast majority of these bacteria do no harm; in fact, they promote health. Playing in the dirt is a good thing (Louv 2008).

Bacteria in soil are not the base of the food chain. That honor for the most part goes to organisms that photosynthesize. There are algae living in soil, especially near the surface, but as a portion of gross primary productivity and net primary productivity (NPP), they are relatively minor players in land-based ecosystems. Plant root systems contribute the most to soil organic material. It is very difficult to get a handle on just how much plants contribute through their roots, because they are so difficult to measure. The fine root hairs, those roots less than 1.5 mm in length and 10–20 microns in diameter, do not last long in the soil.[4] Their purpose is to find and extract nutrients and water from the soil to empower the photosynthesis above ground. While many biology texts and agricultural sources indicate that nutrients are in chemical form when absorbed, it is likely that most nutrients are absorbed as part of larger organic molecules, as broken cell structures, or perhaps even as whole bacteria by these hairs via endocytosis (Pommeresche 2019). The leaves send sugars and other plant-manufactured molecules to the soil to build the roots and to feed other soil organisms like bacteria and mycorrhizal fungi that assist the plant in obtaining nutrients. The amount of overall NPP that is transferred underground is often given as 50%, but the soil science literature indicates a much broader range: from 40% to 90% depending on the species (Coleman, Crossley, and Hendrix 2004). What you see above ground is not a direct indicator of productivity below ground for all species, though management above ground does affect the below-ground biomass in significant ways.

Each plant's root system penetrates the soil in different ways. Dr. Jerry Glover, formerly of The Land Institute in Salina, Kansas, has dramatically shown the difference between the below-ground biomass of an annual wheat plant and the below-ground biomass of a perennial wheatgrass, shown in Figure 10.2. The deep fibrous roots of the perennial wheat grass are both deeper and wider than those of the annual grain, protecting soil and contributing more organic material to the overall soil structure. These roots also provide a continuous source of food to the soil biotic community, which in turn brings a better nutrient supply back to the plant. In these prairie ecosystems, soil bacteria are the major partners with the plants. They eat sugars that the plants contribute, eat sloughed-off root hairs that have extracted what was available from the soil, digest dead organic material, and then excrete nutrient-rich waste that the plants can tap. Because of their continuous presence, the soils in perennial prairie have a richer, more populous bacterial and fungal community and a more robust and complex community of soil organisms than that which is found in mono-cropped agricultural fields. The SOM content of a native mixed-height prairie commonly runs between 2.0kg/m^2 and 6.0kg/m^2 to a depth of 20 cm depending on temperature, rainfall, and soil texture (Burke et al. 1989). On continuously cultivated soils using tillage, these

---

4   The literature on soil root hairs is detailed and complex, giving a range of numbers depending on the species of plant studied. The hairs, which are produced on the root shaft, not on the lengthening tip, grow fast, work hard, and are sloughed off frequently, becoming part of the underground cellular and molecular nutrient exchange system.

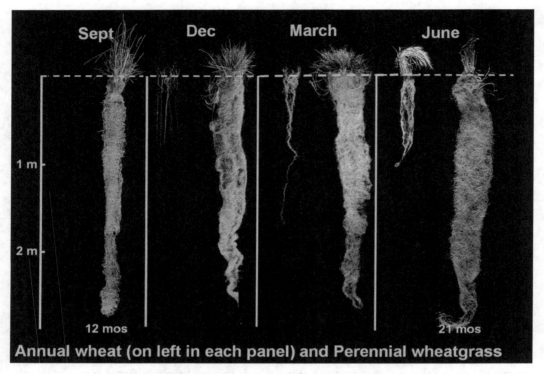

Sept   Dec   March   June

1 m

2 m

12 mos   21 mos

Annual wheat (on left in each panel) and Perennial wheatgrass

FIGURE 10.2   Below-ground biomass of wheat compared to wheatgrass. From the archives of The Land Institute, Salina, Kansas.

numbers drop significantly—from less than 0.2 kg/m² to up to 4.0 kg/m², with an approximate average of some 2 kg/m² less than uncultivated rangeland where management was not specified (Burke et al. 1989). Giving a weight of carbon in soil is generally considered more reliable than giving a percentage of organic matter, because the latter is density-dependent.[5] Soils with a high percentage of SOM commonly have lower bulk densities, greater porosity, better drainage, and greater ability to retain nutrients—as explained earlier, their cation exchange capacity or CEC—than do low-SOM soils (Brady 2007).

Getting carbon back into the soil is the goal, but the way to do this is very dependent on the natural ecological conditions of a place. These conditions will vary in much the same way that soil types vary: according to geological location, climate type, resulting vegetation, and present land use management. Not every place is suited to growing perennial wheatgrasses.

---

5   Soils with 6 kg/m² soil carbon in the top 20 cm at 1.1g/cm³ bulk density have an SOM content of approximately 6.0%. Total soil mass per square meter 20 cm deep is 220 kg. The carbon content of organic matter is approximately 45%. If the bulk density is 1.3g/cm³, the SOM content is 5.1%.

Although every location will vary, broad generalizations can be made about each biome and the soil types within each biome that determine carbon content of soils. There is little or no dispute that all soils can hold more carbon, but how soil carbon can increase in each place is something that must be explored.

Enhancing Soil Carbon by Biome

A study by J. M. Anderson (1992) gives a clear picture of the pools of carbon stored in above-ground biomass and below-ground biomass. This amount varies widely by ecosystem type, by temperature (latitude and elevation), and by annual rainfall. Anderson divides the land-mass of the planet into 13 different categories, or biomes, not including extreme deserts like the Sahara, Gobi, Atacama, and parts of the Australian outback. Table 10.1 below gives a summary of his data about each of these ecosystem categories and their total organic carbon storage. Keep in mind that one petagram equals one billion metric tons, and that one petagram of carbon in the atmosphere is equal to 0.47 ppm CO_2 in the atmosphere.

As shown in table 10.1, each ecosystem has a unique pattern of carbon capture by plants, storage in living primary producers, and total carbon in the soil either as SOM, bacteria, or fungi. It is worthwhile to look at each of these ecosystem types and evaluate their potential for increased carbon storage as a function of their climate type, soil type, and vegetation. To do this, we will start with equatorial environments and then move toward the poles.

Humid Tropical Forests

As shown in table 10.1, humid forests have the greatest ability of any of the ecosystem types to store carbon within their biomass. The most famous humid tropical forest is the Amazon rainforest, two-thirds of which is in Brazil and the rest in Bolivia, Peru, Ecuador, Colombia, Venezuela, Guyana, Surinam, and French Guiana. The forest is huge, and much of it is still intact, but major roads have opened up substantial portions to encroachment. The other major tropical forests of the planet are in much the same shape or worse. The equatorial rainforest of Africa extends from Cameroon and Congo-Brazzaville to the eastern border of the Republic of the Congo. The western and eastern edges of this forest are seeing extensive deforestation for agriculture and mineral extraction. In Indonesia, the island forests of amazing biodiversity, deforestation has reduced some by as much as 90%. Encroachment on the largest island, known as Borneo, is primarily for the planting of oil palm, much of which is used to make biodiesel for European cars at the expense of indigenous peoples and wildlife like the orangutan. Other lesser-known and smaller tropical forests are in trouble as well. Since these forests are nearly unmatched in carbon capture on an annual basis, their loss is felt by the entire planet.

TABLE 10.1 Carbon storage in global ecosystems.

This table shows the approximate area of each global ecosystem type; net primary productivity in terms of carbon captured per meter squared and by the ecosystem; carbon quantity in total biomass per meter squared and in the ecosystem; and carbon in soil per meter squared and in the ecosystem. The data is from Anderson (1992) as found in *Fundamentals of Soil Ecology* (Coleman, Crossley, and Hendrix 2004).

Carbon Capture and Storage by Ecosystems on a Global Scale							
Ecosystem type	Area in million km²	NPP kg C/m² year	NPP Pg/ year*	Carbon quantity in biomass (kg/m²)	Total Pg in biomass	Carbon quantity in soil (kg/m²)	Total petagrams (Pg) in soil
Broad-leafed humid forest	14	0.81	11	15	212	11	156
Taiga	10	0.4	4	9.5	94	17	178
Coniferous forest	5	0.6	3	16.5	81	14	71
Mixed woods	6.9	0.6	4	10.5	69	11	76
Dry forest and woodland	7.1	0.6	4	8	50	11	78
Temperate broad-leaved forest	3.9	0.6	2	10.5	39	16	59
Northern Taiga	4.5	0.4	2	6	27	18	92
Tropical savanna	8	0.5	4	3	24	6	49
Warm grassland	24	0.4	10	1	24	8.8	213
Succulent and thorn wood-land	6	0.33	2	3.7	22	7.3	44
Tundra	11	0.1	1	1	9	18	200
Other dry or highland forest	2	0.3	1	5	7	7	14
Cool grassland	6	0.3	2	1	6	12	72
Totals	108.4		50		664		1302

* P = petagram, or 1×10^{15} grams, or one billion metric tons. 1 Pg C = 0.47 ppm CO_2 in the atmosphere.

Most of the carbon storage in these forests is held in the living organisms of the forest, primarily within the trees' biomass. An intact forest ecosystem is basically at equilibrium for carbon storage. When organic material falls from the trees to the ground, surface organisms—from fungi to ants and beetles—quickly break down the material, respiring CO_2 and releasing nutrients, which are, in turn, quickly recaptured by the shallow surface roots of the forest species. Most of the carbon in soils comes from the roots of the trees, vines, and understory plants. Decomposition is very rapid due to the high moisture levels and high temperatures. Soils in most rainforests are acidic, favoring fungi and ants over bacteria and worms. Soil scientists classify most of these soils as oxisols, fully oxidized soils, often very deep with a crumb structure and moist, sometimes saturated, horizons, which are layers of soil. Finding rock in a flat rainforest is a rarity.

Increasing the carbon content in humid tropical soils is primarily a matter of reforestation. Tropical forests are resilient. They will come back after a trauma, like a fire, a shifting cultivation event, or a logging operation, but the recovery is dependent on the scale of the event. Most species in the closed canopy forest are climax species, meaning they spread slowly and have larger seeds, enabling a seedling to rise above its rivals, but not the type that allows a wide dispersion. A larger deforestation event, like the conversion of land use to agriculture or grassland for beef cattle will make it more difficult for native vegetation to restart. Humans will have to promote reforestation deliberately, perhaps first by planting species with high economic and ecological value. The resulting agroforestry system will act as a bridge, promoting a return to closed canopy forest. Agroforestry will be discussed in more depth in Chapter 13, "The Trillion Tree Project: Tree Crops and the Benefits of Agroforestry." There is considerable evidence that this type of deforestation followed by reforestation has occurred in the Amazon. Places where pre-Columbian peoples lived in the Amazon show a mix of species different than areas with no signs of settlement (Bates 2010).

Another sign of human involvement is a change in forest soils. Some areas of the Amazon have a dark earth soil, referred to as *terra preta* in Portuguese. Studies of this soil show a very high charcoal content (Lehman and Joseph 2009). Carbon-14 dating and archeological evidence strongly suggest that this soil type has an anthropogenic origin. These soils show very high fertility and much higher total carbon content than the oxisols that dominate these regions. It is quite possible that native Amazon peoples discovered a way to improve their soils, making continuous agriculture in the form of agroforestry possible. Through the addition of charcoal, a recalcitrant form of organic carbon often called biochar, the tropical soils can become significant carbon sinks, even rivaling the above-ground biomass that already holds significant carbon, and can serve simultaneously as more productive soils for human production. This topic deserves a chapter to itself. See Chapter 11, "A New Type of Black Gold: An Introduction to the Making and Use of Biochar."

Dry Forest and Woodland

In areas of the tropics where longer periods of water stress occur, both vegetation type and the character of the soils change. Many of these areas have a dry season where water stress occurs three to six months a year. Vegetation responds to this stress by reducing the amount of water lost during photosynthetic activity, either by using a different photosynthetic pathway called C4 or by shedding leaves.[6] The Brachystegia woodland of Africa is such a place. It dominates the landscape of Mozambique across to Angola and north to southern Congo and Tanzania. There is a similar ecosystem, with a different mix of tree species, running across north central Cameroon and Nigeria to the Atlantic Coast in Guinea. Parts of South America and Central America also have dry tropical deciduous forest, well studied by people like Daniel Janzen in Costa Rica. Soils in this region are commonly less acidic, but still relatively infertile, with lower amounts of carbon in their biomass, but with similar amounts in the soil as compared to humid tropical soils. In general, these soils are classified as ultisols, which are deep, old, and slightly acidic, or less commonly as alfisols, which are sandier (more quartz) and nearly neutral in pH. The vegetation is often open canopy trees with deciduous leaves, many of which are nitrogen-fixing, complemented by an understory of shrubs and grasses.

Like in humid tropical soils, the breakdown of organic material on the soil surface is very rapid in this area, but the main actors instead of ants and fungi are termites (Teel 1994). Termite mounds are very common on these soils, and any organic material with nutrient value is quickly consumed. Leaves with a very high carbon-to-nitrogen, or C:N, ratio, on the other hand, like the cashew tree, are not readily eaten because they lack essential nutrients. While agroforestry is a likely candidate for increasing above-ground biomass in these areas, below-ground biomass will require an additive like biochar that is immune to termite attack. Biochar will help productivity on well-drained nutrient-poor soils by increasing water- and nutrient-holding capacity while increasing soil carbon content (Bates 2010).

In some regions, especially on ultisols, these soils can develop a cap, a clay seal that does not allow water penetration, especially during the initial rains of the wet season. In this case, water runs off rapidly, leading to erosion and failure of the first crops. In these cases, it is important that efforts are made to keep the water in the field. P. A. Yeomans developed techniques for doing this in Australia, one of which he called keyline plowing. Instead of

---

6   The C4 pathway is a way of storing precursor sugars in a four-carbon chain. It is used by plants in drier areas so they can close their stomata during the day when water is short and open them up at night to finish photosynthesis. In this way, a plant stays more productive in dry conditions than the more efficient but more water-demanding C3 process.

making terraces, Yeomans used an adapted deep chisel plow to direct water across the slope in a direction slightly off contour away from its natural drainage pattern. By opening the soil to water penetration and directing it toward convex slopes, rather than concave stream valleys, more of the water is stored for vegetation. This redirection of water flow increases net primary productivity on the landscape, changing both above and below-ground carbon storage potential (Yeomans and Yeomans 1993). There is more on this method in Chapter 6, "Water: A Global Issue with Local Solutions."

Tropical Savanna

The crucial image of the savanna consists of great herds of animals, especially the wildebeest of the Serengeti Plain, migrating in mass across a vast expanse of knee-high grass. Around the fringes of the herds are predators like lions and hyenas, waiting for a lone animal they can attack. At rivers or watering points, where trees and water provide cover, leopards and crocodiles sit patiently until an unwary animal gets separated from the rest, and then they pounce. The drama of these events reflects the lost world of American bison in the early nineteenth century or the imagined herds of megafauna at the end of the last ice age. Yet what we do not see, but is part of the reality, are the times when the plains are empty. The great herds always move, and they always come back, but they do not stay in one place. It turns out that this movement of wildlife promotes the health of both the grass and the carbon content of the soil.

Ecologists and wildlife biologists like Allan Savory took a long time to figure out this puzzle, and the key was learning to see the ecosystem in the absence of the wildlife. Grass evolved with the great herds. We think of grass and imagine that its story goes way back to the time of the dinosaurs, but that turns out to be false. The evolutionary history of grass is not that long. Its dominance did not come until after the great rise of the Himalayan Mountains, some 25 million years ago. Two great tectonic plates, the Australian-Indian plate and the vast Eurasian plate, slammed into each other at that time, with the heavier basaltic plateau of India sliding under the lighter granitic plate of Asia. As this basaltic plate went under, it heated and melted, eventually separating the light silicate rock from the heavier aluminum and iron rock of the basalt, with the latter dropping into the molten mantle. When this dropped, the lighter silicates slowly rose, lifting the entire Tibetan plateau and the surrounding mountains. This changed the climate of the planet in profound ways as jet stream patterns adjusted, opening up a niche for the evolving grasses, and in turn, stimulating the rise of the ungulates, from aurochs to eland.

Grasses differ greatly from woody species in many ways, but perhaps most importantly, in their pattern of growth. They do not grow from the tip like woody plants or vines do; instead, they grow from a root collar just under the soil. This is where all new grass stems originate. This enables them to survive a fire or a severe grazing event; in fact, they even need either a fire or grazing events to thrive. When grasses send out shoots from the base, they commonly form multiple stems called tillers. These leaves and stems provide food for the roots to grow deeply into the soil and energy to make seed, but they are not designed for indeterminate growth; they flower, fruit, and die. If these dead stems remain intact, they crowd out and shade the growth of new shoots. Unless a grazing animal or a fire comes along to remove the above-ground biomass, the plant loses energy, roots slough off and die, and eventually the degradation kills the plant. A passing herd of wildebeest solves the grass's problem by eating and stomping on the above-ground biomass, opening up the canopy and permitting new shoot growth. Lions, hyenas, cheetahs, and wild dogs keep the herds moving, allowing the grass to grow anew in the silence between the migrations. When roots stay healthy, they add organic matter to the soil. Savanna soils are often deep, well-drained, and near neutral in pH, with twice as much carbon in the soil as in the above-ground biomass. These systems are rich in soil carbon because of the dry climate, with between six and nine months of dry season per year; but without the action of animals, the soil carbon declines (Pineiro et al. 2010). (The Holistic Management system developed by Allan Savory is explained in Chapter 12, "The Problem of Brittle Landscapes: A Deeply Rooted Solution.")

Succulent and Thorn Woodland

Semiarid and desert lands dominate a large swath of the planet. Hyperarid areas like the Sahara have little to no growth and therefore very little carbon storage potential. Arid and semiarid lands, sometimes called ASALs, do produce some organic matter, commonly in short bursts during and shortly after a brief rainy season. Succulents survive in this region by storing water in their leaves, which commonly have a waxy coating and thick, fleshy growth to reduce transpiration. They grow slowly and have a rich chemical stew that dissuades browsing by mammals or insects. Aloes, cacti, and euphorbia fall into this category. Probably the richest area of succulents in the world is found in the Karoo region of South Africa, with its rich diversity of aloes. Cacti are at their richest in the Sonoran Desert of northwestern Mexico and the American Southwest.

Even more widespread are the ASALs of Africa, Australia, and the Chaco of South America. These regions feature thorns, spines, and prickles of a variety of species, most notably the acacias of Africa.[7] These trees use long, sharp spines to ward off browsing species, though

---

7   The formal name of the genus of African acacias has recently been officially changed. A dispute arose over whether they were indeed in the same genus as Australian acacias, which look very similar to African acacias at first, but then undergo a leaf-altering change from fine pinnate or bipinnate leaves to phyllodes, which are expanded leaf stems. Botanists decided to place African acacias in two different genera, *Vachellia* and *Senegalia*.

browsers have evolved tricks to get around the thorns. Among the species adapted to these woods are the reticulated giraffe and the slender gerenuk. Other tree species, like the Commiphora family, have a greater chemical arsenal to ward off the animals.

As a result of the dry climates, these regions have low levels of biomass and soil carbon. The soils tend toward a basic pH, with limited development of soil horizons. These soils are commonly called aridisols because of the climate, or inceptisols due to their poorly defined horizons related to their slow development through time. A majority of the carbon found in these soils is in the inorganic form of carbonate commonly bonded with calcium, magnesium, or in extreme cases sodium. Trees and shrubs often grow deep root systems to find water in the soils, and the organic matter produced is widely dispersed. Grasses will grow in these regions, but the period of rest required is longer for recovery after grazing or fire; some vulnerable landscapes tolerate only one intense grazing event in a year.

Mixed Woods

Around the Mediterranean Sea, along the South African coast near Cape Town, in southwestern Australia, and along the Southern California coast into northwestern Mexico, the climate follows a winter rainfall pattern. Because the summers are long and dry and the winters cool and wet, the natural vegetation tends toward woody perennials. The trees that thrive here, such as olive, carob, cork oak, and holm oak, seldom get very tall and are well adapted to fires. While there are excellent agricultural areas in these regions, much of the agricultural activity happens in later winter and early spring, with summers reserved for the care of perennial crops like olives, pomegranate, almonds, figs, and grapes. The soils are highly variable depending on slope and parent material. The Italian peninsula with its volcanic activity, and the constantly shifting and rising California coastal zone, have some of the youngest parent material on the planet. This makes for relatively young soils, generally in the inceptisol and alfisol soil orders. South Africa and Australian sites are much older, tending toward the acidic unless there is limestone rock in the area. The amount of carbon in these regions is nearly equally divided between the biomass and the soil, with the biomass carbon often stored in the form of fire-vulnerable wood.

Management of the woody biomass has become a critical issue because of increased human population and the increased frequency of drought. The woody biomass becomes tinder-dry in the hot, low-humidity summers, so fires can quickly consume vast areas. Greece, California, and Australia frequently make the news when these conditions occur. If the woody biomass is thinned regularly, fire probability drops. So what does a manager do with the thinned wood? The answer again may lie in making biochar. This historically has never happened, but the present conditions—of unprecedented levels of human population combined with increased drought from climate change—make a radical shift in management worthwhile. If the dead woody biomass is turned into charcoal, composted with human and agricultural biomass waste, and mixed back into the soil, a win–win situation could result. Thinning reduces fire danger, while the nutrient-enriched biochar improves the soil for plant growth and agriculture, agroforestry, and tree crops.

Temperate Broadleaf

Of all the world's broadly defined ecosystems, the temperate broadleaf forest has become the most disturbed by humans, in part because it sits at a climatic sweet spot for our species. Northern Europe, central China, most of the eastern United States, plus some small pockets in northern India, New Zealand, and southeastern Australia fall into this category, though the vegetation differs in the last two. The soils in these regions vary greatly, from old clay soils to very young soils that are newly derived from glacial tills, but in general the vegetation determines soil type. Deciduous forest adds a thick layer of organic material every fall that tends to sit for a period of slightly longer than one winter, beginning to slowly rot as the temperatures warm in the spring. Rains occur fairly evenly throughout the year, though summer rains are more common overall. Most of this climate seldom has droughts lasting more than a month.

Soils are very active during warmer temperatures especially as they are kept moist. Perhaps the most important creature is the earthworm, native throughout Eurasia but introduced elsewhere as humans moved to different parts of the world. Charles Darwin was the champion of the earthworm in his later years. His last, and some say his best, book was all about earthworms, which he studied in depth with the help of his sons (Montgomery 2007).

FIGURE 10.3   A granular, forest-derived soil with 8% organic matter by weight in the top 15 cm. This is characteristic of limited disturbance soils dominated by the action of worms.

Darwin took detailed measurements of the amount of soil that earthworms deposited on the surface from their below-ground dens. He found that the slow but steady actions of the worms buried rocks in fields at a rate of just over an inch per century, but in some areas it could be much faster, such as in grassy fields where an inch per decade was possible. Worms eat organic material and the duff of the forest floor, so broadleaf forests or tall grass prairies provide perfect habitats. Organic matter on the surface is carried down as the mineral soil below is carried up, with the worms acting as nature's plow, mixing the soil beautifully without the unintended consequence of soil erosion. In fact, worm channels encourage water penetration, making the soil an even better sponge.

Human management of these soils is the real problem. Our agriculture is really a direct descendent of the traditional agriculture of northern Europe. English, Scottish, and Germanic farmers who settled and still manage most of our eastern farmland in the United States brought an agriculture that was based on gentle rains and alternated between sod crops for animals and annual crops for humans. The switch between the two cropping systems kept the soil healthy, rejuvenating the soil ecology as sod and using the available nutrients for row crops. Changing this system to permanent row-cropping using heavy equipment, rather than horses or hoes, led to soil erosion and nutrient depletion that compelled farmers to use fertilizers and other inputs not widely available until the twentieth century. Soil erosion and the loss of SOM was, and remains, common. This ecosystem normally has more carbon in its soils than in its biomass, between 4% and 5% by weight in the top 20 cm; but in areas where agriculture is dominant, the amount of soil carbon commonly drops below 2%. Only a change in management of farmland or complete reforestation can change this pattern. This is explained further in Chapter 3, "The Rise and Pending Fall of Conventional Agriculture," and we will come back to this issue in Chapter 13, "The Trillion Tree Project: Tree Crops and the Benefits of Agroforestry."

Warm Grassland

Though many ecosystems compete for the title of most damaged, a very good case could be made for warm grassland in the temperate zone. It is the largest of the ecosystems on Anderson's list (1992) covering 24 million square kilometers, and it has the largest concentration of carbon in the soil compared to carbon in above-ground biomass, a ratio of 9:1. The photos of perennial grass compared with annual wheat in Figure 10.1 helps to explain this difference. The dominant soils throughout the prairie and steppe environment are mollisols. Mollisols have a top horizon that is loaded with organic matter built up primarily by grasses and the perennial herbaceous plants that accompany them, many of which are legumes and composites. All of these have tremendous root systems. Aldo Leopold describes just one, growing in a small cemetery plot that was not mowed (Leopold 1986). The plant, *Silphium laciniatum*,[8] in the sunflower family, has a taproot that can grow 16 feet deep. Every year the plant grows a new stem from the top of the taproot, providing

---

8   http://plants.usda.gov/factsheet/pdf/fs_sila3.pdf

the energy to both produce seed and probe ever more deeply into the soil. It is a favorite food of ruminants such as cattle and buffalo. If it is grazed frequently or mowed, as happens along highway rights-of-way and "properly" managed cemeteries, the taproot loses energy and eventually the crown dies.

This story repeats itself all over the prairie states in the United States. The grassland is fenced and the cattle freely graze, picking their favorites like *Silphium* first; then the perennials degrade, soil penetration is reduced, and above ground, productivity drops. But this is not the worst thing done to prairie soils; that distinction goes to the conversion of the prairie vegetation—from Ohio to Colorado and from Texas to Canada—into annual crops. We now grow 200 bushels of corn and 70 bushels of wheat per acre on land that once held 20 million buffalo. Some say this is a good thing; it is how we feed the planet. Yet it has an unintended consequence, including the loss of SOM on a massive scale, unseen except by the creatures that live in the soil.

Wes Jackson grew up in Kansas in the 1940s and 1950s. He studied plant breeding in California, but in the 1970s he had a strong urge to return to his roots. He was strongly influenced by writers Aldo Leopold and Wendell Berry, giving him a new perspective on what had been happening to his land. Most agriculture is based on two broad categories of plants: woody perennials (fruits and nuts) and herbaceous annuals (grains and pulses). The prairie, however, is primarily composed of herbaceous perennials that humans cannot consume directly. So we have two choices: We can manage animals to convert these perennials to our food, which is the dominant choice in the drier parts of the prairie and mountain states, or we can break the sod, turning it over to grow annual grains such as corn, wheat, and barley, or pulses like soybeans and lentils. In Kansas, around Jackson's homeland, farmers grow wheat (Jackson 1980).

Jackson decided that the problem causing degradation was modern agriculture, and a potential solution involves developing a perennial herbaceous food for humans. He does not negate the value of conversion of perennials to food by animals, but he reasons that this is not adequate for addressing the problems, and that humans are better off eating lower on the food chain. So how does someone develop a perennial herbaceous agriculture? Very slowly, and by choosing and then breeding the right plants over a long period of time. The Land Institute, based in Salina, Kansas, was founded to become the institutional center for this process. Jackson thought it would take 50 years to develop herbaceous perennial agriculture. The institute is now 40 years into the process and has produced enough success to attract interest and researchers from major universities around the country. The hope is to develop multiple crops that produce edible seed at a sufficient yield to make this form of agriculture worthwhile, while still keeping an extensive root system perennially intact to build and hold the soils. The institute presently has high hopes for a grain developed from perennial wheatgrass called Kernza®, now being tested at a number of sites and being sold locally for bread flour and beer-making.[9]

If this new agriculture works, and half the land presently in annual crops (12 million km²) is converted to perennials, with the side effect of an increase in soil carbon from its present 1.5% back to its historic 4.4%, the amount of carbon stored in this scenario would reach 41 billion metric tons, or 41 petagrams. Since one petagram of carbon equals 0.47 ppm in the atmosphere, the conversion of 6 million km² would reduce atmospheric carbon by nearly 20 ppm.[10] At the same time, using perennials would reduce the amount of fossil fuels needed to grow the food. This is not a simple conversion. There is no system in place for growing this way on a widespread scale, nor can it be done using the same equipment and system used to produce food today. What the experiment does point out dramatically is that soils, in only one of the many ecosystems described, have an amazing potential to store carbon for the long term while at the same time increasing the ecosystem's health. This conversion to herbaceous perennial agriculture involves only a quarter of the total prairie land. This important topic is covered further in Chapter 12, "The Problem of Brittle Landscapes: A Deeply Rooted Solution.

Coniferous Forest

The coniferous forest ecosystem is probably best divided into two pieces: dry and/or warm coniferous forest dominated by pines, and wet coniferous forest dominated by redwood, Douglas fir, and Sitka spruce, depending upon latitude. Conifers exert a strong influence on soil development. Their leaves, or more properly needles, are strongly recalcitrant, breaking down only slowly but releasing humic acids, which can further degrade to become humus. Humic acids speed the breakdown of parent material, release nutrients, and increase the mobility of organic molecules, changing their position in the soil profile. At the same time, the slow breakdown of conifer needles creates a thick duff layer at the surface, inhibiting soil erosion. The thick canopy of many coniferous trees inhibits undergrowth, making the floor of some forests easy to walk through.

Pines are a very broad genus covering a wide range of habitats. They have proven highly adaptable for forest plantations as well, since many are quite happy in near monocultures naturally. North America is home to a number of different types of pine forest. When settlers

---

9   The Land Institute, "Kernza® Grain: Toward a Perennial Agriculture," 2018, https://landinstitute.org/our-work/perennial-crops/kernza/.

10   This is an overstatement. In reality the ocean and atmosphere are in a state of dynamic equilibrium when it comes to carbon dioxide. If atmospheric carbon drops, oceans will release some of their CO_2^- back to the atmosphere, though there will be less than before.

first arrived in the southeast United States, they found the coastal plain dominated by 92 million acres of longleaf pine, *Pinus palustris*. This tree thrived in the well-drained and droughty soils. Longleaf pine is a fire-tolerant species, germinating quickly after fires with an erect vertical growth that rises rapidly above the herbaceous annuals and perennials of the region, and developing a fire-resistant bark that resists low-temperature ground fires. Early settlers found the tree very useful for construction because of its long, branch-free trunk, and a useful pine tar was extracted for the shipping industry as well. This industrial use led to a great deal of deforestation, as the land was converted to agriculture while the trees were logged (Earley 2006). The soils underneath the longleaf pine are commonly sandy loams and acidic, restricting undergrowth. Such soils are termed sandy ultisols by soil scientists. They do not retain fertility for long when used for agriculture, but do they allow a buildup of SOM over time when left alone. For this reason, cotton and tobacco production on these soils was abandoned rather quickly, but the leguminous peanut did just fine. These days, the pine is undergoing a slow process of recovery, partially aided by the Endangered Species Act. The endangered red-cockaded woodpecker finds that old-growth longleaf pine is perfect for its nesting sites, so the protection of the woodpecker resulted in halting the final stages of old-growth longleaf pine elimination and brought the tree back to the public's attention (Earley 2006).

Further north, another pine dominates: *Pinus strobus*, or eastern white pine. It occurs in mixed stands with northern hardwoods like northern red oak, hickory species, beech, and maple. In its more northerly range on granitic soils, it grows among spruce and balsam fir. Soil underneath the eastern white pine has the characteristic thick duff layer of pines. On the granitic soils they produce a spodosol, a sandy soil with highly leached organic matter. If you remove the duff layer of these soils, you often find a white sand that turns very dark further down the profile. The humic acid in the duff mobilizes the organic matter, which leaches out and precipitates deeper in the soil. This leaching takes with it a lot of the nutrients, making for a nutrient-poor plow layer when converted to agriculture. The remaining organic material resists decay, lasting a long time in the soil if undisturbed. Unfortunately, much of this ecosystem is disturbed, and organic matter is vulnerable to degradation.

Further west on the dry, leeward side of the Sierra Nevada and Cascade Mountains, and throughout all but the wettest regions of the Rocky Mountains, from Mexico to Canada, pines dominate the forest. Three species deserve special note: ponderosa pine (*Pinus ponderosa*), a tree of lower-elevation mountains and generally growing with some separation between individuals; lodgepole pine (*Pinus contorta*), characterized by dense stands in areas where fires caused by lightning are common; and whitebark pine (*Pinus albicaulis*), a keystone species of the northern cold Rockies, where its seed provides food for a wide range of animals. The whitebark pine is undergoing a massive dieback from blister rust, a bark disease, and from attacks by the mountain pine beetle—which, due to warmer winters, is not dying during the cold season as it once did. Lodgepole pine is affected by the same beetle and by drought, the latter contributing to some of the massive fires seen in the west in recent years. Fires also lead to substantial erosion once the trees and the forest floor duff are burned off. Ponderosa pine is doing the best of the three species, recolonizing land it lost during the first wave of logging in the late nineteenth century. It is the most commercially viable timber species of these three pines. All three have the same impact on the soils as the pines named earlier; but because of the climate and the relative youth of the soils, they are classified as different soil orders. Most of these soils are considered inceptisols, which have some soil development, or entisols, which have negligible soil development in the profile.

Moving over the Sierra Nevada and the Cascades into the Pacific maritime climate, a completely different situation is encountered. Moist cool air from the ocean hits the coastal hills and mountains and, in the form of fog or rain, bathes the windward side of the mountains in near continuous moisture. Trees respond with seemingly unstoppable growth. Redwoods reach spectacular heights of over 300 feet, while other species easily hit 200 feet and, in old-growth stands, have diameters of six feet or more. What stands out about these forests is the phenomenal amount of above-ground biomass, much of it in standing timber, but also a tremendous volume of woody biomass very slowly rotting on the forest floor. This pattern explains why this ecosystem as a whole has a biomass carbon of 16.5kg/m², higher than any other ecosystem. Relatively high amounts of biomass are found in pine woods, but it is the maritime forests that really stand out.

Below ground in these forests, the soils are relatively poor and highly leached, and they likely consist of very deep, undifferentiated sandy profiles, or spodosols with leached organic horizons. Plant roots dominate these soils in mutualistic relationships with mycorrhizal fungi, and most degradation happens through the action of saprophytic fungi. The mass of fungal mycelia complements the commonly shallow roots of the trees, helping to keep nutrients cycling through living biomass rather than leaching out of the wet environment. Paul Stamets of Fungi Perfecti®,[11] a commercial mycology company, has found that saprophytic fungi are among the largest organisms on the planet and that they grow best in cool, moist conditions, even when the ground is covered with snow.[12] Soil fauna eat the saprophytic fungi as temperatures warm in the spring and through the summer, releasing

11 For more about Paul Stamets, see Andy Isaacson, "Return of the Fungi," *Mother Jones*, Nov./Dec. 2009, http://www.motherjones.com/environment/2009/11/paul-stamets-mushroom.

12 Anne Casselman, 2007, "Strange but True: The Largest Organism on Earth Is a Fungus," *Scientific American*, October 4, 2007. http://www.scientificamerican.com/article/strange-but-true-largest-organism-is-fungus/.

nutrients that are then captured by mycorrhizal fungi and transported back into the trees. This ecosystem's tendency to emphasize mutualistic soil relationships argues for a management system that leaves a continuous cover of trees. Unfortunately, the main management style is a clear-cut rotation of economically valuable Douglas fir in square-mile lots. This management lessens standing biomass volume and opens the soils to leaching and erosion. The potential to store biomass in these systems is very high, but our demand for uniform timber sizes and high-speed extraction processes, which also demand high-energy input, negates these global ecological benefits.

Five Additional Ecosystems: Land We Should Not Touch

In the 1970s, Paul Erlich and John Holdren of Stanford University developed a system to evaluate the human impact on ecosystems. They named it IPAT. The letter I stands for human *impact*, which is equal to or a function of *population*, P, *affluence* or consumption, A, and *technology*, T. Scientists Erlich and Holdren were uncomfortable with Barry Commoner's idea, proposed in his book *The Closing Circle*, that most of the ecological impact following World War II was technological. Their proposal for a broader interpretation of human impact won the debate, but subsequent ecological evaluation prompted the addition of another variable, *sensitivity*, S, which includes the environment's ability to recover from an impact. According to Coleman, Crossley, and Hendrix (2004), highly sensitive environments should inspire careful management or should even be left alone. Allan Savory calls these "brittle environments." Parts of some of the ecosystems already covered are considered brittle, especially those that are dry, steep, or otherwise unstable. Any human activity on these landscapes could lead to irreversible harm in the time span of those who caused it. Such is the case with all the remaining five categories on Anderson's list, described below.

Dry highland forests are found everywhere that there are mountain ranges. They often create their own climate by extracting water from clouds, or they are located in areas where elevation-induced orographic precipitation occurs. By definition, these areas have steep slopes, are heavily exposed to damage if ground cover is inadequate, and are prone to landslides even in good conditions. Human activity induces more hazardous conditions and can lead to catastrophic damage in periods of exceptional rainfall. The recent floods in the northern Colorado Rockies are a case in point. Humans extracted timber and practiced mining in this region, and then prevented fires, all activities that led to a buildup of dry organic material on the surface of the land (see the subsection "Coniferous forests" above). When fires did come, in 2012, they left behind exposed land with only rapidly colonizing annuals as cover, along with a few newly germinating trees. Finally, the freakishly heavy floods of September 2013 washed a lot of land away, as well as housing, roads, and other developments. Developing and managing an extremely sensitive landscape like this one requires a degree of long-term thinking that is rare in modern society.

Cool grassland occurs in places like the highlands of Tibet; the altiplano of Peru, Bolivia, Argentina, and Chile; and the meadows of mountain land in other places around the planet. Such regions have natural resources, but the extraction of such materials involves very damaging operations, which require great care or should be avoided altogether. These are landscapes that store a lot of carbon in their soils, because of their size, but take a long time to build up that carbon initially.

Taiga is the land of jack pine, birch, and white spruce. It extends across vast stretches of Canada and Russia, starting just north of the Russian steppe and the North American prairie. The soils are commonly shallow and the trees spindly. In Siberia, the Chinese are buying up vast tracks to feed their voracious economy. The Canadian forests feed the paper mills of the United States and Japan, among others; the wood is used primarily for paper towels and toilet paper.[13] Yet these trees take a long time to grow, and the cool temperatures mean that the organic matter content in the upper soil horizon is very high. Across vast stretches of this landscape are soils made almost entirely of organic material, called peat when it is mined. Peat appears more frequently in wet areas where soils are almost continually saturated with water. Removing the trees exposes the soil to oxidation, which leads to a loss of organic matter and adds greatly to global atmospheric carbon.

Northern taiga is similar to the taiga but even colder, with deep permafrost. This ecosystem overlaps with taiga, marked by a change in species to black spruce, which can live atop permafrost. On hills, the north side is often dotted with black spruce where soils are colder. Birch and white spruce are found on the southern side of the hills. A new phenomenon has appeared in the northern taiga, the "drunken forest." As the climate has changed, warming more in the Arctic than elsewhere on the planet, the permafrost melts. This makes the ground under the black spruce unstable and the forest begins to tilt awkwardly, sometimes in relation to the winds, other times in relation to the microtopography where the tree sits. These leaning trees look like a bunch of drunken men staggering randomly out of a bar. And just as drunk staggering is not healthy for men, it is not healthy for trees. Weakened trees in the warmer climate are more susceptible to beetle attack. Millions of acres of trees are dying in Alaska and elsewhere because of this change, resulting in a release of carbon as they decay, and the soil is exposed. These weakened trees are also more vulnerable to

13   A lot of this paper goes into the production of paper towels, toilet paper, and tissues. Does it really make
      sense to blow your nose into a tissue made from a slow-growing tree in the ecologically sensitive subarc-
      tic? A handkerchief does the job just fine.

fire—so many fires that the air in Anchorage and other Alaska towns was nearly unbreathable in the summer of 2019.

Tundra marks the end of the trees, whether you go up in elevation or north. The growing season is very short and temperatures so low that vegetation does not survive well unless it remains covered with snow during the long cold season. Here is the land of maximum sensitivity. Anything done on the tundra that damages vegetation remains visible for years, if not decades, even if the action was minor. For example, on Kodiak Island at an elevation just over 1,500 feet, where the trees are gone and little life rises above two feet in height, two young men rode their all-terrain vehicles across the landscape one wet summer day in 1998. They did it only once, but five years later, in 2003, I could still see the dual tracks crossing the hillside until they disappeared over a ridge. Thankfully, the island leaders banned ATVs and they never returned. But imagine what happens to tundra when Chevron, Shell, and Exxon go exploring for North Slope crude oil? How many centuries will be required for the land around Prudhoe Bay to recover? What goes on in the Russian Arctic, where a Greenpeace ship in neutral waters assessing environmental damage caused by oil exploration gets boarded by the Russian military and the entire crew is arrested for spying?

The tundra is the last place on earth we should touch. The land has been ice-free for only a few millennia, yet it now has the highest soil organic content per square meter of any region on the planet. This is the best area for long-term carbon storage on the planet. If we do not keep it that way, the results could be worse than burning tar sands oil.

So Now What Do We Do?

There is no single, overarching answer for capturing and sequestering carbon. The way in which it is done is ultimately a local ecological question. The answer will differ from the state of Pará in Brazil, to Windhoek, the capital of Namibia. The place where the carbon goes, however, will be the same: into the soil. The means by which it gets there will be a function of the ecology of place. What we will look at among the following chapters are three strategies for getting carbon into the soil. There are many more, but these three have been chosen because solid research already exists on their potential, and they can be implemented at a variety of scales at affordable cost. The first strategy we will examine is the making of biochar, the substance called *terra preta* in Brazil. The second is the management strategy developed by Allan Savory and others to improve the productivity of grassland soils—increasing the productivity of the land for humans, and increasing the carbon content of soils at the same time. This material, which the Amazonian peoples used to make their soils more productive, has the ability to do the same elsewhere while sequestering carbon. The third strategy we will examine is the concept of agroforestry, the use of trees on farms to improve productivity, as well as how that approach can be used to capture carbon both above and below ground.

Agroforestry is very similar to permaculture, which was examined in Chapter 4, "From Lawns to Sustainable Perennial Agriculture: Making Permaculture Part of Your Landscape," which lays out a way to decentralize agricultural production, to decrease use of fossil fuels and chemical inputs for growing food, and to increase the storage of carbon in soils.

Study Questions

No matter where you are, you can ask a series of questions about the nature of soils in your place. Some of these will be broad, some relate to history, and some will be very specific.

1. What is your biome? What are the key variables related to soil formation in your locations? Find the parent material, identify the climate, name the dominant vegetation types in your region, see how this varies according to topography and aspect, and finally ask, "How old is this place?"

2. What is the history of land use where you live or study? What has happened in the past that might have affected the soil? Was it a farm? A forest? A prairie? What have been the dominant land uses of this place over time?

3. What is growing on the land now? How does that differ from what might have been there in the past? Is the soil rich with organic material and worms? Does the soil look lifeless and overworked? At this point, you might even want to get a soil sample and have it tested to see what is available for plants.

4. Who is actively changing the nature of soils in your area? Is this action reducing the soil organic richness, or is it increasing it? What ideas are worth mimicking? What actions should be avoided? See if you can name and find the most important plant species that could help improve the soil in your place.

5. What is a good soil improvement plan for your location/area? If this is not known, can you develop one?

References

Anderson, J. M. 1992. "Responses of Soils to Climate Change." *Advances in Ecological Restoration* 22:163–210.

Bates, Albert. 2010. *The Biochar Solution: Carbon Farming and Climate Change.* Gabriola Island, British Columbia, Canada: New Society Publishers.

Brady, Nyle C., and Ray R. Weil. 2007. *The Nature and Properties of Soils.* 14th ed. Essex, UK: Pearson.

Burke, I. C., C. M. Yonker, W. J. Parton, C. V. Cole, K. Flach, and D. S. Schimel. 1989. "Texture, Climate, and Cultivation Effects on Soil Organic Matter Content in U.S. Grassland Soils." *Soil Science Society of America Journal* 53 (3): 800–805. https://doi.org/10.2136/sssaj1989.03615995005300030029x.

Coleman, David C., D. A. Crossley Jr., and P. R. Hendrix. 2004. *Fundamentals of Soil Ecology*, 2nd ed. Elsevier/Academic Press.

Costanza, R., R. d'Arge, R. de Groot, S. Farber, M. Grasso, B. Hannon, K. Limburg, S. Naeem, R. V. O'Neill, J. Paruelo, R. G. Raskin, P. Sutton, and M. van den Belt, 2007. "The Value of the World's Ecosystem Services and Natural Capital." *Nature* 387 (15): 253–260. https://doi.org/10.1038/387253a0.

Diamond, Jared. 2005. *Collapse: How Societies Choose to Fail or Succeed*. New York: Penguin.

Earley, 2006. *Looking for Longleaf: The Fall and Rise of an American Forest*. Chapel Hill: University of North Carolina Press.

Jackson, Wes. 1980. *New Roots for Agriculture*. Lincoln: University of Nebraska Press.

Lehmann, J., and S. Joseph. 2009. *Biochar for Environmental Management*. Sterling, VA: Earthscan Publishing.

Leopold, Aldo. 1986. *A Sand County Almanac*. New York: Ballantine Books.

Louv, Richard. 2008. *Last Child in the Woods: Saving Our Children from Nature Deficit Disorder*. Chapel Hill, NC: Algonquin Books.

Montgomery, David R. 2007. *Dirt: The Erosion of Civilizations*. Berkeley: University of California Press.

Nardi, James B. 2007. *Life in the Soil*. Chicago: University of Chicago Press.

Pineiro, G., J. Paruelo, M. Oesterheld, and E. Jobbagy. 2010. "Pathways of Grazing Effects on Soil Organic Carbon and Nitrogen." *Rangeland Ecology and Management*, 63 (1):109–119. https://doi.org/10.2111/08-255.1.

Pommeresche, Herwig. 2019. *Humusphere: Humus: A Substance or a Living System?* Translated by Paul Lehmann. Greeley, CO: Acres USA.

Teel, Wayne S. 1994. "Catching the Rain: Agroforestry and Soil Conservation in Nampula, Mozambique." PhD diss., Cornell University Graduate School.

Yeomans, P. A., and K. B. Yeomans 2008. *Water for Every Farm: Yeomans Keyline Plan*. Self-published, CreateSpace Independent Publishing Platform.

Credits

Chapter 11

A New Type of Black Gold
An Introduction to the Making and Use of Biochar

Introduction

Our response to climate change has to take many forms. The most obvious is the need to stop burning hydrocarbons such as coal, oil, and natural gas. We also have to remove the greenhouse gases that are already in the atmosphere and put them somewhere else. Chapter 10, "Putting Carbon Where It Belongs: An Introduction to Soil," focuses on getting carbon into the soil, the place where nature likes it. However, soil carbon is labile and biologically active, and it eventually goes back into the atmosphere as carbon dioxide. Keeping carbon out of the atmosphere over a long time frame is critical. This is the premise of the book *Drawdown*, edited by Paul Hawken, and the Project Drawdown® website (https://drawdown.org/), where there are continuous updates on over 100 methods to reduce emissions and capture carbon. As scientists, farmers, and foresters continue to explore ways to capture and store carbon that involve the productivity of plants, the role of black carbon, charcoal, or biochar (the more recent term) becomes more important. This chapter explains why.

What Is Biochar?

Energy conservation, carbon sequestration, and soil enhancement are all part of sustainability and can lead to a product that is familiar to people everywhere. There are times when moving forward can mean looking back with clearer eyes and seeing what you missed, such as the charcoal in the backyard grill. The modern version of charcoal, sold in paper bags with names like Kingsford® on the label, is not the right image. Real charcoal, used by humans for millennia, lacks the compaction and additives of the backyard briquette. You get a better glimpse of reality in a bag of Cowboy® charcoal, made from machined blocks of hardwood scraps, but even this is made at too low a temperature. Real charcoal is made by heating wood in a low-oxygen environment, driving off most of the hydrogen and oxygen in the cellulose and lignin components, and getting a black, lightweight, blocky hunk of 80% to 90% porous carbon that many people in the less-developed world use as their primary fuel.

Today, charcoal is mainly used as fuel. It has another important function that was once widely known to people but essentially has been lost. This story is told more completely by Albert Bates in his 2010 book *The Biochar Solution: Carbon Farming and Climate Change*. The native peoples of the Amazon rainforest discovered this other use for charcoal. After Hernando Pizarro invaded Peru and conquered the Inca, he wanted to find the land of cinnamon. His brother Gonzalo set out to do this and sent one of his captains, a man named Orellana, to explore the Coca River, a tributary of the Napo and then the Amazon. The current of the river and the dense tropical rainforest prevented the group from going back upstream. Instead they continued down the river, becoming the first Europeans, along with a large number of Peruvian natives, to make the trek down the Amazon. Orellana had an assistant named Carvajal who kept detailed notes on the trip. Some people thought the notes were exaggerated in order to persuade Spain to finance a trip back to the Amazon. The second trip failed, and Orellana died near the mouth of the Amazon in 1546.

While the Spanish and the Portuguese were undoubtedly cruel and wrongheaded, in their travels they did uncover some information that anthropologists, archeologists, and soil scientists have only recently confirmed. Carvajal recorded details about cities along the Amazon that they saw and robbed while traveling the river. These were large, well-planned, and fully populated cities, with food markets and thriving economies. Some think this is the origin of the El Dorado myth. When the Amazon was further explored, 30 years later, none of these cities were seen. The Amazon was an empty place, peopled only by hostile groups of hunter-gatherers who wanted nothing to do with Europeans. Carvajal's tales were thought to be the wild imaginings of a sick man starving on an empty river. Now we think he was neither mad nor sick, because signs of these cities have been found, and the soil in and around these sites is black.

Today we recognize that the Amazon was not an untouched wilderness. It certainly had dense vegetation, but it was well populated. Along with the explorers came European and African diseases that the local people had never experienced. Their immune systems were not prepared for this invisible attack, and they expired in massive numbers. Some researchers, including Bates, think that up to 98% of the population that Orellana and Carvajal saw died within 30 years of the journey.[1] Without people, the forest grew quickly, hiding the evidence. It was only during the next great invasion of the Amazon in the late nineteenth and early

---

[1]   The book *1491: New Revelations of the Americas Before Columbus*, by Michael Mann (Alfred A. Knopf, 2005), touches on the same theme, with less detail about biochar.

twentieth centuries that people noticed the soil. At this time, rubber was in high demand. John Boyd Dunlop had invented the pneumatic tire, enabling the bicycle with even-sized wheels. Benz, Mercedes, and others had invented the car, and the Wright brothers invented the airplane. Everyone demanded rubber. The best source of natural rubber on the planet is *Hevea brasiliensis*, the Amazonian rubber tree. In the Amazon this tree is not found in dense stands, but grows singly in isolation from other members of its own species, thereby limiting the spread of diseases. Rubber tappers, often under slave labor conditions, spread out across the southern Amazon basin, tapping the trees. In the process, they gathered information about a black soil that seemed especially fertile. The rubber barons of the time took note.

These black soils look quite different from the dominant red soils of the basin. They are quite fertile and nearly neutral in pH, while the red soils are infertile and acidic. Both soils are deep, but the black soils are also filled with shards of pottery and other human debris. Eventually scientists from Europe and Japan began working on these soils. Even as far back as Justus von Liebig, the German scientist who came up with the idea of limiting factors in soil, charcoal was known as a good soil amendment. Apparently, the Amazonian peoples knew this and deliberately used charcoal to enhance soils close to their compounds. We do not know how they did this, though given the pottery shards, it is likely that they used community organic waste products, including feces, mixed with charcoal and added it all to soil when they threw out their old pots. The result was what the Portuguese-speaking Brazilians call *terra preta dos Indios*, "Indian black earth" (Bates 2010).

In order not to confuse the use of charcoal as a soil amendment with its use as a fuel, scientists and other enthusiasts now use the term *biochar* for the former and talk about it as a soil amendment of great utility. There is an increasing volume of studies on biochar. A major book on the subject, called *Biochar for Environmental Management*, edited by Johannes Lehmann of Cornell University and Stephen Joseph at the University of New South Wales, Australia, came out in 2009. A book called *The Biochar Revolution: Transforming Agriculture and Environment*, edited by Paul Taylor, was published in 2010. These books are compilations of articles that look at the details of biochar: how it is made, its physical and chemical properties, how it is used in the field, what it does to enhance crops, and how it can be used to sequester carbon in the soil for the long term. Thousands of articles have come out subsequently. The International Biochar Initiative is perhaps the best place to find a full list of all the studies and information on the topic.[2] These topics will be summarized in the remainder of this chapter.

---

2   The International Biochar Initiative (IBI) official website is https://biochar-international.org/.

How Biochar Is Made

Biochar is made in the same way as barbecue or Cowboy brand charcoal, but the general consensus in the literature suggests that it should be done at a higher temperature. To learn this, first we need to understand the basics about the composition of biomass in general, and woody biomass in particular. A piece of dry biomass, whether wood, grass stems, vines, or other herbaceous material, is usually between 97% and 99% a combination of cellulose, hemicellulose, and lignin. Proteins, fats, and other components of plant tissues are concentrated in leaves, stems, and growing roots. When these components die or mature, the plant moves them to other tissues. A dead grass stem contains energy, but not much nutrient compared to a living stem. Cellulose, hemicellulose, and lignin are composed of sugars, or more complex derivatives of sugars, which are 44% carbon, 48% oxygen, and 6% hydrogen.[3] The remaining 1%–3% is usually made of proteins and fats combined with minerals like calcium, magnesium, potassium, sulfur, silicon, and traces of others. This mix has an air-dried energy content of approximately 15 MJ (megajoules) per kilogram, which if kiln-dried rises to 18 MJ/kg. Making charcoal involves stripping the hydrogen and oxygen from the carbon chain and leaving behind the carbon skeleton of the organism. Once the chemical reaction is activated (by lighting the fire), it become a self-sustaining exothermic reaction, and if the oxygen supply to the reaction is controlled, charcoal is produced. Charcoal is a variable product, containing between 80% and 90% carbon, some oxygen and hydrogen, and a mix of minerals that are components of ash. All the nitrogen is lost in the process. Charcoal has a concentrated energy content, dependent on the carbon percentage, of 27–31 MJ/kg.

The Traditional African Method

Charcoal is the fuel of choice—and often the only fuel available—for most Africans. Because of the concentrated energy content and lighter weight per unit volume, it lowers transportation costs per unit of "energy value moved" compared to the original wood. As the nations of Africa increased in population, the demand for charcoal in cities created circles of deforestation moving out from the concentrated population. In the 1970s and 1980s, this prompted a lot of soul-searching among development groups and a lot of pushing for reforestation programs by NGOs, bilateral and multilateral aid organizations, and governments. It has

---

3   This is a simplification of the complex organic chemistry of woody biomass. For a more complete discussion, see Boateng et al., "Biochar Production Technology," in *Biochar for Environmental Management: Science, Technology and Implementation*, edited by Johannes Lehmann and Stephen Joseph (New York: Routledge, 2015), pp. 63–87.

not stopped charcoal production, sometimes taking place over 300 kilometers (190 miles) from its urban point of sale.

Making charcoal is not difficult. It requires only an axe or a machete and a digging tool. First, the wood is cut, gathered, and stacked. Next, a pit is dug next to the wood pile, usually deep enough so that half the volume of wood can go in the pit. If the soil is easy to dig, the pit may be made deeper. Then the wood is piled in the pit, as tightly as possible. Some charcoal-makers then use grass or leaves to make a less-permeable cap over the top to prevent dirt from dropping through the pile. Now the dirt from the pit is loaded evenly over the pile of wood, so that very little air can get through. One end of the pile is left open for a bit, and a small hole is left in the other end. A fire is started at the open end of the pile. When the fire is burning well, it is covered with dirt to stop the flames. (These flames are from the burning of hydrogen, carbon monoxide, and methane with a few more complex molecules called volatile organics.) The aerobic combustion slows, and anaerobic combustion continues. Charcoal-makers can see whether they are successful by watching the smoke in the small hole at the opposite end. White smoke is water vapor. Yellow smoke is also good, showing the pyrolysis phase after water is driven off and the volatile gases are released. Blue smoke indicates that too much oxygen is entering the pile—causing partial aerobic combustion, which leads to particulate release and lower yield. The charcoal-makers then look for any narrow places in the dirt cap and fill them to seal off the air flow. Finally, when the smoke turns blue again, the anaerobic combustion is complete because air entering through the smoke hole itself is reaching the wood. At this point, the hole is closed and the pile is allowed to cool. The temperature must drop below 150°C at all points in the pile, or it is liable to ignite upon exposure to air. The final step is to uncover the pile, break it up into pieces, and put the charcoal in bags for shipment to market. Charcoal-sellers do not make a lot of money on this. It is the truck owners controlling transport and street sale who make the real profit.

This system works but it is filled with inefficiencies. Control of air flow is usually problematic. The process normally takes a few days and the pile is not continuously monitored. The type of wood used is generally not always of the same density or dryness, so the resultant quality of the charcoal is variable too. In the end, if things have gone well, the charcoal-maker is left with between 15% and 20% of the original weight of the wood. This means if you start with 1,000 kg of wood, you have 150 to 200 kg of charcoal. At 200 kg, you have lost 63% of the original energy content of the wood. At 150 kg, you have lost 72% of the energy content of the wood. The rest is lost as heat in the pile or, more critically, is lost as gases to the atmosphere. Because this loss includes methane, a potent greenhouse gas, as well as carbon monoxide and particulate matter, both dangerous air pollutants, making charcoal this way is unacceptable.

Improved Methods—The Kiln or Retort

Charcoal-makers have improved this system by using brick, metal, or cement kilns of various types. With these systems, the producer can control air flow much better and add afterburners to combust the gases in the exhaust flow. Some of the carbon is still lost to combustion, because a small amount of oxygen is needed in the chamber to drive the process. Kilns can also be made to allow the continuous flow of wood into the chamber and out as charcoal. As long as air control is maintained and temperatures inside the chamber are monitored, system efficiency is much improved over traditional methods. Even though yields are higher, the cost of making these systems is out of reach for African charcoal-makers. Kilns are primarily the charcoal-makers' choice. Biochar-makers want a higher-temperature product with higher porosity.

A retort is an adaptation of the kiln that eliminates a much higher amount of oxygen from the pyrolysis chamber. *Pyrolysis* is the conversion of biomass to charcoal using heat in the absence of oxygen. The chamber is commonly a metal container with a lid that allows the exit of volatile gases without the entrance of air. The pyrolysis is endothermic, requiring an outside source of heat. The simplest type made from easily obtained materials is the double-barrel retort. This requires two metal barrels, one 200 liters and one 100 to 120 liters. The larger barrel has a series of holes cut into the bottom edge of the sides in order to allow air flow. The smaller barrel is elevated on bricks or stones and filled with small pieces of dry wood or other organic material. The larger barrel is placed upside down over the smaller one, with the bottom of the larger barrel sitting on the top rim of the small barrel. The two barrels are flipped so the small one is upside down in the larger barrel. The empty portion of the larger barrel is filled with wood until full. The lid of the larger barrel has a hole cut in it that is slightly narrower than the diameter of a standard stovepipe. The lid is placed on the large barrel and weighed down. A fire is lit through the hole, and when it is burning well, the stovepipe is added. Air will flow through the bottom of the large barrel and feed the fire, which will burn down, heating the small barrel and pyrolyzing the wood inside. Gases given off by the pyrolyzing wood will be consumed in the fire, helping drive pyrolysis. This can be done without the lid and stovepipe, but the process takes longer. The heat produced could also be used for cooking a meal outdoors while the biochar is being made. When combustion stops, water is poured through the hole in the lid to cool everything; an alternative is to wait until the inner barrel can be touched without the charcoal-maker's hands getting burned. If the newly made biochar is not cooled, it will combust if exposed to air.[4]

---

[4] For an excellent video on making biochar, including the double-barrel process, go to http://forum.driveonwood.com/t/unattended-charcoal-making-process/1466. The video features Bob Wells, of New England Biochar, making biochar using a double-barrel system.

Much more sophisticated retorts are available that further reduce pollution problems and increase the relative amount of biochar produced. Some of these are very efficient, requiring as little as 50 kg of fuel wood to fully char up to 1,500 kg of biomass. In an Adam retort (named for its designer, Chris Adam), the wood to be charred is placed in a brick pyrolysis chamber that sits on top of a wood-burning heating chamber. A layer of steel separates the two; stainless steel may be used to improve durability. Gases produced by the charring wood are channeled through a pipe down into the burn chamber to burn, with the burning wood helping to further heat the pyrolysis chamber. The brick of the retort is surrounded by insulation and cement blocks in order to have the heat continue driving pyrolysis instead of escaping to the environment. A good source for information is BiocharProject, an Australian effort led by Dolph Cooke.[5] Peter Hirst and Bob Wells of New England Biochar developed a mobile Adam retort at their base in Eastham, Massachusetts.[6]

The James Madison University Retort

Between 2009 and 2013, a number of James Madison University (JMU) Integrated Science and Technology (ISAT) students and I developed a dual-purpose retort for making biochar. The first purpose is to make biochar, and the second purpose is to catch the resulting heat to warm a greenhouse or other structure. This means that any smoke produced in the process must be able to leave the structure, and the heat captured by the unit should be stored for a time and released slowly into the indoor environment. The entire system has three interconnected parts: a burn chamber with a chimney, a pyrolysis chamber inside the burn chamber, and above these a water tank for heat capture.

The pyrolysis chamber is adapted from a barrel with a lid, but the barrel is made with heavier steel to make it more robust. The size of this tank can vary. The one illustrated in Figure 11.1, drawn by Maryann Sniezek, has a diameter of 20 inches, a depth of 30 inches, and a volume of 155 liters. The lid has a rim that goes around the barrel and clamps down to make an airtight seal. The tank has a two-inch-diameter pipe coming out of the bottom. The pipe bends 90° six inches below the tank heading toward the front, where it is capped. In this pipe, ten 6-mm holes are drilled, aimed upward toward the pyrolysis chamber to vent the pyrolysis gases. The gases will burn when entering the already-burning fuel of the burn chamber.

The burn chamber is a simple rectangular firebrick structure on a cement block pad. Even the chamber floor is firebrick, to prevent damage to the cement blocks. The walls are mortared

---

5   http://biocharproject.org/charmasters-log/biochar-industries-project-adam-retort-biochar-kiln/

6   See http://www.biochar-international.org/Newenglandbiochar.

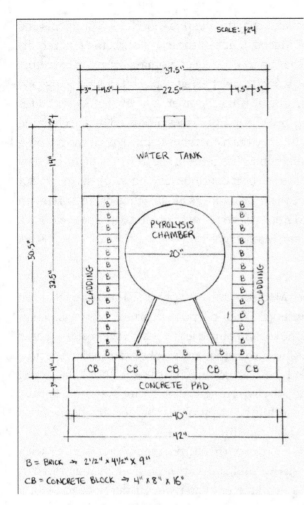

SCALE: 1:4

37.5"

3" 4.5" 22.5" 4.5" 3"

WATER TANK

PYROLYSIS
CHAMBER
20"

CLADDING   CLADDING

B (×15 each side)

50.5"   32.5"   14"   4"

CB   CB   CB   CB   CB

CONCRETE PAD

40"

42"

B = BRICK → 2 1/2" × 4 1/2" × 9"

CB = CONCRETE BLOCK → 4" × 8" × 16"

FIGURE 11.1   Initial design plan for pyrolysis unit. The design was based on variables specific to the location where the unit is located, Hermitage Hill Farm & Stables. Schematic drawn by Maryann Sniezek.

with high-temperature mortar to prevent leaks. The brick walls extend one row of bricks above the top of the pyrolysis chamber, as seen in Figure 11.1. The front door with its dimensions is shown in Figure 11.2. It is closed with a lever system, much like that found on the back of a semitrailer and was designed by Logan Kendle (2013). The door is shown open in Figure 11.3A. It is lined with a high-temperature insulating material to prevent warping that could result from the chamber heat.

The burn chamber is capped with a water tank that is 37.5 inches wide, 45 inches long, and 14 inches high, made of medium 18-gauge steel. This holds 385 liters of water, rust inhibitor, and antifreeze. The tank has an 8-inch-diameter steel pipe welded into it for allowing smoke release from the burn chamber through the tank and into the chimney, the latter taking the smoke outside the hoop house shown in Figure 11.3. Air that feeds the burn chamber fire enters through a series of gaps left in the first layer of bricks, also seen in Figure 11.3C.

Versions of this retort are now operational in four locations in the Shenandoah Valley, all involved in heating structures and providing biochar to farm operations. They are customizable depending on the size of the structure and the amount of heat needed. They are meant to be used once per day in the evening to heat the water tank—which then cools slowly overnight, reducing potential frost damage. The pyrolysis chamber is emptied the next morning when cool. While there is no fixed mass of wood pyrolyzed, depending on wood type and water content, a typical burn chars 30 kg of pine wood, using about the same amount of fuel to drive the process, and produces 10 kg of biochar, or about

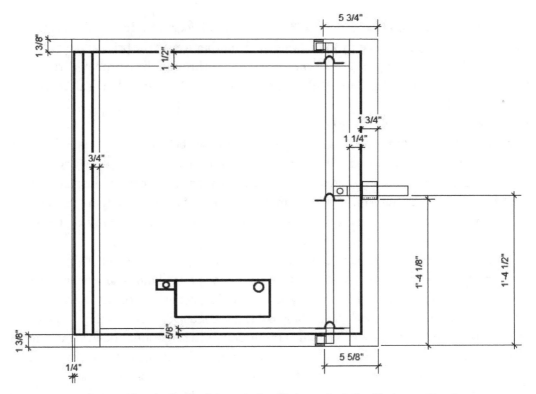

FIGURE 11.2 Schematic for the front of the unit door. Schematic drafted by Logan Kendle.

FIGURE 11.3 Completed pyrolysis unit after stage 1 of construction. Image A is a front view, image B is a side view, and image C is a back view. Image A photographed by Maryann Sniezek; Images B and C photographed by Sarah Mello.

16% of the original wood weight and 31% of the original energy in the wood. The process captures about 11% of the energy in the water and another 10% in the brick and block of the structure, leaving about 50% lost to the environment through the chimney (Brown and Spencer 2013; Sniezek, Mello, and Mulford 2013; Decker et al. 2012; Deitch et al. 2011).

Continuous Feed Production Systems

There is a lot of benefit to the smaller batch systems described above, especially for farms with easy access to waste wood. However, demand for biochar by those who cannot make it for themselves is high. Because batch systems have size limitations, continuous feed systems work better when dealing with very large amounts of material. These systems are designed so that, other than some initial startup energy to activate the process, nearly all the energy driving the process comes from the biomass.

Continuous feed systems can be used to produce other products as well. Pyrolyzed biomass fractionates into gases (methane and carbon monoxide), liquids, and biochar solids. This is the starting point for the company named Cool Planet, whose objective was to make liquid fuels as a primary product and biochar as a secondary product—about 10% of the original biomass. Cool Planet's system is proprietary. The fractionation system is much more complex than most continuous feed systems due to the nature of their final product.[7]

The biggest drawback to a continuous feed system is the startup cost. This complex system requires a relatively uniform feedstock (a grinder or shredder), a feeding system (auger or chain), a pyrolysis chamber with a gas combustion chamber beneath keeping it hot (complex piping and burner heads), an oxygen-free cooling chamber, and a collection system for the liquids and solids produced. The total cost often reaches $750,000, as compared to a JMU retort, costing under $4,000, and a non-mobile Adam retort at $10,000 (not including onsite labor).

Forest Biomass and the Biochar Solution

On the west coast of North America, from Central California to British Columbia, one of the most carbon-rich environments on the planet thrives. Parts of it are temperate rainforest, dominated by redwoods in the southern regions, Douglas fir in the middle, and Sitka spruce to the north. Just inland from this, the climate stays wet in the winter but dries out in the summer. You can see the transition, because in natural areas, where a fragment of

---

7   Cool Planet went bankrupt and liquidated their assets in 2017. The problem was that they did not get the thermodynamics of their system right and could not produce liquid fuel and biochar in the same operation. Only the biochar aspect of their business produced income. Rick Wilson, PhD. Personal communication.

old-growth forest still clings to life, a fire-tolerant ecosystem remains. Summer drought and local ground fires work together to clean out the understory episodically, reducing the woody debris and burning back the buildup of herbaceous biomass. These low-level fires work to stop, or at least reduce, the impact of large-scale fires.

As with most ecosystems on the planet, European immigrants have messed this up. The march of European descendants across the United States picked up speed a generation after Meriwether Lewis and William Clark crossed the continent. They found an old-growth forest with the highest carbon content per unit land in the world. Redwoods topped 300 feet, Douglas fir routinely topped 250 feet with an 8-foot diameter, and many others reached over 200 feet. Over the next 100 years, from 1850 to 1950, these monsters near the Pacific were felled, sometimes to get them out of the way in order to farm, but mostly these logs were sent away, by ship or rail, to build the rest of the country. Most of the land was not suited for farming, and the companies that gorged on the fat logs of old growth recognized that they needed to replant. However, they did so with a monoculture mindset, leaving out the pioneer species like red alder and big leaf maple, other old-growth partners like western hemlock, and the excellent but slow-growing western red cedar. Instead, they chose the fast-growing and most versatile Douglas fir, grown in vast plantations across the variegated landscape in the mountains and foothills of the Cascades, the northern Sierras, the coast range, and the Olympics, all the way to the Canadian Rockies. And the companies prevented natural fires.

Fires were not permitted because it was not known that they were natural in summers. As a result, the debris on the forest floor became deeper and more massive. Because of climate change the droughts of summer have become deeper and longer. When fire did come, whether from blowing power lines in California, poor fire management by campers or companies, or dry lightning throughout the region, it did not stay on the ground. These fires burned into the crown, and when the wind blew, nothing could stop them. They became catastrophic, reaching a peak of fury with events like the Camp Fire that destroyed Paradise, California, in 2018. Preventing fires is really impossible. They are part of the landscape. The real questions are how do we keep them from becoming catastrophic and, perhaps, how can the situation be turned into something good?

A number of people are looking into this issue, and Kelpie Wilson, a member of the US Biochar Initiative, is among them.[8] She is a native of Oregon, and she spent a number of years managing the forest in the Siskiyou region in the southwest part of that state. She sees the forest from her porch and has watched ground fires move across the landscape

---

8   Much of the information that follows can also be found at WilsonBiochar.com. Kelpie Wilson also works closely with both the US Biochar Initiative and IBI.

without harming large trees. She has also seen devastating fires. Part of managing a forest is cleaning up debris. When companies harvest timber, they often do what is called a clear-cut, taking a section of land, often a square mile, and cutting down everything, removing every stem that has economic value, then piling the debris into compact stacks for burning when fire conditions are favorable. The problem with this kind of management is that the stack fires, lit from underneath, are smoky, polluting, and hot—burning everything to ash, and the extreme heat destroying the soil underneath the pile. Kelpie identified a better way to burn, and the result of this is biochar, a product with both ecological and economic value.

When a fire burns wood, three things happen. In the first stage, the water has to be removed, which is why it takes time to get a fire going. The fire has to be started with something quite dry so that the temperatures can get high enough to begin the chemical reaction of oxidation, which takes organic molecules like cellulose and converts them ultimately to carbon dioxide and water. But the process is more complex. First, the heat drives off water, and then it stimulates dissociation of the organic molecules, giving off simpler molecules such as methane, hydrogen, short alcohols like methanol and ethanol, pollutants like carbon monoxide and other gases, and some particulates, which we call smoke. If sufficient oxygen is available, these quickly burn in the air, creating the yellow flames we associate with burning wood. This is the second stage of burning. The third, slower stage is the conversion of the now solid remains of complex carbon chains to carbon dioxide. This process happens in the glowing orange embers in the core of a fire. Kelpie and many others recognized that if the third stage of combustion can be prevented or at least limited, what's left is biochar.

So how do you do this with the waste wood of a forest? Kelpie suggests three different ways, all dependent on the conditions of the place where the debris on the forest floor has built up, making conditions ripe for a major fire. The first, and simplest, method is to make a rick, similar to the type that the Jack Daniel's® Company uses to make charcoal to filter their whiskey. Stack the debris in loose but systematic piles by crisscrossing the wood, the layers made up of equal-sized pieces but shrinking as the pile gets larger. Then light the pile at the top. This reduces smoke, because the fire is not drying out the upper layers at the same time as it consumes the lower material. This reduces the loss of methane and particulates, and more completely consumes the carbon monoxide in the burn. As the pile is burned, the material reaching the third stage of carbon oxidation breaks up and falls to the bottom of the pile, where less oxygen is available. When the pile completes this collapse and the flames shrink, you can quench the fire with water or cover it with soil to prevent oxygen reaching the carbonized material. Once the fire is quenched, the result is a pile of biochar. This can be spread across the forest floor, where it joins the biochar of past natural burns, or it can be moved to where it is used for other purposes.

In this kind of burn, the conversion of biomass to biochar is relatively inefficient, somewhere between 5% and 15% depending on how well the fire is managed. Kelpie sought better efficiency and pursued another idea called the flame-cap kiln (Figure 11.4). In this second method, you need a heat-resistant container. Steel works well, because it can be thinner and mobile. You can also use firebrick, or dig a pit, but these structures are fixed, or less mobile. Kelpie's are variable in size: from small circular or conical steel walls with open bottoms called Kontiki kilns, to large steel oil tanks cut in half or long troughs 3 to 4 feet wide and of variable lengths. Inside these walls, you build a smaller

FIGURE 11.4   A simple flame-cap kiln design. This one is 60 cm (2 feet) high, 130 cm across the top, and 60 cm across the base. Note how the flame has a rough curl pattern. This is a sign that air is being drawn into the kiln from the top, driving the second stage of burning with very little smoke production. It is best to do these burns on days when there is little wind.

version of the rick described above and light a fire on top, letting it burn down. As the fire begins to slow, you add more fuel, again using approximately the same size of material in each layer you add. When I do it, I add smaller pieces in the first layers to get the fire completely covering the surface area of the kiln. Material is added as the flames dictate. The objective is to keep the fire in stage two. Adding layers and keeping the flames active creates a cap, preventing oxygen from reaching the bottom of the kiln, as seen in Figure 11.4. This gives the devices the broader name of flame-cap kilns. Once the pile of carbonized biomass nears the top of the container, controlling the entry of oxygen becomes difficult and carbon is lost to combustion. At this point, you will need to quench the fire with water, or cap the kiln with thick mud and soil, or even use a steel lid sealed around the edges with soil. Once the material is completely cooled, you have biochar. Kelpie's measurements indicate a conversion percentage of around 16%.

The third way to convert forest debris to biochar is more efficient but more expensive. This involves moving the debris to a kiln, which can be a larger batch system or a continuous feed system. Batch systems do not require the material to all be of the same size, but they need to be loaded, and unloaded, all at once. Continuous feed systems require materials that are of relatively uniform size, so the debris must be ground first. There is a greater material cost for these systems, and the need to collect, load, and transport the material from a distance also

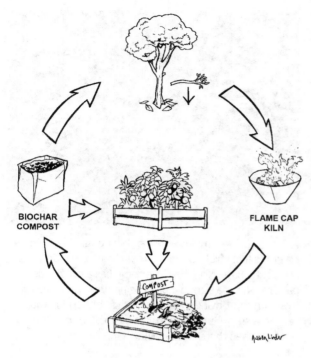

FIGURE 11.5 The cycle of biochar. Woody debris and pruning waste are pyrolyzed in a flame-cap kiln, then ground up and added to a compost pile. Next, that compost goes to the garden or back to the forest. These then produce the material both for manufacturing the biochar and growing the garden. Drawing by Austen Linder.

makes it more expensive. Efforts are underway to develop both types of units as mobile large batch systems, but these are even more expensive. In the right location these systems make sense, especially if you can also capture and use the excess energy for other purposes, like providing heat to buildings or even making electricity. However, transporting woody debris is uneconomic if the distance to the site is much more than 10 miles. One of the benefits of biochar is that it sequesters carbon. Why make biochar if your fossil-energy carbon cost of making it exceeds the carbon sequestered as biochar?

Making biochar from forest debris addresses two problems simultaneously. It eliminates the buildup of fire-enhancing material on the forest floor, and it turns that debris into a recalcitrant material that enhances the soil. (See Figure 11.5.) In many ways this is a win–win suggestion, but it does require labor. Right now, the market for biochar is low, so it is impossible to make a living producing biochar using a mobile flame-cap kiln, unless you are also being paid for providing another service, such as lowering the chances of a catastrophic fire. However, the reputation of biochar as a method for capturing and sequestering carbon and using it in industry and agriculture is growing steadily, as documented on the Project Drawdown website.[9]

Cooking and Making Biochar—Dr. TLUD

At the other end of the cost spectrum is a way to make biochar and cook at the same time. Called the Top-Lit Updraft (TLUD) stove, it is championed by Dr. Paul Anderson, known as

---

9   Biochar Production, Project Drawdown. https://drawdown.org/solutions/biochar-production

Dr. TLUD, and Dr. Hugh McLaughlin. These stoves are fairly easy to make, and when they're operated with the right type of fuel, they burn clean and hot and produce a good-quality biochar. Dr. TLUD's goal is to develop units that eliminate the smoke from "three stone fires" that cause so many health problems in rural, low-development regions, while at the same time making biochar that can improve crop production if used as a soil amendment on those regions' fields.[10]

A TLUD stove is relatively simple in concept. To make biochar, you have to pyrolyze biomass in a limited-oxygen environment. In a TLUD you don't separate the pyrolyzed wood from the fuel; you separate the second and third stages of combustion. In a fire with no control on oxygen, you see two types of oxidation. One comes from the gases given off by the wood, causing flames. The other shows in the glowing red coals from carbon oxidation of the solid surface as oxygen hits it. In a TLUD, the primary oxygen from under the biomass initiates pyrolysis, the chemical separation of gases from the biomass, while the secondary source of air that is provided to the unit goes to the flame oxidation of the gases. The primary oxygen combines with the wood exothermically and gives off the gases of carbon mon-

oxide, methane, and a smaller amount of hydrogen and other volatile organic compounds. There is not sufficient oxygen to consume the gases at that point, and they rise in the chamber to the top where a secondary air source ignites them, giving a wood gas flame. Carbon burns only briefly at the beginning to get the process started. The diagram in Figure 11.6 shows how this works.

There are many different designs of TLUD stoves. One of the simplest is the "two can" method developed by Hugh McLaughlin and Jock Gill.[11] There are several different designs, but they all use the same principle. The bottom can has its top

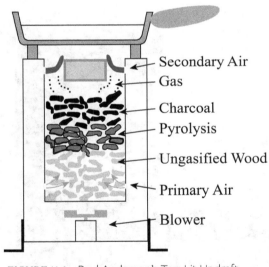

Secondary Air
Gas
Charcoal
Pyrolysis
Ungasified Wood
Primary Air
Blower

FIGURE 11.6 Paul Anderson's Top-Lit Updraft system

10   Dr. Anderson's website, describing the stoves and the fieldwork, is at http://www.drtlud.com/.

11   "1G Toucan TLUD for Biochar Production" by Hugh McLaughlin, PhD, PE, Alterna Biocarbon Inc., January 2010 Version https://www.build-a-gasifier.com/PDF/1G%20Toucan%20TLUD%20for%20 Biochar%20Jan%202010%20-%20final_0.pdf

removed, and its bottom has a number of holes poked in it to allow entry of primary air. Around the top edge of this same can, a number of holes are punched to allow entry of secondary air. This is filled with biomass to the bottom edge of the secondary air holes. The top can, which is of the same size, acts as a chimney. It has its top removed, but the bottom has a hole made that is only half the diameter of the can. This concentrates the gases and air for a better flame. When you cook, the bottom can is held off the ground to allow air entry, and the cooking pot is held above the top edge of the upper can to allow oxidized gases to escape.

Two ISAT senior project students and I designed the JMU TLUD shown in Figure 11.7, following the work of Dr. Anderson. This TLUD has two adaptations from the basic design of Figure 11.6. The outer metal cylinder is flared out to provide a stronger base, and the removable top has three metal flanges added to provide a platform for the pot. We took this design to Kenya in the summer of 2013 and used it with great success for cooking. The biochar-making aspect of the stove was not its main attraction. Most local people are accustomed to smoky, "three stone" fires. This stove produces very little smoke, except

FIGURE 11.7 On the left is a TLUD designed by Cara DiFiore and Kofi Boafa (pictured) during a test burn. Note that the top of the stove is detachable, allowing for easy filling with biomass, in this case wood pellets. On the right, the photo shows a good-quality wood gas flame in the middle of a burn. The burn lasted over an hour, sufficient time to cook most meals. (Pictures by Cara DiFiore)

upon startup, allowing people to cook indoors when it is raining, which is common in western Kenya in the late afternoon. The biochar-making aspect of the stove will have to be introduced later.

The Best Biomass?

Almost any biomass can be used to make biochar, but there are trade-offs. With grasses, it is very difficult to get a lot of biochar because of low density and difficulty of compaction. Baled straw or dry grass insulates itself, so the bale must be broken up. No matter how much grass you stuff into a batch barrel or an Adam retort, the resulting biochar quantity will be low compared to what you get with wood. Thoroughly dried cattle manure makes decent biochar, but it is so valuable as a nutrient source that it is not recommended for making biochar. The charring removes all nitrogen. The same is true for poultry litter, even when it contains a lot of wood chips or another carbon source. Poultry litter biochar does not look or feel like wood or grass biochars, and it is doubtful that it has the same porous characteristics.

In my experience, wood and bamboo make the best biochars, although in circumstances involving nutrient delivery the biochar from grasses and other herbaceous sources is better. The importance of porosity cannot be overstated (Theis and Rillig in Lehmann and Joseph 2009). There is, however, no need to cut down a forest to make biochar. This chilling scenario was and is being used by the people at Biofuel Watch to condemn biochar across the board.[12] No one in the biochar community of researchers and practitioners advocates cutting down trees to make biochar. The recognition that forests are our best mechanism for capturing carbon is widespread in the community. Most makers use waste wood, branch material, woody debris from city streets and backyards, or other biomass that would go into a landfill or a burn pile, becoming the source of biochar rather than a source of pollution. Good logs are good timber; the branches and bark make the biochar.

Physical and Chemical Properties

The most important physical aspect of biochar is its porosity, which is directly proportional to its large surface area. All biomass is essentially a group of cells. Plant biomass in general, and woody biomass in particular, is comprised of cells designed both to support its own weight and to transport materials. Only cells in the leaves are designed to photosynthesize, and roots are designed to find and import water and nutrients. Everything else is a support structure

_____

12   See http://www.biofuelwatch.org.uk/category/reports/biochar/.

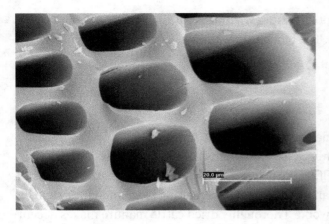

FIGURE 11.8 Yellow pine biochar. The bar has a length of 20.0 microns.

comprised of cellulose, hemicelluloses, and lignin with "supporting" biochemistry. When these cells die, their basic structure is relatively recalcitrant to breakdown. When the biomass is made into biochar, the carbon chemistry simplifies, becoming a higher percentage of carbon, ideally between 80% and 90%, while its basic structure stays the same. Figure 11.8 shows a scanning electron microscope (SEM) image of yellow pine (probably loblolly pine) made at 590°C in a JMU retort.

High-porosity carbon like this has a low density. The JMU team's measurements showed densities of wood biochars between 0.28 and 0.38 g/cm³. These vary by species of wood and the temperature of the pyrolysis process, with lower temperatures ending with higher density. The densest biochar we made came from a Brazilian hardwood and the lightest came from pine. Miscanthus grass is even lighter, though an exact density from this was not determined. The main point of high porosity and low density is the amount of surface area, which is where the chemical activity of biochar takes place. Most of the biochar solids are interconnected carbon ring structures that are primarily planar. In these planes are gaps of less than 2 nm in size called nanopores. Often, at the edges of nanopores are functional groups like carboxyls (COO^-) having a negative charge. These nanopores are too small to see in an SEM image, but the size and thickness of the wall of the micropores that are seen indicate the number of nanopores. It is in these nanopores that chemical interactions take place and nutrients are stored and exchanged with organisms (Theis and Rillig in Lehmann and Joseph 2009). This chemical activity is measured as for soils with cation exchange capacity (CEC) studies. It is clear that biochar in soil increases CEC, which indicates nutrient storage of soils and correlates with plant growth. Having a higher CEC means that nutrients are less likely lost by the soils, and there is greater availability of nutrients for plants (Chan and Xu in Lehman and Joseph 2009).

Biochar is not a nutrient source in itself. Normally, wood does have some ash content, primarily salts of potassium, calcium, and magnesium, all of which form positive ions. These are attracted to the negative ions on the surface of the biochar and in the nanopores. After biochar is made, it has only the nutrients of the plants' ash content. In the soil, it picks up more nutrients because the available charges on the surface are able to hold more nutrients than they have at their application. Thus, an early measure of CEC before addition to soils is generally lower than after the biochar is incorporated into the soil for a time (McLaughlin 2010).

Field Use: Some Ideas from Around the Planet

The impact of biochar was first noted in the Amazon, but scientists wanted to prove that this was an anthropogenic process of adding biochar to soil to get improvements, not a natural phenomenon that people exploited. Cristof Steiner and Johannes Lehmann did a number of studies on upland soils in the Amazon, the deep red aerobic soils of the forest that are nutrient-poor. They added biochar to these soils and measured the nutrient-holding capacity of the soil and its impact on crop production overtime. They found that these soils, when modified with applications of biochar, yielded better than soils without biochar when manure and fertilizer were added to the plots (Steiner et al. 2007). Other scientists have confirmed this observation elsewhere in the tropics.

Bob Wells, a farmer and biochar enthusiast in Cape Cod, grows a variety of crops on a sandy, glacial till soil. A few years ago, he happened across biochar as a soil amendment and started making his own biochar in barrels. He took the biochar and mixed it with compost and applied it to two rows of a local turnip variety. The size of the resulting turnips was double that of the control rows using his normal methods. He then tried it on all his crops, including blueberries, and saw good results across the board. Wells cautions that results don't always show on the plant, but rather with the yield (Wells 2010).

This research has prompted many to try biochar on other soils with various levels of scientific rigor, from informal backyard trials with strictly anecdotal results to full-scale formal efforts. A study in Switzerland provided biochar to a group of 150 farmers and asked them to mix it with their own compost. They grew crops on two side-by-side 10 m^2 plots of land, and one plot had compost with biochar while the other had plain compost (Schmidt et al 2012). The results showed an overall increase in yield of 7.5% for the biochar amended soils, but this varied with a complex mix of crops, soil types and types of compost. It turns out that the mustard family (broccoli, cabbage, and mustard) did much better with biochar than the Solanaceae family (potatoes and tomatoes). This could be a result of biochar raising pH and increasing potassium availability, both of which are preferred by the brassicas (Schmidt and Niggli 2012).

In Quebec, Canada, Barry Husk of BlueLeaf Inc. a commercial farming operation, has tested biochar on a number of different crops, most of which show strong positive impacts from biochar. The first formal article the company published reported an increased yield of 20% in soybean plant biomass when using an application rate of 3.9 tons of biochar to the hectare. The next two years, the same plot had a crop of forage plants. Their yield was only 4.1% higher than the control, but there were significant gains in nutritional content that encouraged further studies in the same field. BlueLeaf has since announced higher yield with biochar in plots of broccoli, blueberries, and other crops (Husk and Major 2011).

Local biochar produced in the JMU retorts are used on the farms where they are located. Results remain anecdotal at this point, though farmers are encouraged enough to keep mixing biochar with their compost or worm castings and putting them on their plots. One farm reports an increase in size of raspberries and a lengthened season to harvest lettuce without the leaves turning bitter (Teel 2012). Another farmer reports that radishes and Swiss chard show increased production, but the increase has not been formally documented.

While the initial focus of biochar was its application on crops, more innovative and interesting uses of biochar keep appearing. Hans Peter Schmidt of the Delinat Institute for Ecology and Climate Farming in Switzerland has come up with a list of 55 uses for biochar (Schmidt 2012a). One of these is as an additive in animal feed. Giving cattle, pigs, and poultry a small amount of biochar reduces their emissions of methane both before and after they defecate. A study done in Thailand on a local cattle breed, which was fed 0.6% biochar with urea at 1.83%, showed a lowering of methane emissions by 29% and an increase in weight gain by 25%, without any increase in rations, when the cattle ate cassava (Leng, Preston, and Sangkhom 2012). Studies using biochar in anaerobic digestion systems producing methane showed that methane production increased while carbon dioxide decreased in the presence of biochar (Schmidt 2012b). Poultry living on bedding with biochar have less trouble with ammonia emissions and foot problems. If the biochar is part of the feed, it also reduces diarrheal diseases and improves growth rates (Gerlach and Schmidt 2012).

Since World War II, global agriculture has consumed a lot of fossil fuels to make nitrogenous fertilizer using the Haber–Bosch process developed in Germany.[13] As a result, global agriculture has expanded significantly and has become a major source of nitrogenous waste and air pollution (Smil 2001). An increasing number of studies have shown conclusively that using biochar in farming systems decreases the emissions of nitrous oxide (N_2O), a potent greenhouse gas that is 300 times as powerful per molecule as CO_2 (University of Tubingen 2013). In addition, the biochar reduces leaching and off-gassing of ammonium and ammonia, attaching ammonium ions, which are positive, to the negative surface charge of biochar, making them available to plants and thus reducing fertilizer demand (Major et al. 2009).

---

13   For more details on this, see Chapter 3, "The Rise and Pending Fall of Conventional Agriculture." in this volume.

An Argument for Decentralized Production and Use

Biochar is potentially a game changer, but it is not the solution. It could serve as part of a broad set of solutions that have a large number of components. Like most every new thing, it attracts a lot of attention and produces avid proponents. Yet even by the biochar community's own admission and numbers, it only gets us part way to drawing down carbon in the atmosphere. More recent literature does indicate a lot of potential. In the book *Drawdown*, written by Paul Hawken and a large team of researchers, biochar is listed at number 72 of their 80 proposed solutions (Hawken 2017). Albert Bates and Kathleen Draper, authors of *Burn: Using Fire to Cool the Earth*, give a convincing argument that biochar has a higher potential than Hawken's team suggests. They don't just promote biochar as a soil amendment. They also suggest using it as an additive in cement and asphalt, in water filtration systems for acid mine drainage, in cattle feedlots, as a feed additive for cattle to reduce methane production, in bedding material for other animals, and more. If used in these ways, and made from forest floor debris of the type that contributes to forest fires in the western United States, biochar can become a key ingredient in drawing down atmospheric carbon (Bates and Draper 2019).

Biochar production depends on the production of a surplus from the local environment. Biochar is made from biomass that is bulky and cumbersome to collect and move. The more you try to scale up the collection of biomass, the more energy you need in order to do so. This is a self-defeating problem. The idea is to get carbon out of the air and back into the ground. If you use fossil fuel energy to do that, you lose whatever benefits you gain. Therefore, any effort to make biochar should use as its driving force only the energy contained in the biomass. Even small efforts like the JMU retort have the problem of using fossil fuel energy to make the retort. Moving steel, brick, cement block and ourselves around require the input of energy, and it takes a lot of production to cover that energy cost. The more centralized and technologically sophisticated means you use to make biochar, the higher the energy input and the longer the payback period. This is the lesson of *emergy*, which is defined as the embodied energy cost of all technological solutions.

The emergy lesson is one that Cool Planet failed to fully acknowledge as the company designed a biochar and liquid fuel production system. Cool Planet attempted to make jet fuel and gasoline from biomass using proprietary fractionator technology involving sophisticated catalysts. They had a startup plant operating in California, and they installed their first production-sized facility in Louisiana. They hoped to make 20 million gallons of fuel a year from the biomass sources, with 10% of the carbon in the process discharged as biochar. If everything had worked as they hoped, they would have a carbon-negative system. The company recognized that 20 million gallons is about all that you can make in one plant annually from locally harvested biomass, and that it is better to set up multiple small-scale plants as semi-independent franchises rather than to have very large production facilities. The economics of large scale don't work.[14] Cool Planet did not include in its literature an ecological evaluation of the process, including an audit on embodied energy costs. The company recently went into Chapter 11 bankruptcy. The only thing that resulted in any income from their process was biochar, but this did not cover their losses when trying to make fuel.

Greater hope lies in small-scale production, such as farmers and gardeners and enthusiasts making biochar from biomass produced on their own land and sequestered in their own soils. Most of the time, biochar-makers might produce one to ten kilos in a batch. Perhaps if they are diligent, they will make one ton a year. A one-acre plot could easily hold 100 tons of biochar, or more if it can go deeper in the soil. The response of crops will depend on other aspects of management as well. Are they mixing it with compost? Are the producers using manure and urine in the process? Are all the nutrients and carbon produced on the land staying within the cycle of life as much as possible? Biochar can do a lot to improve productivity, but only if the entire local ecology is considered and if it is used in the right place and made in the right way.

That we need to sequester carbon is a given. How we sequester carbon involves a number of choices. Biochar is one good choice. There are others, too, some complementary to biochar, others independent. The choice must be made in accordance with the ecology of the place where you live and work.

Study Questions

1. What are the primary sources of carbon presently going to waste in your area? Do a survey of your neighborhood and see what happens to waste biomass, whether it is tree leaves and branches, roadside trimming, yard waste, or timber scrapes. What happens to this material? Who picks it up, and where does it go?

2. What potential do you have for making biochar locally? Why is this far more difficult in urban or suburban environments than in rural areas? How far would you have to go to find a place where making biochar is even possible? Is it reasonable and energetically viable to get the biomass waste of your home area made into biochar locally?

3. Can you capture the energy in the biomass and capture it for further use? Let's say you have identified a way to collect the biomass and make biochar. This takes more effort, but any way to capture this energy is also a way to reduce reliance on fossil fuels. Who could use this energy, and how could they capture it and make biochar simultaneously?

_____

14 Personal communication. Rick Wilson, PhD.

4. Is there a composting location in your yard, neighborhood, or local region that could incorporate the biochar once it is made? Composting adds value to the biochar, making it better for farmers or backyard gardeners. How is your compost process handled presently? Where can biochar fit into this process?

References

Bates, A. 2010. *The Biochar Solution: Carbon Farming and Climate Change.* Gabriola Island, British Columbia, Canada: New Society Publishers.

Bates, Albert, and Kathleen Draper. 2019. *Burn: Using Fire to Cool the Earth.* White River Junction, VT: Chelsea Green Publishing.

Brown, C., and B. Spencer. 2013. "Implementation of Pyrolysis Chamber Adapted to be Used as Heat Source for Hoop House at Wildside Farms, and Production of Biochar to be Used for Study on use as a Soil Amendment and Stream Restoration Tool." Senior thesis, Department of Integrated Science and Technology, James Madison University.

Decker, J., A. Martindale, M. Najamy-Winnick, and D. Spolarics. 2012. "Construction and Implementation of a Pyrolysis Unit for the Production of Biochar in a Sustainable Greenhouse Heating System." Senior thesis, Department of Integrated Science and Technology, James Madison University.

Deitch, C., and K. Gazenski. 2011. "Biochar Production and Heat Capture: Refining the Design on a Small-Scale Production System." Senior thesis, Department of Integrated Science and Technology, James Madison University.

Gerlach, H., and H. P. Schmidt. 2012. "Biochar in Poultry Farming." *Ithaka Journal* 1/2012:262–264. www.ithaka-journal.net. Hawken, Paul, ed. 2017. *Drawdown: The Most Comprehensive Plan Ever Proposed to Reverse Global Warming.* New York: Penguin.

Husk, B., and J. Major. 2011. *Biochar Commercial Agriculture Field Trial in Québec, Canada—Year Three: Effects of Biochar on Forage Plant Biomass Quantity, Quality and Milk Production.* https://www.academia.edu/34462029/Biochar_Commercial_Agriculture_Field_Trial_in_Qu%C3%A9bec_Canada_Year_Three_Effects_of_Biochar_on_Forage_Plant_Biomass_Quantity_Quality_and_Milk_Production

Kendle, L. 2013. "Redesigning Biochar Production Systems to Reduce Steel, Cost, and Decrease Smoke Loss." Senior thesis, Department of Integrated Science and Technology, James Madison University, Harrisonburg, Virginia.

Lehmann, J., and S. Joseph. 2009. *Biochar for Environmental Management: Science, Technology and Implementation.* Abingdon-on-Thames, UK: Earthscan Publishing/Routledge.

Leng, R. A., T. R. Preston, and I. Sangkhom, I. 2012. "Biochar Reduces Enteric Methane and Improves Growth and Feed Conversion in Local 'Yellow' Cattle Fed Cassava Root Chips and Fresh Cassava Foliage." *Livestock Research for Rural Development* 24 (11).

Major, J., C. Steiner, A. Downie, and J. Lehmann. 2009. "Biochar Effects on Nutrient Leaching." In J. Lehman and S. Joseph, *Biochar for Environmental Management: Science, Technology and Implementation*, pp. 271–287. Abingdon-on-Thames, UK: Earthscan Publishing/Routledge.

McLaughlin, H. 2010. *Characterizing Biochars Prior to Addition to Soils*. http://terrapreta.bioenergylists.org/files/Characterizing Biochars - Version I - Jan 2010.pdf.

Schmidt, H. P. 2012a. "55 Uses of Biochar." *Ithaka Journal* 1/2012: 286–289. www.ithaka-journal.net.

Schmidt, H. P. 2012b. "Treating Liquid Manure with Biochar." *Ithaka Journal* 1/2012: 273–276. www.ithaka-journal.net.

Schmidt, H. P., and C. Niggli. 2012. "Biochar Gardening – Results 2011." *Ithaka Journal* 1/2012: 265–269. www.ithaka-journal.net.

Smil, Vaclav. 2001. *Enriching the Earth: Fritz Haber, Carl Bosch, and the Transformation of World Food Production*. Cambridge, MA: MIT Press.

Sniezek, M., S. Mello, and E. Mulford. 2013. "Design, Implementation, and Analysis of Biochar Production at Hermitage Hill Farm & Stables." Senior thesis, Department of Integrated Science and Technology, James Madison University, Harrisonburg, Virginia.

Steiner, C., W.G. Texeira, J. Lehmann, T. Nehls, J. L. V. de Macado, W. E. H. Blum, and W. Zech, 2007. Long Term Effects of Manure, Charcoal, and Mineral Fertilization on Crop Production and Fertility on a Highly Weathered Central Amazonian Upland Soil. *Plant and Soil* 291 (1): 275–290. https://doi.org/10.1007/s11104-007-9193-9.

Taylor, P. 2010. *The Biochar Revolution: Transforming Agriculture and the Environment*. Chirnside Park, Victoria, Australia: Global Publishing Group.

Teel, W. 2012. "Capturing Heat from a Batch Biochar Production System for Use in Greenhouses and Hoop Houses." *Journal of Agricultural Science and Technology* A 2 (12): 1332–1343.

University of Tubegin. 2013. "Biochar in Soils Cuts Greenhouse Gas Emissions." *Science Daily*, October 4, 2013. http://www.sciencedaily.com/releases/2013/10/131004090618.htm.

Wells, B. 2010. "On the Farm: A Biochar Biography." In *The Biochar Revolution: Transforming Agriculture and the Environment*, by P. Taylor, pp. 31–44. Chirnside Park, Victoria, Australia: Global Publishing Group.

Credits

Chapter 12

The Problem of Brittle Landscapes
A Deeply Rooted Solution

Introduction

Grasslands once dominated the North American landscape. From the tallgrass prairies managed by fire in the east to the shortgrass prairies of the great plains near the Rocky Mountains, these vast landscapes were dominated by herbaceous perennial plants. The shorter and drier of these landscapes have proven vulnerable to heavy damage by human management, or mismanagement. They have degraded badly over time with the continuous grazing pressure of protected domestic livestock, extractive road-building, mining, and inappropriate development. The biggest symptom of this is soil erosion. But they can be managed differently, especially if we pay attention to the natural ecological patterns in these places. It took us a long time to learn how to listen. As Aldo Leopold said, "Only a mountain can listen objectively to the cry of a wolf." When we removed the wolf for the sake of cattle, we lost the mountain's objectivity—and with it, the topsoil.

So how do we respond? One way is to relearn the lessons of the ecosystem. Sometimes that takes people who grew up in a different landscape to point out the problem and propose a different management. That is the story of this chapter. How do we manage a landscape, unsuited for agriculture or broad-scale forestry because of dryness, in a way that is both productive and true to its ecological foundation?

Seeing the Brittle Landscape

Imagine yourself in a field in the high plains of the American West. Mountains rise in the distance. Green lines of trees trace the tracks of streams running off the lower slopes of the mountains and foothills. The land you walk on is dry, the soil is exposed and cracked in spots, and vegetation consists of tall dry clumps of tumbleweed, leafy spurge, sage brush, and thorny thistles, or gray clumps of dry grass that look half dead awaiting a rain. The land is fenced, but you can't see the lines of barbed wire as they are too far from the spot where you tread. The flies are a pain and occasionally you get bit by one, usually on the back of your neck. A few cattle pass to one side, widely spaced, rather listless, looking for something edible to nibble while aiming toward the watering spot. The land looks barren, unproductive, rather like a desert. The only stream running across the rangeland is shallow, muddy, meandering aimlessly across its unshaded streambed with its sharp-edged, barren banks. Cattle tracks are everywhere.

You hike across the landscape and reach the barbed wire fence, pick a good spot, and hop across, carefully avoiding the prongs with tufts of cattle hair attached. The transformation is startling. The first patch you cross, also unfenced, has few weeds, the few sage plants are widely spaced and look rather sick, while the grass is lush and rises above your ankles. You angle toward a stream marked by willow and cottonwood. Quite suddenly the landscape changes. The grass is really short, about an inch high, with manure piles visible, though you can see flies and beetles attacking the piles. A few steps later you scare up a grouse that bolts rapidly away. It had ripped apart one of the manure piles. Off to your left you see some cattle, bunched and grazing happily on grass, moving together like coordinated lawn mowers, trampling shrubs and taller weeds while they move. It seems that there is not enough space between the beasts for them to walk around the shrubs. A clump of young ponderosa and pinion pine stands just outside the single strand of electric fence casting shade on a few animals. The grass stands mid-calf high before the cattle eat, and one inch high after. They don't seem to miss anything. In the corner of the field, alongside an access road, is a tanker of water with a hose leading to a watering trough with a float valve. The system is mobile.

You cross the electric fence again and head toward the stream. A small group of elk bound away from the stream. You are not sure if they are running because they see you or if they are fleeing something else. You keep your eyes open. The stream is densely vegetated with grasses and small shrubs forming the understory, and young poplars and willows are growing well. The stream itself is narrow, the water runs clean and clear between tight banks. There are signs that the stream suffered some damage in the past but is healing over as perennial vegetation penetrates the banks with a stabilizing root system. There is no sign of cattle near the stream. In fact, you don't see cattle anywhere except the tight bunch bounded by the electric fence. What you do see and hear are birds. They seem to flit around at every turn. The shrubs and trees of the bank are a wonderful habitat. Most of the species are insectivores, and you notice that you are untroubled by insects here. You silently thank the birds. The soil on the far side of the stream is not visible; it is completely covered by grasses and some legumes. Occasionally a taller composite, looking something like a tiny sunflower, rises above the grass. On impulse, you reach down to the soil and scrape up a bit. It is darker than the dry, baked soils of the first range. This soil smells rich, crumbles in your hand, and even has a tiny worm trying to escape your disturbance. You wonder, what is going on?

Though the previous paragraphs describe an imaginary walk, the physical reality of these types of landscape transformations is not hard to find. Unfortunately, they are still rare, but word about the possibility of change is spreading from the American West, described above, to Zimbabwe, Australia, Argentina, and Mexico. The impetus comes from a movement started by Allan Savory called Holistic Management. It starts with an understanding of systems: energy systems, water systems, nutrient cycling systems, ecosystems, and not least, economic systems that penetrate to the family level. To understand how all this started, it is best to go back to Savory's story.

Allan Savory is from Zimbabwe, though when he was growing up the land was called Rhodesia, a self-governing colony of the United Kingdom. Today's Zimbabwe lies on the Southern African plateau, south of the Zambezi River, and most of the country is between 600 and 2,000 meters in elevation. The highest ridges in the country lie along the Mozambican border to the east, but the heart of the country is a broad, high plain that runs from northeast to southwest, with high-quality soils and good rainfall. This plain, which was free of malaria and other diseases that had stopped European settlement elsewhere in Africa, attracted Cecil Rhodes and colonial settlers. Starting around 1890, they took the highlands and used it to create a highly successful agricultural economy. Land is the wealth of Zimbabwe, and the whites had the best land. On either side of this high central plain, the land is drier, harsher, stony, and prone to drought. The best sites are occupied by African farmers, the rest is rangeland used by white and black ranchers. Along the western and southern borders of the country are a series of parks, established well before independence to attract tourists for the wildlife of the region. The full range of African wildlife once coursed across Zimbabwe, though now most wildlife is confined to the parks.

This is the setting where Savory grew up and worked in his early years. He had ranching experience and connections as a youth, but he chose to work in wildlife management after he finished school. Like Aldo Leopold in the United States, he was a keen observer of patterns in nature. His early observation was that elephants in the country were overpopulating the landscape, which led to its degradation. Like Leopold shooting wolves, Savory culled elephants, but the results showed no improvement. To his lasting dismay, he had killed elephants for no gain, only loss.[1] There had to be another reason for the degradation. Savory noticed that in the parks, the grasses were doing fine. In the rangeland occupied by cattle, however, even on ranches with the best management practices, the grassland ecology

---

1 Details on this story come from Allan Savory's TED Talk, "How to Fight Desertification and Reverse Climate Change," in February 2013: http://www.ted.com/talks/allan_savory_how_to _green_the_world_s_deserts_and_reverse_climate_change.

was degrading. What was the difference? By narrowing his focus to one species, really a collection of species but dominated by wildebeest, he saw a pattern that could explain the grasses' demise. Wildebeest and their companion animals—zebra, hartebeest, topi, and various gazelle—move in sizeable herds, not as large as the Serengeti migrations, but still a large group. They move together across the landscape in a bunch, eating everything in an area and trampling a lot of what they do not eat. Lions, hyenas, and wild dogs follow them across the land, picking off individuals that stray from the tightly packed groups. These loners are commonly injured, old, young and foolish, or sick. Leopards and crocodiles keep them from staying long at watering holes. The pattern was constant; dense, intense grazing that affected all the plants in an area was followed by a long period where the animals were gone. Even Cape buffalo followed this bunch-and-move pattern, though their range was not as extensive as the wildebeest association.

In contrast, how do ranchers manage cattle? First of all, ranchers of European background, wherever they are found on the planet, tend to follow a land ownership pattern. They buy, borrow, or steal a large spread of land in these drier environments and fence off the borders. Steal, borrow, or buy is really the correct order of these activities. We do not like to acknowledge the fact that the land was occupied by other people before Europeans came, and that those people had a completely different management approach that was totally ignored. The fenced land was typically within the same ecological type, with wide expanses of dry plains or hills interspersed with widely spaced, intermittent, or perennial streams that promoted woody perennial growth, including trees, vines, and shrubs of various types. Cattle were put into the rangeland and, for the most part, simply left to fend for themselves. Sometimes a rancher might have two pastures, one for summer or rainy-season grazing and another for winter or dry-season grazing, but the field management for both is the same. Twice yearly, the animals are grouped to assess health, to account for growth, to select for sale, and to brand or mark newborn animals. Once released, the cattle could go wherever they wanted. They were spread across the ranch, finding and grazing in their favorite spots, along streams, in well-watered lowlands, in shade. The animals had no incentive to stay together. There were no predators and no cowherds.

This neglect of cattle's original ecological niche is the cause of the decline. Cattle are thought to be the domesticated descendants of the aurochs, a Eurasian animal that falls into the same bovine family as American bison, water buffalo, musk ox, Himalaya yaks, European bison, and others. They naturally bunch and move in association with predators. Without this predator pressure, they spread out. Instead of eating everything, they overgraze their favorite plants, mainly succulent grasses, composites, legumes, and herbs, while they avoid anything unpleasant. In fact, they don't even step on the unpleasant plants. The result is that the unpleasant plants, such as thorny woody shrubs in Africa and Australia, or sage, tumbleweed, and spurge in temperate North America, and mesquite and paddle cacti in Mexico and Texas, thrive, while the grasses and forbs (a term for herbaceous perennials in a wide number of families edible by ruminants) slowly degrade and fail.

Savory noted this pattern among cattle and plants and began thinking about how to manage animals following a different protocol. Along the way, he made another important observation while visiting the American Southwest. In this part of the world, the problem of overgrazing was observed and noted by environmentalists concerned with the erosion of the American West. Although damage rates peaked in the period known as the Dust Bowl, degradation did not stop at its conclusion; it only slowed slightly with the return of the rains. Environmental groups pushed for an end to grazing on selected landscapes of aesthetic and recreational value owned or controlled by federal and state governments. This is a substantial percentage of the land in the American West. The groups won a number of battles, taking land away from ranchers and putting it into parks and wilderness areas, or simply making National Forest lands off-limits to grazing. When Savory looked at this land, he noted that it was not improving as the environmentalists had hoped; rather, it was continuing to degrade with a slightly different pattern.

Grasses did not disappear because they were constantly eaten; instead, they disappeared because they were not eaten at all. Many grasses grow naturally in clumps; many shoots derive from one crown just below the soil surface at the top of a perennial root system of great depth. When stems fully mature, they seed and die. If they are not eaten or stomped on, these stems remain above the plant to degrade by oxidation, turning gray, shading the crown, and limiting potential for growth when temperatures or rains permit development of new shoots. If this pattern continues, the root systems of the grasses begin to fail. Other plants follow a similar pattern. Savory realized that grasses evolved with the herd animals that eat them. It was not just that the grazers needed the grassland; the grassland needs the grazers just as much. Both overgrazing and no grazing result in the same degraded landscape.

At this point, Savory reached an understanding of grassland ecology that allowed him to think of a new way to manage what he terms "brittle landscapes." These are areas with climates that permit only seasonal growth, are subject to long periods of drought, and have specific requirements to stay healthy. To manage brittle landscapes successfully, you need a different tool bag than for other ecoregions. The Holistic Management tool bag that Savory developed includes components related to animals, to rest, to fire, and to fencing. The animals' job is to eat the grasses and forbs on a regular basis. To do this, they need to eat everything edible on a landscape, not just their favorites, and trample the inedible. The fence in this case is used not as a passive border marker, but as an active tool that is moved regularly to keep the animals in a tighter area, ideally an area that they can eat in one day, or perhaps just a few days. Then they must move, so the electric fence must move too. This gives the animals a new stock of ready-to-eat grass and forbs, and it allows the land that was just eaten down a chance to recover without a cap of old growth blocking the sunlight. Weeds such as thistles and leafy spurge and seedlings of acacia and mesquite are trampled, while the grasses and forbs, being better equipped to handle the damage, recover quickly and shade them out. Rest leads to recovery, and to the recurring need for grazing when the time is right. On some landscapes, where woody plants have overtaken the herbaceous vegetation, fire is used as the key tool to reduce their dominance. When woody vegetation becomes totally dominant in dry landscapes, fire danger gets very high. By reducing the woody biomass and establishing a regular cycle of grazing and rest, the land improves.

An ecological aside is needed here. It is easy to think that woody biomass is a good thing, especially for those of us who live in deciduous forests of the East Coast or in the wet Pacific rainforest. In brittle landscapes, the woody biomass never gets as dense as in these wetter situations. The trees and shrubs are often thorny and are commonly small. They have shallow root systems, though some may have a deep taproot to get water. They mainly grow quickly when rains come, then go dormant for much of the year and fail to keep the soil well-covered. The overall gain in biomass happens with initial growth and then stops. Below-ground biomass peaks at a low level and usually does not rise above about 2% by weight in the top foot of soil. Grasses and forbs, in contrast, produce a much deeper and more fibrous root system. More than half the total biomass production of these species occurs below ground. Root hairs and side roots are continually produced and sloughed off, feeding a rich population of bacteria, fungi, and other organisms in a complex underground food web. This production increases underground soil carbon to well beyond the 2% level of woody plant systems. The potential of soils to store carbon in these brittle landscapes is an untapped reserve for storage of atmospheric carbon, but using it will take a drastic change in the management of rangeland on a planetary scale.

Unfortunately, there is no such thing as planetary-scale action. There is only local action, one ranch at a time. This brings in other factors besides the four tools that Savory mentions. When dealing with humans and culture, things become more complicated than simply looking at the natural processes. Holistic Management is not just about the use of the four tools; you also have to consider what humans want and need in the system. For example, what kind of lifestyle do people want to live? How much money do they need to make? How large is their family? What are relationships like within that family? What are their goals, both long-term and short-term? Do they like to work with people? Do they prefer independence and privacy? Are they fascinated with wildlife, or focused on the management of animals? All these factors come into consideration when designing a holistic system for a given piece of land. In fact, social system healing often supersedes ecological system healing; you cannot do the latter until you correct the former. An example of this comes from the book *Beyond the Rangeland Conflict* by Dan Dagget (1995). A ranch in Colorado, in the mountains west of Denver, was having trouble because of overgrazing and frequent flooding in the heavy, but widely spaced, storms of the region. Without grasses and healthy forest on the mountain slopes, rainfall simply washed off the land. The extended family that owned the farm wanted to implement Holistic Management practices but could not get things established smoothly. When the advisors from the Holistic Management Institute, founded by Allan Savory and based in Santa Fe, New Mexico, went to help, they found that a dysfunctional marriage lay at the heart of the problem, since the couple served as primary managers but did not agree on a solution. It was not until this relationship difficulty was resolved that the broader farm management strategy could be implemented.

Another story from the same book illustrates some of the institutional problems that implementation of Holistic Management can butt up against. Tony and Jerrie Tipton operate a ranch on land in Nevada that, like many in the region, is partly their own land and partly owned by the federal government under the jurisdiction of the Bureau of Land Management (BLM). Adjacent to their land was a large abandoned mine with a long ridge of saline, eroding mine tailings that leaked onto their property. They wanted to manage these mine tailings, but the BLM did not believe that using cattle to heal the mine tailings slope was a wise thing to do, even though the BLM's previous attempts to sow grass had failed many times. Eventually the BLM relented and allowed the couple to try. The Tiptons fenced off the slope using temporary electric fencing and spread hay from their own property across the slope. Then they let their cattle in to eat the hay. The cattle ate, trampled, urinated, and defecated all over the slope, eating most of the hay and driving seeds, nutrients, and mulch into the soil. Then the cattle were removed. When the rare rains came, grass sprouted and grew. It was grass adapted to the climate, and it thrived. The land had its rest. About a year later, the Tiptons were ready to graze the land again, but the BLM refused to allow them to do so, citing the improved conditions of the slope and the problem of overgrazing by cattle. The Tiptons argued that over-resting land was as bad as overgrazing, but the BLM refused. The bickering went on until the BLM again saw signs of degradation on the slopes. They relented and decided to let the Tiptons bring their cattle back onto half the area. The cattle had to have supplemental hay because the grasses were old and decaying, but this strategy did the trick and the slope healed again. Now the relationship with the BLM has improved. Unfortunately, these lessons do not spread easily, because entrenched opinions on all sides, including those of environmentalists, ranchers, and government land managers, are not easily swayed by other positions. Nor should it be said that Holistic Management for grassland is perfect for all environments or needs. It is a solution for rangeland management that deserves consideration, but it must be done within the social, political, economic, and ecological context of a particular place, and each place requires a nuanced, carefully tailored management plan.

Savory has specifically aimed his method for managing beef operations at farmers and ranchers using brittle landscapes, the semiarid lands that make up about 24 million square kilometers of the planet's surface. Chapter 10, "Putting Carbon Where It Belongs: An Introduction to Soil," explores in depth the benefits and potential carbon capture that could occur on such landscapes. Even a rise of 1% in soil carbon on this land use type could reduce atmospheric carbon by 26 ppm.[2] This tool could prove to be a key component of any plan to address our present climate emergency. At the same time, stocking rates for cattle would go up, not down. It turns out that using the grazing techniques Savory advocates will increase the land's carrying capacity for both cattle and wildlife, while reducing erosion and other forms of land degradation.

Proving this point involves bringing two other sources into the discussion. The first is Andre Voisin of Normandy in Northwest France, a place with a long history of agriculture and a maritime climate quite different from the brittle climates that Savory inhabits. Voisin was a biochemist and farmer who worked with animals in a veterinary school and on his own land. Like Savory, he was a keen observer of his cattle, as well as an academic who read what others had done with cattle in the past. He noticed that cattle are happiest when moved into a field with fresh grass, untainted by their own recent presence. As he studied their behavior, he also recognized how the grass responded. In Normandy's moist climate with low temperatures and high humidity much of the year, grasses grew continuously. When the grasses were grazed too short, less than 5 cm, it took them some time to put on a new burst of growth. If the animals were not allowed to graze them too short, then the grasses came back more quickly after the cattle were removed. Voisin slowly developed the idea that if you rotate the animals from smaller fields more frequently, you had a better yield of grass and cattle growth than if you leave them in one place for too long. On the flip side, if you do not graze for a long time, the grass goes to seed and becomes unpalatable for the animals. Not content with his own observations, Voisin looked for other information in the cattle management literature and found this gem from 1777 in Scotland:

---

2   This is an equivalent value, but it is not the whole story. Ocean carbonates are in equilibrium with atmospheric carbon dioxide. Any reduction in atmospheric CO_2 opens up the ocean to release its excess carbonate back into the atmosphere CO_2 These re-equilibrate constantly. While sequestering atmospheric carbon of the quantity is a good thing, the actual drawdown is less because of oceanic release. The scientists who cooperatively developed the book *Drawdown* (Hawken 2017) have more information on this at the Project Drawdown® website (https://drawdown.org/).

To obtain this constant supply of fresh grass, let us suppose that a farmer who has any extent of pasture ground, should have it divided into fifteen or twenty divisions, nearly of equal value; and that, instead of allowing his beasts to roam indiscriminately through the whole at once, he collects the whole number of beasts that he intends to feed into one flock, and turns them all at once into one of these divisions; which, being quite fresh, and of a sufficient length for a full bite, would please their palate so much as to induce them to eat of it greedily, and fill their bellies before they thought of roaming about, and thus destroying it with their feet. And if the number of beasts were so great as to consume the best part of the grass of one of these enclosures in one day, they might be allowed to remain there no longer;—giving them a fresh park every morning, so as that the same delicious repast might be again repeated. And if there were just so many parks as there required days to make the grass of these fields advance to a proper length after being eaten bare down, the first field would be ready to receive them by the time they had gone over all the others; so that they might thus be carried round in a constant rotation.[3]

Out of this personal experience and reading, Voisin developed what has become known widely as "rapid rotation grazing." An illustration of this grazing pattern is shown in Figure 12.1. Voisin published his book on the topic in 1957, and it has influenced people like Allan Savory and Joel Salatin. (Salatin was made famous in Michael Pollan's *Omnivore's Dilemma*; he is an author himself, with several books published about his experience on his own Polyface Farm.)

Since I live in the Shenandoah Valley, own a share in a cattle farm, and work with farmers as part of my teaching activities, I have made a point of visiting Polyface Farm frequently. I even purchase meat from this farm, mostly chicken and pork since we already have our own beef supply. Joel's father bought the land that is now Polyface in 1961. At that time, it was a degraded farm that raised animals and annual crops. It was sold cheaply because it really was not worth much. The land could not support a farmer by itself, so Joel's father worked off-site and began a program to improve the land, removing junk and devising a system for grazing cattle that would fit the ecology of the land. Voisin's advice on rotational grazing was part of his vision. Grazing in the woods and taking out loans to improve farm infra-structure were not acceptable to him. By 1980, Joel was out of school, had started a family,

---

3   From A. Voisin's *Grass Productivity* (Washington, DC: Island Press 1988), taken from http://upthelane-farm.wordpress.com/2009/12/31/rotational-grazing-past-present-future/, a blog site by grass farmers on Up the Lane Farm in central Ohio.

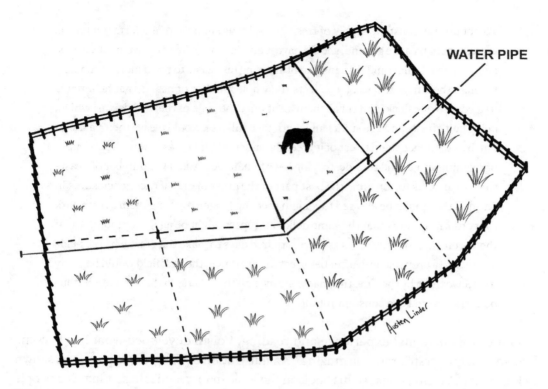

WATER PIPE

FIGURE 12.1 Rotational grazing means keeping all the cattle, or other grazers, concentrated in one paddock and moving frequently. A key aspect and limiting factor in this is access to water. This can be resolved by a piping system that is central, allowing use of a mobile watering spot that is fed from the mainline pipe. This is essential in hot, dry conditions where animals need to drink more often. The perimeter of the large field is fixed with an electric wire; then a temporary wire is used to mark the daily grazing area, which can vary in size depending on conditions. In periods of rapid growth the fields are smaller, which allows the making of hay. In times of slow growth, fields are larger to provide one day's worth of fodder. Rotation allows many days, or even months, of rest and regrowth before the animals return for another day of feeding.

and was ready to take on farming full-time. He and his father set up a watering system that allowed them to gravity-feed water to all parts of the pasture using connections to a main line from a pond high on the land they owned. This enabled Joel to adhere to a rapid rotational grazing cycle. It took a while to get the rhythm of this system. Unlike Normandy, France, the Shenandoah Valley is hot and dry with seasonally adjusted growth patterns. In spring, things grow quickly and one day of grazing requires a small patch. As summer progresses and growth slows, bigger patches are needed. Observation of growth cycles and cattle needs informed their management system.

As they began to get the grazing pattern right, they began integrating chickens into the farm following the cattle. The birds were in two systems. One group consisted of pastured broilers kept in 10 × 12-foot pens that were moved daily across a large field. Cattle grazed the land before and after the broilers crossed, but the broilers passed over a given piece of grass only once a year. Feeding broilers grass and insect larvae associated with cow manure cut their daily grain consumption by 30%, though it increased holding time to slaughter. But unlike in a poultry house situation, there is no manure problem; chicken manure is a directly applied input benefiting the grass. This reduces chicken stress due to ammonia release in the poultry house, and it increases the amount of nitrogen available for use by plants.

The second poultry management activity is the egg mobile. A flock of egg-laying hens, trained to live in and around a mobile chicken hutch with nesting boxes, follows the cattle by three days. These chickens have two tasks: lay eggs and rip apart cow patties. They do the latter with gusto, as the fly larvae in the patties provide excellent nutrition. This action helps the grass by eliminating the smothering of the growing crown and by evenly distributing the fertility of the cow pie. The chickens also break the parasite cycle in the pasture, so that when the cattle pass by for the next grazing period, they are free of flies and other troubling critters that could cause problems with the herd.

As time went on, Salatin noticed that large rocks that had been in his pastures began disappearing. The gullies, badly eroded when the farm was purchased, had filled with organic debris and growth, even becoming swampy during rains. The soil then became deeper, darker, pocked with worm channels, and easier to penetrate with portable electric fence posts. This was not due to the rapid formation of mineral soil; rather, it came about because the organic fraction of the soil increased and the bulk density stemming from overuse of farm equipment was reversing. Polyface Farm became a carbon sink by managing the cattle correctly.

Now it is time for some numbers, using another farm to compare with Polyface. That farm is mine, co-owned with five other families. We have 28 acres of pasture, about the same amount of woodland, and we usually run around 30 head of Black Angus in a cow calf operation, selling registered Black Angus bulls. Normally our cattle are on pasture from mid-March until the end of October, though the exact dates vary according to conditions such as rainfall and temperature. We feed hay from November to mid-March. This means our animals are on pasture about 230 days. We have eight pastures carved out of our 28 acres, and the cattle are rotated from one pasture to the next as needed. We are not systematic about this in the way that Polyface manages and Voisin recommends. Virginia Cooperative Extension uses a metric called "grazing days per acre" as a measure of grassland productivity. Since we have 30 animals on 28 acres for 230 days, we are getting about 245 cow days per acre, but this includes calves, which don't eat quite as much, so the actual value is about 210 cow days per acre for fully grown animals. The average in the Shenandoah Valley is between 80 and 100 cow days per acre. The difference is due to our rotational grazing pattern. Admittedly, we are not consistent with this. Polyface has 150 animals on 100 acres and grazes longer:

270 days in an average year. This gives them a measurement of over 400 cow days per acre, including the calves. The difference is just like the Scottish farmer reported in 1777; if you move your cows every day, the pasture is tastier and recovers better. Good management means more cattle and less erosion. When the land is fully healthy, there will be no erosion at all in typical years, and only limited erosion in extreme climate events, basically the background erosion rate of one ton per acre per year.

In an attempt to move our farm toward the Voisin recommendations, we chose to participate in a USDA and state program called the Conservation Reserve Enhancement Program. In return for excluding our cattle from our ephemeral stream, woodland, and ponds for a minimum of 15 years, the program pays for fencing and an alternative watering system. This program allowed us to increase our number of grazing paddocks from five to eight and to decrease the number of days the animals spend in each paddock. The key feature is to increase the intensity of grazing but simultaneously increase rest time. Having available water in each paddock allows us to do this, since water was the limiting factor in permitting a rotational grazing strategy. Now we monitor the health of both our new grazing land and the separated stream and woodland to get a sense of the ecological impact. In 2015 we increased the cow days per acre to 265.[4] Healing the land will take some time. So will changing our farm management habits, but the process has started.

So now we can circle back to brittle landscapes and Holistic Management. Having a deeply rooted solution to the problem of brittle landscapes requires a variety of different conditions and tools. Above all else, there needs to be a strong, culturally sound base of operation. This might arise from a stable family or extended family, from a strong community, town, or village, or from a culture of cooperation on a wide landscape. Second, you need a common set of goals, and a plan of action to reach those goals. You have to know what you want as a person, as a family, and as a larger group before you can decide on the steps needed to reach those goals. Third, you need a sound ecological understanding of your place, its soils, its climate, its species composition, and the collection of biotic and abiotic factors that define the place. With these three items—cultural awareness, common goals, and a deep ecological understanding based on observations of natural patterns—you can then implement the regenerative management strategy. This means starting slowly and perhaps starting small, then growing into a system that covers the land in the way that works for you, your family and community, and the ecology of that place.

---

4   This may be partly due to rainfall in 2015. Each year the numbers will vary depending upon climatic conditions. Droughts happen, as they did from 1999 to 2002, and so do extra-high rainfall years, like 2018. The extremes bring problems quite different than the norm for a farm.

Study Questions

1. Have you ever thought about where your beef comes from and how it is grown? Can you trace the meat you eat back to its point of origin, or perhaps just to the company that packed it for sale? What impact did that beef have on the ecosystem where it was raised?

2. The western United States, especially from the Rocky Mountains to the Sierra Nevada and the Cascades, is a mix of land owned by the BLM, the National Forest Service, Indian reservations, large private ranchers, and a growing number of wealthy ranchette owners who live on the land only episodically in a second home. How does this land ownership pattern impact ecosystems?

3. Is the absence of animals really just as bad as having too many poorly managed ones, as Allan Savory claims? What further evidence can you find to support your view?

4. Do the lessons that Allan Savory learned apply to landscapes that are not as brittle, such as the agricultural landscapes of Iowa or the forested regions of Kentucky and the Appalachians? What are the implications of applying his recommendations more broadly?

References

Brown, Gabe. 2018. *Dirt to Soil*. White River Junction, VT: Chelsea Green Publishing.

Dagget, D. 1995. *Beyond the Rangeland Conflict: Toward a West That Works*. Kaysville, UT: Gibbs Smith. (2nd edition published by the Good Steward Project, January 2000).

Hawken, Paul, ed. 2017. *Drawdown: The Most Comprehensive Plan Ever Proposed to Reverse Global Warming*. New York: Penguin.

Ohlson, Kristin. 2014. *The Soil Will Save Us: How Scientists, Farmers and Foodies Are Healing the Soil to Save the Planet*. New York: Rodale Books.

Pollan, M. 2006. *The Omnivore's Dilemma: A Natural History of Four Meals*. New York: Random House.

Rueschel, J. 2006. *Grass-Fed Cattle: How to Produce and Market Natural Beef*. North Adams, MA: Storey Publishing.

Salatin, J. 1995. *Salad Bar Beef*. Swoope, VA: Polyface Inc.

Salatin, J. 1998. *You Can Farm: The Entrepreneur's Guide to Start & Succeed in a Farming Enterprise*. Brattleboro, VT: Echo Point Books & Media.

Savory, A., and J. Butterfield. 2006. *Holistic Management Handbook*. Washington, DC: Island Press.

Voisin, A. 1988. *Grass Productivity*. Washington, DC: Island Press. (Originally published in 1957).

White, Courtney. 2014. *Grass, Soil, Hope: A Journey through Carbon Country*. White River Junction, VT: Chelsea Green Publishing.

Chapter 13

The Trillion Tree Project
Tree Crops and the Benefits of Agroforestry

Introduction

Though the phrase is catchy and alliterative, is planting a trillion trees possible? We need to start with the data about how much potential forest there is on the planet. The land mass of Earth is approximately 29% of the surface area of the planet, which equals 148.94 million kilometers squared (km^2). Of this, about 20% is extreme desert that grows little except in isolated and tiny oases, which are locally important but do not amount to much on a global scale. Another 11 million km^2 is ice, also unavailable for human use. Tundra, northern taiga, and taiga, 25.5 million km^2, really should be off-limits to human exploitation. After replanting the trees that have already been removed, humanity should leave these places alone. With these areas unavailable or off-limits, 83 million km^2 remain that could have trees. However, 25% of the global total is ecologically dominated by cool, warm, and savanna grassland. This leaves 45 million km^2—4.5 billion hectares, or 30% of the planet—dominated by some type of forest ecosystem.[1] A map of the global forest is given in Figure 13.1. One trillion trees divided by 4.5 billion hectares gives you a total of 222 trees per hectare, or about 45 m^2 per tree, which is more space than most trees need in a closed canopy forest setting, except perhaps a giant sequoia or a baobab reaching maturity. There is room for one trillion more trees on the planet. The real question is how we grow and manage them.[2]

---

1   These numbers are derived from table 6.1 in Chapter 10, "Putting Carbon Where It Belongs: An Introduction to Soil."

2   Since this was written, the journal *Nature* has published a new study, entitled "Mapping Tree Density at a Global Scale." The article's authors estimate that the global population of trees is now just above three trillion, and that this represents a decline of some 46% since the dawn of human civilization (Crowther et al. 2015).

FIGURE 13.1   Global forests with changes in total covered between 2000 and 2012 based on satellite imagery.[3]

One method widely promoted to both increase trees in the ground and use them to benefit agriculture is called agroforestry. It is the integrated and intentional use of trees in association with crops that takes a variety of forms globally. The most widely known institution promoting agroforestry is the International Center for Research in Agroforestry (ICRAF), headquartered in Nairobi, Kenya. ICRAF defines *agroforestry* this way:

> A dynamic, ecologically based, natural resources management system that, through the integration of trees on farms and in the agricultural landscape, diversifies and sustains production for increased social, economic and environmental benefits for land users at all levels.[4]

This chapter explains the nature of agroforestry in more detail in the larger context of planting more trees planet-wide as a response to climate change.

The Precursor to Agroforestry in North America

In the mid-1930s, the Midwest region of the United States went through an economic depression and a "Dust Bowl." The latter was caused by a severe drought following years of inappropriate farming on shortgrass prairies that left a barren landscape. It was

---

3   For a wonderful interactive map on the global forest, run by the University of Maryland and powered by Google Earth, go to http://earthenginepartners.appspot.com/google.com/science-2013-global-forest.

4   http://www.worldagroforestry.org/

less well-known that the eastern, northern, and far western parts of the United States had already suffered from landscape calamities. Shenandoah National Park, much of Appalachia, and a large part of the Piedmont actually consisted of a long stretch of partially abandoned farmland, deforested during the nineteenth century to grow oats and other small grains for feeding horses, the transportation system of that era. When the horses gave way to the automobile, these farms collapsed because they could not produce wheat and corn competitively with those further west. There are more trees in the Piedmont and Appalachian regions of the East now than there were between the Civil War (1860s) and World War II (1940s).

In the 1920s, one of the most forward-thinking and innovative foresters in the United States presented an idea that would have radically healed the American eastern forest and reduced much of the agricultural shift to the middle of the country. J. Russell Smith was a professor of economic geography at Columbia University and a professor of industry at the Wharton School, as well as being closely associated with the US Department of Agriculture and the Northern Nut Growers Association. He had a passion for using trees to provide more than just timber. In 1929, J. Russell Smith published a book called *Tree Crops*. His working thesis was simple: the agriculture that dominated much of the warm temperate belt from the subtropics to latitude 50° north was inappropriately practiced on steep hillsides in the foothills and mountains of Appalachia, the loess hills of China, and across much of the Middle East and the Mediterranean basin. The European farming systems exported to the United States were designed for light rains on relatively flat land. The Appalachians (analogous to hilly land everywhere) were subject to heavy thunderstorms that could rapidly strip barren land of its topsoil. Any agriculture that left the land uncovered was dangerous. Smith documented sheet erosion damage in Algeria, extreme gully erosion in China near the Great Wall, as well as deep loss of topsoil on gently sloping land in Illinois and steeper corn land in Alabama and Georgia in the southern Appalachian foothills. Agriculture could work in these areas only if they grew permanent crops. He pushed tree crops: fruit-, nut-, and fodder-producing trees.

This requires a change in mindset. Today, American agriculture is dominated by two energy-intensive crops, corn and soybeans, and much of our food production system is based on these two primary sources. When we eat beef, pork, chicken, turkey, and even farm-raised salmon, we are eating corn and soybeans. As Michael Pollan famously said, "You are what you eat eats."[5] Until recently, over half of all the corn in the United States, and an even higher

---

5   Michael Pollan, *In Defense of Food* (New York: Penguin, 2009).

percentage of soy, was fed to livestock.[6] These domestic animals did not live on corn and soybeans until the twentieth century. What if they ate what was normal for them? Cattle eat grass and herbaceous perennials. Pigs, turkeys, and goats gobble tree crops (acorns, chestnuts, fruits, and leaves). Chickens scratch for grubs, worms, bugs, fly larvae, and almost any seeds and greens they can find.

Smith documents a number of species that do well throughout the eastern part of the United States and beyond that could help change agriculture. His first example comes from the island of Corsica, a fiercely independent province of France, located in the Mediterranean Sea off the coast of Italy and Southern France. The island is mountainous, rugged, and rocky, but it is covered with trees and shows little sign of erosion. Most of the trees between 1,000 and 3,000 feet in elevation are the European chestnut (*Castanea sativa*). Americans have little knowledge of chestnuts except from a Christmas song that starts, "Chestnuts roasting on an open fire." We lost the American chestnut between 1904 and 1926 when a fungal disease was accidentally imported to the Brooklyn Botanical Garden on a Chinese chestnut and spread to the nonresistant American chestnut. The European and Chinese trees are resistant to the fungus. On Corsica, the European version thrives on the steep slopes, producing an annual bounty of chestnuts eaten directly by humans and fed to pigs, goats, and other animals. The agriculture of Corsica is based around this harvest, and it requires neither tillage nor fertilizer, and limited mechanization. For Smith, it became a model for a hill country agricultural revolution. While we lack a native chestnut at this time,[7] the European and Chinese (*Castanea mollissima*) varieties do well in the mid-Atlantic region. The number of chestnuts grown in the United States is presently very low. We have locked our agriculture into unsustainable crops with antiecological reasoning. It is time that we start looking at the details of Smith's 1929 proposal and implementing them.

Smith looked at the many resources within the eastern deciduous forest of the United States that qualify. Chestnuts are essentially equivalent to a grain crop. They are sweeter than grains when roasted, but the amount of oils and protein is similar. Grazing pigs in a

---

6   Only recently has that percentage for corn dropped, though the amount fed to livestock has not. The recent rise in corn production goes to produce alcohol for fuel.

7   The American Chestnut Foundation (ACF) is working on backcrossing American Chestnut (*Castanea dentata*) with Chinese Chestnut, which suffers only minor cosmetic damage from the blight. The ACF's work has progressed to the point that they are now testing a 15/16 American/Chinese cross that is intercrossed to eliminate genetic susceptibility to blight. Once these highly resistant crosses are confirmed, the ACF will begin to introduce them widely across the American chestnut's former range, which extended from Mississippi and Alabama to Maine and southern Ontario along Lake Erie. Regional adaptations will be required, but ACF has farms in many places working on genetic stock. See www.acf.org.

chestnut woodland makes sense, because pigs will eat chestnuts from the forest floor without hesitation. They will also eat acorns. These seeds are mostly inedible for people, because, unlike pigs, we lack the proper bacteria and digestive system to deal with the acorn's high tannin content. Many ruminants, such as goats, deer, llamas, and camels, can handle acorns without a problem, whether from red or white oak groups. Red oak acorns are full of tannin and were seldom consumed as human food.[8] White oak acorns have less tannin, and they served as a major part of the diet for Native Americans in California and throughout the United States when available. In some cases, up to 25% of these people's calories came from acorns. The white oak acorn is quite nutritious and is higher in fat than grains are, about 18% dry weight. Before eating, the acorn needs to be ground and leached in water to get the tannins out.[9] Sometimes this takes three washings. Once washed, the acorn can be mixed with grain flour to make breads or can be eaten as porridge by itself. The high oil content, according to Smith, makes it taste like a bread-and-butter mix. Species potentially eaten in the United States include the swamp white oak (*Quercus bicolor*), white oak (*Q. alba*), chestnut oak (*Q. montana*), and bur oak (*Q. macrocarpa*), as well as a number of California species. In the Mediterranean, the evergreen holly oak (*Q. ilex*) produces an acorn that can be roasted like a chestnut, as it has low tannin content. The swamp chestnut oak (*Q. micheauxii*) is also edible without leaching the seed.[10]

The eastern deciduous forest has many fodder species other than oaks. Among them is the mulberry. Though we normally think of mulberries in association with silk (the silkworm caterpillars prefer mulberry leaves), the fruits and leaves are eaten by a number of farm animals. Ruminants go for the leaves, while pigs and chickens prefer the berries. These animals eat both from the ground, so there is no need for harvesting. Although the berries are not easily stored, apart from freezing, drying, or canning them, some varieties have a very long fruiting season and will provide food for the animals over a two-month production period. This often happens in summer before acorns or chestnuts are ripe. When animals are allowed to forage for themselves, having a diet that produces food over time is critical.

---

8   This is not as definitive as originally thought. You can eat red oak acorns if you grind them up, soak them in water, discard the water and repeat. Two or three washing removes most of the tannin and the resulting flour is easily used in baking.

9   Tannins were once used for treating leather to make it stiff for shoes. Because this is a difficult process, most leather shoes, especially the soles, use the toxic metal chromium as documented in McDonough and Brungart's book *Cradle to Cradle* (New York: North Point Press, 2002). The tannins extracted from acorns are useful for this task and far less toxic than chromium when floating in the environment.

10   *The USDA Field Guide to Native Oak Species of Eastern North America*, by J. Stein, D. Binion, and R. Acciavatti (2003), is an excellent resource: http://www.fs.fed.us/foresthealth/technology/pdfs/fieldguide.pdf

Depending on one species to supply all of an animal's needs is foolish. In Smith's day, when pigs were not factory-farmed but lived on pasture, mulberries were part of the food system. Mulberry plants were important for the mix; they are easily planted, they grow quickly, they fruit early, consistently, and heavily, and they provide timber, posts, and firewood. The mulberry on farms disappeared with the rush to industrialize agriculture. Ripe mulberries are also tasty food for people and can be dried and eaten later, but in the long term they are more important as animal food.

There are some exceptions to the use of mulberry. In Tajikistan and Afghanistan, among the Pamirs along the old China Silk Road, the white mulberry (*Morus alba*) holds a special place. Legend has it that the trees were smuggled out of China when a Pamir leader married a Chinese princess, who brought the mulberry and silk moth with her. Though the production of silk never took off in the region, the fruit became part of the diet. To the Pamir in the lowlands of that very elevated region, the mulberry is the single most important fruit. When the Soviet Union collapsed and Tajikistan went through a period of violence and instability with the absence of food imports, the mulberry became a major part of the diet. Dried fruit was used like a grain (van Oudenhoven and Haider 2017). Unfortunately, the red mulberry (*M. rubra*) of the eastern United States does not hold the same lofty place as the white mulberry of Asia.

Another underappreciated tree is the American persimmon (*Diospyrus virginiana*), which produces an edible fruit. It is not the large flavorful yellow of the Asiatic persimmon (*D. kaka*) found in the supermarket. If an American persimmon is picked before the first frost, even though soft and ripe in appearance, it has a mouth-puckering astringency. With a bit of patience, a good frost, and a willingness to pick the fruit off the ground, these persimmons are as delicious as any purchased in the market—if the opossums, bears, and deer don't get them first. During the slave era and later, blacks in the US South often hunted possums at night in persimmon trees where the animals flocked to the fruit in season. Pigs, chickens, turkeys, and most other farm animals relish the fruit. Yet the tree has never gained a foothold in the United States. It grows over a broad range, on poor, eroded, or sandy soils. It also has a very long fruiting season, dropping ripe fruit from September to February. It is a perfect complement to the mulberry for foraging pigs, cattle, horses, turkeys, and chickens. The persimmon tree is harder to start than the mulberry or other fruit like apples, but because its leaves are basically inedible, once it starts growing, it requires less care and lives for a long time. Naturally occurring trees also support grafted stock of better varieties quite easily. Though they provide fairly dense shade, persimmons do well next to crops and do not seem to compete with them for nutrients and moisture. Smith pleaded for more research on the persimmon in 1929, and some research has gone into improving the American varieties and importing Asian types. Some new varieties have less astringent fruit and larger sizes. The market for persimmon has improved since Smith's day, but it remains limited.

The argument about the impact of eating meat assumes that the meat animals are fed corn and soybeans, slaughtered in centralized industrial plants, and shipped to stores around the country. Smith has pointed us to trees that provide food for pigs, chickens, turkeys, and goats. What about cattle? They are grazers and they belong on the prairie, but they like shade too. Smith identifies the honey locust (*Gleditsia triacanthos*) as the perfect tree for these animals in the eastern half of the United States. The honey locust thrives in moist lowland habitats but will grow on drier sites with deeper soils. It is a legume, producing prolific numbers of sweet pods that cattle and other animals like to eat either green or dry. The tree has an open canopy that allows some light through it and does not shade out or otherwise inhibit grass growth. It is a great pasture tree, with one notable exception. The honey locust evolved in the presence of now-departed megafauna like the mammoth and giant ground sloths, which loved the leaves and pods. In order to prevent an annual stripping of all photosynthesizing parts, the plant developed wickedly long thorns that stabbed anything larger than a squirrel attempting to grab its trunk or branches. The fiendish thorns allowed the honey locust to thrive, and the trees were spread by the same animals that eagerly ate fallen pods.[11] These animals are gone now, but the thorns remain on most wild trees. Humans have found some varieties without them and have propagated those varieties. Cattle can now take over the duties formerly accomplished by sloths and put on weight at the same time. People are able to eat the honey locust pods, but the pods take a lot of time to prepare. The tree feeds us best via milk or meat of the cattle and goats that eat the pods.

The honey locust is a tree of the temperate deciduous forests, but other ecosystems have trees that serve a similar role. In the semiarid tropics, the acacia species provide both pods and foliage that make excellent fodder for goats and camels. *Acacia tortillis*[12] and *Faidherbia albida* (formerly *A. albida*) are excellent examples. In the Americas, the mesquite group accomplishes this job. *Prosopis glandulosa*, called honey mesquite, has sweet pods that are made into flour and eaten by native peoples in northwestern Mexico and the US Southwest. Cattle and horses can eat these pods directly, and the seed passes through their gut ready to germinate in the provided fertilizer. If the pods are ground, however, the nutritional value of the seed becomes available to the animals, making it nearly equivalent to feeding cattle grain mixed with a high fiber source. *Prosopis juliflora, P. chiliensis,* and *P. velutina* are

---

11   Whit Bronaugh, "The Trees That Miss the Mammoths," *American Forests* Magazine, http://www.americanforests.org/magazine/article/trees-that-miss-the-mammoths/.

12   The Acacia genus in Africa has been divided into two new genera. *Acacia tortillis* is now *Vachellia tortilis*.

excellent fodder producers, too. Acacias and mesquite are also thorny to protect their vegetation in dry landscapes. The trees do not become weedy in their natural habitat, but they do so with poor grazing management. The lessons Smith learned in the early twentieth century have been ignored in most of the United States. Mesquite is treated as a weed by ranchers in places such as western Texas, because these people tend to work against, rather than with, natural systems. However, Kenyan pastoralists will bag and sell *A. tortillis* pods in dry years to areas that do not have access to their own supply. For them, *A. tortillis* is the single most important tree for their cattle, sheep, and goats.

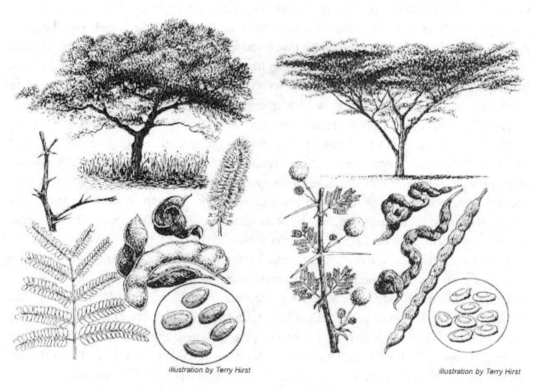

illustration by Terry Hirst   illustration by Terry Hirst

FIGURE 13.2 Two trees in Africa widely used for agroforesty: *Faidherbia albida* is shown on the left and *Vachellia tortillis* on the right. The former is used in association with crops throughout its range, but perhaps most widely across the Sahel from Senegal to Sudan. *V. tortillis* is even more tolerant of arid conditions and is primarily used as a fodder tree for camels and goats, with pods sometimes collected and sold in the market.[13]

13   These illustrations were drawn by Terry Hirst for the website Agroforestry Trees of Kenya based on *A Pocket Directory of Trees and Seeds in Kenya* (Teel 1984). See http://agroforesttrees.cisat.jmu.edu/.

In the season of the black walnut (*Juglans nigra*) every fall, around early September, the wood's edge becomes a bit more dangerous, causing twisted ankles and bumps on the head. The tree grows on bottomland soils, usually well-drained and moist, throughout the eastern part of the United States. It has dark wood of excellent quality that is easy to work. It has edible nuts that are encased in a hard shell, sometimes used for industrial purposes as a grinding agent, and a soft outer covering that stains just about everything it touches a dark brown. Squirrels work hard to get at the nutmeat. It is rich, and very high in protein, oils, and calories. It makes good food for people, but is considered too strong to eat by itself, so it ends up mostly in ice cream and confectionaries. The squirrels commonly plant it for storage, then maybe forget about it or do not need it for food later, so it grows everywhere soils are suitable. The roots exude a chemical called juglone that has a strong allopathic effect on the Solanaceae family, including tomatoes, potatoes, eggplant, and peppers, and also other plants, like blueberries, blackberries, and apples. A number are unaffected by the black walnut, including most grasses and pasture species. In general, well-aerated compost over two months old made from black walnut leaves and seed husks will not harm any plants.[14] Smith felt that black walnut deserved a lot more attention from plant breeders than it had received in his day. The nuts are naturally better than most wild nuts, and improvements could make them superior to the English/Carpathian/Persian walnut, *J. regia*.

One of the themes that makes Smith's book stand out is his willingness to see things in a different way than Americans of his and our generations. His chapter on the Persian walnut is an excellent example. Americans tend to think in grand visions, like "amber waves of grain" stretching to the horizon, and we like monocultures. Smith did not. He wanted fields that produced but didn't erode. So he looked for ways to grow food that preserved the environment. When he considered Persian walnuts in Europe and Asia, he saw trees growing alone or scattered around fields in spots less useful for annual crops. He asked a farmer in France why he grew isolated walnuts and the farmer responded, "You see, monsieur, it is zis way. It is income wizout labor." Smith identified what we now call agroforestry: the deliberate management of trees in a diverse farming system.

Most of Smith's chapter on the Persian walnut is devoted to developing varieties suitable for the climate of the eastern United States. The varieties we imported from Europe are adapted to cool, moist winters and mild summers. This area of the United States is hotter in the summer, with powerful rains and higher humidity, and colder in the winter, with frequent killing frosts. We needed a variety suitable for this climate, but instead we grew the walnuts in California and Oregon in monoculture orchards and shipped them

---

14   https://www.hort.net/lists/perennials/jul03/msg00029.html.

around the country. The idea of breeding a variety of walnut for the East Coast had not occurred to anyone, especially to people with enough money to support such a long-term enterprise. Smith also felt that we had not looked into developing commercially viable varieties of American native nut species, except for the pecan. Among these are black walnut, butternut, shagbark hickory, and shellbark hickory. According to Smith, if we made such an effort, perhaps nut crops could change the way we eat and could save the soil on sloping land at the same time.

There is another way to deal with black walnut and hickory nuts that is gaining interest now. Most of these nuts are characterized by hard, difficult shells that resist attempts to extract the whole nut. We can get the nutrient value of these nuts by breaking them into pieces and putting the entire nut, shell and all, into a boiling pot of water. This frees the oil, causing it to float to the surface, where it is easily decanted, filtered, and used as an edible oil. The remaining seed and shells can be fed to chickens, pigs, and turkeys, replacing the ubiquitous corn and soybeans with a more nutritious and local feed (Mudge and Gabriel 2014). The hickories that are best suited for this include shagbark hickory (*Carya ovata*), shellbark hickory (*C. laciniosa*), mockernut hickory (*C. tomentosa*), pignut hickory (*C. glabra*), and bitternut hickory (*C. cordiformus*).[15] The last of these, bitternut hickory, is better used for nonedible purposes. The most well-known hickory is the pecan (*C. illinoiensis*), which has a thin shell and an easily extracted nut that has enabled widespread commercial development, especially in the state of Georgia.

Smith's ideas did not rise to the top of the American agricultural research agenda, which was hijacked by corporate agriculture, giant mechanization, and a collection of chemical companies. However, those ideas did not die in the 1930s, but survived in the quiet parts of university research and on the farms of mavericks who wanted to do things differently. One such maverick, named Philip Rutter, lives in southeastern Minnesota on Badgersett Research Farm, which he started in 1978. He is not connected to any university or to other nonprofit research-oriented groups like the American Chestnut Foundation® (ACF) or the Northern Nut Growers Association, though at one time he headed both groups and he maintains contact with them. He started working with American chestnut hybridization early on, but true to his maverick attitude, the relationship with ACF did not last. Rutter made the conscious decision to go with first-generation and second-generation hybrid chestnuts that are of blended American and Chinese chestnut heritage. The nuts are smaller and more flavorful, like the American nut, but their growth pattern and productivity are more like

---

15   Steve Nix, "Identify Common Major Hickory Species in North America," ThoughtCo., January 29, 2019, https://www.thoughtco.com/identify-major-hickory-species-north-america-1341859.

the Chinese chestnut. The ACF is attempting to get a timber tree back again, concentrating on combining the growth pattern of the American tree with the resistance to blight of the Chinese variety.[16]

If anything, Badgersett and Philip Rutter are more excited about hybrid hazelnuts than they are about chestnuts. The European hazelnut was perhaps the single most important plant source of nutrients for hunter-gatherer peoples from what is now Kazakhstan to the Balkan Peninsula. It remains one of the most important exports of Turkey, the world's largest producer. However, the European hazelnut, called the *filbert* in the United States, does not tolerate the climate of the northern Great Plains and can hardly tolerate the frosts of Virginia; further, it does not do well in the humidity of the Southeast, nor does it handle diseases native to that part of the world. The American hazelnut, on the other hand, thrives in these conditions and is very nutritious, but it produces smaller nuts that are not competitive on the market. Badgersett has had considerable success hybridizing these two species, working with American varieties from Wisconsin and Iowa as well as European varieties grown in Oregon. Badgersett breeders advocate planting hazelnuts in contour rows on farms. It is possible to grow row crops between the hedges of hazelnuts, but the nuts are shallow-rooted and could be damaged by tillage. They do well, though, when associated with pasture or other perennials like cane fruits or blueberries, depending on soil type. Rutter thinks that the hazelnut has the potential, with continued breeding, to replace soybeans on farms. This means a chemical-free perennial crop would replace an annual that requires frequent tillage or needs chemical treatment in no-till systems. The replacement would greatly please J. Russell Smith (Rutter, Wiegrefe, and Rutter-Daywater 2015).

Alley Cropping

Alley cropping is a method of agroforestry in which widely spaced rows of perennial trees are grown with crops between the rows. In the United States, this idea was developed best by H. E. Garrett, a research scientist at the University of Missouri's Center for Agroforestry (Garrett and Harper 1999). Garrett thinks the black walnut is really made up of two types of trees. To get the best timber with the least effort, the tree must grow densely in a closed forest system, keeping lateral branches to a minimum and straight vertical growth to a

---

16   All the information from this paragraph comes from the Badgersett Research Corporation website (http:// www.badgersett.com/) and the book *American Chestnut: The Life, Death, and Rebirth of a Perfect Tree* by Susan Freinkel (Berkeley: University of California Press, 2007).

maximum. The tree in these settings produces a timber or veneer grade log in 50–80 years, depending on conditions. A nut tree requires a more open setting. It's grown at a 30 × 30-foot spacing, and then thinned slowly to 60 × 60-foot spacing, giving the tree adequate light and reduced nutrient competition in order to maximize seed production. While it is common practice to emphasize one production system or the other, agroforestry can work for both—using alley cropping with an emphasis on mixed production across a landscape. The walnut trees are planted in a row with relatively tight spacing, even as crowded as 15 feet between trees. These should be grafted trees, meant to provide commercial nuts from a known cultivar (Reid et al. 2009). The spacing between rows is based on what is being farmed and the equipment used, but normally 60 feet is considered a good spacing. Crops are then grown between the rows of trees. In early years, corn, soybeans, and small grains are possible. As the walnuts grow, side branches are trimmed, reducing nut yield but keeping the trees growing straight. Nut production can start in as little as three to five years, depending on the cultivar chosen, but production does not peak until year 15 or later. Once trees reach this age, they usually cast too much shade for light-demanding crops like corn and soybeans. Small grains are grown, or the switch is made to pasture crops like alfalfa or mixed grass with legumes. Hay or pasture and nuts become the annual crops. Between 15 and 25 years, thinning of the black walnut trees occurs within the row. Trees are selected for form and length of the clear bole or trunk to maximize timber value when harvested. Often, about half the trees are thinned out. This also increases nut production on the thinned trees, though it never reaches the level of a true nut orchard. Full timber value is reached between 50 and 80 years. The amount earned on timber harvest can match the value of crops grown over the entire period of the agroforestry system if logs are of veneer quality. They are normally not as long as those found in a closed canopy forest, but they can still reach a high value. Agroforestry like this requires long-term, intergenerational planning and serves as a great example of a sustainable practice.

The National Agroforestry Center (NAC), based in Lincoln, Nebraska,[17] established in 1990 and expanded in 1995, serves as the American counterpart to the World Agroforestry Center, also called the International Center for Research in Agroforestry (ICRAF), based in Nairobi, Kenya.[18] Alley cropping was conceived by ICRAF as a way to increase nutrient availability for crops while reducing erosion; the idea is conceptually simple, but more difficult to implement. The plan is to grow a tree or a shrub that accumulates nutrients, like *Leucaena leucocephala* or the *Tephrosia* genus (both of which fix nitrogen on their roots),

---

17   https://www.fs.usda.gov/nac/
18   http://www.worldagroforestrycentre.org/

FIGURE 13.3   This illustration gives a glimpse at the places where agroforestry systems could occupy a landscape. The wooded areas shown in the top and bottom corners of the illustration act as shelterbelts and places for woodlot understory farming. In the upper right corner, a riparian area surrounds a stream. On the left side is an alley cropping system following the contour lines, in much the way as Badgersett Research Farm does with hazelnuts. In the bottom center is a silvopastoral system that can work in multiple climate types with differing tree species. Drawing by Austen Linder.

on contour lines or in straight rows within crop fields to provide nutrients as needed from trimmed leaves and stems. Contour lines of trees along a terrace riser are a good way to stabilize the steep banks and limit erosion. Complications arise in situations where the limiting factor in agriculture is light or water, since the rows of trees will compete for these. However, the technique can be successful on appropriate sites. It was also found that alley cropping was only one of a myriad of ways trees could integrate with overall farm productivity. Alley cropping is one of five agroforestry practices identified by the NAC and ICRAF.

Windbreaks and Shelterbelts

Back in the Dust Bowl of the 1930s, it was very apparent that wind erosion was a major hazard. The newly formed Soil Conservation Service (now called the Natural Resources Conservation Service) focused on planting trees to act as windbreaks and shelterbelts throughout the Great Plains states. Windbreaks and shelterbelts work by slowing wind at field level and forcing it above the height of the tree. Their impact is usually effective to a horizontal distance 20 times the height of the tree, so a 30-foot tree would slow wind 600 feet away from the tree row. This impact is important both for protecting livestock and for reducing energy cost in heating homes. In October of 2013, a freak snowstorm in the western Dakotas killed thousands of cattle in areas where no protection was available.[19] In fields protected by windbreaks, the animals fared better, even though this storm arrived before the cattle had added their winter coats. Windbreaks around homes can reduce heating costs by 10% to 25%, depending on the aspect and quality of the house.

In the 1930s, the recommended windbreaks were wide. Today, the recommendation is for a narrower break of two to three rows of trees. Trees used in the windbreaks vary according to location. At least one row of evergreen trees is recommended to keep the effect through winter, and the short-needled spruce and fir species are commonly used. Pines are important in drier areas, but they commonly have a more open growth habit and the needles strongly inhibit growth under the trees by changing soil pH. A second or even third row of deciduous trees is recommended as well. These are commonly of a shorter species and could have additional uses. Serviceberries or saskatoon berries in Canada (*Amelanchier* genus) provide edible fruit for people and livestock. They taste a bit like blueberries and are about the same size but are harder to harvest. Osage orange (*Maclua pomifera*) has spiny branches, which can root if forced into the soil, forming a nearly impenetrable hedge that keeps even goats from passing through if done correctly.[20] There is an excellent guide for doing this in *Mother*

---

19   Irina Zhorov, "Why Did South Dakota Snowstorm Kill So Many Cattle?" *National Geographic*, October 22, 2013, http://news.nationalgeographic.com/news/2013/10/131022-cattle-blizzard-south-dakota-winter-storm-atlas/.

20   Osage orange has a very large fruit, bigger than grapefruit, quite hard and heavy. It was found on a limited range in the Red River valley on the border between Texas and Oklahoma. It proved very useful for fencing and providing rot-resistant fence posts, so it spread all over the country. Evolutionary ecologists think that its limited range is a recent phenomenon caused by the extinction of mammoths and giant ground sloths, animals large enough to eat the fruit and spread the seed. Humans took over that role in

Earth News.[21] Black locust (*Robinia pseudoacacia*) is another useful species in combination with evergreens in windbreaks; also, it provides highly durable wood for posts and makes excellent firewood. The National Agroforestry Center is an excellent source for more information on windbreaks and shelterbelts.

Riparian Buffers

Water erosion is the problem in the Appalachian region and more broadly in the East. While sheet erosion, the more or less even loss of soil from the surface through the action of rain drops and resultant runoff, has decreased due to implementation of best management practices pushed by the NRCS and others, erosion along stream banks persists in too many places. The best way to reduce this is to establish riparian buffers. A buffer is an exclusion zone on each side of a stream that prevents cattle entry and allows the growth of deeply rooted perennials, mainly trees. National and state programs like the Conservation Reserve Program and the Conservation Reserve Enhancement Program help farmers fence out cattle and other domestic animals, set up alternative watering systems, and plant trees. The recommended trees include many that Smith would have liked, such as swamp white oak, bitternut hickory, and black walnut. These are commonly called mast species, trees that produce seeds eaten by wildlife, including deer and turkeys. The trees evolutionary strategy is to overwhelm the seedeaters with food, so they are satiated, and leave some for reproduction, but they tend to do this in alternate years.[22] These buffers could be managed for human or domestic animal food production as long as the tree, shrub, or perennial grasses of the stream bank protection system remain intact. Other trees used in buffers include poplars, sycamores, willows, birch, honey locust, some dogwood, and red maple.

---

the nineteenth century. Horses and cattle will eat the fruit in winter when fresh grass is not available (http://en.wikipedia.org/wiki/Maclura_pomifera).

21 Harvey Ussery, "Living Fences: How-to, Advantages and Tips." *Mother Earth News*, October/November 2010. https://www.motherearthnews.com/homesteading-and-livestock/sustainable-farming/living-fences-zmaz10onzraw.

22 https://www.britannica.com/science/mast-seeding

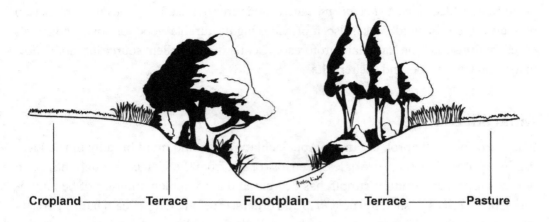

Cropland ——————— **Terrace** ——————— **Floodplain** ——————— **Terrace** ——————— **Pasture**

FIGURE 13.4   A cross section of a riparian buffer. Most of the time, the stream flows in a narrow channel, confined by non-erosive rock and a bank locked in place by the root system of plants. With heavy rains, the flow expands into the terrace area, reaching what is called "bank-full" flow. Extreme events may raise water levels into the broader floodplain. If the stream banks are well vegetated with deeply rooted perennials, this slows water, allowing sand and silt to settle out and add to the stream bank and floodplain. In the absence of these trees, shrubs, and deeply rooted grasses, the floods carry away soil, leaving behind a deeply scarred riparian zone.[23] Drawing by Austin Linder.

Silvopasture and the Importance of Shade

When working in East Africa, I visited a farm in the northwestern part of Tanzania on the east side of Lake Victoria, and west of the Serengeti. The area is high and relatively dry hill country, suitable for agriculture. People grow sorghum, millet, cowpeas, cassava, beans, and a mix of other crops. They also keep cattle, and since the area is elevated, there was some effort to bring in high-milk-producing breeds to improve local stock yields. A German government project used Brown Swiss cattle, a breed known for excellent milk production. Their pastures were good, and because it was a trial project they kept careful records of daily milk yields from individual fields. A pattern in daily yields was observed: when cattle grazed in certain fields, yields went up. Analysis showed that the only significant difference between fields was the amount of shade provided by remnant trees: the large fig (*Ficus thonningii*) and the umbrella thorn (*Acacia abyssinica*). Cattle have a highly predictable consumption pattern.

---

23   For a detailed examination of riparian landscapes, see David Rosgen. *Applied River Morphology*, 2nd ed (Fort Collins, CO: Wildland Hydrology, 1996) and Luna Leopold, *Water, Rivers and Creeks* (Sausalito, CA: University Science Books, 1997).

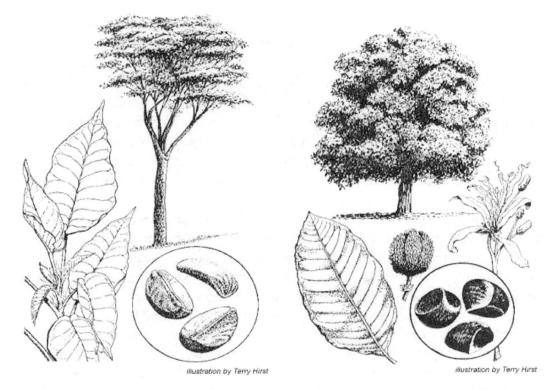

FIGURE 13.5 (a) *Croton megalocarpus* and (b) *Calodendron capense*, drawn by Terry Hirst for the website Agroforestry Trees of Kenya based on *A Pocket Directory of Trees and Seeds in Kenya* (Teel 1984) (http://agroforesttrees.cisat.jmu.edu/).

They graze for about four hours, from dawn to mid-morning, then lie or stand around for four hours chewing the cud (which is rechewing the material eaten in the morning), grazing again in the afternoon to dusk, and spending the night sleeping and chewing more. Without shade in the heat of the day, cattle spend far less time chewing, reducing digestibility of their food and subsequently reducing yield. Adding shade increased yields by 20% or more. The project added a tree-planting component and asked for ideal shade trees. I recommended three additional species based on my work in Kenya: *Croton megalocarpus*, *Albizia gummifera*, and *Calodendrum capense*. These were suitable for the local elevation and rainfall, and all three were known locally by farmers.[24]

One of the harshest landscapes on the planet is found in the Sahel, the southern "shore" of the Sahara desert stretching from Senegal and Mauritania in the west to Sudan in the

---

24   For more information on these trees and others in East Africa, see http://agroforesttrees.cisat.jmu.edu/.

east. It is a land that receives only 200 to 600 millimeters of rain each year, most falling in one short rainy season when the intertropical convergence zone passes overhead between May and August. The Sahel experiences frequent droughts and at one point had a shortage of wood, the fuel used by most living in the region. This shortage is diminishing because a change of attitude and land use has slowly transformed the landscape. People are both planting trees and encouraging regrowth of those trees that survived the deforestation that dominated in the 1970s. The trees grown include many pod-producing species, such as the apple-ring acacia (*Faidherbia albida*), that are used to produce fodder and shade for the animals in the dry season. The animals, in turn, leave their droppings and urine behind for next season's production of crops.

In the tropics, trees give cattle more benefits than just shade. Some shrubs, notably *Calliandra calothyrsus*, provide fodder and increase the butterfat content of milk. *Harrisonia abyssinica* is another important fodder shrub, commonly found in hedgerows and a favorite of milk goats (Teel 1984). Hedgerow planting was started on the smaller East African farms because of the multiple uses for the trees and shrubs. Hedgerows can be planted on contours and used for living fences, and the cuttings provide firewood and fodder use.[25]

Shade benefits cattle in the United States as well. Farmers in the southeastern United States grow widely spaced pines for this purpose. Pines have the advantage of being non-palatable when young, so cattle do not browse them. Oak, hickory, maple, and black walnut are useful shade trees, but they require protection until they reach a size—usually at least four inches in diameter at the height of a cow's back—where cattle will not rub off their bark or eat any new growth. Cattle will congregate under the tree's shade during the heat of the day in almost every part of the country, and this will enhance their growth or milk production. If there are only small patches of shade, cattle will trample the areas, allowing little to grow in the understory and damaging the tree's root system.[26]

From 1987 to 1989, I worked on a master's thesis in Lewis County, New York, looking at dairy farms and their use of trees on the farm. The most enjoyable use of trees involved the making of maple syrup from sugar bushes. These are groves of trees dominated by sugar maple (*Acer saccharum*) that are codominant species with beech trees throughout much of New England, west to Minnesota, and into Ontario and Quebec. Maple syrup is made from the free-flowing spring sap of maples that begins when temperatures in spring rise above

---

25   Regarding fodder trees and milk production in East Africa, see the World Agroforestry Centre 2009 Policy Brief, http://www.worldagroforestry.org/downloads/publications/PDFs/BR09326.PDF.

26   These are personal observations of my own farm, and of farms in the Shenandoah Valley, in Lancaster, Pennsylvania, in Lewis County, New York, and in Western Washington.

freezing during the day and fall back to below freezing at night. This period can last for up to a month. The sap contains between 1% and 4% sugar, though a few isolated trees can have even more. Usually, the trees having the highest percentage of sugar had full canopies and grew in open or widely spaced settings around the edges of farms. These same trees provided shade to cattle in the heat of summer and probably benefited from the increase in nutrients that the cattle deposited around the base. At least a few farmers I interviewed planted the trees deliberately for this dual purpose. Most of their sugar production was based in the woods.

Overstory and Understory Trees

This brings us to the fourth use of trees in agricultural systems: an overstory tree for understory crops. Here again ecology comes into sharp focus. Most ecosystems have a wide variety of niches for producers and consumers. The plants that humans use come naturally from a niche in their native ecosystems. Commonly, humans have pushed the plants into niches that differ from their natural ones in order to enhance production. Coffee and cocoa are two outstanding examples of this, as both are widely grown and economically valuable. Coffee as a commodity is exceeded only by petroleum in value on the world trade market. Cocoa is in the top ten of globally traded crops. They share the characteristic of originating as understory bushes to small trees in tropical forests. Arabica coffee, preferred by lovers of premium brews, is a native of Ethiopia's southwestern forests and grows as a small tree of variable habits in cool highland areas with a dry season of four to six months. Cocoa comes from the Caribbean region of South America and Central America, growing in dense lowland forests that also have a seasonal dry period. Both prefer partial to full shade. People did not keep them there, because shade reduces energy input to the plant and in turn reduces potential yield. To maximize yield, plantation owners took these two plants and grew them in monocultures. This came with a price. More inputs in the form of fertilizer, herbicides, fungicides, and insecticides were required to keep the plants healthy. There was also a heavy environmental cost in terms of biodiversity, erosion, water quality, and human health.

Coffee is the world's largest agricultural commodity. It grows in the tropics of places like the Atlantic forests of Brazil; the mountainous midlands and highlands of Colombia, Central America, Mexico, Kenya, and Ethiopia; and the hilly forests of Indonesia and Vietnam. These forests are some of the most diverse on the planet and also the most endangered. Conversion of these forests to coffee production is one of the key factors in this endangerment. Brazil and Vietnam produce primarily robusta coffee (*Coffea robusta*), which is tolerant of the warmer temperatures found in Uganda where it is a native understory tree. Colombia and Ethiopia focus on *Coffea arabica* production. The relatively recent recognition that deforestation has had a profound effect on wildlife, especially birds and primates, has led some farmers to pursue shade-grown coffee. The results have proven to be very positive. An online article by the Smithsonian Migratory Bird Center that reviewed 50 academic studies of shade-grown or forest-grown coffee shows that the overstory forest has a strong positive impact on bird life, insect life, reduced insect damage because of increased predation, better pollination, lower erosion rates, higher income from noncoffee farm enterprises, and much more.[27] Agroforestry-grown coffee might reduce production, but the overall improvement of farm-land ecology and farm income offsets this loss, and, in a less well-documented conclusion, consumers also think the coffee tastes better.[28]

There is an irony in the farming of coffee and cocoa. Coffee is a leading cause of defor-estation in the Atlantic forest of Brazil and mid-elevation mountains of Colombia, while cocoa is a leading cause of deforestation in West Africa, especially the lowland forests of Cote d'Ivoire and Ghana. Why do these crops flip originating continents? The answer lies in colonial history and the presence of disease in their places of origin. Plants evolve in an ecological context, and in the tropics they are usually found in highly diverse ecosys-tems. When forced into monocultures, or at least more-intensive cultivation strategies, insects and diseases that coevolved with the plants gain an advantage. These organisms are not found on the new continent. While this was conventional wisdom for a long time, and holds true for some species like the rubber tree of the Amazon, it is not a universal truth. Sometimes, the problem is the loss of biodiversity associated with the intended crop. When you take an understory tree away from its ecological context, you lose the birds, insect predators, and other beneficial organisms as well as some of the problems. The plants, now in a context where environmental stimuli have changed, do not respond the same way, and more inputs are required. Agroforestry is an attempt to establish an ecosystem that simulates an original ecosystem context while still intensifying produc-tion on a given piece of land. The jury is still out for both crops when it comes to details (Asare 2006), but there is little doubt that bird populations, erosion control, and overall carbon capture are improved in an agroforestry setting, just not to the degree present in the original ecosystem of those places.

Like the Atlantic forest of Brazil, the West African forest that extends from Guinea to Cameroon is now highly fragmented and endangered. Cocoa, coffee, oil palm, and rubber are major contributors to this problem. All four are components of tropical forest ecosystems, but

---

27   Robert Rice, with assistance from Mauricio Bedoya, *The Ecological Benefits of Shade-Grown Coffee*, September 2010, http://nationalzoo.si.edu/scbi/migratorybirds/coffee/bird_friendly/ecological-bene-fits-of-shade-grown-coffee.cfm

28   All Ground Up: http://www.allgroundup.com/light_en/sustainability/

only oil palm is native to this part of Africa.[29] Ghana, Cote d'Ivoire, Nigeria, and Cameroon are the world's leading cocoa producers. After deforestation, the biggest problem now is child slavery. Cocoa as it is now grown requires thinning and pruning to maximize production. Since the trees have relatively fragile branches, it is best to use lightweight boys for the task. "Buying" or kidnapping young boys from poor families is an easy way to get the labor. A simple internet search of "chocolate child labor Africa" leads to numerous news stories and groups working to end the problem. Cote d'Ivoire is the center of this activity, but it extends to the other countries as well.

In Cameroon and Ghana, efforts are underway to change the nature of cocoa production, moving from monoculture to understory production. The latter was practiced during the introduction of cocoa, but monoculture became dominant from the 1950s through the 1970s. As the plantations aged, opportunities arose to adapt these systems. While growing canopy trees of fruits like avocado and mango is possible, both these trees have very dense shade, so they are probably best suited for the edges of cocoa groves. More success comes with growing open canopy timber species, though Asare's (2006) review indicates that no verdict has been reached on productivity and the reduction of inputs. He also provides a set of guidelines needed to assure the success of agroforestry-based cocoa production. Systems must be *ecologically possible* (appropriate for the best genetic expression of the tree), *socially acceptable* (plausible for local systems given available labor and conditions), and *economically viable* (people have to make a reasonable living). At present, even more than coffee, cocoa is subject to the needs of the corporations that control the market. Making a profit while being ecologically and socially appropriate has proven elusive—thus the problem with child slavery.

Montgomery (2017) adds another dimension relevant to both coffee production and cocoa production. He visited a farm in Ghana run by Kofi Boa, near Kumasi to the northwest of the capital city of Accra. Mr. Boa is an advocate of the soil-first paradigm. He emphasizes that mulch is the main ingredient of his success. He uses all dead organic material as a source for mulch, uses far fewer inputs like fertilizer and herbicides, and basically uses no insecticides. Birds and other predators, taking advantage of the overstory trees, remove most of the problem insects, which also reduces plant diseases where the insects are carriers. The thick mulch suppresses weed growth, so Mr. Boa is able to avoid the normal practice of burning crop residues in the area. In fact, Kofi Boa is a leading practitioner of Albert Howard's Law of Return, and his success promotes the spread of the ideas to the wider community (Montgomery 2017).

---

29 Oil palm is a major factor in the deforestation of Borneo and Sumatra in Indonesia. See the Rainforest Action Network and the Nature Conservancy for their work on this issue. The rate of deforestation, as a percentage of total area, is the highest in the world in this region.

Cocoa is less problematic in Central America and South America. Even though less than a third of global supply comes from cocoa's native range, more efforts to grow it with agroforestry systems are underway. The "Fair Trade" and environmental movements have promoted these efforts. Just as for coffee, evidence acquired by the Smithsonian's Migratory Bird Center shows that cocoa planted with an overstory of native trees, the more species the better, has substantially increased the habitat for migratory birds. Cocoa yields underneath trees are somewhat less than in open plantations but require fewer inputs. The Smithsonian's article on the subject also indicates that cocoa trees have not had serious selection trials for yield when growing in these shade situations. Some trees do very well, while others bear very few fruits (Somarriba and Beer n.d.). Rolim and Chiarello (2004) caution that simply having an overstory of selected shade trees is not enough to save the Atlantic forest of Brazil, or by implication other tropical forests. Most of the trees that do well in this setting are early succession species, and later emerging canopy trees are not allowed to compete. The result is a slow degradation of the natural forest instead of a rapid deforestation. The end result for the ecosystem may be the same. It is important to recognize that agroforestry with cocoa and coffee is really in the early stages of development.

We are still learning about the agroforestry systems of cocoa, coffee, and other crops. We know they work, but it is unclear how they work best. The source for the best information is in the natural system that we are destroying. Even in agroforestry, the systems studied are often not a mimic of a natural ecosystem. There may be an attempt to overlay a natural ecosystem on a cocoa or coffee production system, even though done in a monoculture. Overall habitat is still reduced for natural inhabitants of an area. In addition, these are often relatively large plantation efforts, not mixed systems on a scale where a healthy natural system is adjacent to an agroforestry system and thereby allows genetic diversity and easy movement of insect, bird, and mammal species. The large-scale plantation model is part of the problem. On a smaller scale, more single-family-size operations interspersed with natural forest in a mosaic would prove better and more productive. Unfortunately, the human population pressure of the planet does not provide a lot of space to make the effort.

Forest Management: Farming the Woods[30]

This brings us to a final component of agroforestry that ties into the larger issue of how we manage and use forests on a broader scale. Historically, most farms had a woodlot or a

---

30 This title is deliberately borrowed from the excellent book by Ken Mudge and Steve Gabriel: *Farming the Woods: An Integrated Permaculture Approach to Growing Food and Medicinals in Temperate Forests* (White

woodland commons that every farm family could access. These woods provided a host of products: mulch and green manure, fodder, fruit and other food, fiber, timber and other construction materials, fuel wood, and medicine. These were things that were essential for the operation of the household economy but did not require collection every day, so it was fine to have the lot some distance away. Less well known, and certainly not well remembered, is that the plants of this ecosystem were managed. People needed certain items from their woods, so they tended and promoted the species that provided their needs and removed those species that they did not require. A weed in this system was not a waste; it was selected for use as green manure, mulch, firewood, or even biochar. A plant that provided fiber or medicine was left to grow until needed for that use. Good straight timber trees were left to grow, while crooked, forked, or spindly trees of the same species would go on the wood pile. This is called low-grade management, with the removal of the poorest members first, while encouraging the growth and reproduction of the best-quality stock.

The United States had the dubious distinction of having destroyed native ecosystems faster than any other country on the planet—until Australia (and perhaps now China) broke our record. Before we Europeans destroyed the place, Native Americans had lived here for millennia. We do not know the role of the early Clovis people in destruction of megafauna, but since that period the native peoples, still called Indians even by themselves, managed the North American landscape in ways that looked so natural that the Europeans did not recognize management. It was not "natural" in the sense that there were no human fingerprints on the landscape. Indians did manipulate fire and promote some species and reduce others. What they did not do was change ecosystems in wholesale ways as the Europeans did. As just one example, starting in the 1830s, settlers began claiming land and clearing forest in the northern states of Michigan, Wisconsin, and Minnesota. This process sped up rapidly during the Civil War, supplying a substantial portion of the resources needed for the war effort, including railway ties and eventually supplying the ties and other timber materials for the transcontinental railway. The forests were stripped willy-nilly, giving rise to some of the most spectacular and destructive fires in US history, exceeding even the recent spate of fires in the American West. The native Indians of Wisconsin were confined to small tracts of land—reservations. One group, the Menominee, received a 235,000-acre piece northwest of Green Bay. Tribal elder and chief Oshkosh (yes, the one the clothing company is named after) introduced a style of sustainable management to this forest in 1865 amid the destruction

---

River Junction, VT: Chelsea Green Publishing, 2014).

of the rest of the state.[31] It takes people with a true vision to buck the prevailing paradigm of a dominant culture. Here is the mission statement of Menominee Tribal Enterprises:

> Menominee Tribal Enterprises is committed to excellence in the sustainable management of our forest, and the manufacturing of our lumber and forest products providing a consistently superior product while serving the needs of our forest, employees, wood products customers, tribal community, and future *generations*. (http://www.mtewood.com/)
>
> It is said of the Menominee that the sacredness of the land is their very body, the values of the culture are their very soul, the water is their very blood. It is obvious, then, that the forest and its living creatures can be viewed as food for their existence. (Marshall Pecore, MTE Forest Manager, *Journal of Forestry*, July 1992)

In the Pacific Northwest, and to a lesser extent everywhere, the forest is basically managed for timber. This leads to an even-age forest of one high-value species growing at the same rate. The Menominee turned this on its head. They manage for the full range of forest products and the full health of the forest with the active participation of the people. Trout, good walks, and mushrooms are all considered products that have value, even though they don't bring in money the same way that other products, like cabinets or molding, of the Menominee Tribal Enterprise (MTE) do. The key is managing for a healthy ecosystem. MTE wants a diverse ecosystem with mixed-age stands of every tree. The people monitor the trees closely on a regular basis, measuring 58,000 trees a year to track growth in a 15-year cycle. They remove trees that exhibit ill health or bad form, and they leave trees to form old-growth stands in places to maintain good genetics. They have harvested more wood than most single-product management systems, and they have more standing timber value now than when they began these practices 140 years ago.[32]

The same thing is true for the management of the Almanor Forest, owned and managed by the Collins Pine Company in northeastern California, just east of Lassen Volcanic National Park. The company has owned land in the area since 1902 and started managing it as an intact 94,000-acre forest on a sustained yield basis in 1941.[33] The forest is primarily coniferous, but species vary according to aspect, elevation, and soils: lodgepole pine,

---

31   http://www.mtemillwork.com/forest/index.php

32   Christopher and Barbara Johnson, "Menominee Forest Keepers," *American Forests Magazine*, Spring 2012, http://www.americanforests.org/magazine/article/menominee-forest-keepers/.

33   http://www.collinsco.com/almanor-fsc/

ponderosa pine, other pine, Douglas fir, a variety of true firs, and incense cedar. The company was certified by the Forestry Stewardship Council® in 1992. Nattrass and Altomare (1999) cited the work of the company as an example of The Natural Step™ management practices in the book *The Natural Step for Business: Wealth, Ecology and the Evolutionary Corporation*. The result of the selective harvest management system is a forest with sustained yield, increasing wood content, an intact ecosystem (birds, mammals, and other wildlife), and healthy streams (where they are not impacted by preexisting dams). The Collins Pine website is highly transparent with respect to management systems, and the company is open to visitors. This contrasts greatly with the dominant model of private forests represented by Weyerhaeuser, Boise Cascade®, and Georgia Pacific that use square-mile clear-cuts and have "Keep Out" signs on their access roads.

While these forests are small in comparison to the total land found in major corporate forests or in the National Forest System, they represent a model much more in tune with how farmers or forest landowners could manage their personal land. Woodlots have a size range, from backyard trees to 500-acre forests. Most of them are ignored as a resource, with the possible exception of firewood, until they are turned over to a contract harvester to strip the woods of valuable trees. Unfortunately, they are still ignored after being stripped, and they come back with a combination of pioneer trees and weedy species of lower value. This degradation affects wildlife and soil and water quality. Using a woods well does not have to become an all-consuming exercise, but it does take planning and some ecological understanding. A few simple rules will suffice here to sum up the process of managing a sustainable woods with multiple products and a constant storage of carbon.

1. *Low-grade the woodlots.* Most woods almost everywhere in the United States are regenerated from forests heavily logged in the nineteenth and early twentieth centuries. Our wood products come from second- or third-generation forests farmed commercially. Most small woods came from what could easily and quickly recover. These woods are commonly a mix of weedy species, early succession species, and a few good-quality trees growing slowly in their midst. Low-grading means selective removal of trees that have little value as either timber, because of poor form or disease, or an alternative product like nuts, acorns, fruit, or medicine. When weeds like *Ailanthus altissima* (tree of heaven, which does make excellent firewood when larger), eastern red cedar, or autumn olive are removed, space is freed for higher-value species like white oak, shagbark hickory, or white pine.

2. *Plant species you want.* Many farm or family woodlots are disconnected from an extended region of forests, and there is no seed source available for high-value species that commonly have heavier seed that cannot be carried by the wind. Choosing and planting these trees is essential. Since they are not growing in an open situation,

they do not need a lot of care, especially once they reach a height where deer cannot nip them, or a thickness of bark where rabbits or voles cannot girdle them. It may take some initial effort to protect what you plant, or you can simply overwhelm the pests by sowing a lot of seed and letting nature make the selection of the best new seedlings (Shepard 2013).

3. *Thin the growth.* Often, new growth comes in already very densely packed, since sunlight is not limiting at first. Once the canopy closes, growth of individual trees will slow if they are tightly packed. This can even slow overall carbon capture. Thinning to a spacing where the canopy is no longer closed will open the woods up and maximize growth. Selecting the trees to thin may involve cutting out a good tree. Do not be afraid to do this. Leaving two good trees could lead to growing two bad trees. It is best to thin to one good tree. Thinning to between 15 and 20 feet between trees in every direction is common in well-managed woods.

4. *Use the understory.* There are a lot of species that like limited light. The second highest value export in early America was ginseng. It was Daniel Boone's major source of financing for his exploration of Kentucky. Other high-value understory plants include goldenseal, black cohosh, and Virginia snakeroot in the East, Canadian and Pacific yew in the northern forests, Oregon grape and salal in the Pacific Northwest, and many more. Often, all these plants need is a space to grow and someone to plant them. Most are competitive native perennials that need only a chance to get started again in a formerly degraded habitat (Teel and Buck 1998).

5. *Think differently about management.* In the past, before fossil fuels and massive urbanization, people managed the woods for a variety of goods. Perhaps the most important part of the woods was the coppice woodlot. Most of us today do not know what coppicing is. Many tree species, when cut near the ground at between 15 and 50 cm, will sprout new stems. These will grow more rapidly than the original single stem, especially if thinned to two or three stems, and they will provide a continuous supply of poles and firewood on a rotational basis. Harvest of these stems was often every 7 to 10 years, yielding good volumes of easily harvested and cut firewood and above-ground construction poles. Many species, including oak, hickory, basswood, eucalyptus, redwood, willow, and poplar, coppice well. Mark Krawczyk and Dave Jacke are presently working on a book about coppice woodlots, hoping to reinvigorate the practice in the United States and elsewhere.[34]

34 More information is available on their website: http://www.coppiceagroforestry.com/index.html.

Edible Forests in Your Backyard (or Front Yard)

For most of us, having land on which to plant an extensive number of trees is simply a dream. The best we can hope for is an area of maybe a quarter or half an acre, 10,000 to 20,000 square feet (930 to 1,860 m²). For most Americans, this space is made into a manicured lawn with a few flower beds scattered around the edges. Lawns are basically green deserts. When you keep grass under four inches most of the time, you also keep the root system of grass approximately the same length. This is part of the reason why the lawn dries out so fast if we don't get a good weekly rain. What if the lawns, the largest area of managed land in the United States for a single crop (yes, larger than corn), were to transform into an edible perennial landscape?

This is the working premise behind Dave Jacke and Eric Toensmeier's two-volume work, *Edible Forest Gardens*. Their work is based on understanding the ecology of a forest as managed in a garden. Their premise is that humans need food, but have dissociated their food supply from their residence and need to put the two back together. The authors also recognize that most people do not have time for full-time gardening, but that perennials, once established in the correct arrangement, take care of themselves. People normally have problems figuring out the correct arrangement because they have lost touch with the ecology and genetic character of the species we use for food. So people plant six fruit trees in their backyard, too close together and in uncomplimentary arrangements. They fail to recognize that short sun-loving plants should go on the south side of taller species and a reasonable distance from the shade of the house. For Jacke and Toensmeier, less is often more. Yield is dependent on creating the right abiotic and biotic conditions of a yard. This is ecosystem thinking scaled to the backyard level.

In *Edible Forest Gardens*, they provide two excellent case studies of edible forest gardens. The first example is from Greensboro, North Carolina. The homeowner, Charlie Headington, has a standard quarter-acre lot with a driveway along the south side of the house, a front yard facing east, and a larger backyard of 50 ×100 feet. The front yard is filled with a small meadow, and flowering shrubs decorate the entrance to the house. The hot south side is now protected in summer by a trellis with muscadine grapes and three dwarf pear trees. The north side of the house has taller shade trees that rise above the roof. The roof serves as a water catchment, draining into 55-gallon drums, with the water used to irrigate the garden as needed. The backyard is a mix of fruit trees, including five plums, a grape, a kiwi, a persimmon, a fig, two apples, two peaches, a red bud, and a large mulberry in the south corner, with an ash, an elm, and a red maple along the north fence. In the middle of all this is a vegetable garden of annuals and perennials, like asparagus. The whole is a beautiful but very crowded space. The large trees prevent more productivity, and the crowding reduces the yield of some individual plants—yet the overall effect of the garden is stunning, even in the pictures. Charlie did not plan this space from the beginning. It was more ad hoc. The authors make a case for deliberate planning before planting, so the needs of each species are properly identified. When this is done, you get an aesthetically pleasing and productive yard with a relatively low-maintenance system. High maintenance is commonly a sign that the ecological conditions are wrong.

The second example comes from the home and garden of Martin Crawford in Devon in South West England. Martin developed his garden with a deeper understanding of the ecology of his place. His focus is on native species, and those plants are naturalized and developed for the cool, moist conditions of Devon. Though the garden is only two acres, Martin has 31 families of woody plants in the canopy and 550 total species growing on the property. Many of these he is simply testing both for individual plant yield and for interactions with other species. Even with this high diversity, Martin leaves a lot of space between the canopy trees. Around 40% of the canopy is open to allow light to reach the understory and ground plants. His original intent remains: to test species in relation to each other, measure yield, assess ideal growth conditions, and expose their usefulness to the wider public. He grows species like linden (*Tilia cordata*)—which has leaves that people do not know are edible—in a coppice that does not get above head height so the leaves are easy to harvest. The details of this garden are very complex and best explained by Martin himself.[35] He estimates that his garden can feed 10–12 people year-round.

The Trillion Tree Project: Reversing Climate Change One Local Planting at a Time

A trillion trees is a huge goal. It is not reachable with the mindset of our planet's inhabitants at present. We must recognize first that a problem exists and second that we are part of the problem. An interesting survey has been completed by Stanford University professors and students on the attitudes of US citizens about climate change and global warming. It found that even people in Texas and Mississippi were aware that global warming was a reality. Fewer people thought that regulation should induce business to lower carbon emissions. However, when the question turned to paying more for gasoline or electricity, the negatives outweighed the positives. Among survey respondents in Virginia, 81% were aware of global warming happening, 75% thought businesses should limit emissions, only

---

35 For a brief summary and videos see this site: http://permaculturenews.org/2011/06/08/martin-craw-fords-forest-garden/. Crawford also has a book: *Creating a Forest Garden: Working with Nature to Grow Edible Crops* (Devon, UK: Green Books, 2010).

28% thought we should pay a consumption tax for electricity, and 41% thought the same for gasoline.[36] We are fine when it is someone else's problem, but we're not so interested in owning the problem ourselves. However, since the study was completed, the awareness of, and the need to act on, climate change has grown. The 2018 Congressional election and the climate strike actions of Greta Thunberg have made an impact even in the age of presidential climate denial.

It is not enough to stop putting carbon into the air. To reduce climate change, we have to get the carbon out—and tree planting is a major way of doing that. Yet tree planting is a very diffuse activity. It must be done over millions of square kilometers. No government is going to take on that responsibility unless its people model that behavior and push the government to participate. No person has modeled that dual effort more than Wangari Mathaii in Kenya. She planted trees with women in the Green Belt movement, focusing on land in and around cities, in public rights of way, and on barren or abandoned land. With her group, she planted 30 million trees and was aiming for a billion. Her vision continues though she has passed.

Another Kenyan, Patrick Musyimi of Makueni District (now called Makueni County), models this in a different way. Patrick owns a farm on the dry slopes of the Mbooni Hills, where less than 800 mm of rain fall in two annual rainy seasons, and the probability of rainfall failure is high. His area is limited by that availability of water. He heads a community self-help group called Nzaaya Muisya that came together to reduce the water problems by building a series of sand dams on the Mwea River, a seasonal stream that carries a lot of sand. The sand dams store water in a way that reduces evaporation and makes the water available throughout the year. Patrick uses this water to grow vegetables and fruit trees, but he does not stop there. Even before the sand dam, he planted trees, mostly eucalyptus and *Grevillea robusta* and some native species. With the help of his family, Patrick has planted over 10,000 trees, and the number continues to climb. He does not have a lot of land, his land is steep and dry, and the soils are not particularly good; yet he persists, and he now has an oasis of green that even shows up in satellite data (Ryan 2012).

These are examples of where we need to plant trees. We begin with our own yards, fencerows, and woodlots, and we grow to windbreaks on the prairie, riparian buffers on every stream, new woods along every highway, forest gardens in Europe, the deforested land of the Amazon, green belts in the Sahel, and terrace trees in the dry hills of Kenya.

---

36   For more information on Virginia and other states, see http://climatepublicopinion.stanford.edu/

Study Questions

1. How many trees and shrubs can you identify on your property? What are the trees in your area that have good value as shade trees, fruit and nut trees, and riparian trees?

2. Communities, college campuses, stream banks, and public commons often have spaces where trees would be appropriate. Take a walk around a selection of these areas and look. What trees can you find? How many can you identify? How many spaces are there where planting more would work? Add this up. How many trees could grow in the locations you identify?

3. As you move from city through suburbia to countryside, the space for trees expands. The number and type will change by region, climate, and soil conditions. The tools we have for identifying these areas geographically have improved greatly overtime. Google Earth is just one resource. Select an area and explore it. What agroforestry possibilities do you find in that area? How could you participate in making a tree-planting project in this region happen?

4. Do you have a favorite tree? What is it, and why is it your favorite? How does it fit, or how would it fit, in your yard, neighborhood, or region?

References

Asare, R. 2006. "A Review on Cocoa Agroforestry as a Means for Biodiversity Conservation." Paper presented at World Cocoa Foundation Partnership Conference, Brussels, May 2006. http://www.bio.miami.edu/horvitz/bil235/cacao/cacao06/ms/ms%20Cacao/cocoa%2520review.pdf

Crowther, T. W. , H. B. Glick, K. R. Covey, C. Bettigole, D. S. Maynard, S. M. Thomas, J. R. Smith, G. Hintler, M. C. Duguid, G. Amatulli, M.-N. Tuanmu, W. Jetz, C. Salas, C. Stam, D. Piotto, R. Tavani, S. Green, G. Bruce, S. J. Williams, S. K. Wiser, M. O. Huber, G. M. Hengeveld, G.-J. Nabuurs, E. Tikhonova, and P. Borchardt. 2015. "Mapping Tree Density at a Global Scale." *Nature* 525:201–205. doi:10.1038/nature14967.

Freinkel, Susan. 2007. *American Chestnut: The Life, Death, and Rebirth of a Perfect Tree*. Berkeley: University of California Press.

Garrett, H. E., and L. S. Harper. 1999. "The Science and Practice of Black Walnut Agroforestry in Missouri, USA: A Temperate Zone Assessment." In *Agroforestry in Sustainable Agricultural Systems*, edited by L. E. Buck, J. P. Lassoie, and E. C. M. Fernandes, pp. 97–110. New York: CRC Press.

Jacke, Dave, and E. Toensmeier. 2005. *Edible Forest Gardens*. 2 vols. White River Junction, VT: Chelsea Green Publishing.

McDonough, William, and Michael Brungart. 2002. *Cradle to Cradle: Remaking the Way We Make Things*. New York: North Point Press.

Montgomery, David. 2017. *Growing a Revolution: Bringing Our Soil Back to Life*. New York: W. W. Norton.

Mudge, Ken, and Gabriel, Steve. 2014. *Farming the Woods: An Integrated Permaculture Approach to Growing Food and Medicinals in Temperate Forests*. White River Junction, VT: Chelsea Green Publishing.

Nattrass, B., and M. Altomare. 1999. *The Natural Step for Business: Wealth, Ecology and the Evolutionary Corporation*. Gabriola Island, British Columbia, Canada: New Society Publishers.

Reid, W., M. Coggeshall, H. Garrett, and J. Van Sambek. 2009. "Growing Black Walnut for Nut Production. Agroforestry in Action." University of Missouri Center for Agroforestry. AF 1011–2009. http://www.centerforagroforestry.org/pubs/walnutNuts.pdf.

Rolim, G. R., and A. G. Chiarello. 2004. "Slow Death of Atlantic Forest Trees in Cocoa Agroforestry in Southeastern Brazil." *Biodiversity and Conservation* 13:2679–2694. https://doi.org/10.1007/s10531-004-2142-5.

Rutter, Philip, Susan Wiegrefe, and Brandon Rutter-Daywater. 2015. *Growing Hybrid Hazelnuts: The Resilient Crop for a Changing Climate*. White River Junction, VT: Chelsea Green Publishing.

Ryan, C. 2012. *The Potential for Sand Dams to Increase the Adaptive Capacity of Drylands to Climate Change*. PhD diss., Climate Change Management, Birkbeck College, University of London.

Shepard, Mark. 2013. *Restoration Agriculture*. Austin, TX: Acres USA.

Smith, J. Russell. 1929. *Tree Crops*. https://soilandhealth.org/wp-content/uploads/01aglibrary/010175.tree%20crops.pdf.

Somarriba, E., and J. Beer. "Cocoa Based Agroforestry Production Systems." http://nationalzoo.si.edu/conservationandscience/migratorybirds/research/cacao/somarriba.cfm.

Teel, W. 1984. *A Pocket Directory of Trees and Seeds in Kenya*. Nairobi: KENGO.

Teel, W. 1989. "An Assessment of Farm Management Strategies and Agroforestry Potential in Lewis County, New York." Master's Thesis, Cornell University.

Teel, W., and L. Buck. 1998. "From Wildcrafting to Intentional Cultivation: The Potential for Producing Specialty Forest Products in Agroforestry Systems in Temperate North America." Paper presented at the North American Conference on Enterprise Development Through Agroforestry: Farming the Agroforest for Specialty Products, Minneapolis, MN, October 4–7, 1998. https://nfs.unl.edu/documents/SpecialtyForest/Teel%20&%20Buck.pdf.

Trosper, R. L. 2007. "Indigenous Influence on Forest Management on the Menominee Indian Reservation." *Forest Ecology and Management* 249:134–139. http://courses.washington.edu/dts-class/TEK-Menominee.pdf.

Von Oudenhoven, Frederik, and Jamila Haider. 2017. *With Our Own Hands: A Celebration of Food and Life in the Pamir Mountains of Afghanistan and Tajikistan*. Volendam, the Netherlands: LM Publishers.

Printed in the USA
CPSIA information can be obtained
at www.ICGtesting.com
LVHW060431200724
785912LV00016B/59